# The Philosophy of John Dewey
## THE STRUCTURE OF EXPERIENCE

*Books Edited by John J. McDermott*

THE WRITINGS OF WILLIAM JAMES

THE BASIC WRITINGS OF JOSIAH ROYCE

THE PHILOSOPHY OF JOHN DEWEY

# The Philosophy of John Dewey

## Volume I

### THE STRUCTURE OF EXPERIENCE

*Edited with an Introduction
and Commentary by*

## John J. McDermott

*Capricorn Books*

## G. P. PUTNAM'S SONS
### New York

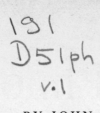

COPYRIGHT © 1973 BY JOHN J. McDERMOTT

*Putnam SBN: 399–10956–0*
*Capricorn SBN: 399–50288–2*
*Library of Congress Catalog*
*Card Number: 73–175269*

PRINTED IN THE UNITED STATES OF AMERICA

FOR

*Marise McDermott*

1953–

*Our First Born—A Life of Loyalty*
*and Celebration*

# Contents

VOLUME II
THE LIVED EXPERIENCE

# Preface

Who was John Dewey? Despite a staggering output of lectures, articles, and books, an incredibly long career of almost a century, an engendering of fascination, controversy, and widespread influence in many areas of human activity, the question is difficult to answer in any depth. No modern philosopher has exerted such influence while being hidden from view. This vagueness in our grasp of the qualities of his person, his motivations, sufferings, and delights cannot proceed from his having lived a sheltered life. His personal and intellectual odyssey ranged from Burlington, Vermont, to David Dubinsky and the trade unions of New York City, from Chicago to China, the Soviet Union, Turkey, and the Trotsky Commission in Mexico.

Embroiled and embattled at every level of human endeavor, we find John Dewey responding to technical philosophical disputes, as well as to highly inflammatory issues of the public arena. Yet at this writing we have only a thin autobiographical statement, "From Absolutism to Experimentalism," and a few biographical sketches. We are promised more, with the most encouraging news being the announcement of a definitive biography by Geroge Dykhuizen, to be published by Southern Illinois University Press as part of its distinguished series of the complete writings of John Dewey. Whether these future biographical studies will provide adequate insight into the life of this extraordinary man or whether it is of his very person to remain elusive and out of reach of such studies remains an open question.

The corollary to our limited understanding of the person of John Dewey is the acknowledgment of the importance and power of his writings. And it is with this in mind that we present these two volumes. In view of the fact that the Co-operative Research Project on Dewey publications at Southern Illinois University is now issuing critical editions of all of Dewey's writings, it has not been necessary for me to provide a full critical and bibliographical apparatus. Nor do the present volumes supplant the excellent edition of Dewey's writings by Richard

J. Bernstein, *On Experience, Nature, and Freedom,* which has as its
scope the development of Dewey's *Experience and Nature* after 1925.

What is needed, however, is a presentation of Dewey's thought as it
has developed both chronologically and thematically. Within the omni-
present limitation of space, I have tried to offer as wide a range of
Dewey's interests as possible and to set those interests into the
framework of the development and growth of his thought. Given the
massiveness of Dewey's bibliography, these selections, although running to approximately 1,000 pages of his own writing, constitute but a
small sampling. Nonetheless, they yield access to almost every major
theme in his writings, and they do this by representation of the full
range of his thought. Students and teachers of all disciplines will find in
these pages a renewed call to the majesty and importance of Dewey's insight into "creative intelligence." It is especially hoped that the present
generation, so often fired by a sense of social responsibility and a
feeling for the "lived body" but so woefully lacking in "accrued
wisdom," will find in Dewey's thought a dramatic instance of their
being brought together.

By way of acknowledgment, I again cite the imaginative teaching and
writing of Robert C. Pollock, whose "Process and Experience" is still
the best essay on the philosophy of John Dewey. Over the years, I have
learned much about John Dewey from my colleagues at Queens College: Eugene Fontinell, Peter T. Manicas, John B. Noone, Jr., and especially Ralph W. Sleeper. From among the vast amount of writings about
John Dewey, I am especially indebted to the work of Sidney Hook, H.
S. Thayer, Richard J. Bernstein, and John Herman Randall, Jr., whose
book *Nature and Historical Experience* is thus far the only successor to
Dewey's *Nature and Experience.* As for all Dewey scholarship, the
bibliographical research of Milton Halsey Thomas has been invaluable.
And I wish to acknowledge the cooperation and good fellowship offered
to me by Morris and Elizabeth Eames, Jo-Ann Boydston, Garth Gillan,
George McClure, and Lewis Hahn during my visit to the Center for
Dewey Studies at Southern Illinois University. I have also enjoyed a
conversation with John Dewey's son, Sabino, now deceased.

With regard to the preparation of the manuscript, I am indebted to
Peter T. Manicas, who facilitated its acceptance, and to Marsha
Treiber, who provided expert and cordial secretarial services. Eugene
Fontinell provided a perceptive critique of the Introduction. My editor,
Mr. Walter C. Betkowski, has been properly firm but understanding, su-
premely long on patience, and kind throughout. In past work, I have
acknowledged the extensive editorial assistance of my wife, Virginia.

Since that time, Deweyan by instinct as well as by learning, she has chosen to teach elementary school children in an open-corridor experiment. Her contribution has been to tell of the lives of children in a way which people who write and edit books tend to forget, if they ever knew.

JOHN J. MCDERMOTT

*Huntington, New York*
1972

# Introduction

## John Dewey: A Biographical Sketch

American philosophy of the nineteenth century is often said to lack a sense of the tragic. This charge is addressed particularly at the thought of John Dewey, so often typed for its overall optimism, its confidence in the potentialities of men, and its leaning toward an ameliorated future. If, however, we dig beneath the bland commentaries on the American philosophers and proceed to study their lives in depth, the tragic dimensions of the lives and thought of Ralph Waldo Emerson,[1] Charles Peirce,[2] William James,[3] and Josiah Royce[4] become painfully obvious. The life of Emerson reads like a long chapter from *A Cool Million* by Nathaniel West, riven throughout with illness and premature deaths, culminating in the destruction by fire of his home. William James, who lost an infant son by whooping cough, suffered all his life from severe psychoneurosis and major family crises and was plagued in the last decade of his life by increasing heart failure. Charles Peirce was a dissolute, debt-ridden public failure, whose life was capped by a lingering, painful illness. And Josiah Royce, despite the bravado of his public presence, hid from view his own considerable mental anguish and the tragic lives of some of his children. Perhaps it can be said that the confidence and optimism which characterizes their doctrines are partially in the form of compensation, as Emerson, for one, would be quick to acknowledge. Certainly, it cannot be said that these philosophers are naïve about the meaning of suffering and tragedy.

A similar judgment can be offered about the thought of John Dewey, although, with some notable exceptions, his life was not laced with the violent upheavals just cited. Further, Dewey lived so actively, for so long (1859-1952), that the major events of his life seem to fade into an almost unreal historical tapestry. Aside from Dewey's brief autobiographical piece, "From Absolutism to Experimentalism,"* published in 1930, and some isolated reminiscences of colleagues and friends,[5] the only substantial statement we have of Dewey's life is that of Jane Dewey,[6] who edited a brief biography written by herself and

xv

her two sisters, Evelyn and Lucy, from material provided by their father. Virtually all of the biographical material written by subsequent commentators thus far is a reduction of portions of this material. Yet, in most instances the death of two of Dewey's children and the personal stress involved in the collapse of the laboratory school at the University of Chicago are either passed over or mentioned briefly and without assessment, as though they might mar the cool logic of Dewey's thought. But Dewey's philosophy never strays from his insight into the irreducible presence of the tension between the "precarious" and the "stable," while, more than most philosophers, he integrates the experience of loss and setback with that of growth.

John Dewey was born in Burlington, Vermont, on October 20, 1859. He was the third of four sons born to Lucina Rich Dewey and Archibald Sprague Dewey. A quartermaster of a Vermont regiment during the Civil War, Dewey's father made his living in Burlington as a grocer. With the exception of a winter stay in the war-devastated area of northern Virginia, John Dewey's childhood was uneventful, and at age fifteen he entered the University of Vermont. In addition to a classical education, Dewey also studied the evolutionary thought of T. H. Huxley, which widened his outlook. He studied the reigning "Scotch realism" with H. A. P. Torrey and was introduced to German philosophy through the teaching of James Marsh. In 1879, Dewey graduated with honors and went on to teach high school for two years at Oil City, Pennsylvania. In retrospect, his experience in Oil City was very significant. He learned to live in comparative isolation, devoted to his thoughts and his teaching. And it was during this period that he resolved to continue with philosophy. His experience with the school and the children began an abiding interest in the affairs and problems of education.

In 1881 Dewey returned to Vermont, where he taught in a village school and studied philosophy on a tutorial basis with Professor Torrey. After reading *Speculative Philosophy,* a journal edited by W. T. Harris, Dewey sent off an essay on "The Metaphysical Assumptions of Materialism," asking Harris if the author should contemplate a career in philosophy. Harris answered yes and published the essay, and Dewey went to the new graduate school at Johns Hopkins University. Although Dewey studied with Charles Peirce at Johns Hopkins, he was unaware of the vast learning and importance of Peirce until many years later. The most powerful philosophical and personal influence on John Dewey at that time was that exercised by George S. Morris, who was responsible for Dewey's early interest and commitment to idealism and especially to the philosophy of Hegel. Despite subsequent vast changes in his thought, Dewey was fond of saying throughout his life that Hegel "left a permanent deposit in my thinking." Of particular importance to Dewey was Hegel's view that the individual is not isolated from history, culture, or environment, thereby providing a basis for Dewey's later fascination with social psychology.

In 1884 George Morris was influential in obtaining for Dewey an instructorship in philosophy at the University of Michigan, where, with the exception of a year at the University of Minnesota (1888-89), he taught until 1894. This period was to begin his long friendship and collaboration with the distinguished philosopher George Herbert Mead, who was to have a pervasive influence on the development of Dewey's thought. And during his stay at Michigan, on July 28, 1886, Dewey married Alice Chipman (1859-1927), a graduate of the University of Michigan. Six children were born to them: in Michigan, Frederick (1887-1967), Evelyn (1889-1965), and Morris (1893-95); and in Chicago, Gordon (1896-1904), Lucy (1897-   ), and Jane (1900-   ).

In 1894 Dewey accepted a position as professor of philosophy and chairman of the Department of Philosophy, Psychology, and Education at the University of Chicago—a most important decision. Such a troika of responsibilities might seem the height of pretense, but for Dewey it was merely a symbol of what we now call the interdisciplinary approach to human activity. He had become increasingly concerned with the social dimensions of behavior, particularly in the genetic state, and therefore wished to organize a program around the philosophical and psychological problems of inquiry as found in the education of children. Also, during his time at Michigan, Dewey's view of the meaning of psychology and its relationship to other approaches to human activity underwent a tremendous change due to the publication in 1890 of William James' *Principles of Psychology*. In a later essay on "The Development of American Pragmatism,"* Dewey details the importance of James' *Principles* both in his own thought and for the subsequent direction of American philosophy.

The Chicago years are crucially important for an understanding of Dewey's personal development and the evolution of his thought. In the first place, he gathered around him a group of philosophers and thinkers from other disciplines who, upon the publication of a group effort in 1903, *Studies in Logical Theory*, were dubbed by William James as the Chicago School.[7] Of them, Darnell Rucker writes:

Because the Chicago philosophy reflected an awareness of the interconnections among the advances being made in biology, psychology, and sociology, it was able to provide a method and a perspective for an array of disciplines. And so it was that the Chicago School was a school, not merely in the sense that several men were working together evolving (not just defending) a philosophy, but in the fuller sense that their work had effects in a cluster of fields of thought around philosophy; it was a school with a university full of its progeny.[8]

John Dewey was the acknowledged leader of the Chicago School, although in retrospect we see the pervasive influence of George Herbert Mead as well. Dewey also exercised that leadership, albeit indirectly, after he left the University of Chicago in 1904. His abrupt departure at that time also signalized the end of a second major event in Dewey's Chicago years: his founding of "the laboratory school."[9] At its maximum size in 1904, this school served well over 100 children, ranging from ages four to fifteen. Dewey saw the school as not only a laboratory for pedagogy but also a way to pursue experimentally the wider problems of inquiry in an interdisciplinary context. Dewey had great support from the parents and the community, but a combination of personal and financial strains, set in the environment of the politics of the comparatively new University of Chicago, spelled its demise. The ending of the laboratory school was a very unpleasant affair for Dewey. While he was away, the president of the University of Chicago arranged a merger of Dewey's school with the Chicago Institute under the direction of the University School of Education. He also arranged for the resignation of Mrs. Dewey as principal of the laboratory school. Upon returning home, Dewey was appalled at the high-handedness of this decision, and he promptly resigned from all three of his positions at the University of Chicago. At the age of forty-four, he accepted a position as professor of philosophy at Columbia University in New York City, which was to be his home for close to half a century.

Two other events, both catastrophic, intruded upon Dewey's life during the ten years of his Chicago period. The first, in 1895, was the death of his third child, Morris, of diphtheria in Milan at the age of two and a half. Even at such a young age, he was apparently a child of rare promise, and his tragic death inflicted a lifelong wound on John and Alice Dewey. Not quite ten years later untimely death struck again, this time felling the Dewey's fourth child, Gordon. Only eight years of age and very gifted, Gordon was a victim of typhoid fever, dying in a hospital in Ireland while the Deweys were vacationing before beginning their life at Columbia University. The death of Gordon revisited the Deweys with all the sadness and inexplicability of the death of Morris. Evelyn Dewey writes of this event that "the blow to Mrs. Dewey was so serious that she never fully recovered her former energy."[10]

Many years later, in *Experience and Education*, John Dewey wrote that "We always live at the time we live and not at some other time, and only by extracting at each present time the full meaning of each present experience are we prepared for doing the same thing in the future. This is the only preparation which in the long run amounts to anything."[11] A typical interpretation of this kind of statement from Dewey holds that he is present-minded, locked in immediacy, without adequate sense of the ravages or joys of the past. Reading Dewey through the experience of the death of his two sons yields a different point of view. I offer that for Dewey the above text and many others point to the irreducible presence of loss and suffering in all events, an experiential shadow accompanying our efforts at ". . . extracting at each present time the full meaning of each present experience. . . ." Dewey's way of confronting the death of Gordon was to return to Italy, the site of the earlier death of Morris, where he and his wife adopted an orphan boy, Sabino. This child grew wise in ways different from those anticipated for Morris and Gordon. In some ways, however, he was distinctively a Dewey child. Gifted with his hands, a master of the sea, Sabino taught and innovated programs in the industrial arts. At more than seventy years of age, he was seen picketing in New York City on behalf of a young pacifist sentenced to five years for refusal to serve in the Vietnam War. The loss of Morris and Gordon—the precarious—the adoption and odyssey of Sabino—the stable—is what John Dewey means by the relationship between suffering and celebration, the precarious and the stable.

The years from 1904 to his retirement in 1930 found Dewey teaching at Columbia University and at Teachers College. He also made a series of lecture trips and educational surveys to Japan, China, Turkey, Mexico, and the Soviet Union.[12] His involvements in public matters of a social, political, and educational nature during this time and after his retirement from teaching are too numerous to even list.[13] It should be noted, however, that he was a founder and first president of the American Association of University Professors. He was also involved in the founding of the teacher union movement in New York City and was a charter member of the New York Teachers' Guild of the American Federation of Teachers.[14] In 1937, at the age of seventy-eight, John

Dewey served in Mexico City as chairman of the Commission of Inquiry into the Charges Made Against Leon Trotsky in the Moscow Trials.[15] The international observers of the trial were extremely impressed with Dewey's tact, wisdom and, not least, energy during the proceedings. Despite his extraordinary involvement in public affairs, Dewey still wrote voluminously and addressed himself to philosophical problems, both those long-standing and those emerging with each generation. He was invited to a number of prestigious lecture series, among them the Carus Lectures (*Experience and Nature*), the Gifford Lectures (*The Quest for Certainty*), and the William James Lectures (*Art as Experience*).

In 1927 Dewey's wife Alice died of arteriosclerosis. Actually, the loss of her position in the laboratory school in Chicago and the death of her two sons made even more inroads on her person than on her husband. Not having the vast distractions, which characterize the life of a public figure, her world was more inundated by the loss. After her death Dewey depended increasingly on his children for care and concern until 1946, when he remarried. His second wife was Roberta Lowitz Grant, who came originally from Oil City, Pennsylvania, and whose family knew Dewey for many years. John and Roberta Dewey adopted two children, John and Adrienne. It is of note that the first John Dewey II, Dewey's grandson, the child of Frederick and Elizabeth Dewey, was killed in an automobile accident at age thirteen in 1934.

After a series of what turned out to be premature *Festschriften* and farewell birthday celebrations in 1929,[16] 1939,[17] and 1949,[18] Dewey, publicly active to the very end, died on June 1, 1952, at his home, 1158 Fifth Avenue, New York City. He was ninety-two years of age. His second wife, Roberta Dewey, died in Florida on May 6, 1970.

This short biographical summary has no doubt failed to indicate Dewey's charm and the lighter side of his person. Although far too little of that quality of Dewey is on record, some gleaning of his person can be found in the aforementioned essay by Eastman and in the reminiscing found in Lamont's edition of the *Dialogue on John Dewey*. Most of us who are intrigued by Dewey have heard delightful stories about him, but we just as often hear them from someone else with all the data changed. The likely apocryphal nature of these stories is cautioning.

It is known that John Dewey was not an especially adept teacher if flamboyance of personal style is the criterion. But if depth of insight, concentration, loyalty to students, and original thinking in the classroom become the criteria, then Dewey was a superb teacher. And it is also known that Dewey was a man of extraordinary personal integrity, who often risked his reputation in a defense of others, even when the cause was as unpopular as it was transitory. An obvious case in point is his well-known defense of Bertrand Russell, with whom he had little personal or philosophical sympathy, when Russell was denied his appointment to City College in New York on alleged moral grounds.[19] More revealing, perhaps, of Dewey's person was his reaction to the Maxim Gorki affair. Gorki arrived in New York to obtain support for the Russian Revolution and was accompanied by his common-law wife. Under great attack by czarist elements in America, Gorki's moral character was ridiculed, and he was reportedly ousted from a number of hotels. Support for him was difficult to rally, and even Mark Twain reneged, stating that "laws can be evaded and punishment escaped, but an openly transgressed custom brings sure punishment."[20] In the midst of this public outcry, John Dewey offered his home to Gorki and his mistress. The publicity in this instance was unusual but the hospitality was not, for the Deweys often housed on a temporary basis people fleeing or making one revolution or another, be they Irish or Chinese. Of course, even without visitors the Dewey house was always filled with children and later with grandchildren. It is legend that Dewey, despite his involvements and the complexity of his domestic life, was able to persist in his work, as if his ever-present typewriter were an extension of his body, reflecting and producing all the while.

Although it is true that at the present time extensive and trustworthy information about Dewey's personal life is difficult to obtain, nonetheless one aspect of his later life has been brought posthumously to public awareness—namely, his extensive correspondence with Arthur Bentley[21] (1870-1957), which not only casts profound light on Dewey's thought and on the rigor of his mind but also tells us of his sensitivity, his modesty, and his ability to cultivate a deep friendship without any pandering or false affection. And this despite the fact that the published correspondence is that which met the criterion of philosophical viability, thereby lamentably leaving out the more personal commentary.

The story quite simply is this: When Arthur Bentley was a young lecturer in sociology in the late 1890's at the University of Chicago, he audited some of Dewey's courses. He did not make Dewey's acquaintance at that time and went on to a career in political journalism and free-lance speculation in logic and mathematics. In 1932, almost forty years later, he sent Dewey the following letter from Paoli, Indiana:

My Dear Professor Dewey:

    While you were at Chicago, I had a place at the outer edge of one of your courses, where I secured a certain manner of vision which, so far as I can appraise such things, I have long regarded as one of the three or four most valuable aids I have received. I have at length found a region of investigation in which some tentative results can be secured, and I am permitting myself to send you a copy of the resulting book, *Linguistic Analysis of Mathematics*. I do this, I may add, entirely for my own satisfaction by way of making acknowledgements.

    With the strongest wishes for success in your present political work.

Sincerely yours,

ARTHUR F. BENTLEY[22]

Some two and a half years later Dewey answered this letter. Addressed to "Dear Mr. Bentley," the first few lines read as follows:

    Some time ago I received a copy of your *Linguistic Analysis of Mathematics*. I fear I didn't acknowledge it. At all events as I was occupied with other matters, I didn't read it. Recently I have read it, and am still re-reading it. It has given me more enlightenment and intellectual help than any book I have read for a very long time. . . .[23]

Thus began a correspondence that was to last for almost twenty years, covering Dewey's age-span from seventy-three to ninety-two and Bentley's from sixty-two to eighty-one. They ranged over the full spectrum of contemporary philosophy, made visits into the past, and challenged friends and foes alike. They doubted and recast philosophical term after term, and in passing they offered brilliant analyses of ordinary language. Bentley, often acidic in style, was mostly on the attack as directed to their philosophical peers. Dewey was forthright in opinion but gentle in manner, ever cutting through Bentley's rhetoric to state their shared position with acumen and dignity. Slow to be informal in address,[24] they became companions in inquiry, seemingly sensing that the end of the correspondence would be the end of everything. In 1945, when eighty-five years of age, Dewey wrote to Bentley that "there is no doubt you are right in feeling that we are leaving out lots of good stuff, but it isn't as if we weren't going to have a chance to write more in the future."[25] And indeed they did, publishing thirteen articles between 1945 and 1949 and revising them for their book *Knowing and the Known*. Throughout the correspondence Dewey evoked a freshness of approach and a constant willingness to begin over. In 1951 he formulated a new and massive task but hinted that he might not be able to manage it. Prescient to the end, he pointed to the problem at the center of what we now call bio-feedback in our attempt to humanize the new media. Dewey wrote to Bentley that "If I ever get the needed strength, I want to write on *knowing* as the way of behaving in which linguistic artifacts transact business with physical artifacts, tools, implements, apparatus, both kinds being planned for the purpose and rendering *inquiry* of necessity an *experimental* transaction. . . ."[26] It is then with considerable sadness that we read the opening lines of the next and last letter from Bentley to Dewey: "Dear John: I haven't heard from you for some time. In much the same figure of speech, however, I might say that I have not heard even from myself."[27] In not quite seven months from that letter John Dewey was dead.

## John Dewey: A Philosophical Perspective

The selections contained in the present volumes constitute an ample representation of John Dewey's philosophy. They are chosen with both Dewey's chronological development and thematic presentation in mind. The editorial commentaries prior to each selection attempt to focus on a root concern of the piece, whether it be historical or problematic. The titles of each volume and the titles of the eight section headings have been chosen with an eye to providing an interpretive context for Dewey's philosophy.[28]

In *The Philosophy of John Dewey* I have subtitled the first volume *The Structure of Experience* and the second *The Lived Experience*. It would be an unfortunate irony if the reader took this separation to be indicative of a bifurcation in the thought of Dewey. To the contrary, Dewey held to no such separation in any fundamental sense, and indeed it can be said that the "lived experience" is precisely the ground from which the "structure of experience" is obtained. His point of departure and style of explication very much depended on the nature of the problem under consideration, although he usually found a way to integrate both concerns in even the most topical piece of writing. Consequently, although the ideal is to read these two volumes consecutively, they also stand on their merits independent of each other.

Dewey once described philosophy as "a generalized theory of criticism."[29] He also wrote that metaphysics is defined by its search for a "generic insight into existence."[30] Both of these positions indicate a concern for structure, but they also locate that structure in an ongoing process, and as a matter of fact, the attempt to delineate the meaning of existence is itself a factor to be considered. For example, in "Existence, Value and Criticism," Dewey writes that:

> The generic insight into existence which alone can define metaphysics in any empirically intelligible sense is itself an added fact of interaction, and is therefore subject to the same requirement of intelligence as any other, natural occurrence: namely, inquiry into the bearings, leadings, and consequences of what it discovers. The universe is no infinite self-representative series, if only because the addition within it of a representation makes it a different universe.[31]

From the sense of the above text, we could rightfully conclude that the search for the structure of experience *is* the lived experience. Thus for Dewey, in the most fundamental sense, philosophy deals with experience which is "had"—that is, undergone, lived. Yet, in functional terms, in this case the pedagogy of presentation, a difference does obtain between Dewey's writings on the meaning of experience and his writings on those specific clusterings of experiences which constitute problematic situations for man such that they elicit direction and possible resolution. Dewey's writings, then, on politics, the arts, society, education, and religion are not to be construed as merely applications of principles derived from his metaphysics. Rather, these writings should be seen as working from a change in venue, sensitized to the qualities of new data and new patterns of organization but nonetheless faithful to the experimental mode of inquiry, which runs consistently throughout all of his work. The "structure of experience" and "the lived experience" represent two contexts from which Dewey proceeds to articulate the nature of the human endeavor.

It is important to note that the term "experience" occurs in both subtitles and in five of the eight section headings. Indeed, it is a crucial term in most of the selections and throughout the entire corpus of Dewey's work. The very obviousness of the term "experience" makes it an unlikely candidate for a root philosophical notion, and Dewey agrees with William James that it is a double-barreled word, as with "history" and "life," referring both to *what* men do and *how* they are acted upon. The ambiguity here is not of semantic origin but is of the nature of man, who in touching is thereby touched. In "Experience and Philosophic Method"\* Dewey elaborates on his comment that "experience is *of* as well as *in* nature."

> It is not experience which is experienced, but nature—stones, plants, animals, diseases, health, temperature, electricity, and so on. Things interacting in certain ways *are* experience; they are what is experienced. Linked in certain other ways with another natural object—the human organism—they are *how* things are experienced as well. Experience thus reaches down into nature; it has depth. It also has breadth and to an indefinitely elastic extent. It stretches. That stretch constitutes inference.

This text, as much as any single text can, conveys the core of Dewey's philosophy. Opening it up slightly, we have the following themes, corresponding in a general way to the concerns of the eight sections of these present volumes. The setting is the interaction of the human organism with nature or with the environment. Nature has a life of its own, undergoing its own relatings, which in turn become what we experience. Our own transaction[32] with the affairs of nature cuts across the givenness of nature and our ways of relating. This is *how* we experience *what* we experience. Dewey was a realist in the sense that the world exists independent of our thought of it, but the meaning *of* the world is inseparable from our *meaning* the world. Experience, therefore, is not headless, for it teems with relational leads, inferences, implications, comparisons, retrospections, directions, warnings, and so on. The rhythm of *how* we experience is an aesthetic, having as its major characteristic the relationship between anticipation and consummation, yet having other perturbations, as mishap, loss, boredom, and listlessness. Pedagogy becomes then the twin effort to integrate the directions of experience with the total needs of the person and to cultivate the ability of an individual to generate new potentialities in his experiencing and to make new relationships so as to foster patterns of growth. And politics is the struggle to construct an optimum environment for the realizing and sanctioning of the aesthetic processes of living. Finally, the entire human endeavor should be an effort to apply the method of creative intelligence in order to achieve optimum possibilities in the never-ending moral struggle to harmonize the means-end relationship[33] for the purpose of enhancing human life and achieving growth. In "The Construction of Good"* Dewey writes:

> The problem of restoring integration and cooperation between man's beliefs about the world in which he lives and his beliefs about the values and purposes that should direct his conduct is the deepest problem of modern life. It is the problem of any philosophy that is not isolated from that life.

Terms such as "integration," "interaction," "transaction," and "means-end relationships" are not objects of Dewey's philosophy so much as they are descriptions of both the affairs of nature and the method of inquiry. Frequently, working from two points of view or from two apparently isolated fields of inquiry, Dewey has the extraordinary capacity to cut across the conceptual and terminological gaps presented by engendering a version of the underlying problem which binds them, in a language closer to our actual experiencing.[34] This approach of Dewey finds him rarely introducing a technical term as a shortcut for the describing of the ongoing experience. The use of technical terms often gains clarity but at the price of isolating the language of the discipline from that of other disciplines and from common recognition by the larger community of inquiry. Dewey's awareness of the difficulty in achieving a rapprochement between philosophic purpose and fidelity to ordinary language is made clear in one of his letters to Arthur Bentley. Commenting on his preparation of a new edition of *Experience and Nature* in 1951, Dewey wrote that he decided to change the title to *Nature and Culture*: "I was dumb not to have seen the need for such a shift when the old text was written. I was still hopeful that the [philosophic] word 'Experience' would be redeemed by [being] returned to its idiomatic usages—which was a piece of historic folly, the hope, I mean. . . ."[35] The many critics of Dewey's prose style should be more aware that the gnarled character of some of his writing traces to a determined effort to articulate the character of our experiences in a language faithful to our way of having them and in as rich a descriptive version as possible.

A knowledge of two other general themes in Dewey's philosophy will be of assistance to the reader of these volumes. The first, which is at the center of Dewey's logic and epistemology, is his affirmation that "knowing is one mode of experiencing." Stated most clearly in "The

Postulate of Immediate Empiricism"* but often elsewhere and in different ways, Dewey's position is that the process of inquiry is that specific way of having experience in which things are "experienced as known things," as "compared with things experienced esthetically, or morally, or economically or technologically." Put another way, things are what they are experienced to be, only one way of which is to know them. One implication of this position taken by Dewey is that there are multiple ways of experiencing the world which do not necessarily translate into the specific conceptual apparatus that accompanies knowing about something. Without challenging, at this point, the too exhaustive distinction between the cognitive and noncognitive,[36] suffice it to say that for Dewey experiencing is a learning consistent with the variety of ways of experiencing. One such way is to experience by knowing about things and structuring their relationship in a logic of inquiry. His text in "The Postulate of Immediate Empiricism"* will prove helpful here:

> By our postulate, things are what they are experienced to be; and unless knowing is the sole and only genuine mode of experiencing, it is fallacious to say that Reality is just and exclusively what it is or would be to an all-competent all-knower; or even that it *is* relatively and piece-meal, what it is to a finite and partial knower. Or, put more positively, knowing is one mode of experiencing, and the primary philosophic demand (from the standpoint of immediatism) is to find out *what* sort of an experience knowing is—or, concretely how things are experienced when they are experienced *as* known things.

In our discussion of approaches to these selections from the writings of John Dewey, one further general theme should be mentioned—namely, the role of the body in his philosophy. Less obvious than the concerns already examined and discussed rarely by commentators, it is nonetheless of central importance. Of course, for readers who are familiar with phenomenological and existential writings, Dewey's references to the body will seem tame and indirect. And for those who are acquainted with the work of Freud and the host of thinkers with allied concerns, the comparative absence of sexual themes in Dewey's writing may lead to the view that his interests were mainly cerebral and detached from the activities of the lived body. In effect, one does not find in Dewey's writing those hyperpersonal metaphors and descriptions that characterize so vividly the contemporary self-consciousness about bodily states and psychosexual activity. Even were Dewey to have had access to contemporary literature, it is doubtful that he would have altered his style dramatically. For one thing, despite his cosmopolitan experiences, he maintained a Yankee simplicity to his person, and the experience of the "underground" man or the world of a Kafka and Genet would be extremely peripheral to his vision. Also, Dewey was very wary of the seductive character of language and strove to avoid the use of the flamboyant phrase, choosing rather to make his point in the "plain style."

These limitations of perspective and style should not mislead us, however, into thinking that Dewey had no sense of the body or of the themes so central to contemporary thought. To the contrary, if we make some concessions to Dewey's style and allow him to speak in his own language, we discover at least three concerns that occupied him throughout his entire life and that attest dramatically to the presence of the lived body at the center of all of his philosophy. First, he insisted that the meaning of life was to be found in "growth"—that is, in an embodied process—rather than in a state of being, such as happiness or success. Second, he had unusual insight into nonsexual repression—that is, to the damage done to our person by the insensitivity, irrelevance, and manipulation of many of our institutions. As a case in point, Dewey's attempt to create a school distinctively for children, environmentally as well as intellectually, ranks with the work of Maria Montessori as one of the two early major efforts to liberate children in their bodily experience. Third, Dewey early maintained and finally articulated in detail in *Art as Experience* that the affective dimension of human activity was to be considered as central rather than peripheral in any evaluation of its worth. Further, he held that we learn of the affective not so much in the perusal of the affairs and objects of high culture but in sensitizing ourselves to the aesthetic rhythm of our bodies as we live our daily lives.

The body, then, is not alien to Dewey's philosophy. And given the rarity of his references to our sexual situation, we should remember that Dewey's philosophy had as its starting point the transaction of the organism with the world. Although agreeing to the primary role of the biological in any assessment of human life, some thinkers, such as Freud in *Civilization and Its Discontents*[37] and Norman O. Brown in *Life Against Death*,[38] are pessimistic about the outcome of such transactions. For them, and for countless other thinkers, repression and alienation necessarily dominate the life of man. John Dewey, while not pollyanna in his approach or naïve in his expectations, sees it differently. In "The Live Creature"* Dewey wrote that:

> Life itself consists of phases in which the organism falls out of step with the march of surrounding things and then recovers unison with it—either through effort or by some happy chance. And, in a growing life, the recovery is never mere return to a prior state, for it is enriched by the state of disparity and resistance through which it has successfully passed. If the gap between organism and environment is too wide, the creature dies. If its activity is not enhanced by the temporary alienation, it merely subsists. Life grows when a temporary falling out is a transition to a more extensive balance of the energies of the organism with those of the conditions under which it lives.

At first glance this text may appear gentle and comforting. A closer look, however, reveals that alienation and death present themselves in the course of events, and the line between the temporary alienation necessary to the enhancement of life and the gap of permanent alienation which spells death, physical or spiritual, is a thin one. The blame for crossing it is placed not on nature, or on civilization, or on a *deus ex machina,* but on ourselves. In John Dewey's philosophy, the task of overcoming alienation and reconstituting the processes of living is one which is laced with chance, but the responsibility is ours and ours alone.

# Notes

1 Cf. Ralph L. Rusk, *The Life of Ralph Waldo Emerson* (New York, Charles Scribner's Sons, 1949), and Stephen E. Whicher, "Emerson's Tragic Sense," Milton Konvitz and Stephen Whicher, eds., *Emerson* (New York, Prentice Hall 1962), pp. 39-45.

2 Until we receive the long-awaited biography of Peirce by Max H. Fisch, *cf*. Paul K. Conkin, *Puritans and Pragmatists* (New York, Dodd, Mead & Co., 1968), pp. 193-207.

3 For the literature about James, *cf*. John J. McDermott, "Introduction," *The Writings of William James* (New York, Random House, 1967), pp. xiii-xliv.

4 For the literature about Royce, *cf*. John J. McDermott, "Introduction," *The Basic Writings of Josiah Royce* (Chicago, University of Chicago Press, 1969), Vol. I, pp. 3-18.

5 *Cf. e.g.* Corliss Lamont, ed., *Dialogue on John Dewey* (New York, Horizon Press, 1959), and Max Eastman, *Great Companions* (New York, Farrar, Straus and Cudahy, 1959), pp. 249-98.

6 Jane Dewey, ed., "Biography of John Dewey," in Paul Arthur Schilpp, ed., *The Philosophy of John Dewey* (New York, Tudor Publishing Co., 1951) (1939), pp. 3-45.

7 *Cf*. Darnell Rucker, *The Chicago Pragmatists* (Minneapolis, University of Minnesota Press, 1969), for a detailed history of this movement. *Cf*. also Charles Morris, *The Pragmatic Movement* (New York, George Braziller, 1970), pp. 174-91 for a discussion of the Chicago School.

8 Rucker, *op. cit.*, p. vi.

9 *Cf*. Katherine Camp Mayhew and Anna Camp Edwards, *The Dewey School* (New York, Appleton-Century Co., 1936); Melvin C. Baker, *Foundations of John Dewey's Educational Theory* (New York, Atherton Press, 1966), pp. 136-57; and George Dykhuizen, "John Dewey: The Chicago Years," *Journal of the History of Philosophy*, II (October, 1964), pp. 227-53; "John Dewey in Chicago:

Some Biographical Notes,'' *Journal of the History of Philosophy*, III (October, 1965) pp. 217-33.

10 Jane Dewey, ed., ''The Biography of John Dewey,'' p. 35. *Cf.* also Eastman, *op. cit.*, pp. 279-80.

11 John Dewey, *Experience and Education* (New York, Macmillan Co., 1956) (1938), p. 51.

12 *C.f e.g.* William W. Brickman, *John Dewey's Impressions of Soviet Russia and the Revolutionary World, Mexico—China—Turkey, 1929* (New York, Teacher's College, 1964).

13 A sample of Dewey's range of interests and the astonishing level of competence he maintained in addressing public issues can be found in Joseph Ratner, ed., *Characters and Events—Popular Essays in Social and Political Philosophy* (New York, Henry Holt and Co., 1929), 2 Vols. Much of Dewey's sensitivity to these matters can be traced to Jane Addams and her work at Hull House in Chicago.

14 Dewey participated widely in the labor movement. *Cf.* his sympathetic account of the president of the International Ladies Garment Workers Union in *David Dubinsky—A Pictorial Biography* (New York, Inter-Allied Publications, 1951), pp. 13-19, 21-28.

15 *Cf. The Case of Leon Trotsky* (New York, Merit Publishers, 1968) (1937), *passim,* and *Not Guilty* (New York, Harper and Bros., 1938).

16 *Essays in Honor of John Dewey* (New York, Henry Holt and Co., 1929). Of particular interest in this book is the large number of Columbia University colleagues and students of Dewey who join with his older Chicago colleagues in tribute. Thus, F. J. E. Woodbridge, an important philosophical influence on Dewey, and Herbert Schneider, John Herman Randall, Jr., and Sidney Hook, each to become a distinguished interpreter of Dewey's thought, are among the contributors.

17 *The Philosopher of the Common Man—Essays in Honor of John Dewey* (New York, Greenwood Press, 1968) (1940).

18 Sidney Hook, ed., *John Dewey—Philosopher of Science and Freedom* (New York, Dial Press, 1950).

19 *Cf.* John Dewey and Horace M. Kallen, ed., *The Bertrand Russell Case* (New York, Viking Press, 1941), and Bertrand Russell, *The Autobiography of Bertrand Russell—The Middle Years: 1914-1944* (New York, Bantam Books, 1969), pp. 341-44.

20 *Cf.* Howard Mumford Jones, *The Age of Energy—Varieties of American*

*Experience, 1865-1915* (New York, Viking Press, 1971), p. 184. *Cf.* also, Eastman, *op. cit.*, pp. 288-89.

21 Sidney Ratner, Jules Altman, and James E. Wheeler, eds., *John Dewey and Arthur F. Bentley, A Philosophical Correspondence—1932-1951* (New Brunswick, Rutgers University Press, 1964). Surperbly introduced, edited, and printed, this book is a selection of almost 600 pages of correspondence from among 2,000 pieces collected by the editors. It also contains two previously unpublished essays by Dewey and drafts of material used subsequently in Dewey and Bentley's collaborative book, *Knowing and the Known* (Boston, Beacon Press, 1949).

22 Ratner *et. al.*, *Dewey and Bentley*, *op. cit.*, p. 51.

23 *Ibid.*

24 Dewey didn't drop the "Mr." in his salutation until 1939, while Bentley waited until 1942. And they did not use first names until 1945.

25 Ratner *et. al.*, *Dewey and Bentley*, *op. cit.*, p. 387.

26 *Ibid.*, p. 646.

27 *Ibid.*

28 There are a variety of sources available for the continued study of Dewey's thought. From among the vast array of writings about John Dewey, informative and trustworthy analyses of the philosophy can be found in Sidney Hook, Morton G. White, H. S. Thayer, and Richard J. Bernstein. Imaginative efforts to relate Dewey's thought to other philosophical and cultural traditions characterize recent work by Robert C. Pollock, Ralph W. Sleeper, Reginald Archambault, and Richard J. Bernstein. A thorough survey of Dewey's main interests is provided in Jo-Ann Boydston's *Guide to the Works of John Dewey* (Carbondale, Southern Illinois University Press, 1969).

29 John Dewey, *Experience and Nature* (New York, Dover Publications, 1958), p. xvi.

30 *Ibid.*, p. 414.

31 The criticism of a "self-representative series" refers to a doctrine held for a time by Josiah Royce.

32 In order to overcome the dualism possibly associated with the term "interaction," Dewey, late in life, came to prefer "transaction." *Cf.* Ratner *et al.*, *Dewey and Bentley*, *op. cit.*, pp. 613-14.

33 *Cf.* John Dewey, *Reconstruction in Philosophy* (Boston, Beacon Press, 1948), p. 73. "When we take means for ends we indeed fall into moral material-

xxxiv NOTES

ism. But when we take ends without regard to means we degenerate into sentimentalism. In the name of the ideal we fall back upon mere luck and chance and magic or exhortation and preaching; or else upon a fanaticism that will force the realization of preconceived ends at any cost.''

34 *Cf.* the comment on Dewey's ability to cut across different and even polarized fields of inquiry in C. Wright Mills, *Sociology and Pragmatism* (New York, Paine-Whitman Publishers, 1964), pp. 314-15.

35 Ratner *et al.*, *Dewey and Bentley, op. cit.*, p. 643.

36 Dewey did not hold to a rigid distinction between cognitive and noncognitive experiences. *Cf.* John Dewey, ''Experience, Knowledge and Value,'' in Schilpp, *op. cit.*, pp. 532-33. ''My theory of the relation of cognitive experiences to other modes of experience is based upon the fact that *connections* exist in the most immediate non-cognitive experience, and when the experienced situation becomes problematic, the connections are developed into distinctive objects of knowledge, whether of common sense or of science.''

37 Sigmund Freud, *Civilization and Its Discontents* (London, Hogarth Press, 1953) (1930).

38 Norman O. Brown, *Life Against Death* (Middletown, Wesleyan University Press, 1959).

# Chronology

1859  Born on October 20, in Burlington, Vermont
1879  Graduates from University of Vermont
      Begins teaching high school at Oil City, Pennsylvania
1881  Teaches in Charlotte, Vermont, and studies philosophy with H. A.
      P. Torrey
1882  Graduate student, Johns Hopkins University
1884  PhD, Johns Hopkins University
      Begins teaching philosophy at the University of Michigan, 1884-88
1886  Marries Alice Chipman
1888  Professor of philosophy, University of Minnesota
1889  Professor of philosophy, University of Michigan, 1889-94
1894  Professor of philosophy and chairman of the Department of
      Philosophy, Psychology, and Education, University of Chicago,
      1894-1904
1899  President of the American Psychological Association, 1899-1900
1904  Professor of philosophy, Columbia University, 1904-30
1905  President of the American Philosophical Association, 1905-06
1915  A founder and first president of the American Association of
      University Professors
1919  Lectures in Japan
      Lectures in China, 1919-21
1924  Visits schools in Turkey
1926  Visits schools in Mexico
1927  Death of Alice Chipman Dewey
1928  Visits schools in Soviet Russia
1930  Professor Emeritus, Columbia
1946  Married to Roberta (Lowitz) Grant
1952  Dies on June 1, in New York City

# Bibliography

Three major bibliographies of John Dewey's writing are now extant. Two of them are arranged chronologically and the third is by subject matter.

1) "Writings of John Dewey, 1882-1950," in Paul Arthur Schilipp, ed., *The Philosophy of John Dewey*. New York, Tudor Publishing Company, 1951, pp. 609-86.

2) "Writings of John Dewey," in *John Dewey: A Centennial Bibliography (1882-1962)*, edited and annotated by Milton Halsey Thomas. Chicago, University of Chicago Press, 1962, pp. 1-153, 298.

3) Jo-Ann Boydston, ed., *Guide to the Works of John Dewey*. Carbondale, Southern Illinois University Press, 1970 (Paperback edition, 1972).

John Dewey's writings have been translated into many other languages. For this information, consult Jo-Ann Boydston and Robert L. Andresen, eds., *John Dewey: A Checklist of Translations, 1900-1967*. Carbondale, Southern Illinois University Press, 1969. For a list of "Writings About John Dewey" consult Thomas, *John Dewey: A Centennial Bibliography*, pp. 195-293.

The following bibliography serves as an introductory list of Dewey's most important books and collections of essays.

### Writings of John Dewey
#### 1882-98

1) *The Early Works of John Dewey*. Carbondale, Southern Illinois University Press, 1967, 1967, 1969, 1971, 1972, 5 vols.

#### 1900

2) *The School and Society*. Chicago, University of Chicago Press, 129 pp. (Rev. ed. 1915, Paperback, Phoenix Books, 1956).

3) *The Child and the Curriculum*. Chicago, University of Chicago Press, 40 pp. (Paperback, Phoenix Books, 1956).

### 1910

4) *How We Think*. Boston, D. C. Heath and Co., 224 pp. (Rev. ed. 1933).
5) *The Influence of Darwin and Other Essays on Contemporary Thought*. New York, Henry Holt and Co., 309 pp. (Paperback, Midland Books, 1965).

### 1916

6) *Democracy and Education*. New York, Macmillan Co., 434 pp. (Macmillan Paperbacks, 1961).
7) *Essays in Experimental Logic*. Chicago, University of Chicago Press, 444 pp. (Paperback, Dover Books, n.d.).

### 1917

8) "The Need for a Recovery of Philosophy," in *Creative Intelligence, Essays in the Pragmatic Attitude*. New York, Henry Holt and Co., pp. 3-69.

### 1920

9) *Reconstruction in Philosophy*. New York, Henry Holt and Co., 224 pp. (Paperback, enlarged edition, Beacon Press, 1957).

### 1922

10) *Human Nature and Conduct*. New York, Henry Holt and Co., 336 pp. (Modern Library edition, 1930).

### 1925

11) *Experience and Nature*. Chicago, Open Court Publishing Co., 443 pp. (Rev. ed., New York, W. W. Norton and Co., 1929). (Paperback, Dover Books, 1958.)

### 1927

12) *The Public and Its Problems*. New York, Henry Holt and Co., 224 pp. (Paperback, Alan Swallow, 1957).

### 1929

13) Joseph Ratner, ed., *Characters and Events: Popular Essays in Social and Political Philosophy*. New York, Henry Holt and Co., 2 vols.
14) *The Quest for Certainty*. New York, Minton, Balch and Co., 318 pp. (Paperback, Capricorn Books, 1960).

### 1930
15) *Individualism Old and New*. New York, Minton, Balch and Co., 171 pp. (Paperback, Capricorn Books, 1962).

### 1931
16) *Philosophy and Civilization*. New York, Minton, Balch and Co., 334 pp. (Paperback, Capricorn Books, 1963).

### 1932
17) John Dewey and James H. Tufts, *Ethics—Revised Edition*. New York, Henry Holt and Co., 528 pp.

### 1934
18) *Art as Experience*. New York, Minton, Balch and Co., 355 pp. (Paperback, Capricorn Books, 1959).
19) *A Common Faith*. New Haven, Yale University Press, 87 pp. (Paperback, Yale, 1960).

### 1935
20) *Liberalism and Social Action*. New York, G. P. Putnam's Sons, 93 pp. (Paperback, Capricorn Books, 1963).

### 1938
21) *Logic: The Theory of Inquiry*. New York, Henry Holt and Co., 546 pp.
22) *Experience and Education*. New York, Macmillan Co., 116 pp. (Paperback, Collier Books, 1963).

### 1939
23) Joseph Ratner, ed., *Intelligence in the Modern World: John Dewey's Philosophy*. New York, Modern Library, 1,077 pp.
24) *Freedom and Culture*. New York, G. P. Putnam's Sons, 176 pp. (Paperback, Capricorn Books, 1963).
25) *Theory of Valuation*. Chicago, University of Chicago Press, 67 pp. (Published originally in the *International Encyclopedia of Unified Science*, Vol. II, No. 4).
26) "Experience, Knowledge and Value: A Rejoinder," in Paul Arthur Schilpp, ed., *The Philosophy of John Dewey*. Evanston, Northwestern University Press, pp. 517-608.

1946

27) *Problems of Men*. New York, Philosophical Library, 424 pp.

1949

28) John Dewey and Arthur F. Bentley, *Knowing and the Known*. Boston, Beacon Press, 334 pp. (Paperback).

1960

29) Richard J. Bernstein, ed., *Dewey on Experience, Nature and Freedom*. New York, Library of Liberal Arts, 293 pp. (Paperback).

1963

30) Joseph Ratner, ed., *Philosophy, Psychology and Social Practice*. New York, G. P. Putnam's Sons, 315 pp. (Paperback, Capricorn Books, 1965).

1964

31) Reginald D. Archambault, ed., *John Dewey on Education*. New York, Modern Library, 439 pp.

32) William W. Brickman, ed., *John Dewey's Impression of Soviet Russia and the Revolutionary World: Mexico—China—Turkey*. New York, Teachers College Publications, 178 pp. (Paperback).

33) Sidney Ratner and Jules Altman, eds., *John Dewey and Arthur Bentley: A Philosophical Correspondence, 1932-1951*. New Brunswick, Rutgers University Press, 737 pp.

1966

34) Reginald D. Archambault, ed., *John Dewey—Lectures in the Philosophy of Education: 1899*. New York, Random House, 366 pp.

# Editor's Note on the Text

The selections in these volumes are each complete in themselves. They were originally chapters in books or essays written for journals and collections of essays. With the exception of an occasional transitional sentence at the beginning or end of a selection, no editorial excisions have been made. A few typographical errors in the original text have been corrected.

Southern Illinois University Press is publishing a complete critical edition of Dewey's work. At this writing, four volumes have appeared, with the fifth imminent. Thus far, only three of the selections in the present volumes have been edited critically by Southern Illinois University Press. They are: "Kant and Philosophic Method," "The Psychological Standpoint," and "Psychology as Philosophic Method." These essays as printed in the critical editions of *The Early Works* are not altered in any substantial way. The critical apparatus, however, that accompanies those editions is very informative as to verifying and providing Dewey's source material. The most signal contribution of this critical apparatus is to make it clear that Dewey was notoriously careless in citing the texts of other thinkers. Serious students of John Dewey are encouraged to utilize the critical editions as they appear. It is to be hoped that the impressive work of the Center for Dewey Studies at Southern Illinois University is to be followed by similar efforts on behalf of William James and Josiah Royce.

The material in the present volumes is cited as to the edition used. If the date of this edition is later than that of the original publication, the latter date is added in parentheses. I have used the latest version of Dewey's writings except in the case of "The Reflex Arc Concept in Psychology." That was chosen for historical reasons over the later, slightly changed, retitled piece "The Unit of Behavior." When Dewey refers to previous or subsequent material, the reference is to the original source and not to the selections in these volumes, unless consecutive chapters have been reprinted. Finally, an asterisk accompanying a reference in the Preface or Introduction indicates that the selection is contained in these volumes.

*Respect for experience is respect for its possibilities in thought and knowledge as well as an enforced attention to its joys and sorrows. Intellectual piety toward experience is a precondition of the direction of life and of tolerant and generous cooperation among men. Respect for the things of experience alone brings with it such a respect for others, the centres of experience, as is free from patronage, domination and the will to impose.*

—JOHN DEWEY, *Experience and Nature, 1925*

# I

## Historical Roots
## and Reflections

With the exception of his early works on Immanuel Kant and Gottfried Wilhelm von Leibniz and some subsequent isolated pieces, Dewey's concern with the history of philosophy was not pronounced, although it exercised a subtle influence on all of his writings. The material collected in this section indicates the range of Dewey's concerns and some of his judgments about prior philosophical efforts. Throughout these two columes many other *aperçus* on the history of philosophy will emerge from Dewey's point of view. It should be kept in mind that Dewey approached philosophy contextually—that is, as inseparable from wider cultural issues.

## 1. From Absolutism to Experimentalism*

Although sparse in detail about his personal life, this essay yields a number of judgments by Dewey which are crucial to any understanding of his life and work. In addition to the influence of some of his first teachers, Dewey stresses the significance of Hegel as "a permanent deposit" in his thinking and points especially to the work of William James as the "one specifiable philosophic factor which entered into my thinking so as to give it a new direction and quality."

The reader should note also Dewey's admission of a "certain skepticism about the depth and range of purely contemporary issues" and his belief that on the whole, the forces that have influenced him "have come from persons and from situations more than books." Finally, as he points to the philosophical significance of his classic work on *Democracy*

---

* From *Contemporary American Philosophers*, George Plimpton Adams and William Pepperell Montague, eds. (New York, 1930), Vol. II, pp. 13-27.

1

*and Education,* we should heed Dewey's chastisement that
philosophers have failed to take education seriously, for this
criticism is still pertinent.

In the late 'seventies, when I was an undergraduate, "electives" were
still unknown in the smaller New England colleges. But in the one I attended, the University of Vermont, the tradition of a "senior-year
course" still subsisted. This course was regarded as a kind of intellectual coping to the structure erected in earlier years, or, at least, as an in-
sertion of the key-stone of the arch. It included courses in political
economy, international law, history of civilization (Guizot), psychology,
ethics, philosophy of religion (Butler's *Analogy*), logic, etc., not history
of philosophy, save incidentally. The enumeration of these titles may
not serve the purpose for which it is made; but the idea was that after
three years of somewhat specialized study in languages and sciences, the
last year was reserved for an introduction into serious intellectual topics
of wide and deep significance—an introduction into the world of ideas.
I doubt if in many cases it served its alleged end; however, it fell in with
my own inclinations, and I have always been grateful for that year of
my schooling. There was, however, one course in the previous year that
had excited a taste that in retrospect may be called philosophical. That
was a rather short course, without laboratory work, in Physiology, a
book of Huxley's being the text. It is difficult to speak with exactitude
about what happened to me intellectually so many years ago, but I have
an impression that there was derived from that study a sense of in-
terdependence and interrelated unity that gave form to intellectual stir-
rings that had been previously inchoate, and created a kind of type or
model of a view of things to which material in any field ought to conform. Subconsciously, at least, I was led to desire a world and a life that
would have the same properties as had the human organism in the picture of it derived from study of Huxley's treatment. At all events, I got
great stimulation from the study, more than from anything I had had
contact with before; and as no desire was awakened in me to continue
that particular branch of learning, I date from this time the awakening
of a distinctive philosophic interest.

The University of Vermont rather prided itself upon its tradition in
philosophy. One of its earlier teachers, Dr. Marsh, was almost the first
person in the United States to venture upon the speculative and
dubiously orthodox seas of German thinking—that of Kant, Schelling,
and Hegel. The venture, to be sure, was made largely by way of Coleridge; Marsh edited an American edition of Coleridge's *Aids to Reflec-*

*tion*. Even this degree of speculative generalization, in its somewhat obvious tendency to rationalize the body of Christian theological doctrines, created a flutter in ecclesiastical dovecots. In particular, a controversy was carried on between the Germanizing rationalizers and the orthodox representatives of the Scottish school of thought through the representatives of the latter at Princeton. I imagine—although it is a very long time since I have had any contact with this material—that the controversy still provides data for a section, if not a chapter, in the history of thought in this country.

Although the University retained pride in its pioneer work, and its atmosphere was for those days theologically "liberal"—of the Congregational type—the teaching of philosophy had become more restrained in tone, more influenced by the still dominant Scotch school. Its professor, Mr. H. A. P. Torrey, was a man of genuinely sensitive and cultivated mind, with marked esthetic interest and taste, which, in a more congenial atmosphere than that of northern New England in those days, would have achieved something significant. He was, however, constitutionally timid, and never really let his mind go. I recall that, in a conversation I had with him a few years after graduation, he said: "Undoubtedly pantheism is the most satisfactory form of metaphysics intellectually, but it goes counter to religious faith." I fancy that remark told of an inner conflict that prevented his native capacity from coming to full fruition. His interest in philosophy, however, was genuine, not perfunctory; he was an excellent teacher, and I owe to him a double debt, that of turning my thoughts definitely to the study of philosophy as a life-pursuit, and of a generous gift of time to me during a year devoted privately under his direction to a reading of classics in the history of philosophy and learning to read philosophic German. In our walks and talks during this year, after three years on my part of high-school teaching, he let his mind go much more freely than in the classroom, and revealed potentialities that might have placed him among the leaders in the development of a freer American philosophy—but the time for the latter had not yet come.

Teachers of philosophy were at that time, almost to a man, clergymen; the supposed requirements of religion, or theology, dominated the teaching of philosophy in most colleges. Just how and why Scotch philosophy lent itself so well to the exigencies of religion I cannot say; probably the causes were more extrinsic than intrinsic; but at all events there was a firm alliance established between religion and the cause of "intuition". It is probably impossible to recover at this date the almost sacrosanct air that enveloped the idea of intuitions; but somehow the cause of all holy and valuable things was supposed to stand or fall with the validity of intuitionalism; the only vital issue was that between intuitionalism and a sensational empiricism that explained away the reality of all higher objects. The story of this almost forgotten debate, once so urgent, is probably a factor in developing in me a certain scepticism about the depth and range of purely contemporary issues; it is likely that many of those which seem highly important to-day will also in a generation have receded to the status of the local and provincial. It also aided in generating a sense of the value of the history of philosophy; some of the claims made for this as a sole avenue of approach to the study of philosophic problems seem to me misdirected and injurious. But its value in giving perspective and a sense of proportion in relation to immediate contemporary issues can hardly be overestimated.

I do not mention this theological and intuitional phase because it had any lasting influence upon my own development, except negatively. I learned the terminology of an intuitional philosophy, but it did not go deep, and in no way did it satisfy what I was dimly reaching for. I was brought up in a conventionally evangelical atmosphere of the more "liberal" sort; and the struggles that later arose between acceptance of that faith and the discarding of traditional and institutional creeds came from personal experiences and not from the effects of philosophical teaching. It was not, in other words, in this respect that philosophy either appealed to me or influenced me—though I am not sure that Butler's *Analogy,* with its cold logic and acute analysis, was not, in a reversed way, a factor in developing "scepticism".

During the year of private study, of which mention has been made, I decided to make philosophy my life-study, and accordingly went to Johns Hopkins the next year (1884) to enter upon that new thing, "graduate work". It was something of a risk; the work offered there was almost the only indication that there were likely to be any self-supporting jobs in the field of philosophy for others than clergymen. Aside from the effect of my study with Professor Torrey, another influence moved me to undertake the risk. During the years after graduation I had kept up philosophical readings and I had even written a few articles which I sent to Dr. W. T. Harris, the well-known Hegelian, and the editor of the *Journal of Speculative Philosophy,* the only philosophic journal in the country at that time, as he and his group formed almost the only group of laymen devoted to philosophy for non-theological reasons. In sending an article I asked Dr. Harris for advice as to the possibility of my successfully prosecuting philosophic studies. His reply was so encouraging that it was a distinct factor in deciding me to try philosophy as a professional career.

The articles sent were, as I recall them, highly schematic and formal; they were couched in the language of intuitionalism; of Hegel I was then ignorant. My deeper interests had not as yet been met, and in the absence of subject-matter that would correspond to them, the only topics at my command were such as were capable of a merely formal treatment. I imagine that my development has been controlled largely by a struggle between a native inclination toward the schematic and formally logical, and those incidents of personal experience that compelled me to take account of actual material. Probably there is in the consciously articulated ideas of every thinker an over-weighting of just those things that are contrary to his natural tendencies, an emphasis upon those things that are contrary to his intrinsic bent, and which, therefore, he has to struggle to bring to expression, while the native bent, on the other hand, can take care of itself. Anyway, a case might be made out for the proposition that the emphasis upon the concrete, empirical, and "practical" in my later writings is partly due to considerations of this nature. It was a reaction against what was more natural, and it served as a protest and protection against something in myself which, in the pressure of the weight of actual experiences, I knew to be a weakness. It is, I suppose, becoming a commonplace that when anyone is unduly concerned with controversy, the remarks that seem to be directed against others are really concerned with a struggle that is going on inside himself. The marks, the stigmata, of the struggle to weld together the characteristics of a formal, theoretic interest and the material of a maturing experience of contacts with realities also showed themselves, naturally, in style of writing and manner of presentation. During the time when the schematic interest predominated, writing was comparatively easy; there were even compliments upon the clearness of my style. Since then thinking and writing have been hard work. It is easy to give way to the dialectic development of a theme; the pressure of concrete experiences was, however, sufficiently heavy, so that a sense of intellectual honesty prevented a surrender to that course. But, on the other hand, the formal interest persisted, so that there was an inner demand for an intellectual technique that would be consistent and yet capable of flexible adaptation to the concrete diversity of experienced things. It is hardly necessary to say that I have not been among those to whom the union of abilities to satisfy these two opposed requirements, the formal and the material, came easily. For that very reason I have been acutely aware, too much so, doubtless, of a tendency of other thinkers and writers to achieve a specious lucidity and simplicity by the mere process of ignoring considerations which a greater respect for concrete materials of experience would have forced upon them.

It is a commonplace of educational history that the opening of Johns Hopkins University marked a new epoch in higher education in the United States. We are probably not in a condition as yet to estimate the extent to which its foundation and the development of graduate schools in other universities, following its example, mark a turn in our American culture. The 'eighties and 'nineties seem to mark the definitive close of our pioneer period, and the turn from the civil war era into the new industrialized and commercial age. In philosophy, at least, the influence of Johns Hopkins was not due to the size of the provision that was made. There was a half-year of lecturing and seminar work given by Professor George Sylvester Morris, of the University of Michigan; belief in the "demonstrated" (a favourite word of his) truth of the substance of German idealism, and of belief in its competency to give direction to a life of aspiring thought, emotion, and action. I have never known a more single-hearted and whole-souled man—a man of a single piece all the way through; while I long since deviated from his philosophic faith, I should be happy to believe that the influence of the spirit of his teaching has been an enduring influence.

While it was impossible that a young and impressionable student, unacquainted with any system of thought that satisfied his head and heart, should not have been deeply affected, to the point of at least a temporary conversion, by the enthusiastic and scholarly devotion of Mr. Morris, this effect was far from being the only source of my own "Hegelianism". The 'eighties and 'nineties were a time of new ferment in English thought; the reaction against atomic individualism and sensationalistic empiricism was in full swing. It was the time of Thomas Hill Green, of the two Cairds, of Wallace, of the appearance of the *Essays in Philosophical Criticism,* co-operatively produced by a younger group under the leadership of the late Lord Haldane. This movement was at the time the vital and constructive one in philosophy. Naturally its influence fell in with and reinforced that of Professor Morris. There was but one marked difference, and that, I think, was in favour of Mr. Morris. He came to Kant through Hegel instead of to Hegel by way of Kant, so that his attitude toward Kant was the critical one expressed by Hegel himself. Moreover, he retained something of his early Scotch philosophical training in a common-sense belief in the existence of the external world. He used to make merry over those who thought the *existence* of this world and of matter were things to be proved by philosophy. To him the only philosophical question was as to the *meaning* of this existence; his idealism was wholly of the objective type. Like his contemporary, Professor John Watson, of Kingston, he combined a logical and idealistic metaphysics with a realistic epistemology. Through his teacher at Berlin, Trendelenburg, he had acquired a great reverence for Aristotle, and he had no difficulty in uniting Aristoteleanism with Hegelianism.

There were, however, also "subjective" reasons for the appeal that Hegel's thought made to me; it supplied a demand for unification that was doubtless an intense emotional craving, and yet was a hunger that only an intellectualized subject-matter could satisfy. It is more than difficult, it is impossible, to recover that early mood. But the sense of divisions and separations that were, I suppose, borne in upon me as a consequence of a heritage of New England culture, divisions by way of isolation of self from the world, of soul from body, of nature from God, brought a painful oppression—or, rather, they were an inward laceration. My earlier philosophic study had been an intellectual gymnastic. Hegel's synthesis of subject and object, matter and spirit, the divine and the human, was, however, no mere intellectual formula; it operated as an immense release, a liberation. Hegel's treatment of human culture, of institutions and the arts, involved the same dissolution of hard-and-fast dividing walls, and had a special attraction for me.

As I have already intimated, while the conflict of traditional religious beliefs with opinions that I could myself honestly entertain was the source of a trying personal crisis, it did not at any time constitute a leading philosophical problem. This might look as if the two things were kept apart; in reality it was due to a feeling that any genuinely sound religious experience could and should adapt itself to whatever beliefs one found oneself intellectually entitled to hold—a half unconscious sense at first, but one which ensuing years have deepened into a fundamental conviction. In consequence, while I have, I hope, a due degree of personal sympathy with individuals who are undergoing the throes of a personal change of attitude, I have not been able to attach much importance to religion as a philosophic problem; for the effect of that attachment seems to be in the end a subornation of candid philosophic thinking to the alleged but factitious needs of some special set of convictions. I have enough faith in the depth of the religious tendencies of men to believe that they will adapt themselves to any required intellectual change, and that it is futile (and likely to be dishonest) to forecast prematurely just what forms the religious interest will take as a final consequence of the great intellectual transformation that is going on. As I have been frequently criticized for undue reticence about the problems of religion, I insert this explanation: it seems to me that the great solicitude of many persons, professing belief in the universality of the need for religion, about the present and future of religion proves that in fact they are moved more by partisan interest in a particular religion than by interest in religious experience.

The chief reason, however, for inserting these remarks at this point is to bring out a contrast effect. Social interests and problems from an early period had to me the intellectual appeal and provided the intellectual sustenance that many seem to have found primarily in religious questions. In undergraduate days I had run across, in the college library, Harriet Martineau's exposition of Comte. I cannot remember that his law of "the three stages" affected me particularly; but his idea of the disorganized character of Western modern culture, due to a disintegrative "individualism", and his idea of a synthesis of science that should be a regulative method of an organized social life, impressed me deeply. I found, as I thought, the same criticisms combined with a deeper and more far-reaching integration in Hegel. I did not, in those days when I read Francis Bacon, detect the origin of the Comtean idea in him, and I had not made acquaintance with Condorcet, the connecting link.

I drifted away from Hegeliansim in the next fifteen years; the word "drifting" expresses the slow and, for a long time, imperceptible character of the movement, though it does not convey the impression that there was an adequate cause for the change. Nevertheless I should never think of ignoring, much less denying, what an astute critic occasionally refers to as a novel discovery—that acquaintance with Hegel has left a permanent deposit in my thinking. The form, the schematism, of his system now seems to me artificial to the last degree. But in the content of his ideas there is often an extraordinary depth; in many of his analyses, taken out of their mechanical dialectical setting, an extraordinary acuteness. Were it possible for me to be a devotee of any system, I still should believe that there is greater richness and greater variety of insight in Hegel than in any other single systematic philosopher—though when I say this I exclude Plato, who still provides my favourite philosophic reading. For I am unable to find in him that all-comprehensive and overriding system which later interpretation has, as it seems to me, conferred upon him as a dubious boon. The ancient sceptics overworked another aspect of Plato's thought when they treated him as their spiritual father, but they were nearer the truth, I think, than those who force him into the frame of a rigidly systematized doctrine. Although I have not the aversion to system as such that is sometimes attributed to me, I am dubious of my own ability to reach inclusive systematic unity, and in consequence, perhaps, of that fact also dubious about my contemporaries. Nothing could be more helpful to present philosophizing than a "Back to Plato" movement; but it would have to be back to the dramatic, restless, co-operatively inquiring Plato of the Dialogues, trying one mode of attack after another to see what it might yield; back to the Plato whose highest flight of metaphysics always terminated with a social and practical turn, and not to the artificial Plato constructed by unimaginative commentators who treat him as the original university professor.

The rest of the story of my intellectual development I am unable to record without more faking than I care to indulge in. What I have so far related is so far removed in time that I can talk about myself as another person; and much has faded, so that a few points stand out without my having to force them into the foreground. The philosopher, if I may apply that word to myself, that I became as I moved away from German idealism, is too much the self that I still am and is still too much in process of change to lend itself to record. I envy, up to a certain point, those who can write their intellectual biography in a unified pattern, woven out of a few distinctly discernible strands of interest and influence. By contrast, I seem to be unstable, chameleon-like, yielding one after another to many diverse and even incompatible influences; struggling to assimilate something from each and yet striving to carry it forward in a way that is logically consistent with what has been learned from its predecessors. Upon the whole, the forces that have influenced me have come from persons and from situations more than from books—not that I have not, I hope, learned a great deal from philosophical writings, but that what I have learned from them has been technical in comparison with what I have been forced to think upon and about because of some experience in which I found myself entangled. It is for this reason that I cannot say with candour that I envy completely, or envy beyond a certain point, those to whom I have referred. I like to think, though it may be a defence reaction, that with all the inconveniences of the road I have been forced to travel, it has the compensatory advantage of not inducing an immunity of thought to experiences—which perhaps, after all should not be treated even by a philosopher as the germ of a disease to which he needs to develop resistance.

While I cannot write an account of intellectual development without giving it the semblance of a continuity that it does not in fact own, there are four special points that seem to stand out. One is the importance that the practice and theory of education have had for me: especially the education of the young, for I have never been able to feel much optimism regarding the possibilities of "higher" education when it is built upon warped and weak foundations. This interest fused with and brought together what might otherwise have been separate interests— that in psychology and that in social institutions and social life. I can recall but one critic who has suggested that my thinking has been too much permeated by interest in education. Although a book called *Democracy and Education* was for many years that in which my philosophy, such as it is, was most fully expounded, I do not know that philosophic critics, as distinct from teachers, have ever had recourse to it. I have wondered whether such facts signified that philosophers in general, although they are themselves usually teachers, have not taken education with sufficient seriousness for it to occur to them that any rational person could actually think it possible that philosophizing should focus about education as the supreme human interest in which, moreover, other problems, cosmological, moral, logical, come to a head. At all events, this handle is offered to any subsequent critic who may wish to lay hold of it.

A second point is that as my study and thinking progressed, I became more and more troubled by the intellectual scandal that seemed to me involved in the current (and traditional) dualism in logical standpoint and method between something called "science" on the one hand and something called "morals" on the other. I have long felt that the construction of a logic, that is, a method of effective inquiry, which would apply without abrupt breach of continuity to the fields designated by both of these words, is at once our needed theoretical solvent and the supply of our greatest practical want. This belief has had much more to do with the development of what I termed, for lack of a better word, "instrumentalism", than have most of the reasons that have been assigned.

The third point forms the great exception to what was said about no very fundamental vital influence issuing from books; it concerns the influence of William James. As far as I can discover, one specifiable philosophic factor which entered into my thinking so as to give it a new direction and quality, it is this one. To say that it proceeded from his *Psychology* rather than from the essays collected in the volume called *Will to Believe*, his *Pluralistic Universe,* or *Pragmatism,* is to say something that needs explanation. For there are, I think, two unreconciled strains in the *Psychology*. One is found in the adoption of the subjective tenor of prior psychological tradition; even when the special tenets of that tradition are radically criticized, an underlying subjectivism is retained, at least in vocabulary—and the difficulty in finding a vocabulary which will intelligibly convey a genuinely new idea is perhaps the obstacle that most retards the easy progress of philosophy. I may cite as an illustration the substitution of the "stream of consciousness" for discrete elementary states: the advance made was enormous. Nevertheless the point of view remained that of a realm of consciousness set off by itself. The other strain is objective, having its roots in a return to the earlier biological conception of the *psyche,* but a return possessed of a new force and value due to the immense progress made by biology since the time of Aristotle. I doubt if we have as yet begun to realize all that is due to William James for the introduction and use of this idea; as I have already intimated, I do not think that he fully and consistently realized it himself. Anyway, it worked its way more and more into all my ideas and acted as a ferment to transform old beliefs.

If this biological conception and mode of approach had been prematurely hardened by James, its effect might have been merely to substitute one schematism for another. But it is not tautology to say that James's sense of life was itself vital. He had a profound sense, in origin artistic and moral, perhaps, rather than "scientific", of the difference between the categories of the living and of the mechanical; some time, I think, someone may write an essay that will show how the most distinctive factors in his general philosophic view, pluralism, novelty, freedom, individuality, are all connected with his feeling for the qualities and traits of that which lives. Many philosophers have had much to say about the idea of organism; but they have taken it structurally and hence statically. It was reserved for James to think of life in terms of life in action. This point, and that about the objective biological factor in James's conception of thought (discrimination, abstraction, conception, generalization), is fundamental when the rôle of psychology in philosophy comes under consideration. It is true that the effect of its introduction into philosophy has often, usually, been to dilute and distort the latter. But that is because the psychology was bad psychology.

I do not mean that I think that in the end the connection of psychology with philosophy is, in the abstract, closer than is that of other branches of science. Logically it stands on the same plane with them. But historically and at the present juncture the revolution introduced by James had, and still has, a peculiar significance. On the negative side it is important, for it is indispensable as a purge of the heavy charge of bad psychology that is so embedded in the philosophical tradition that it is not generally recognized to be psychology at all. As an example, I would

say that the problem of "sense data", which occupies such a great bulk
in recent British thinking, has to my mind no significance other than as
a survival of an old and outworn psychological doctrine—although
those who deal with the problem are for the most part among those who
stoutly assert the complete irrelevance of psychology to philosophy. On
the positive side we have the obverse of this situation. The newer objective psychology supplies the easiest way, pedagogically if not in the
abstract, by which to reach a fruitful conception of thought and its
work, and thus to better our logical theories—provided thought and
logic have anything to do with one another. And in the present state of
men's minds the linking of philosophy to the significant issues of actual
experience is facilitated by constant interaction with the methods and
conclusions of psychology. The more abstract sciences, mathematics
and physics, for example, have left their impress deep upon traditional
philosophy. The former, in connection with an exaggerated anxiety about
formal certainty, has more than once operated to divorce philosophic
thinking from connection with questions that have a source in existence.
The remoteness of psychology from such abstractions, its nearness to
what is distinctively human, gives it an emphatic claim for a sympathetic
hearing at the present time.

In connection with an increasing recognition of this human aspect,
there developed the influence which forms the fourth heading of this
recital. The objective biological approach of the Jamesian psychology
led straight to the perception of the importance of distinctive social
categories, especially communication and participation. It is my conviction that a great deal of our philosophizing needs to be done over again
from this point of view, and that there will ultimately result an integrated synthesis in a philosophy congruous with modern science and
related to actual needs in education, morals, and religion. One has to
take a broad survey in detachment from immediate prepossessions to
realize the extent to which the characteristic traits of the science of to-
day are connected with the development of social subjects—an-
thropology, history, politics, economics, language and literature, social
and abnormal psychology, and so on. The movement is both so new, in
an intellectual sense, and we are so much of it and it so much of us, that
it escapes definite notice. Technically the influence of mathematics
upon philosophy is more obvious; the great change that has taken place
in recent years in the ruling ideas and methods of the physical sciences
attracts attention much more easily than does the growth of the social
subjects, just because it is farther away from impact upon us. Intellectual prophecy is dangerous; but if I read the cultural signs of the times

aright, the next synthetic movement in philosophy will emerge when the significance of the social sciences and arts has become an object of reflective attention in the same way that mathematical and physical sciences have been made the objects of thought in the past, and when their full import is grasped. If I read these signs wrongly, nevertheless the statement may stand as a token of a factor significant in my own intellectual development.

In any case, I think it shows a deplorable deadness of imagination to suppose that philosophy will indefinitely revolve within the scope of the problems and systems that two thousand years of European history have bequeathed to us. Seen in the long perspective of the future, the whole of western European history is a provincial episode. I do not expect to see in my day a genuine, as distinct from a forced and artificial, integration of thought. But a mind that is not too egotistically impatient can have faith that this unification will issue in its season. Meantime a chief task of those who call themselves philosophers is to help get rid of the useless lumber that blocks our highways of thought, and strive to make straight and open the paths that lead to the future. Forty years spent in wandering in a wilderness like that of the present is not a sad fate—unless one attempts to make himself believe that the wilderness is after all itself the promised land.

# 2. Kant and Philosophic Method*

Written when he was a young graduate student at Johns Hopkins University, this essay of Dewey's attempts to locate a mooring point, a point of departure, for philosophic method. This piece is very cluttered and Dewey is yet to discover the importance of William James, who this very year, 1884, was to publish "On Some Omissions of Introspective Psychology," but even at this early date it is clear that for Dewey "experience" is a key term, and he is wary of abstract schema in philosophical inquiry.

On its subjective side, so far as individuals are concerned, philosophy comes into existence when men are confronted with problems and contradictions which common sense and the special sciences are able neither to solve nor resolve. There is felt the need of going deeper into

* From *Journal of Speculative Philosophy*, XVIII (April, 1884), pp. 162-74.

things, of not being content with haphazard views or opinions derived from this or that science, but of having some principle which, true on its account, may also serve to judge the truth of all besides. It is no matter of accident that modern philosophy begins, in Descartes, with a method which doubts all, that it may find that wherewith to judge all; nor is it meaningless that Kant, the founder of modernist philosophy, commences his first great work with a similar demand, and "calls upon Reason to undertake the most difficult of tasks, self-knowledge, and establish a tribunal to decide all questions according to its own eternal and unchangeable laws." This self-knowledge of Reason, then, is the Method and criterion which Kant offers.

Before we may see what is involved in this, it is necessary to see what in gist the previous methods had been, and why they had failed. The method of "intellectualism" begun by Descartes and presented to Kant through Wolff was (in one word): Analysis of conceptions, with the law of identity or non-contradiction for criterion. To discover truth is to analyze the problem down to those simple elements which cannot be thought away, and reach a judgment whose predicate may be clearly and distinctly seen to be identical with its subject. Analytic thought, proceeding by the law of identity, gives the method for philosophic procedure. Now, Kant in his pre-critical period[1] had become convinced that analysis does not explain such a conception as that which we have of causation: "How one thing should arise out of another, when it is not connected with it, according to the law of identity, this is a thing which I should much like to have explained." Nor again, while it may be, and undoubtedly is, the method for pure thought, does it give any means for passing from thought to existence. This, he would say, is no predicate of anything; it is part of no conception, and can be got by no analysis. Reality is added to our notions from without, not evolved from them. But, if logical thought is not adequate to such notions as cause, nor able to reach existence, it can be no method for discovering Absolute truth.

So Kant finds himself thrown into the arms of the Empiricists. It is experience which shows us the origin of an effect in a cause, and experience which adds reality or existence to our thoughts. What, then, is the method of "Empiricism"? Beginning with Bacon, at first it merely asserted that the mind must be freed from all subjective elements, and become a mirror, to reflect the world of reality. But this, as criterion, is purely negative, and required the positive complement of Locke. This

[1] See especially his essay on attempt to introduce the idea of negative quantity into philosophy.

method in a word is, *Analysis of perceptions with agreement as criterion.* In contrast with the intellectual school, which began with conceptions supposed to be found ready-made in the human mind, it begins with the perceptions impressed upon that blank tablet, the Mind, by external objects, and finds "knowledge to consist in the perception of the connection or agreement or disagreement of these ideas." But two questions arise: If truth or knowledge consists in perceptions, how, any more than from conceptions, shall we get to an external world? This question was answered by Berkeley in showing that, if knowledge were what this theory made it to be, the external world was just that whose *esse* is *percipi.* The second question is: What is agreement of perception? Agreement certainly means, as Locke said, "connexion," that is, mutual reference, or Synthesis. But how can this synthesis occur? The mind is a blank, a wax tablet, a *tabula rasa,* whose sole nature is receptivity, and certainly it can furnish no synthesis. Locke had avoided the difficulty by assuming that ideas come to us or are "given" more or less conjoined— that one has naturally some bond of union with another. But this, of course, cannot be. Simple impressions or perceptions are, as Hume stated, such as admit of no distinction or separation, and these are the ultimate sensations. These have no connection with each other, except perhaps the accidental one of following or occurring together in time, and so it is that "every distinct perception is a separate existence." Necessary connection among them, therefore, there can be none. Sensations are purely contingent, accidental, and external in their relations to each other, with no bonds of union. Any agreement is the result of chance or blind custom. Knowledge as the necessary connection of perceptions does not exist.

Kant consequently discovers, by a more thorough study of empiricism, that it too betrays him. It, no more than his former guides, can furnish him with a way of getting to an external world nor to knowledge at all. Nay, even self, some ghost of which was left him by the other method, has disappeared too.

What has been the difficulty? Descartes did not come to a standstill at once, for he had tacitly presupposed the synthetic power of thought in itself—had even laid the ground for a theory of it in his reference to the Ego, or self-consciousness. But his successors, neglecting this, and developing only the analytic aspect of thought, had produced a vacuum, where no step to existence or actual relations, being synthetic, could be taken. "Conceptions are empty." Nor had Locke been estopped immediately, for he presupposed some synthesis in the objective world; but it turns out that he had no right to it, and world, self, and all actual relations, being synthetic, have gone. "Perceptions are blind." The problem, then, is clearly before Kant, as is the key to its solution. Synthesis is the *sine qua non*. Knowledge is synthesis, and the explanation of knowledge or truth must be found in the explanation of synthesis. Hence the question of Method is now the question: How are synthetic judgments *a priori* possible? *A priori* means simply belonging to Reason in its own nature, so the question is, How and to what extent is Reason the source of synthesis?

The case stands thus: Pure thought is purely analytic; experience *per se* gives only a blind rhapsody of particulars, without meaning or connection—actual experience, or knowledge involves, *is* synthesis. How shall it be got? One path remains open. We may suppose that while thought *in itself* is analytic, it is synthetic when applied to a material given it, and that from this material, by its functions, it forms the objects which it knows. And such, in its lowest terms, is the contribution Kant makes. The material, the manifold, the particulars, are furnished by Sense in perception; the conceptions, the synthetic functions from Reason itself, and the union of these two elements are required, as well for the formation of the object known, as for its knowing.

To characterize Kant's contribution to Method, it remains to briefly examine these two sides of his theory: First, for the part played by the synthetic functions or the categories. These, in first intention, are so many conceptions of the understanding, and, as such, subject to analysis according to the law of identity, and thus furnish the subject matter of Logic. But they also have relation to objects, and as such, are synthetic and furnish the subject matter of Transcendental Logic, whose work is to demonstrate and explain their objective validity. This is done by showing that "the categories make experience and its objects for the first time possible." That is to say, Kant, after showing that the principles of identity and contradiction, though the highest criteria of logical thought, can give no aid in determining the truths of actual experience, inquires what is the criterion of truth for the latter, or what comes to the same thing, of the synthetic use of the categories as Transcendental Logic—and the answer he finds to be "possible experience" itself. In other words, the categories have objective validity or synthetic use because without them no experience would be possible. If Hume, for example, asks how we can have assurance that the notion of causality has any worth when applied to objects, he is answered by showing that without this notion experience as an intelligible connected system would not exist. By the categories the objects of experience are constituted, and hence their objective validity.

It follows, accordingly, that the system of experience may be determined, as to its form, by a completely made out system of categories. In them, as synthetic functions, constituting experience, we find the criterion of truth. But they themselves have a higher condition. As synthetic functions, they must all be functions of a higher unity which is subject to none of them. And this Kant calls the synthetic *unity* of Apperception or, in brief, self-consciousness. This is the highest condition of experience, and in the developed notion of self-consciousness we find the criterion of truth. The theory of self-consciousness is Method.

But this abstract statement must be further developed. It comes to saying, on the one hand, that the criterion of the categories is possible experience, and on the other, that the criterion of possible experience is the categories and their supreme condition. This is evidently a circle, yet a circle which, Kant would say, exists in the case itself, which expresses the very nature of knowledge. It but states that in knowledge there is naught but knowledge which knows or is known—the only judge of knowledge, of experience, is experience itself. And experience is a system, a real whole made up of real parts. It as a whole is necessarily implied in every fact of experience, while it is constituted in and through these facts. In other terms, the relation of categories to experience is the relation of members of an organism to a whole. The criterion of knowledge is neither anything outside of knowledge, nor a particular conception within the sphere of knowledge which is not subject to the system as a whole; it is just this system which is constituted, so far as its form is concerned, by the categories.

Philosophic Method, or the discovering of the criterion of truth, will consist, then, in no setting up of a transcendent object as the empiricists did, or of an abstract principle after the manner of the intellectual school. Since the categories, in and through self-consciousness, constitute experience, Method will consist in making out a complete table of these categories in all their mutual relations, giving each its proper placing, with the full confidence that when so placed each will have its proper place in experience, *i.e.,* its capacity for expressing reality determined.

But we have now strayed far from Kant. While having said nothing which is not deducible from his Transcendental Logic, we have abstracted from the fact that this holds only of the *form* of our knowledge; that there is also an *aesthetic,* and that thought is synthetic, not in itself, but only upon a material supplied to it from without. Turning to this, we find the aspect of affairs changed. Though the categories make experience, they make it out of a foreign material to which they bear a purely external relation. They constitute objects, but these objects are not such in universal reference, but only to beings of like capacities of receptivity as ourselves. They respect not existence in itself, but ourselves as *affected* by that existence. The system of categories furnished the criterion for all the knowledge we have, but this turns out to be no real knowledge. It is, Hegel says, as if one ascribed correct insight to a person, and then added that he could see only into the untruth, not the truth. Nor does the deficiency of our method end here. We had previously assumed that the categories as a system, or in their organic relation to self-consciousness, could be known. But it now turns out that nothing can be known except that to which this feeling of external matter through sensibility is given. To know this subject, or self-consciousness, is to make an object of it, and every object is sensible, that is, has a feeling which tells us how we are affected. But such a knowledge is evidently no knowledge of self-consciousness in its own nature. Thus, so far as knowledge is concerned, it must remain a bare form of self-identity, of "I = I," into definite organic relations with which the categories can never be brought. Hence, it appears that our picture of a method was doubly false—false in that after all it could not reach truth; false in that after all no such method was in itself possible. Our organic system of categories cannot constitute absolute truth—and no such organic system is itself knowable. Criterion and method we are still without. The golden prize, which seemed just within our hands as long as we confined ourselves to the Transcendental Logic, turns out to be a tinsel superfluity.

Yet, none the less, there was the suggestion of a method there, which is exactly what we wish. The only question is: Is its reference to the Aesthetic necessary? Is the latter a necessary part of Kant's theory, or, so far as it concerns the reception of external matter, an excrescence? The question is just here: Previous methods failed because they made no allowance for synthesis—Kant's because the synthesis can occur only upon matter foreign to it. Thought in the previous theories was *purely* analytic; in Kant's it is *purely* synthetic, in that it is synthesis of foreign material. Were thought at once synthetic *and* analytic, differentiating and integrating in its own nature, both affirmative and negative, relating to self at the same time that it related to other—indeed, through this relation to other—the difficulty would not have arisen.

Is the state of the case as Kant supposes? Must we say that Reason is synthetic only upon condition that material be given it to act upon, or, may it be, that while we must say that for the individual the material, nay, the form as indissolubly connected with the material, is given, yet, to Reason itself, nothing is given in the sense of being foreign to it?

A slight examination will show us that, at least as far as Kant is concerned, the former supposition is but an arbitrary limitation or assumption which Kant imposed upon himself, or received without question from previous philosophy. On one side, he had learned that pure thought is analytic; on the other, that the individual is affected with sensations impressed upon it by external objects. At the same that he corrects both of these doctrines with his own deduction of the categories, he formally retains both errors.

So we have him asking at the very outset, as a matter of course: "In what other way is it to be conceived that the knowing power can be excited to activity, except by objects which affect our senses?" That is to say, he assumes at the outset that there is something external to Reason by which it must be excited. He perceives, what all admit, that an individual organized in a certain specific way with certain senses, and external things acting upon these senses, are conditions to our knowledge, and then proceeds to identify respectively this individual with the subject, and these things with the object, in the process of knowledge. But here it is that we ask with what right does he make this identification. If it is made, then surely the case stands with Reason as he says it does—it acts only upon a material foreign to it. Yet this individual and these things are but known objects already constituted by the categories, and existing only for the synthetic unity of apperception or self-consciousness. This, then, is the real subject, and the so-called subject and object are but the forms in which it expresses its own activity. In short, the relation of subject and object is not a "transcendent" one, but an "immanent," and is but the first form in which Reason manifests that it is both synthetic and analytic; that it separates itself from itself, that it may thereby reach higher unity with itself. It is the highest type of the law which Reason follows everywhere. The material which was supposed to confront Reason as foreign to it is but the manifestation of Reason itself. Such, at least, are the results which we reach in the Transcendental Deduction, and such are the results we consider ourselves justified to keep in opposition to Kant's pure assumptions.

We see the same thing in Kant's theory of phenomenon. Just as, concerning the process of knowledge, he assumes that subject and object are in external relation to each other, and hence Reason in contact with a foreign material, so here he assumes that the character of phenomenality consists in relation to an unknowable noumenon. The phenomenon is referred to something outside of experience, instead of being defined by its relation within experience—in which case it would be seen to be a phenomenon in its own nature, in that the categories which constitute it as such are not adequate to truth.

We have but to turn to Kant's derivation of the categories, to be again assured that Kant's theory of Reason as synthetic only in reference to foreign material is one purely assumed. As is notorious, these he took from the Logic of the School, which he held to give a complete table of all the forms of pure thought. When we turn to this table we find the highest point reached in it to be reciprocity. Now, reciprocity is precisely that external relation of two things to each other that we have already found existing, in Kant's theory, between subject and object in Knowledge—the relations of things that are independent of each other but mutually act upon each other. So, too, it is but another way of stating that Thought, analytic in itself, is synthetic when applied to an external material, or that this material, blind and haphazard in itself, is formed by something acting upon it. When Kant tells us, therefore, that the categories are not limited in their own nature, but become so when applied, as they must be, to determine space and time, we have in our hands the means of correcting him. They are limited, and express just the limitation of Kant himself. And Kant confesses their insufficiency as soon as he takes up the questions of moral and aesthetic experience and of life itself. Here we find the categories of freedom determined by ends, free production, organism to be everywhere present, while all through his *Critiques* is woven in the notion of an intuitive understanding which is the ultimate criterion of all truth, and this understanding is just what we have already met as the organic system of experience or self-consciousness.

Whether we consider the relations of subject and object, or the nature of the categories, we find ourselves forced into the presence of the notion of organic relation. The relation between subject and object is not an external one; it is one in a higher unity which is itself constituted by this relation. The only conception adequate to experience as a whole is organism. What is involved in the notion of organism? Why, precisely the Idea which we had formerly reached of a Reason which is both analytic and synthetic, a Reason which differentiates itself that it may integrate itself into fuller riches, a Reason that denies itself that it may become itself. Such a Reason, and neither an analytic Thought, nor an analytic Experience, nor a Reason which is analytic in itself, and synthetic for something else, is the ultimate criterion of truth, and the theory of this Reason is the Philosophic Method.

The two defects which we found before in Kant's theory now vanish. The method is no longer one which can reach untruth only, nor is it a

method which cannot be made out. The track which we were upon in-
following the course of the Transcendental Deduction was the right one.
The criterion of experience is the system of categories in their organic
unity in self-consciousness, and the method consists in determining this
system and the part each plays in constituting it. The method takes the
totality of experience to pieces, and brings before us its conditions in
their entirety. The relations of its content, through which alone this content has character and meaning, whereby it becomes an intelligible, connected whole, must be made to appear.

It was the suggestion of this method, it was the suggestion of so many
means for its execution, it was the actual carrying of it out in so many
points that makes Kant's *Philosophy* the *critical* philosophy, and his
work the *crisis,* the separating, dividing, turning point of modern
philosophy, and this hurried sketch would not be complete if we did not
briefly point out what steps have been taken toward the fulfilling of the
Ideal. This is found chiefly in Hegel and his *Logic*. We can only discuss
in the light of what has already been said why Hegel begins with Logic;
why the negative plays so important a part in his philosophy, and what
is the meaning of Dialectic. (1) Logic. One of Hegel's repeated charges
against Kant is, that he examines the categories with reference to their
*objective* character, and not to determine their own meaning and worth.
At first it might seem as if this were the best way to determine their
worth, but it ought now to be evident that such a procedure is both to
presuppose that they are subjective in themselves, and that we have a
ready-made conception of object by which to judge them—in short, it
amounts to saying that these conceptions are purely analytic, and have
meaning only in relation to an external material. Hence the method
must examine the categories without any reference to subjective or objective existences; or, to speak properly, since we now see that there are
no purely subjective or objective existences, without any relation to
things and thoughts as two distinct spheres. The antithesis between
them is not to be blinked out of sight, but it must be treated as one
which exists within Reason, and not one with one term in and the other
out. The categories which, for the individual, determine the nature of
the object, and those which state how the object is brought into the subjective form of cognition, must be deduced from Reason alone. A
theory performing this task is what Hegel calls Logic, and is needed not
only to overcome Kant's defects, but is immediately suggested by his
positive accomplishments. In our account of the Transcendental Deduction we saw that self-consciousness was the supreme condition of all the
categories, and hence can be subject in itself to none of them. When it is

made subject we have no longer the absolute self-consciousness, but the empirical ego, the object of the inner sense. In short, the categories constitute the individuals as an object of experience, just as much as they do the material known. Hence they are no more subjective than objective. We may call them indifferently neither or both. The truth is, they belong to a sphere where the antithesis between subject and object is still potential, or *an sich*. It is evident, therefore, that logic, in the Hegelian use, is just that criterion of truth which we thought at first to find in Kant's transcendental Logic—it is an account of the conceptions or categories of Reason which constitute experience, internal and external, subjective and objective, and an account of them as a system, an organic unity in which each has its own place fixed. It is the completed Method of Philosophy.

(2) The Negative in Hegel. It ought now to be evident that any Philosophy which can pretend to be a Method of Truth must show Reason as both Analytic *and* Synthetic. If History can demonstrate anything, it has demonstrated this, both by its successes and its failures. Reason must be that which separates itself, which differentiates, goes forth into differences, that it may then grasp these differences into a unity of its own. It cannot unite unless there be difference; there can be no synthesis where there is not analysis. On the other hand, the differences must remain forever foreign to Reason unless it brings them together; there can be no analysis where there is not synthesis, or a unity to be dirempted. If there be no synthesis in Reason, we end in the impotence of the former school of intellectualism, or in the helpless skepticism of Hume; if Reason be synthetic only upon a foreign material, we end in the contradictions of Kant. If there is to be *knowledge*, Reason must include both elements within herself. It is Hegel's thorough recognition of this fact that causes him to lay such emphasis on the negative. Pure affirmation or identity reaches its summit in Spinoza, where all is lost in the infinite substance of infinite attributes, as waves in the sea. Yet even Spinoza was obliged to introduce the negative, the determinations, the modes, though he never could succeed in getting them by any means from his pure affirmation. In Hume we find pure difference or negation, the manifold particularization of sensations, but even he is obliged to introduce synthetic principles in the laws of association, though he never succeeds in legitimately deriving them from sensations, for a "consistent sensationalism is speechless." Kant had tried a compromise of the principle, synthesis from within, difference from without. That, too, failed to give us knowledge or a criterion of Truth. Hegel comprehends the problem, and offers us Reason af-

firmative *and* negative, and affirmative only in and through its own negations, as the solution.

(3) Dialectic. We have now the notion of Dialectic before us in its essential features. We have seen that the desired object is a theory of the Conceptions of Reason in an organic system, and that Reason is itself both integrating and differentiating. Dialectic is the construction by Reason, through its successive differentiations and resumptions of these differences into higher unities, of just this system. If we take any single category of Reason—that is to say, some conception which we find involved in the system of experience—this is one specific form into which Reason has unified or "synthesized" itself. Reason itself is immanent in this category; but, since Reason is also differentiating or analytic, Reason must reveal itself as such in this category, which accordingly passes, or is reflected, or develops into its opposite, while the two conceptions are then resumed into the higher unity of a more concrete conception.

Since the system of knowledge is implicit in each of its members, each category must judge itself, or rather, Reason, in its successive forms, passes judgment on its own inadequacy until the adequate is reached—and this can be nothing but Reason no longer implicit, but developed into its completed system. Reason must everywhere, and in all its forms, propose itself as what it is, *viz.*, absolute or adequate to the entire truth of experience; but, since at first its *form* is still inadequate, it must show what is absolutely implicit in it, *viz.*, the entire system. That at first it does, by doing what it is the nature of the Reason which it manifests to do, by differencing itself, or passing into its opposite, its other; but, since Reason is also synthetic, grasping together, these differences must resolve themselves into a higher unity. Thus, Reason continues until it has developed itself into the conception which is in form equal to what itself is in content, or, until it has manifested all that it is implicitly. A twofold process has occurred. On the one hand, each special form of Reason or Category has been placed; that is, its degree of ability to state absolute truth fixed by its place in the whole organic system. On the other, the system itself has been developed; that is to say, as Reason goes on manifesting its own nature through successive differences and unities, each lower category is not destroyed, but retained—but retained at its proper value. Each, since it is Reason, has its relative *truth;* but each, since Reason is not yet adequately manifested, has only a *relative* truth. The Idea is the completed category, and this has for its meaning or content Reason made explicit or manifested; that is, all the stages or types of Reason employed in reaching it. "The categories are not errors, which one goes through on the way to the truth, but phases of truth. Their completed system in its organic wholeness is *the* Truth." And such a system is at once philosophic Method and Criterion; method, because it shows us not only the way to reach truth, but truth itself in construction; criterion, because it gives us the form of experience to which all the facts of experience as organic members must conform.

It will be seen, I hope, that we have not left our subject, "Kant's Relation to Philosophic Method"; for a crisis in nothing in itself. It is a crisis only as it is the turning point; and a turning point is the old passing into the new, and can be understood only as the old and the new are understood. The criterion of Kant is just this turning point; it is the transition of the old abstract thought, the old meaningless conception of experience, into the new concrete thought, the ever growing, ever rich experience.

# 3. Ralph Waldo Emerson*

In 1907, when commenting on Santayana's multivolumed *Life of Reason,* John Dewey wrote that "we are grateful to Mr. Santayana for what he has given us, the most adequate contribution America has yet made, always excepting Emerson, to moral philosophy." Although this essay on Emerson was first written in 1903, readers of the later John Dewey will be struck by the anticipation here of Deweyan themes: the affection for the ordinary, a logic of inquiry, and the close relationship of philosophy and poetry.

It is said that Emerson is not a philosopher. I find this denegation false or true according as it is said in blame or praise—according to the reasons proffered. When the critic writes of lack of method, of the absence of continuity, of coherent logic, and, with the old story of the string of pearls loosely strung, puts Emerson away as a writer of maxims and proverbs, a recorder of brilliant insights and abrupt aphorisms,

* From John Dewey, *Characters and Events: Popular Essays in Social and Political Philosophy*, Joseph Ratner, ed., Vol. I, pp. 69-77. Copyright 1929 by Holt, Rinehart and Winston, Inc. Copyright © 1957 by Joseph Ratner. Reprinted by permission of Holt, Rinehart and Winston, Inc. (Published originally in 1903.)

the critic, to my mind, but writes down his own incapacity to follow a logic that is finely wrought. "We want in every man a logic; we cannot pardon the absence of it, but it must not be spoken. Logic is the procession or proportionate unfolding of the intuition; but its virtue is as silent method; the moment it would appear as propositions and have a separate value, it is worthless." Emerson fulfills his own requisition. The critic needs the method separately propounded, and not finding his wonted leading-string is all lost. Again, says Emerson, "There is no compliment like the addressing to the human being thoughts out of certain heights and presupposing his intelligence"—a compliment which Emerson's critics have mostly hastened to avert. But to make this short, I am not acquainted with any writer, no matter how assured his position in treatises upon the history of philosophy, whose movement of thought is more compact and unified, nor one who combines more adequately diversity of intellectual attack with concentration of form and effect. I recently read a letter from a gentleman, himself a distinguished writer of philosophy, in which he remarked that philosophers are a stupid class, since they want every reason carefully pointed out and labelled, and are incapable of taking anything for granted. The condescending patronage by literary critics of Emerson's lack of cohesiveness may remind us that philosophers have no monopoly of this particular form of stupidity.

Perhaps those are nearer right, however, who deny that Emerson is a philosopher, because he is more than a philosopher. He would work, he says, by art, not by metaphysics, finding truth "in the sonnet and the play." "I am," to quote him again, "in all my theories, ethics and politics, a poet"; and we may, I think, safely take his word for it that he meant to be a maker rather than a reflector. His own preference was to be ranked with the seers rather than with the reasoners of the race, for he says, "I think that philosophy is still rude and elementary; it will one day be taught by poets. The poet is in the right attitude; he is believing; the philosopher, after some struggle, having only reasons for believing." Nor do I regard it as impertinent to place by the side of this utterance, that other in which he said, "We have yet to learn that the thing uttered in words is not therefore affirmed. It must affirm itself or no forms of grammar and no plausibility can give it evidence and no array of arguments." To Emerson, perception was more potent than reasoning; the deliverances of intercourse more to be desired than the chains of discourse; the surprise of reception more demonstrative than the conclusions of intentional proof. As he said, "Good as is discourse, silence is better, and shames it. The length of discourse indicates the distance of thought betwixt the speaker and the hearer." And again, "If I speak, I define and confine, and am less.'' "Silence is a solvent that destroys personality and gives us leave to be great and universal.''

I would not make hard and fast lines between philosopher and poet, yet there is some distinction of accent in thought and of rhythm in speech. The desire for an articulate, not for silent, logic is intrinsic with philosophy. The unfolding of the perception must be stated, not merely followed and understood. Such conscious method is, one might say, the only thing of ultimate concern to the abstract thinker. Not thought, but reasoned thought, not things, but the ways of things, interest him; not even truth, but the paths by which truth is sought. He construes elaborately the symbols of thinking. He is given over to manufacturing and sharpening the weapons of the spirit. Outcomes, interpretations, victories, are indifferent. Otherwise is it with art. That, as Emerson says, is "the path of the Creator to his work''; and again "a habitual respect to the whole by an eye loving beauty in detail.'' Affection is towards the meaning of the symbol, not to its constitution. Only as he wields them, does the artist forge the sword and buckler of the spirit. His affair is to uncover rather than to analyze; to discern rather than to classify. He reads but does not compose.

One, however, has no sooner drawn such lines than one is ashamed and begins to retract. Euripides and Plato, Dante and Bruno, Bacon and Milton, Spinoza and Goethe, rise in rebuke. The spirit of Emerson rises to protest against exaggerating his ultimate value by trying to place him upon a plane of art higher than a philosophic platform. Literary critics admit his philosophy and deny his literature. And if philosophers extol his keen, calm art and speak with some depreciation of his metaphysic, it also is perhaps because Emerson knew something deeper than our conventional definitions. It is indeed true that reflective thinkers have taken the way to truth for their truth; the method of life for the conduct of life—in short, have taken means for end. But it is also assured that in the completeness of their devotion, they have expiated their transgression; means become identified with end, thought turns to life, and wisdom is justified not of herself but of her children. Language justly preserves the difference between philosopher and sophist. It is no more possible to eliminate love and generation from the definition of the thinker than it is to eliminate thought and limits from the conception of the artist. It is interest, concern, caring, which makes the one as it makes the other. It is significant irony that the old quarrel of philosopher and poet was brought off by one who united in himself more than has another individual the qualities of both artist and metaphysician. At bottom the quarrel is not one of objectives nor yet of methods, but of the affections. And in the divisions of love, there always abides the unity of him who loves. Because Plato was so great he was divided in his affections. A lesser man could not brook that torn love, because of which he set poet and philosopher over against one another. Looked at in the open, our fences between literature and metaphysics appear petty—signs of an attempt to affix the legalities and formularies of property to the things of the spirit. If ever there lived not only a metaphysician but a professor of metaphysics it was Immanuel Kant. Yet he declares that he should account himself more unworthy than the day laborer in the field if he did not believe that somehow, even in his technical classifications and remote distinctions, he too, was carrying forward the struggle of humanity for freedom—that is for illumination.

And for Emerson of all others, there is a one-sidedness and exaggeration, which he would have been the first to scorn, in exalting overmuch his creative substance at the expense of his reflective procedure. He says in effect somewhere that the individual man is only a method, a plan of arrangement. The saying is amply descriptive of Emerson. His idealism is the faith of the thinker in his thought raised to its *nth* power. "History," he says, "and the state of the world at any one time is directly dependent on the intellectual classification then existing in the minds of men." Again, "Beware when the great God lets loose a thinker on this planet. Then all things are at risk. The very hopes of man, the thoughts of his heart, the religion of nations, the manner and morals of mankind are all at the mercy of a new generalization." And again, "Everything looks permanent until its secret is known. Nature looks provokingly stable and secular, but it has a cause like all the rest; and when once I comprehend that, will these fields stretch so immovably wide, these leaves hang so individually considerable?" And finally, "In history an idea always overhangs like a moon and rules the tide which rises simultaneously in all the souls of a generation." There are times, indeed, when one is inclined to regard Emerson's whole work as a hymn to intelligence, a paean to the all-creating, all-disturbing power of thought.

And so, with an expiatory offering to the Manes of Emerson, one may proceed to characterize his thought, his method, yea, even his system. I find it in the fact that he takes the distinctions and classifications which to most philosophers are true in and of and because of their systems, and makes them true of life, of the common experience of the everyday man. To take his own words for it, "There are degrees in idealism. We learn first to play with it academically, as the magnet was once a toy. Then we see, in the hey-day of youth and poetry, that it may be true, that it is true in gleams and fragments. Then, its countenance waxes stern and grand, and we see that it must be true. It now shows itself ethical and practical.'' The idealism which is a thing of the academic intellect to the professor, a hope to the generous youth, an inspiration to the genial projector, is to Emerson a narrowly accurate description of the facts of the most real world in which all earn their living.

Such reference to the immediate life is the text by which he tries every philosopher. "Each new mind we approach seems to require," he says, "an abdication of all our past and present possessions. A new doctrine seems at first a subversion of all our opinions, tastes and manner of living." But while one gives himself "up unreservedly to that which draws him, because that is his own, he is to refuse himself to that which draws him not, because it is not his own. I were a fool not to sacrifice a thousand Aeschyluses to my intellectual integrity. Especially take the same ground in regard to abstract truth, the science of the mind. The Bacon, the Spinoza, the Hume, Schelling, Kant, is only a more or less awkward translator of things in your consciousness. Say, then, instead of too timidly poring into his obscure sense, that he has not succeeded in rendering back to you your consciousness. Anyhow, when at last, it is done, you will find it is not recondite, but a simple, natural state which the writer restores to you." And again, take this other saying, "Aristotle or Bacon or Kant propound some maxim which is the key-note of philosophy thenceforward, but I am more interested to know that when at last they have hurled out their grand word, it is only some familiar experience of every man on the street." I fancy he reads the so-called eclecticism of Emerson wrongly who does not see that it is reduction of all the philosophers of the race, even the prophets like Plato and Proclus whom Emerson holds most dear, to the test of trial by the service rendered the present and immediate experience. As for those who condemn Emerson for superficial pedantry because of the strings of names he is wont to flash like beads before our eyes, they but voice their own pedantry, not seeing, in their literalness, that all such things are with Emerson symbols of various uses administered to the common soul.

As Emerson treated the philosophers, so he treats their doctrines. The Platonist teaches the immanence of absolute ideas in the World and in Man, that every thing and every man participates in an absolute Meaning, individualized in him and through which one has community with others. Yet by the time this truth of the universe has become proper and fit for teaching, it has somehow become a truth of philosophy, a truth of private interpretation, reached by some men, not others, and consequently true for some, but not true for all, and hence not wholly true for any. But to Emerson all "truth lies on the highway." Emerson says, "We lie in the lap of immense intelligence which makes us organs of its activity and receivers of its truth," and the Idea is no longer either an academic toy nor even a gleam of poetry, but a literal report of the experience of the hour as that is enriched and reinforced for the individual through the tale of history, the appliance of science, the gossip of conversation and the exchange of commerce. That every individual is at once the focus and the channel of mankind's long and wide endeavor, that all nature exists for the education of the human soul—such things, as we read Emerson, cease to be statements of a separated philosophy and become natural transcripts of the course of events and of the rights of man.

Emerson's philosophy has this in common with that of the transcendentalists; he prefers to borrow from them rather than from others certain pigments and delineations. But he finds truth in the highway, in the untaught endeavor, the unexpected idea, and this removes him from their remotenesses. His ideas are not fixed upon any Reality that is beyond or behind or in any way apart, and hence they do not have to be bent. They are versions of the Here and the Now, and flow freely. The reputed transcendental worth of an overweening Beyond and Away, Emerson, jealous for spiritual democracy, finds to be the possession of the unquestionable Present. When Emerson, speaking of the chronology of history, designated the There and Then as "wild, savage and preposterous," he also drew the line which marks him off from transcendentalism—which is the idealism of a Class. In sorry truth, the idealist has too frequently conspired with the sensualist to deprive the pressing and so the passing Now of value which is spiritual. Through the joint work of such malign conspiracy, the common man is not, or at least does not know himself for, an idealist. It is such disinherited of the earth that Emerson summons to their own. "If man is sick, is unable, is mean-spirited and odious, it is because there is so much of his nature which is unlawfully withholden from him."

Against creed and system, convention and institution, Emerson stands for restoring to the common man that which in the name of religion, of philosophy, of art and of morality, has been embezzled from the common store and appropriated to sectarian and class use. Beyond any one we know of, Emerson has comprehended and declared how such malversation makes truth decline from its simplicity, and in becoming partial and owned, become a puzzle of and trick for theologian, metaphysician and litterateur—a puzzle of an imposed law, of an unwished for and refused goodness, of a romantic ideal gleaming only from afar, and a trick of manipular skill, of specialized performance.

For such reasons, the coming century may well make evident what is just now dawning, that Emerson is not only a philosopher, but that he is the Philosopher of Democracy. Plato's own generation would, I think, have found it difficult to class Plato. Was he an inept visionary or a subtle dialectician? A political reformer or a founder of the new type of literary art? Was he a moral exhorter, or an instructor in an Academy? Was he a theorist upon education, or the inventor of a method of knowledge? We, looking at Plato through the centuries of exposition and interpretation, find no difficulty in placing Plato as a philosopher and in attributing to him a system of thought. We dispute about the nature and content of this system, but we do not doubt it is there. It is the intervening centuries which have furnished Plato with his technique and which have developed and wrought Plato to a system. One century bears but a slender ratio to twenty-five; it is not safe to predict. But at least, thinking of Emerson as the one citizen of the New World fit to have his name uttered in the same breath with that of Plato, one may without presumption believe that even if Emerson has no system, none the less he is the prophet and herald of any system which democracy may henceforth construct and hold by, and that when democracy has articulated itself, it will have no difficulty in finding itself already proposed in Emerson. It is as true to-day as when he said it: "It is not propositions, not new dogmas and the logical exposition of the world that are our first need, but to watch and continually cherish the intellectual and moral sensibilities and woo them to stay and make their homes with us. Whilst they abide with us, we shall not think amiss." We are moved to say that Emerson is the first and as yet almost the only Christian of the Intellect. From out such reverence for the instinct and impulse of our common nature shall emerge in their due season propositions, systems and logical expositions of the world. Then shall we have a philosophy which religion has no call to chide and which knows its friendship with science and with art.

Emerson wrote of a certain type of mind: "This tranquil, well-founded, wide-seeing soul is no express-rider, no attorney, no magistrate. It lies in the sun and broods on the world." It is the soul of Emerson which these words describe. Yet this is no private merit nor personal credit. For thousands of earth's children, Emerson has taken away the barriers that shut out the sun and has secured the unimpeded, cheerful circulation of the light of heaven, and the wholesome air of day. For such, content to endure without contriving and contending, at the last all express-riders journey, since to them comes the final service of all commodity. For them, careless to make out their own case, all attorneys plead in the day of final judgment; for though falsehoods pile mountain high, truth is the only deposit that nature tolerates. To them who refuse to be called "master, master," all magistracies in the end defer, for theirs is the common cause for which dominion, power and principality is put under foot. Before such successes, even the worshipers of that which to-day goes by the name of success, those who bend to millions and incline to imperialisms, may lower their standard, and give at least a passing assent to the final word of Emerson's philosophy, the identity of Being, unqualified and immutable, with Character.

## 4. The Influence of Darwinism on Philosophy*

The doctrine of evolution was of central importance to the development of classical American philosophy, particularly as found in the writings of C. S. Peirce, William James, G. H. Mead, and John Dewey. In this essay, Dewey sketches the climate of opinion which contexts the publication of the *Origin of the Species*, and he points to the new mode of inquiry that has emerged from the controversy about evolution. Of particular interest to present readers is Dewey's last paragraph, where he stresses the social-psychological character of the struggle over ideas and, in a vein anticipatory of recent work by Thomas Kuhn, contends that "in fact intellectual progress usually occurs through sheer abandonment of questions together with both of the alternatives they assume—an abandonment that results from their decreasing vitality and a change of urgent interest. We do not solve them: we get over them."

I

That the publication of the "Origin of Species" marked an epoch in

* From John Dewey, *The Influence of Darwin on Philosophy: And Other Essays in Contemporary Thought*, pp. 1-19. Copyright 1910 by Holt, Rinehart and Winston, Inc. Copyright 1938 by John Dewey. Reprinted by permission of Holt, Rinehart and Winston, Inc.

the development of the natural sciences is well known to the layman. That the combination of the very words origin and species embodied an intellectual revolt and introduced a new intellectual temper is easily overlooked by the expert. The conceptions that had reigned in the philosophy of nature and knowledge for two thousand years, the conceptions that had become the familiar furniture of the mind, rested on the assumption of the superiority of the fixed and final; they rested upon treating change and origin as signs of defect and unreality. In laying hands upon the sacred ark of absolute permanency, in treating the forms that had been regarded as types of fixity and perfection as originating and passing away, the "Origin of Species" introduced a mode of thinking that in the end was bound to transform the logic of knowledge, and hence the treatment of morals, politics, and religion.

No wonder, then, that the publication of Darwin's book, a half century ago, precipitated a crisis. The true nature of the controversy is easily concealed from us, however, by the theological clamor that attended it. The vivid and popular features of the anti-Darwinian row tended to leave the impression that the issue was between science on one side and theology on the other. Such was not the case—the issue lay primarily within science itself, as Darwin himself early recognized. The theological outcry he discounted from the start, hardly noticing it save as it bore upon the "feelings of his female relatives." But for two decades before final publication he contemplated the possibility of being put down by his scientific peers as a fool or as crazy; and he set, as the measure of his success, the degree in which he should affect three men of science: Lyell in geology, Hooker in botany, and Huxley in zoology.

Religious considerations lent fervor to the controversy, but they did not provoke it. Intellectually, religious emotions are not creative but conservative. They attach themselves readily to the current view of the world and consecrate it. They steep and dye intellectual fabrics in the seething vat of emotions; they do not form their warp and woof. There is not, I think, an instance of any large idea about the world being independently generated by religion. Although the ideas that rose up like armed men against Darwinism owed their intensity to religious associations, their origin and meaning are to be sought in science and philosophy, not in religion.

## II

Few words in our language foreshorten intellectual history as much as does the word species. The Greeks, in initiating the intellectual life of Europe, were impressed by characteristic traits of the life of plants and animals; so impressed indeed that they made these traits the key to defining nature and to explaining mind and society. And truly, life is so wonderful that a seemingly successful reading of its mystery might well lead men to believe that the key to the secrets of heaven and earth was in their hands. The Greek rendering of this mystery, the Greek formulation of the aim and standard of knowledge, was in the course of time embodied in the word species, and it controlled philosophy for two thousand years. To understand the intellectual face-about expressed in the phrase "Origin of Species," we must, then, understand the long dominant idea against which it is a protest.

Consider how men were impressed by the facts of life. Their eyes fell upon certain things slight in bulk, and frail in structure. To every appearance, these perceived things were inert and passive. Suddenly, under certain circumstances, these things—henceforth known as seeds or eggs or germs—begin to change, to change rapidly in size, form, and qualities. Rapid and extensive changes occur, however, in many things—as when wood is touched by fire. But the changes in the living thing are orderly; they are cumulative; they tend constantly in one direction; they do not, like other changes, destroy or consume, or pass fruitless into wandering flux; they realize and fulfil. Each successive stage, no matter how unlike its predecessor, preserves its net effect and also prepares the way for a fuller activity on the part of its successor. In living beings, changes do not happen as they seem to happen elsewhere, any which way; the earlier changes are regulated in view of later results. This progressive organization does not cease till there is achieved a true final term, a       , a completed, perfected end. This final form exercises in turn a plentitude of functions, not the least noteworthy of which is production of germs like those from which it took its own origin, germs capable of the same cycle of self-fulfilling activity.

But the whole miraculous tale is not yet told. The same drama is enacted to the same destiny in countless myriads of individuals so sundered in time, so severed in space, that they have no opportunity for mutual consultation and no means of interaction. As an old writer quaintly said, "things of the same kind go through the same formalities"—celebrate, as it were, the same ceremonial rites.

This formal activity which operates throughout a series of changes and holds them to a single course; which subordinates their aimless flux to its own perfect manifestation; which, leaping the boundaries of space and time, keeps individuals distant in space and remote in time to a uniform type of structure and function: this principle seemed to give insight into the very nature of reality itself. To it Aristotle gave the name, . This term the scholastics translated as *species*.

The force of this term was deepened by its application to everything in the universe that observes order in flux and manifests constancy through change. From the casual drift of daily weather, through the uneven recurrence of seasons and unequal return of seed time and harvest, up to the majestic sweep of the heavens—the image of eternity in time—and from this to the unchanging pure and contemplative intelligence beyond nature lies one unbroken fulfilment of ends. Nature as a whole is a progressive realization of purpose strictly comparable to the realization of purpose in any single plant or animal.

The conception of     , species, a fixed form and final cause, was the central principle of knowledge as well as of nature. Upon it rested the logic of science. Change as change is mere flux and lapse; it insults intelligence. Genuinely to know is to grasp a permanent end that realizes itself through changes, holding them thereby within the metes and bounds of fixed truth. Completely to know is to relate all special forms to their one single end and good: pure contemplative intelligence. Since, however, the scene of nature which directly confronts us is in change, nature as directly and practically experienced does not satisfy the conditions of knowledge. Human experience is in flux, and hence the instrumentalities of sense-perception and of inference based upon observation are condemned in advance. Science is compelled to aim at realities lying behind and beyond the processes of nature, and to carry on its search for these realities by means of rational forms transcending ordinary modes of perception and inference.

There are, indeed, but two alternative courses. We must either find the appropriate objects and organs of knowledge in the mutual interactions of changing things; or else, to escape the infection of change, we *must* seek them in some transcendent and supernal region. The human mind, deliberately as it were, exhausted the logic of the changeless, the final, and the transcendent, before it essayed adventure on the pathless wastes of generation and transformation. We dispose all too easily of the efforts of the schoolmen to interpret nature and mind in terms of real essences, hidden forms, and occult faculties, forgetful of the seriousness and dignity of the ideas that lay behind. We dispose of them by laughing at the famous gentleman who accounted for the fact that opium put people to sleep on the ground it had a dormitive faculty. But the doctrine, held in our own day, that knowledge of the plant that yields the poppy consists in referring the peculiarities of an individual to a type, to a universal form, a doctrine so firmly established that any other method of knowing was conceived to be unphilosophical and un-scientific, is a survival of precisely the same logic. This identity of conception in the scholastic and anti-Darwinian theory may well suggest greater sympathy for what has become unfamiliar as well as greater humility regarding the further unfamiliarities that history has in store.

Darwin was not, of course, the first to question the classic philosophy of nature and of knowledge. The beginnings of the revolution are in the physical science of the sixteenth and seventeenth centuries. When Galico said: "It is my opinion that the earth is very noble and admirable by reason of so many and so different alterations and generations which are incessantly made therein," he expressed the changed temper that was coming over the world; the transfer of interest from the permanent to the changing. When Descartes said: "The nature of physical things is much more easily conceived when they are beheld coming gradually in-to existence, than when they are only considered as produced at once in a finished and perfect state," the modern world became self-conscious of the logic that was henceforth to control it, the logic of which Darwin's "Origin of Species" is the latest scientific achievement. Without the methods of Copernicus, Kepler, Galileo, and their successors in as-tronomy, physics, and chemistry, Darwin would have been helpless in the organic sciences. But prior to Darwin the impact of the new scien-tific method upon life, mind, and politics, had been arrested, because between these ideal or moral interests and the inorganic world in-tervened the kingdom of plants and animals. The gates of the garden of life were barred to the new ideas; and only through this garden was there access to mind and politics. The influence of Darwin upon philosophy resides in his having conquered the phenomena of life for the principle of transition, and thereby freed the new logic for applica-tion to mind and morals and life. When he said of species what Galico had said of the earth, *e pur se muove,* he emancipated, once for all, genetic and experimental ideas as an organon of asking questions and looking for explanations.

III

The exact bearings upon philosophy of the new logical outlook are, of course, as yet, uncertain and inchoate. We live in the twilight of intellectual transition. One must add the rashness of the prophet to the stubbornness of the partizan to venture a systematic exposition of the influence upon philosophy of the Darwinian method. At best, we can but inquire as to its general bearing—the effect upon mental temper and complexion, upon that body of half-conscious, half-instinctive intellectual aversions and preferences which determine, after all, our more deliberate intellectual enterprises. In this vague inquiry there happens to exist as a kind of touchstone a problem of long historic currency that has also been much discussed in Darwinian literature. I refer to the old problem of design *versus* chance, mind *versus* matter, as the casual explanation, first or final, of things.

As we have already seen, the classic notion of species carried with it the idea of purpose. In all living forms, a specific type is present directing the earlier stages of growth to the realization of its own perfection. Since this purposive regulative principle is not visible to the senses, it follows that it must be an ideal or rational force. Since, however, the perfect form is gradually approximated through the sensible changes, it also follows that in and through a sensible realm a rational ideal force is working out its own ultimate manifestation. These inferences were extended to nature: (*a*) She does nothing in vain; but all for an ulterior purpose. (*b*) Within natural sensible events there is therefore contained a spiritual causal force, which as spiritual escapes perception, but is apprehended by an enlightened reason. (*c*) The manifestation of this principle brings about a subordination of matter and sense to its own realization, and this ultimate fulfilment is the goal of nature and of man. The design argument thus operated in two directions. Purposefulness accounted for the intelligibility of nature and the possibility of science, while the absolute or cosmic character of this purposefulness gave sanction and worth to the moral and religious endeavors of man. Science was underpinned and morals authorized by one and the same principle, and their mutual agreement was eternally guaranteed.

This philosophy remained, in spite of sceptical and polemic outbursts, the official and the regnant philosophy of Europe for over two thousand years. The expulsion of fixed first and final causes from astronomy, physics, and chemistry had indeed given the doctrine something of a shock. But, on the other hand, increased acquaintance with the details of plant and animal life operated as a counterbalance and perhaps even strengthened the argument from design. The marvelous adaptations of organisms to their environment, of organs to the organism, of unlike parts of a complex organ—like the eye—to the organ itself; the foreshadowing by lower forms of the higher; the preparation in earlier stages of growth for organs that only later had their functioning—these things were increasingly recognized with the progress of botany, zoology, paleontology, and embryology. Together, they added such prestige to the design argument that by the late eighteenth century it was, as approved by the sciences of organic life, the central point of theistic and idealistic philosophy.

The Darwinian principle of natural selection cut straight under this philosophy. If all organic adaptations are due simply to constant variation and the elimination of those variations which are harmful in the struggle for existence that is brought about by excessive reproduction, there is no call for a prior intelligent causal force to plan and preordain them. Hostile critics charged Darwin with materialism and with making chance the cause of the universe.

Some naturalists, like Asa Gray, favored the Darwinian principle and attempted to reconcile it with design. Gray held to what may be called design on the installment plan. If we conceive the "stream of variations" to be itself intended, we may suppose that each successive variation was designed from the first to be selected. In that case, variation, struggle, and selection simply define the mechanism of "secondary causes" through which the "first cause" acts; and the doctrine of design is none the worse off because we know more of its *modus operandi*.

Darwin could not accept this mediating proposal. He admits or rather he asserts that it is "impossible to conceive this immense and wonderful universe including man with his capacity of looking far backwards and far into futurity as the result of blind chance or necessity."[1]. But nevertheless he holds that since variations are in useless as well as useful directions, and since the latter are sifted out simply by the stress of the conditions of struggle for existence, the design argument as applied to living beings is unjustifiable; and its lack of support there deprives it of scientific value as applied to nature in general. If the variations of the pigeon, which under artificial selection give the pouter pigeon, are not pre-ordained for the sake of the breeder, by what logic do we argue that variations resulting in natural species are predesigned?[2].

---

[1] "Life and Letters," Vol. I., p. 282; cf. 285.
[2] "Life and Letters," Vol. II., pp. 146, 170, 245; Vol. I., pp. 283-84. See also the closing portion of his "Variations of Animals and Plants under Domestication."

## IV

So much for some of the more obvious facts of the discussion of design *versus* chance, as causal principles of nature and of life as a whole. We brought up this discussion, you recall, as a crucial instance. What does our touchstone indicate as to the bearing of Darwinian ideas upon philosophy? In the first place, the new logic outlaws, flanks, dismisses—what you will—one type of problems and substitutes for it another type. Philosophy foreswears inquiry after absolute origins and absolute finalities in order to explore specific values and the specific conditions that generate them.

Darwin concluded that the impossibility of assigning the world to chance as a whole and to design in its parts indicated the insolubility of the question. Two radically different reasons, however, may be given as to why a problem is insoluble. One reason is that the problem is too high for intelligence; the other is that the question in its very asking makes assumptions that render the question meaningless. The latter alternative is unerringly pointed to in the celebrated case of design *versus* chance. Once admit that the sole verifiable or fruitful object of knowledge is the particular set of changes that generate the object of study together with the consequences that then flow from it, and no intelligible question can be asked about what, by assumption, lies outside. To assert—as is often asserted—that specific values of particular truth, social bonds and forms of beauty, if they can be shown to be generated by concretely knowable conditions, are meaningless and in vain; to assert that they are justified only when they and their particular causes and effects have all at once been gathered up into some inclusive first cause and some exhaustive final goal, is intellectual atavism. Such argumentation is reversion to the logic that explained the extinction of fire by water through the formal essence of aqueousness and the quenching of thirst by water through the final cause of aqueousness. Whether used in the case of the special event or that of life as a whole, such logic only abstracts some aspect of the existing course of events in order to reduplicate it as a petrified eternal principle by which to explain the very changes of which it is the formalization.

When Henry Sidgwick casually remarked in a letter that as he grew older his interest in what or who made the world was altered into interest in what kind of a world it is anyway, his voicing of a common experience of our own day illustrates also the nature of that intellectual transformation effected by the Darwinian logic. Interest shifts from the wholesale essence back of special changes to the question of how special changes serve and defeat concrete purposes; shifts from an intelligence that shaped things once for all to the particular intelligences which things are even now shaping; shifts from an ultimate goal of good to the direct increments of justice and happiness that intelligent administration of existent conditions may beget and that present carelessness or stupidity will destroy or forego.

In the second place, the classic type of logic inevitably set philosophy upon proving that life *must* have certain qualities and values—no matter how experience presents the matter—because of some remote cause and eventual goal. The duty of wholesale justification inevitably accompanies all thinking that makes the meaning of special occurrences depend upon something that once and for all lies behind them. The habit of derogating from present meanings and uses prevents our looking the facts of experience in the face; it prevents serious acknowledgment of the evils they present and serious concern with the goods they promise but do not as yet fulfil. It turns thought to the business of finding a wholesale transcendent remedy for the one and guarantee for the other. One is reminded of the way many moralists and theologians greeted Herbert Spencer's recognition of an unknowable energy from which welled up the phenomenal physical processes without and the conscious operations within. Merely because Spencer labeled his unknowable energy "God," this faded piece of metaphysical goods was greeted as an important and grateful concession to the reality of the spiritual realm. Were it not for the deep hold of the habit of seeking justification for ideal values in the remote and transcendent, surely this reference of them to an unknowable absolute would be despised in comparison with the demonstrations of experience that knowable energies are daily generating about us precious values.

The displacing of this wholesale type of philosophy will doubtless not arrive by sheer logical disproof, but rather by growing recognition of its futility. Were it a thousand times true that opium produces sleep because of its dormitive energy, yet the inducing of sleep in the tired, and the recovery to waking life of the poisoned, would not be thereby one least step forward. And were it a thousand times dialectically demonstrated that life as a whole is regulated by a transcendent principle to a final inclusive goal, none the less truth and error, health and disease, good and evil, hope and fear in the concrete, would remain just what and where they now are. To improve our education, to advance our politics, we must have recourse to specific conditions of generation.

Finally, the new logic introduces responsibility into the intellectual life. To idealize and rationalize the universe at large is after all a confession of inability to master the courses of things that specifically concern us. As long as mankind suffered from this impotency, it naturally shifted a burden of responsibility that it could not carry over to the more competent shoulders of the transcendent cause. But if insight into specific conditions of value and into specific consequences of ideas is possible, philosophy must in time become a method of locating and interpreting the more serious of the conflicts that occur in life, and a method of projecting ways for dealing with them: a method of moral and political diagnosis and prognosis.

The claim to formulate *a priori* the legislative constitution of the universe is by its nature a claim that may lead to elaborate dialectic developments. But it is also one that removes these very conclusions from subjection to experimental test, for, by definition, these results make no differences in the detailed course of events. But a philosophy that humbles its pretensions to the work of projecting hypotheses for the education and conduct of mind, individual and social, is thereby subjected to test by the way in which the ideas it propounds work out in practice. In having modesty forced upon it, philosophy also acquires responsibility.

Doubtless I seem to have violated the implied promise of my earlier remarks and to have turned both prophet and partisan. But in anticipating the direction of the transformations in philosophy to be wrought by the Darwinian genetic and experimental logic, I do not profess to speak for any save those who yield themselves consciously or unconsciously to this logic. No one can fairly deny that at present there are two effects of the Darwinian mode of thinking. On the one hand, there are making many sincere and vital efforts to revise our traditional philosophic conceptions in accordance with its demands. On the other hand, there is as definitely a recrudescence of absolutistic philosophies; an assertion of a type of philosophic knowing distinct from that of the sciences, one which opens to us another kind of reality from that to which the sciences give access; an appeal through experience to something that essentially goes beyond experience. This reaction affects popular creeds and religious movements as well as technical philosophies. The very conquest of the biological sciences by the new ideas has led many to proclaim an explicit and rigid separation of philosophy from science.

Old ideas give way slowly; for they are more than abstract logical forms and categories. They are habits, predispositions, deeply engrained attitudes of aversion and preference. Moreover, the conviction persists—though history shows it to be a hallucination—that all the questions that the human mind has asked are questions that can be answered in terms of the alternatives that the questions themselves present. But in fact intellectual progress usually occurs through sheer abandonment of questions together with both of the alternatives they assume—an abandonment that results from their decreasing vitality and a change of urgent interest. We do not solve them: we get over them. Old questions are solved by disappearing, evaporating, while new questions corresponding to the changed attitude of endeavor and preference take their place. Doubtless the greatest dissolvent in contemporary thought of old questions, the greatest precipitant of new methods, new intentions, new problems, is the one effected by the scientific revolution that found its climax in the "Origin of Species."

# 5. The Development of American Pragmatism*

John Dewey once wrote "that we are no longer a colony of any European nation nor of them all collectively. We are a new body and a new spirit in the world." In the present essay, Dewey gives a balanced account of the European origins as well as the originality of American philosophy, particularly as found in the work of William James. Dewey also denies that pragmatism is simply a philosophical version of the popular American mind, seeing it rather as a method for bringing intelligence to bear on the problems of moral and social life and as an antidote to the often "unreflective and brutal" individualism which pervades American life.

The purpose of this article is to define the principal theories of the philosophical movements known under the names of Pragmatism, Instrumentalism, or Experimentalism. To do this we must trace their historical development; for this method seems to present the simplest way of comprehending these movements, and at the same time avoiding certain current misunderstandings of their doctrines and their aims. The origin of Pragmatism goes back to Charles Sanders Peirce, the son of one of the most celebrated mathematicians of the United States, and himself very proficient in the science of mathematics; he is one of the founders of the modern symbolic logic of relations. Unfortunately

* From John Dewey, *Philosophy and Civilization* (New York, Capricorn Books, 1963) (1931), pp. 13-35. Reprinted by permission of G. P. Putnam's Sons. (Published originally in French in 1922 and then in English, as translated by Herbert W. Schneider, 1925.)

Peirce was not at all a systematic writer and never expounded his ideas in a single system. The pragmatic method which he developed applies only to a very narrow and limited universe of discourse. After William James had extended the scope of the method, Peirce wrote an exposition of the origin of pragmatism as he had first conceived it; it is from this exposition that we take the following passages.

The term "pragmatic," contrary to the opinion of those who regard pragmatism as an exclusively American conception, was suggested to him by the study of Kant. In the *Metaphysic of Morals* Kant established a distinction between *pragmatic* and *practical*. The latter term applies to moral laws which Kant regards as *a priori,* whereas the former term applies to the rules of art and technique which are based on experience and are applicable to experience. Peirce, who was an empiricist, with the habits of mind, as he put it, of the laboratory, consequently refused to call his system "practicalism," as some of his friends suggested. As a logician he was interested in the art and technique of real thinking, and especially interested, as far as pragmatic method is concerned, in the art of making concepts clear, or of construing adequate and effective definitions in accord with the spirit of scientific method.

Following his own words, for a person "who still thought in Kantian terms most readily, "*praktisch*" and "*pragmatisch*" were as far apart as the two poles; the former belonging in a region of thought where no mind of the experimental type can ever make sure of solid ground under his feet, the latter expressing relation to some definite human purpose. Now quite the most striking feature of the new theory was its recognition of an inseparable connection between rational cognition and rational purpose."[1].

In alluding to the experimental type of mind, we are brought to the exact meaning given by Peirce to the word "pragmatic." In speaking of an experimentalist as a man whose intelligence is formed in the laboratory, he said: "Whatever assertion you may make to him, he will either understand as meaning that if a given prescription for an experiment ever can be and ever is carried out in act, an experience of a given description will result, or else he will see no sense at all in what you say." And thus Peirce developed the theory that "the rational purport of a word or other expression, lies exclusively in its conceivable bearing upon the conduct of life; so that, since obviously nothing that might not result from experiment can have any direct bearing upon conduct, if one can define accurately all the conceivable experimental phenomena

[1] *Monist*, vol. 15, p. 163.

which the affirmation or denial of a concept could imply, one will have therein a complete definition of the concept.[2]

The essay in which Peirce developed his theory bears the title: *How to Make Our Ideas Clear*.[3] There is a remarkable similarity here to Kant's doctrine. Peirce's effort was to interpret the universality of concepts in the domain of *experience* in the same way in which Kant established the law of practical reason in the domain of the *a priori*. "The rational meaning of every proposition lies in the future. . . . But of the myriads of forms into which a proposition may be translated, what is that one which is to be called its very meaning? It is, according to the pragmatist, that form in which the proposition becomes applicable to human conduct, not in these or those special circumstances, nor when one entertains this or that special design, but that form which is most directly applicable to self-control under every situation, and to every purpose."[4] So also, "the pragmatist does not make the *summum bonum* to consist in action, but makes it to consist in that process of evolution whereby the existent comes more and more to embody generals . . . "[5] in other words—the process whereby the existent becomes, with the aid of action, a body of rational tendencies or of habits generalized as much as possible. These statements of Peirce are quite conclusive with respect to two errors which are commonly committed in regard to the ideas of the founder of pragmatism. It is often said of pragmatism that it makes action the end of life. It is also said of pragmatism that it subordinates thought and rational activity to particular ends of interest and profit. It is true that the theory according to Peirce's conception implies essentially a certain relation to action, to human conduct. But the rôle of action is that of an intermediary. In order to be able to attribute a meaning to concepts, one must be able to apply them to existence. Now it is by means of action that this application is made possible. And the modification of existence which results from this application constitutes the true meaning of concepts. Pragmatism is, therefore, far from being that glorification of action for its own sake which is regarded as the peculiar characteristic of American life.

It is also to be noted that there is a scale of possible applications of concepts to existence, and hence a diversity of meanings. The greater the extension of the concepts, the more they are freed from the restric-

---

[2] *Ibid.*, p. 162.
[3] *Popular Science Monthly*, 1878.
[4] *Monist*, vol. 15, pp. 173-4.
[5] *Ibid.*, p. 178.

tions which limit them to particular cases, the more is it possible for us to attribute the greatest generality of meaning to a term. Thus the theory of Peirce is opposed to every restriction of the meaning of a concept to the achievement of a particular end, and still more to a personal aim. It is still more strongly opposed to the idea that reason or thought should be reduced to being a servant of any interest which is pecuniary or narrow. This theory was American in its origin in so far as it insisted on the necessity of human conduct and the fulfillment of some aim in order to clarify thought. But at the same time, it disapproves of those aspects of American life which make action an end in itself, and which conceive ends too narrowly and too "practically." In considering a system of philosophy in its relation to national factors it is necessary to keep in mind not only the aspects of life which are incorporated in the system, but also the aspects against which the system is a protest. There never was a philosopher who has merited the name for the simple reason that he glorified the tendencies and characteristics of his social environment; just as it is also true that there never has been a philosopher who has not seized upon certain aspects of the life of his time and idealized them.

The work commenced by Peirce was continued by William James. In one sense James narrowed the application of Peirce's pragmatic method, but at the same time he extended it. The articles which Peirce wrote in 1878 commanded almost no attention from philosophical circles, which were then under the dominating influence of the neo-kantian idealism of Green, of Caird, and of the Oxford School, excepting those circles in which the Scottish philosophy of common sense maintained its supremacy. In 1898 James inaugurated the new pragmatic movement in an address entitled, "Philosophical Conceptions and Practical Results," later reprinted in the volume, *Collected Essays and Reviews*. Even in this early study one can easily notice the presence of those two tendencies to restrict and at the same time to extend early pragmatism. After having quoted the psychological remark of Peirce that "beliefs are really rules for action, and the whole function of thinking is but one step in the production of habits of action," and that every idea which we frame for ourselves of an object is really an idea of the possible effects of that object, he expressed the opinion that all these principles could be expressed more broadly than Peirce expressed them. "The ultimate test for us of what a truth means is indeed the conduct it dictates or inspires. But it inspires that conduct because it first foretells some particular turn to our experience which shall call for just that conduct from us. And I should prefer to express Peirce's principle by saying that the effective meaning of any philosophic proposition can always be brought down to some particular consequence, in our future practical experience, whether active or passive; the point lying rather in the fact that the experience must be particular, than in the fact that it must be active.''[6] In an essay written in 1908 James repeats this statement and states that whenever he employs the term "the practical," he means by it, "the distinctively concrete, the individual, the particular and effective as opposed to the abstract, general and inert—'Pragmata' are things in their plurality—particular consequences can perfectly well be of a theoretic nature.''[7]

William James alluded to the development which he gave to Peirce's expression of the principle. In one sense, one can say that he enlarged the bearing of the principle by the substitution of particular consequences for the general rule or method applicable to future experience. But in another sense this substitution limited the application of the principle, since it destroyed the importance attached by Peirce to the greatest possible application of the rule, or the habit of conduct—its extension to universality. That is to say, William James was much more of a nominalist than Peirce.

One can notice an extension of pragmatism in the above passage. James there alludes to the use of a method of determining the meaning of truth. Since truth is a term and has consequently a meaning, this extension is a legitimate application of pragmatic method. But it should be remarked that here this method serves only to make clear the meaning of the term "truth," and has nothing to do with the truth of a particular judgment. The principal reason which led James to give a new color to pragmatic method was that he was preoccupied with applying the method to determine the meaning of philosophical problems and questions, and that moreover, he chose to submit to examination philosophical notions of a theological or religious nature. He wished to establish a criterion which

[6] *Collected Essays and Reviews*, p. 412.

[7] *The Meaning of Truth*, pp. 209-210. In a footnote James gave an example of the errors which are committed in connection with the term "Practical," quoting M. Bourdeau who had written that "Pragmatism is an Anglo Saxon reaction against the intellectualism and rationalism of the Latin mind. . . . It is a philosophy without words, a philosophy of gestures and of facts, which abandons what is general and holds only to what is particular." In his lecture at California, James brought out the idea that his pragmatism was inspired to a considerable extent by the thought of the British philosophers, Locke, Berkeley, Hume, Mill, Bain, and Shadworth Hodgson. But he contrasted this method with German transcendentalism, and particularly with that of Kant. It is especially interesting to notice this difference between Peirce and James: the former attempted to give an experimental, not an *a priori* interpretation of Kant, whereas James tried to develop the point of view of the British thinkers.

would enable one to determine whether a given philosophical question has an authentic and vital meaning or whether, on the contrary, it is trivial and purely verbal; and in the former case, what interests are at stake when one accepts and affirms one or the other of two theses in dispute. (Peirce was above all a logician; whereas James was an educator and humanist and wished to force the general public to realize that certain problems, certain philosophical debates, have a real importance for mankind, because the beliefs which they bring into play lead to very different modes of conduct. If this important distinction is not grasped, it is impossible to understand the majority of the ambiguities and errors which belong to the later period of the pragmatic movement.

James took as an example the controversy between theism and materialism. It follows from this principle that if the course of the world is considered as completed, it is equally legitimate to assert that God or matter is its cause. Whether one way or the other, the facts are what they are, and it is they which determine whatever meaning is to be given to their cause. Consequently the name which we can give to this cause is entirely arbitrary. It is entirely different if we take the future into account. God then has the meaning of a power concerned with assuring the final triumph of ideal and spiritual values, and matter becomes a power indifferent to the triumph or defeat of these values. And our life takes a different direction according as we adopt one or the other of these alternatives. In the lectures on pragmatism published in 1907, he applies the same criticism to the philosophical problem of the One and the Many, that is to say of Monism and Pluralism, as well as to other questions. Thus he shows that Monism is equivalent to a rigid universe where everything is fixed and immutably united to others, where indetermination, free choice, novelty, and the unforeseen in experience have no place; a universe which demands the sacrifice of the concrete and complex diversity of things to the simplicity and nobility of an architectural structure. In what concerns our beliefs, Monism demands a rationalistic temperament leading to a fixed and dogmatic attitude. Pluralism, on the other hand, leaves room for contingence, liberty, novelty, and gives complete liberty of action to the empirical method, which can be indefinitely extended. It accepts unity where it finds it, but it does not attempt to force the vast diversity of events and things into a single rational mold.

From the point of view of an educator or of a student or, if you will, of those who are thoroughly interested in these problems, in philosophical discussions and controversies, there is no reason for contesting the value of this application of pragmatic method, but it is no less important to determine the nature of this application. It affords a means of discovering the implications for human life of philosophical conceptions which are often treated as of no importance and of a purely dialectical nature. It furnishes a criterion for determining the vital implications of beliefs which present themselves as alternatives in any theory. Thus as he himself said, "the whole function of philosophy ought to be to find the characteristic influences which you and I would undergo at a determinate moment of our lives, if one or the other formula of the universe were true." However, in saying that the whole function of philosophy has this aim, it seems that he is referring rather to the teaching than to the construction of philosophy. For such a statement implies that the world formulas have already all been made, and that the necessary work of producing them has already been finished, so that there remains only to define the consequences which are reflected in life by the acceptance of one or the other of these formulas as true.

From the point of view of Peirce, the object of philosophy would be rather to give a fixed meaning to the universe by formulas which correspond to our attitudes or our most general habits of response to the environment; and this generality depends on the extension of the applicability of these formulas to specific future events. The *meaning* of concepts of "matter" and of "God" must be fixed before we can even attempt to reach an understanding concerning the *value* of our belief in these concepts. Materialism would signify that the world demands on our part a single kind of constant and general habits; and God would signify the demand for another type of habits; the difference between materialism and theism would be tantamount to the difference in the habits required to face all the detailed facts of the universe. The world would be one in so far as it would be possible for us to form a single habit of action which would take account of all future existences and would be applicable to them. It would be many in so far as it is necessary for us to form several habits, differing from each other and irreducible to each other, in order to be able to meet the events in the world and control them. In short, Peirce wrote as a logician and James as a humanist.

William James accomplished a new advance in Pragmatism by his theory of the will to believe, or as he himself later called it, the right to believe. The discovery of the fundamental consequences of one or another belief has without fail a certain influence on that belief itself. If a man cherishes novelty, risk, opportunity and a variegated esthetic reality, he will certainly reject any belief in Monism, when he clearly perceives the import of this system. But if, from the very start, he is attracted by esthetic harmony, classic proportions, fixity even to the extent of absolute security, and logical coherence, it is quite natural that he should put faith in Monism. Thus William James took into account those motives of instinctive sympathy which play a greater rôle in our choice of a philosophic system than do formal reasonings; and he thought that we should be rendering a service to the cause of philosophical sincerity if we would openly recognize the motives which inspire us. He also maintained the thesis that the greater part of philosophic problems and especially those which touch on religious fields are of such a nature that they are not susceptible of decisive evidence one way or the other. Consequently he claimed the right of a man to choose his beliefs not only in the presence of proofs or conclusive facts, but also in the absence of all such proof. Above all when he is forced to choose between one meaning or another, or when by refusing to choose he has a right to assume the risks of faith, his refusal is itself equivalent to a choice. The theory of the will to believe gives rise to misunderstandings and even to ridicule; and therefore it is necessary to understand clearly in what way James used it. We are always obliged to act in any case; our actions and with them their consequences actually change according to the beliefs which we have chosen. Moreover it may be that, in order to discover the proofs which will ultimately be the intellectual justification of certain beliefs—the belief in freedom, for example, or the belief in God—it is necessary to begin to act in accordance with this belief.

In his lectures on pragmatism, and in his volume of essays bearing the title *The Meaning of Truth,* which appeared in 1909, James extended the use of the pragmatic method to the problem of the nature of truth. So far we have considered the pragmatic method as an instrument in determining the meaning of words and the vital importance of philosophic beliefs. Now and then we have made allusion to the future consequences which are implied. James showed, among other things, that in certain philosophic conceptions, the affirmation of certain beliefs could be justified by means of the nature of their consequences, or by the differences which these beliefs make in existence. But then why not push the argument to the point of maintaining that the meaning of truth in general is determined by its consequences? We must not forget here that James was an empiricist before he was a pragmatist, and repeatedly stated that pragmatism is merely empiricism pushed to its legitimate conclusions. From a general point of view, the pragmatic attitude consists in "looking away from first things, principles, 'categories,' supposed necessities; and of looking towards last things, fruits, consequences, facts." It is only one step further to apply the pragmatic method to the problem of truth. In the natural sciences there is a tendency to identify truth in any particular case with a verification. The verification of a theory, or of a concept, is carried on by the observation of particular facts. Even the most scientific and harmonious physical theory is merely an hypothesis until its implications, deduced by mathematical reasoning or by any other kind of inference, are verified by observed facts. What direction, therefore, must an empirical philosopher take who wishes to arrive at a definition of truth by means of an empirical method? He must, if he wants to apply this method, and without bringing in for the present the pragmatic formula, first find particular cases from which he then generalizes. It is therefore in submitting conceptions to the control of experience, in the process of verifying them, that one finds examples of what is called truth. Therefore any philosopher who applies this empirical method without the least prejudice in favor of pragmatic doctrine, can be led to conclude that truth "means" verification, or if one prefers, that verification, either actual or possible, is the definition of truth.

In combining this conception of empirical method with the theory of pragmatism, we come upon other important philosophical results. The classic theories of truth in terms of the coherence or compatibility of terms, and of the correspondence of an idea with a thing, hereby receive a new interpretation. A merely mental coherence without experimental verification does not enable us to get beyond the realm of hypothesis. If a notion or a theory makes pretense of corresponding to reality or to the facts, this pretense cannot be put to the test and confirmed or refuted except by causing it to pass over into the realm of action and by noting the results which it yields in the form of the concrete observable facts to which this notion or theory leads. If, in acting upon this notion, we are brought to the fact which it implies or which it demands, then this notion is true. A theory corresponds to the facts when it leads to the facts which are its consequences, by the intermediary of experience. And from this consideration the pragmatic generalization is drawn that all knowledge is prospective in its results, except in the case where notions and theories after having been first prospective in their application, have already been tried out and verified. Theoretically, however, even such verifications or truths could not be absolute. They would be based upon practical or moral certainty, but they are always subject to being corrected by unforeseen future consequences or by observed facts which had been disregarded. Every proposition concerning truths is really in the last analysis hypothetical and provisional, although a large number of these propositions have been so frequently verified without failure that we are justified in using them as if they were absolutely true. But, logically, absolute truth is an ideal which cannot be realized, at least not until all the facts have been registered, or as James says "bagged," and until it is no longer possible to make other observations and other experiences.

Pragmatism, thus, presents itself as an extension of historical empiricism, but with this fundamental difference, that it does not insist upon antecedent phenomena but upon consequent phenomena; not upon the precedents but upon the possibilities of action. And this change in point of view is almost revolutionary in its consequences. An empiricism which is content with repeating facts already past has no place for possibility and for liberty. It cannot find room for general conceptions or ideas, at least no more than to consider them as summaries or records. But when we take the point of view of pragmatism we see that general ideas have a very different rôle to play than that of reporting and registering past experiences. They are the bases for organizing future observations and experiences. Whereas, for empiricism, in a world already constructed and determined, reason or general thought has no other meaning than that of summing up particular cases, in a world where the future is not a mere word, where theories, general notions, rational ideas have consequences for action, reason necessarily has a constructive function. Nevertheless the conceptions of reasoning have only a secondary interest in comparison with the reality of facts, since they must be confronted with concrete observations.[8]

Pragmatism thus has a metaphysical implication. The doctrine of the value of consequences leads us to take the future into consideration. And this taking into consideration of the future takes us to the conception of a universe whose evolution is not finished, of a universe which is still, in James' term, "in the making," "in the process of becoming," of a universe up to a certain point still plastic.

Consequently reason, or thought, in its more general sense, has a real, though limited, function, a creative, constructive function. If we form general ideas and if we put them in action, consequences are pro-

---

[8] William James said in a happy metaphor, that they must be "cashed in," by producing specific consequences. This expression means that they must be able to lead to concrete facts. But for those who are not familiar with American idioms, James' formula was taken to mean that the consequences themselves of our rational conceptions must be narrowly limited by their pecuniary value. Thus Mr. Bertrand Russell wrote recently that pragmatism is merely a manifestation of American commercialism.

duced which could not be produced otherwise. Under these conditions the world will be different from what it would have been if thought had not intervened. This consideration confirms the human and moral importance of thought and of its reflective operation in experience. It is therefore not true to say that James treated reason, thought, and knowledge with contempt, or that he regarded them as mere means of gaining personal or even social profits. For him reason has a creative function, limited because specific, which helps to make the world other than it would have been without it. It makes the world really more reasonable; it gives to it an intrinsic value. One will understand the philosophy of James better if one considers it in its totality as a revision of English empiricism, a revision which replaces the value of past experience, of what is already given, by the future, by that which is as yet mere possibility.

These considerations naturally bring us to the movement called instrumentalism. The survey which we have just made of James' philosophy shows that he regarded conceptions and theories purely as instruments which can serve to constitute future facts in a specific manner. But James devoted himself primarily to the moral aspects of this theory, to the support which it gave to "meliorism" and moral idealism, and to the consequences which followed from it concerning the sentimental value and the bearing of various philosophical systems, particularly to its destructive implications for monistic rationalism and for absolutism in all its forms. He never attempted to develop a complete theory of the forms or "structures" and of the logical operations which are founded on this conception. Instrumentalism is an attempt to establish a precise logical theory of concepts, of judgments and inferences in their various forms, by considering primarily how thought functions in the experimental determinations of future consequences. That is to say, it attempts to establish universally recognized distinctions and rules of logic by deriving them from the reconstructive or mediative function ascribed to reason. It aims to constitute a theory of the general forms of conception and reasoning, and not of this or that particular judgment or concept related to its own content, or to its particular implications.

As far as the historical antecedents of instrumentalism are concerned, two factors are particularly important, over and above this matter of experimental verification which we have already mentioned in connection with James. The first of these two factors is psychological, and the second is a critique of the theory of knowledge and of logic which has resulted from the theory proposed by Neo-Kantian idealism and expounded in the logical writings of such philosophers as Lotze,

Bosanquet, and F. H. Bradley. As we have already said, Neo-Kantian influence was very marked in the United States during the last decade of the nineteenth century. I myself, and those who have collaborated with me in the exposition of instrumentalism, began by being Neo-Kantians, in the same way that Peirce's point of departure was Kantianism and that of James was the empiricism of the British School.

The psychological tendencies which have exerted an influence on in-strumentalism are of a biological rather than a physiological nature. They are, more or less, closely related to the important movement whose promoter in psychology has been Doctor John Watson and to which he has given the name of Behaviorism. Briefly, the point of departure of this theory is the conception of the brain as an organ for the co-ordination of sense stimuli (to which one should add modifica-tions caused by habit, unconscious memory, or what are called today "conditioned reflexes") for the purpose of effecting appropriate motor responses. On the basis of the theory of organic evolution it is main-tained that the analysis of intelligence and of its operations should be compatible with the order of known biological facts, concerning the in-termediate position occupied by the central nervous system in making possible responses to the environment adequate to the needs of the liv-ing organism. It is particularly interesting to note that in the *Studies in Logical Theory* (1903), which was their first declaration, the instrumen-talists recognized how much they owed to William James for having forged the instruments which they used, while at the same time, in the course of the studies, the authors constantly declared their belief in a close union of the "normative" principles of logic and the real processes of thought, in so far as these are determined by an objective or biological psychology and not by an introspective psychology of states of consciousness. But it is curious to note that the "instruments" to which allusion is made, are not the considerations which were of the greatest service to James. They precede his pragmatism and it is among some of the pages of his *Principles of Psychology* that one must look for them. This important work (1890) really developed two distinct theses.

The one is a re-interpretation of introspective psychology, in which James denies that sensations, images and ideas are discrete and in which he replaces them by a continuous stream which he calls "the stream of consciousness." This conception necessitates a consideration of rela-tions as an immediate part of the field of consciousness, having the same status as qualities. And throughout his *Psychology* James gives a philosophical tinge to this conception by using it in criticizing the atomism of Locke and of Hume as well as the *a-priorism* of the synthesis of rational principles by Kant and his successors, among whom should be mentioned in England, Thomas Hill Green, who was then at the height of his influence.

The other aspect of his *Principles of Psychology* is of a biological nature. It shows itself in its full force in the criterion which James established for discovering the existence of mind. "The pursuance of future ends and the choice of means for their attainment are thus the mark and criterion of the presence of mentality in a phenomenon."[9] The force of this criterion is plainly shown in the chapter on Attention, and its relation to Interest considered as the force which controls it, and its teleological function of selection and integration; in the chapter on Discrimination and Comparison (Analysis and Abstraction), where he discusses the way in which ends to be attained and the means for attaining them evoke and control intellectual analysis; and in the chapter on Conception, where he shows that a general idea is a mode of signifying particular things and not merely an abstraction from particular cases or a super-empirical function,—that it is a teleological instrument. James then develops this idea in the chapter on reasoning where he says that "the only meaning of essence is teleological, and that classification and conception are purely teleological weapons of mind."

One might complete this brief enumeration by mentioning also the chapter of James' book in which he discusses the Nature of Necessary Truths and the Rôle of Experience, and affirms in opposition to Herbert Spencer, that many of our most important modes of perception and conception of the world of sensible objects are not the cumulative products of particular experience, but rather original biological sports, spontaneous variations, which are maintained because of their applicability to concrete experiences after once having been created. Number, space, time, resemblance and other important "categories" could have been brought into existence, he says, as a consequence of some particular cerebral instability, but they could by no means have been registered on the mind by outside influence. Many significant and useless concepts also arise in the same manner. But the fundamental categories have been cumulatively extended and reinforced because of their value when applied to concrete instances and things of experience. It is therefore not the origin of a concept, it is its application which becomes the criterion of its value; and here we have the whole of pragmatism in embryo. A phrase of James' very well summarizes its import: "the popular notion that 'Science' is forced on the mind *ab extra*,

[9] *Psychology*, vol. I, p. 8.

and that our interests have nothing to do with its constructions, is utterly absurd."

Given the point of view which we have just specified, and the interest attaching to a logical theory of conception and judgment, and there results a theory of the following description. The adaptations made by inferior organisms, for example their effective and co-ordinated responses to stimuli, become teleological in man and therefore give occasion to thought. Reflection is an indirect response to the environment, and the element of indirection can itself become great and very complicated. But it has its origin in biological adaptive behavior and the ultimate function of its cognitive aspect is a prospective control of the conditions of the environment. The function of intelligence is therefore not that of copying the objects of the environment, but rather of taking account of the way in which more effective and more profitable relations with these objects may be established in the future.

How this point of view has been applied to the theory of judgment is too long a story to be told here. We shall confine ourselves here to saying that, in general, the "subject" of a judgment represents that portion of the environment to which a reaction must be made; the predicate represents the possible response or habit or manner in which one should behave towards the environment; the copula represents the organic and concrete act by which the connection is made between the fact and its signification; and finally the conclusion, or the definitive object of judgment, is simply the original situation transformed, a situation which implies a change as well in the original subject (including its mind) as in the environment itself. The new and harmonious unity thus attained verifies the bearing of the data which were at first chosen to serve as subject and of the concepts introduced into the situation during the process as teleological instruments for its elaboration. Until this final unification is attained the perceptual data and the conceptual principles, theories, are merely hypotheses from a logical point of view. Moreover, affirmation and negation are intrinsically a-logical: they are acts.

Such a summary survey can hardly pretend to be either convincing or suggestive. However, in noting the points of resemblance and difference between this phase of pragmatism and the logic of Neo-Hegelian idealism, we are bringing out a point of great importance. According to the latter logic, thought constitutes in the last analysis its object and even the universe. It is necessary to affirm the existence of a series of forms of judgment, because our first judgments, which are nearest to sense, succeed in constituting objects in only a partial and fragmentary fashion, even to the extent of involving in their nature an element of contradiction. There results a dialectic which permits each inferior and partial type of judgment to pass into a more complete form until we finally arrive at the total judgment, where the thought which comprehends the entire object or the universe is an organic whole of interrelated mental distinctions. It is evident that this theory magnifies the rôle of thought beyond all proportion. It is an objective and rational idealism which is opposed to and distinct from the subjective and perceptual idealism of Berkeley's school. Instrumentalism, however, assigns a positive function to thought, that of reconstituting the present stage of things instead of merely knowing it. As a consequence, there cannot be intrinsic degrees, or a hierarchy of forms of judgment. Each type has its own end, and its validity is entirely determined by its efficacy in the pursuit of its end. A limited perceptual judgment, adapted to the situation which has given it birth, is as true in its place as is the most complete and significant philosophic or scientific judgment. Logic, therefore, leads to a realistic metaphysics in so far as it accepts things and events for what they are independently of thought, and to an idealistic metaphysics in so far as it contends that thought gives birth to distinctive acts which modify future facts and events in such a way as to render them more reasonable, that is to say, more adequate to the ends which we propose for ourselves. This ideal element is more and more accentuated by the inclusion progressively of social factors in human environment over and above natural factors; so that the needs which are fulfilled, the ends which are attained are no longer of a merely biological or particular character, but include also the ends and activities of other members of society.

It is natural that continental thinkers should be interested in American philosophy as it reflects, in a certain sense, American life. Thus it should be clear after this rapid survey of the history of pragmatism that American thought continues European thought. We have imported our language, our laws, our institutions, our morals, and our religion from Europe, and we have adapted them to the new conditions of our life. The same is true of our ideas. For long years our philosophical thought was merely an echo of European thought. The pragmatic movement which we have traced in the present essay, as well as neo-realism, behaviorism, the absolute idealism of Royce, the naturalistic idealism of Santayana, are all attempts at re-adaptation; but they are not creations *de novo*. They have their roots in British and European thought. Since these systems are re-adaptations they take into consideration the distinctive traits of the environment of American life. But as has already been said, they are not limited to reproducing what is worn and imperfect in this environment. They do not aim to glorify the energy and the love of action which the new conditions of American life exaggerated. They do not reflect the excessive mercantilism of American life. Without doubt all these traits of the environment have not been without a certain influence on American philosophical thought; our philosophy would not be national or spontaneous if it were not subject to this influence. But the fundamental idea which the movements of which we have just spoken have attempted to express, is the idea that action and opportunity justify themselves only to the degree in which they render life more reasonable and increase its value. Instrumentalism maintains in opposition to many contrary tendencies in the American environment, that action should be intelligent and reflective, and that thought should occupy a central position in life. That is the reason for our insistence on the teleological phase of thought and knowledge. If it must be teleological in particular and not merely true in the abstract, that is probably due to the practical element which is found in all phases of American life. However that may be, what we insist upon above all else is that intelligence be regarded as the only source and sole guarantee of a desirable and happy future. It is beyond doubt that the progressive and unstable character of American life and civilization has facilitated the birth of a philosophy which regards the world as being in continuous formation, where there is still place for indeterminism, for the new, and for a real future. But this idea is not exclusively American, although the conditions of American life have aided this idea in becoming self-conscious. It is also true that Americans tend to underestimate the value of tradition and of rationality considered as an achievement of the past. But the world has also given proof of irrationality in the past and this irrationality is incorporated in our beliefs and our institutions. There are bad traditions as there are good ones: it is always important to distinguish. Our neglect of the traditions of the past, with whatever this negligence implies in the way of spiritual impoverishment of our life, has its compensation in the idea that the world is recommencing and being remade under our eyes. The future as well as the past can be a source of interest and consolation and give meaning to the present. Pragmatism and instrumental experimentalism bring into prominence the importance of the individual. It is he who is the carrier of creative thought, the author of action, and of its application. Subjectivism is an old story in philosophy; a story which began in Europe and not in America. But American philosophy, in the systems which we have expounded, has given to the subject, to the individual mind, a practical rather than an epistemological function.

The individual mind is important because only the individual mind is the organ of modifications in traditions and institutions, the vehicle of experimental creation. One-sided and egoistic individualism in American life has left its imprint on our practices. For better or for worse, depending on the point of view, it has transformed the esthetic and fixed individualism of the old European culture into an active individualism. But the idea of a society of individuals is not foreign to American thought; it penetrates even our current individualism which is unreflective and brutal. And the individual which American thought idealizes is not an individual *per se,* an individual fixed in isolation and set up for himself, but an individual who evolves and develops in a natural and human environment, an individual who can be educated.

If I were asked to give an historical parallel to this movement in American thought I would remind my reader of the French philosophy of the enlightenment. Every one knows that the thinkers who made that movement illustrious were inspired by Bacon, Locke, and Newton; what interested them was the application of scientific method and the conclusions of an experimental theory of knowledge to human affairs, the critique and reconstruction of beliefs and institutions. As Höffding writes, they were animated "by a fervent faith in intelligence, progress, and humanity." And certainly they are not accused to-day, just because of their educational and social significance, of having sought to subordinate intelligence and science to ordinary utilitarian aims. They merely sought to free intelligence from its impurities and to render it sovereign. One can scarcely say that those who glorify intelligence and reason in the abstract, because of their value for those who find personal satisfaction in their possession, estimate intelligence more truly than those who wish to make it the indispensable guide of intellectual and social life. When an American critic says of instrumentalism that it regards ideas as mere servants which make for success in life, he only reacts, without reflection, to the ordinary verbal associations of the word "instrumental," as many others have reacted in the same manner to the use of the word "practical." Similarly a recent Italian writer, after having said that pragmatism and instrumentalism are characteristic products of American thought, adds that these systems "regard intelligence as a mere mechanism of belief, and consequently attempt to re-establish the dignity of reason by making of it a machine for the production of beliefs useful to morals and society." This criticism does not hold. It is by no means the production of beliefs useful to morals and society which these systems pursue. It is the formation of a faith in intelligence, as the one and indispensable belief necessary to moral and social life. The more one appreciates the intrinsic esthetic, immediate value of thought and of science, the more one takes into account what intelligence itself adds to the joy and dignity of life, the more one should feel grieved at a situation in which the exercise and joy of reason are limited to a narrow, closed and technical social group and the more one should ask how it is possible to make all men participators in this inestimable wealth.

# 6. The Need for a Recovery of Philosophy*

With the exception of his major work on *Experience and Nature,* this is Dewey's most extensive effort to locate experience as the central concern of philosophical method. Paramount to this consideration is Dewey's effort to distinguish by virtue of five comparisons the "orthodox description of experience and that congenial to present conditions." Dewey is also prescient about contemporary philosophy in America when he writes: "I believe that philosophy in America will be lost between chewing a historic cud long since reduced to woody fiber, or an apologetics for lost causes (lost to natural science), or a scholastic, schematic formalism, unless it can somehow bring to consciousness America's own needs and its own implicit principle of successful action."

Intellectual advance occurs in two ways. At times increase of knowledge is organized about old conceptions, while these are expanded, elaborated and refined, but not seriously revised, much less abandoned. At other times, the increase of knowledge demands qualitative rather than quantitative change; alteration, not addition. Men's minds grow cold to their former intellectual concerns; ideas that were burning fade; interests that were urgent seem remote. Men face in another direction; their older perplexities are unreal; considerations passed over as negligible loom up. Former problems may not have been solved, but they no longer press for solution.

Philosophy is no exception to the rule. But it is unusually conservative—not, necessarily, in proffering solutions, but in clinging to problems. It has been so allied with theology and theological morals as

* From John Dewey *Creative Intelligence: Essays in the Pragmatic Attitude*, et al., pp. 3-69. Copyright 1945 by John Dewey. Reprinted by permission of Holt, Rinehart and Winston, Inc. (Published originally in 1917.)

representative of men's chief interests, that radical alteration has been shocking. Men's activities took a decidedly new turn, for example, in the seventeenth century, and it seemed as if philosophy, under the lead of thinkers like Bacon and Descartes, was to execute an about-face. But, in spite of the ferment, it turned out that many of the older problems were but translated from Latin into the vernacular or into the new terminology furnished by science.

The association of philosophy with academic teaching has reinforced this intrinsic conservatism. Scholastic philosophy persisted in universities after men's thoughts outside of the walls of colleges had moved in other directions. In the last hundred years intellectual advances of science and politics have in like fashion been crystallized into material of instruction and now resist further change. I would not say that the spirit of teaching is hostile to that of liberal inquiry, but a philosophy which exists largely as something to be taught rather than wholly as something to be reflected upon is conducive to discussion of views held by others rather than to immediate response. Philosophy when taught inevitably magnifies the history of past thought, and leads professional philosophers to approach their subject matter through its formulation in received systems. It tends, also, to emphasize points upon which men have divided into schools, for these lend themselves to retrospective definition and elaboration. Consequently, philosophical discussion is likely to be a dressing out of antithetical traditions, where criticism of one view is thought to afford proof of the truth of its opposite (as if formulation of views guaranteed logical exclusives). Direct preoccupation with contemporary difficulties is left to literature and politics.

If changing conduct and expanding knowledge ever required a willingness to surrender not merely old solutions but old problems it is now. I do not mean that we can turn abruptly away from all traditional issues. This is impossible; it would be the undoing of the one who attempted it. Irrespective of the professionalizing of philosophy, the ideas philosophers discuss are still those in which Western civilization has been bred. They are in the backs of the heads of educated people. But what serious-minded men not engaged in the professional business of philosophy most want to know is what modifications and abandonments of intellectual inheritance are required by the newer industrial, political, and scientific movements. They want to know what these newer movements mean when translated into general ideas. Unless professional philosophy can mobilize itself sufficiently to assist in this clarification and redirection of men's thoughts, it is likely to get more and more sidetracked from the main currents of contemporary life.

This essay may, then, be looked upon as an attempt to forward the emancipation of philosophy from too intimate and exclusive attachment to traditional problems. It is not in intent a criticism of various solutions that have been offered, but raises a question *as to the genuineness, under the present conditions of science and social life, of the problems.*

The limited object of my discussion will, doubtless, give an exaggerated impression of my conviction as to the artificiality of much recent philosophizing. Not that I have wilfully exaggerated in what I have said, but that the limitations of my purpose have led me not to say many things pertinent to a broader purpose. A discussion less restricted would strive to enforce the genuineness, in their own context, of questions now discussed mainly because they have been discussed rather than because contemporary conditions of life suggest them. It would also be a grateful task to dwell upon the precious contributions made by philosophic systems which as a whole are impossible. In the course of the development of unreal premises and the discussion of artificial problems, points of view have emerged which are indispensable possessions of culture. The horizon has been widened; ideas of great fecundity struck out; imagination quickened; a sense of the meaning of things created. It may even be asked whether these accompaniments of classic systems have not often been treated as a kind of guarantee of the systems themselves. But while it is a sign of an illiberal mind to throw away the fertile and ample ideas of a Spinoza, a Kant, or a Hegel, because their setting is not logically adequate, it is surely a sign of an undisciplined one to treat their contributions to culture as confirmations of premises with which they have no necessary connection.

I

A criticism of current philosophizing from the standpoint of the traditional quality of its problems must begin somewhere, and the choice of a beginning is arbitrary. It has appeared to me that the notion of experience implied in the questions most actively discussed gives a natural point of departure. For, if I mistake not, it is just the inherited view of experience common to the empirical school and its opponents which keeps alive many discussions even of matters that on their face are quite remote from it, while it is also this view which is most untenable in the light of existing science and social practice. Accordingly I set out with a brief statement of some of the chief contrasts between the orthodox description of experience and that congenial to present conditions.

(i) In the orthodox view, experience is regarded primarily as a knowledge-affair. But to eyes not looking through ancient spectacles, it assuredly appears as an affair of the intercourse of a living being with its physical and social environment. (ii) According to tradition experience is (at least primarily) a psychical thing, infected throughout by "subjectivity." What experience suggests about itself is a genuinely objective world which enters into the actions and sufferings of men and undergoes modifications through their responses. (iii) So far as anything beyond a bare present is recognized by the established doctrine, the past exclusively counts. Registration of what has taken place, reference to precedent, is believed to be the essence of experience. Empiricism is conceived of as tied up to what has been, or is, "given." But experience in its vital form is experimental, an effort to change the given; it is characterized by projection, by reaching forward into the unknown; connection with a future is its salient trait. (iv) The empirical tradition is committed to particularism. Connections and continuities are supposed to be foreign to experience, to be by-products of dubious validity. An experience that is an undergoing of an environment and a striving for its control in new directions is pregnant with connections. (v) In the traditional notion experience and thought are antithetical terms. Inference, so far as it is other than a revival of what has been given in the past, goes beyond experience; hence it is either invalid, or else a measure of desperation by which, using experience as a springboard, we jump out to a world of stable things and other selves. But experience, taken free of the restrictions imposed by the older concept, is full of inference. There is, apparently, no conscious experience without inference; reflection is native and constant.

These contrasts, with a consideration of the effect of substituting the account of experience relevant to modern life for the inherited account, afford the subject matter of the following discussion.

Suppose we take seriously the contribution made to our idea of experience by biology—not that recent biological science discovered the facts, but that it has so emphasized them that there is no longer an excuse for ignoring them or treating them as negligible. Any account of experience must now fit into the consideration that experiencing means living; and that living goes on in and because of an environing medium, not in a vacuum. Where there is experience, there is a living being. Where there is life, there is a double connection maintained with the environment. In part, environmental energies constitute organic functions; they enter into them. Life is not possible without such direct support by the environment. But while all organic changes depend upon the natural energies of the environment for their origination and occurrence, the natural energies sometimes carry the organic functions prosperously forward, and sometimes act counter to their continuance. Growth and decay, health and disease, are alike continuous with activities of the natural surroundings. The difference lies in the bearing of what happens upon future life activity. From the standpoint of this future reference environmental incidents fall into groups: those favorable-to-life activities, and those hostile.

The successful activities of the organism, those within which environmental assistance is incorporated, react upon the environment to bring about modifications favorable to their own future. The human being has upon his hands the problem of responding to what is going on around him so that these changes will take one turn rather than another, namely, that required by its own future functioning. While backed in part by the environment, its life is anything but a peaceful exhalation of environment. It is obliged to struggle—that is to say, to employ the direct support given by the environment in order indirectly to effect changes that would not otherwise occur. In this sense, life goes on by means of controlling the environment. Its activities must change the changes going on around it; they must neutralize hostile occurrences; they must transform neutral events into co-operative factors or into an efflorescence of new features.

Dialectic developments of the notion of self-preservation, of the *conatus essendi,* often ignore all the important facts of the actual process. They argue as if self-control, self-development, went on directly as a sort of unrolling push from within. But life endures only in virtue of the support of the environment. And since the environment is only incompletely enlisted in our behalf, self-preservation—or self-realization or whatever—is always indirect—always an affair of the way in which our present activities affect the direction taken by independent changes in the surroundings. Hindrances must be turned into means.

We are also given to playing loose with the conception of adjustment, as if that meant something fixed—a kind of accommodation once for all (ideally at least) of the organism *to* an environment. But as life requires the fitness of the environment to the organic functions, adjustment to the environment means not passive acceptance of the latter, but acting so that the environing changes take a certain turn. The "higher" the type of life, the more adjustment takes the form of an adjusting of the factors of the environment to one another in the interest of life; the less the significance of living, the more it becomes an adjustment to a given environment till at the lower end of the scale the differences between living and the nonliving disappear.

These statements are of an external kind. They are about the conditions of experience, rather than about experiencing itself. But assuredly experience as it concretely takes place bears out the statements. Experience is primarily a process of undergoing: a process of standing something; of suffering and passion, of affection, in the literal sense of these words. The organism has to endure, to undergo, the consequences of its own actions. Experience is no slipping along in a path fixed by inner consciousness. Private consciousness is an incidental outcome of experience of a vital objective sort; it is not its source. Undergoing, however, is never mere passivity. The most patient patient is more than a receptor. He is also an agent—a reactor, one trying experiments, one concerned with undergoing in a way which may influence what is still to happen. Sheer endurance, side-stepping evasions, are, after all, ways of treating the environment with a view to what such treatment will accomplish. Even if we shut ourselves up in the most clam-like fashion, we are doing something; our passivity is an active attitude, not an extinction of response. Just as there is no assertive action, no aggressive attack upon things as they are, which is all action, so there is no undergoing which is not on our part also a going on and a going through.

Experience, in other words, is a matter of *simultaneous* doings and sufferings. Our undergoings are experiments in varying the course of events; our active tryings are trials and tests of ourselves. This duplicity of experience shows itself in our happiness and misery, our successes and failures. Triumphs are dangerous when dwelt upon or lived off from; successes use themselves up. Any achieved equilibrium of adjustment with the environment is precarious because we cannot evenly keep pace with changes in the environment. These are so opposed in direction that we must choose. We must take the risk of casting in our lot with one movement or the other. Nothing can eliminate all risk, all adventure; the one thing doomed to failure is to try to keep even with the whole environment at once—that is to say, to maintain the happy moment when all things go our way.

The obstacles which confront us are stimuli to variation, to novel response, and hence are occasions of progress. If a favor done us by the environment conceals a threat, so its disfavor is a potential means of hitherto unexperienced modes of success. To treat misery as anything but misery, as for example a blessing in disguise or a necessary factor in good, is disingenuous apologetics. But to say that the progress of the race has been stimulated by ills undergone, and that men have been moved by what they suffer to search out new and better courses of action is to speak veraciously.

The preoccupation of experience with things which are coming (are now coming, not just to come) is obvious to any one whose interest in experience is empirical. Since we live forward; since we live in a world where changes are going on whose issue means our weal or woe; since every act of ours modifies these changes and hence is fraught with promise, or charged with hostile energies—what should experience be but a future implicated in a present! Adjustment is no timeless state; it is a continuing process. To say that a change takes time may be to say something about the event which is external and uninstructive. But adjustment of organism to environment takes time in the pregnant sense; every step in the process is conditioned by reference to further changes which it effects. What is going on in the environment is the concern of the organism; not what is already "there" in accomplished and finished form. In so far as the issue of what is going on may be affected by intervention of the organism, the moving event is a challenge which stretches the agent-patient to meet what is coming. Experiencing exhibits things in their unterminated aspect moving toward determinate conclusions. The finished and done with is of import as affecting the future, not on its own account: in short, because it is not, really, done with.

Anticipation is therefore more primary than recollection; projection than summoning of the past; the prospective than the retrospective. Given a world like that in which we live, a world in which environing changes are partly favorable and partly callously indifferent, and experience is bound to be prospective in import; for any control attainable by the living creature depends upon what is done to alter the state of things. Success and failure are the primary "categories" of life; achieving of good and averting of ill are its supreme interests; hope and anxiety (which are not self-enclosed states of feeling, but active attitudes of welcome and wariness) are dominant qualities of experience. Imaginative forecast of the future is this forerunning quality of behavior rendered available for guidance in the present. Day-dreaming and castle-building and esthetic realization of what is not practically achieved are offshoots of this practical trait, or else practical intelligence is a chastened fantasy. It makes little difference. Imaginative recovery of the bygone is indispensable to successful invasion of the future, but its status is that of an instrument. To ignore its import is the sign of an undisciplined agent; but to isolate the past, dwelling upon it for its own sake and giving it the eulogistic name of knowledge, is to substitute the reminiscence of old age for effective intelligence. The movement of the agent-patient to meet the future is partial and passionate; yet detached and impartial study of the past is the only alternative to luck in assuring success to passion.

## II

This description of experience would be but a rhapsodic celebration of the commonplace were it not in marked contrast to orthodox philosophical accounts. The contrast indicates that traditional accounts have not been empirical, but have been deductions, from unnamed premises, of what experience *must* be. Historic empiricism has been empirical in a technical and controversial sense. It has said, Lord, Lord, Experience, Experience; but in practice it has served ideas *forced into* ·experience, not *gathered from* it.

The confusion and artificiality thereby introduced into philosophical thought is nowhere more evident than in the empirical treatment of relations or dynamic continuities. The experience of a living being struggling to hold its own and make its way in an environment, physical and social, partly facilitating and partly obstructing its actions, is of necessity a matter of ties and connections, of bearings and uses. The very point of experience, so to say, is that it doesn't occur in a vacuum; its agent-patient instead of being insulated and disconnected is bound up with the movement of things by most intimate and pervasive bonds. Only because the organism is in and of the world, and its activities correlated with those of other things in multiple ways, is it susceptible to undergoing things and capable of trying to reduce objects to means of securing its good fortune. That these connections are of diverse kinds is irresistibly proved by the fluctuations which occur in its career. Help and hindrance, stimulation and inhibition, success and failure mean specifically different modes of correlation. Although the actions of things in the world are taking place in one continuous stretch of existence, there are all kinds of specific affinities, repulsions, and relative indifferencies.

Dynamic connections are qualitatively diverse, just as are the centers of action. *In this sense,* pluralism, not monism, is an established empirical fact. The attempt to establish monism from consideration of the very nature of a relation is a mere piece of dialectics. Equally dialectical is the effort to establish by a consideration of the nature of relations an ontological Pluralism of Ultimates: *simple and independent beings.* To attempt to get results from a consideration of the "external" nature of relations is of a piece with the attempt to deduce results from their "internal" character. Some things are relatively insulated from the influence of other things; some things are easily invaded by others; some things are fiercely attracted to conjoin their activities with those of others. Experience exhibits every kind of connection[1] from the most intimate to mere external juxtaposition.

Empirically, then, active bonds of continuities of all kinds, together with static discontinuities, characterize existence. To deny this qualitative heterogeneity is to reduce the struggles and difficulties of life, its comedies and tragedies, to illusion: to the nonbeing of the Greeks or to its modern counterpart, the "subjective." Experience is an affair of facilitations and checks, of being sustained and disrupted, being let alone, being helped and troubled, of good fortune and defeat in all the countless qualitative modes which these words pallidly suggest. The existence of genuine connections of all manner of heterogeneity cannot be doubted. Such words as conjoining, disjoining, resisting, modifying, saltatory, and ambulatory (to use James's picturesque term) only hint at their actual heterogeneity.

Among the revisions and surrenders of historic problems demanded by this feature of empirical situations, those centering in the rationalistic-empirical controversy may be selected for attention. The implications of this controversy are two-fold: First, that connections are as homogeneous in fact as in name; and, secondly, if genuine, are all due to thought, or, if empirical, are arbitrary by-products of past particulars. The stubborn particularism of orthodox empiricism is its outstanding trait; consequently the opposed rationalism found no justification of bearings, continuities, and ties save to refer them in gross to the work of a hyper-empirical Reason.

Of course, not all empiricism prior to Hume and Kant was sensationalistic, pulverizing "experience" into isolated sensory qualities or simple ideas. It did not all follow Locke's lead in regarding the entire content of generalization as the "workmanship of the understanding." On the Continent, prior to Kant, philosophers were content to draw a line between empirical generalizations regarding matters of fact and

[1] The word relation suffers from ambiguity. I am speaking here of *connection*, dynamic and functional interaction. "Relation" is a term used also to express logical reference. I suspect that much of the controversy about internal and external relations is due to this ambiguity. One passes at will from existential connections of things to logical relationship of terms. Such an identification of existences with *terms* is congenial to idealism, but is paradoxical in a professed realism.

necessary universals applying to truths of reason. But logical atomism was implicit even in this theory. Statements referring to empirical fact were mere quantitative summaries of particular instances. In the sensationalism which sprang from Hume (and which was left unquestioned by Kant as far as any strictly empirical element was concerned) the implicit particularism was made explicit. But the doctrine that sensations and ideas are so many separate existences was not derived from observation nor from experiment. It was a logical deduction from a prior unexamined concept of the nature of experience. From the same concept it followed that the appearance of stable objects and of general principles of connection was but an appearance.[2]

Kantianism, then, naturally invoked universal bonds to restore objectivity. But, in so doing, it accepted the particularism of experience and proceeded to supplement it from nonempirical sources. A sensory manifold being all which is really empirical in experience, a reason which transcends experience must provide synthesis. The net outcome might have suggested a correct account of experience. For we have only to forget the apparatus by which the net outcome is arrived at, to have before us the experience of the plain man—a diversity of ceaseless changes connected in all kinds of ways, static and dynamic. This conclusion would deal a deathblow to both empiricism and rationalism. For, making clear the nonempirical character of the alleged manifold of unconnected particulars, it would render unnecessary the appeal to functions of the understanding in order to connect them. With the downfall of the traditional notion of experience, the appeal to reason to supplement its defects becomes superfluous.

The tradition was, however, too strongly entrenched; especially as it furnished the subject matter of an alleged science of states of mind which were directly known in their very presence. The historic outcome was a new crop of artificial puzzles about relations; it fastened upon philosophy for a long time the quarrel about the *a priori* and the *a posteriori* as its chief issue. The controversy is today quiescent. Yet it is not at all uncommon to find thinkers modern in tone and intent who regard any philosophy of experience as necessarily committed to denial of the existence of genuinely general propositions, and who take empiricism to be inherently averse to the recognition of the importance of an organizing and constructive intelligence.

---

[2] There is some gain in substituting a doctrine of flux and interpenetration of psychical states *à la* Bergson, for that of rigid discontinuity. But the substitution leaves untouched the fundamental misstatement of experience, the conception of experience as directly and primarily "inner" and psychical.

The quiescence alluded to is in part due, I think, to sheer weariness. But it is also due to a change of standpoint introduced by biological conceptions; and particularly the discovery of biological continuity from the lower organisms to man. For a short period, Spencerians might connect the doctrine of evolution with the old problem, and use the long temporal accumulation of "experiences" to generate something which, for human experience, is *a priori*. But the tendency of the biological way of thinking is neither to confirm or negate the Spencerian doctrine, but to shift the issue. In the orthodox position *a posteriori* and *a priori* were affairs of knowledge. But it soon becomes obvious that while there is assuredly something *a priori*—that is to say, native, unlearned, original—in human experience, that something is *not* knowledge, but is activities made possible by means of established connections of neurones. This empirical fact does not solve the orthodox problem; it dissolves it. It shows that the problem was misconceived, and solution sought by both parties in the wrong direction.

Organic instincts and organic retention, or habit-forming, are undeniable factors in actual experience. They are factors which effect organization and secure continuity. They are among the specific facts which a description of experience cognizant of the correlation of organic action with the action of other natural objects will include. But while fortunately the contribution of biological science to a truly empirical description of experiencing has outlawed the discussion of the *a priori* and *a posteriori*, the transforming effect of the same contributions upon other issues has gone unnoticed, save as pragmatism has made an effort to bring them to recognition.

III

The point seriously at issue in the notion of experience common to both sides in the older controversy thus turns out to be the place of thought or intelligence in experience. Does reason have a distinctive office? Is there a characteristic order of relations contributed by it?

Experience, to return to our positive conception, is primarily what is undergone in connection with activities whose import lies in their objective consequences—their bearing upon future experiences. Organic functions deal with things as things in course, in operation, in a state of affairs not yet given or completed. What is done with, what is just "there," is of concern only in the potentialities which it may indicate. As ended, as wholly given, it is of no account. But as a sign of what may come, it becomes an indispensable factor in behavior dealing with changes, the outcome of which is not yet determined.

The only power the organism possesses to control its own future depends upon the way its present responses modify changes which are tak-. ing place in its medium. A living being may be comparatively impotent, or comparatively free. It is all a matter of the way in which its present reactions to things influence the future reactions of things upon it. Without regard to its wish or intent every act it performs makes some difference in the environment. The change may be trivial as respects its own career and fortune. But it may also be of incalculable importance; it may import harm, destruction, or it may procure well-being.

Is it possible for a living being to increase its control of welfare and success? Can it manage, in any degree, to assure its future? Or does the amount of security depend wholly upon the accidents of the situation? Can it learn? Can it gain ability to assure its future in the present? These questions center attention upon the significance of reflective intelligence in the process of experience. The extent of an agent's capacity for inference, its power to use a given fact as a sign of something not yet given, measures the extent of its ability systematically to enlarge its control of the future.

A being which can use given and finished facts as signs of things to come; which can take given things as evidences of absent things, can, in that degree, forecast the future; it can form reasonable expectations. It is capable of achieving ideas; it is possessed of intelligence. For use of the given or finished to anticipate the consequence of processes going on is precisely what is meant by "ideas," by "intelligence."

As we have already noted, the environment is rarely all of a kind in its bearing upon organic welfare; its most wholehearted support of life activities is precarious and temporary. Some environmental changes are auspicious; others are menacing. The secret of success—that is, of the greatest attainable success—is for the organic response to cast in its lot with present auspicious changes to strengthen them and thus to avert the consequences flowing from occurrences of ill-omen. Any reaction is a venture; it involves risk. We always build better or worse than we can foretell. But the organism's fateful intervention in the course of events is blind, its choice is random, except as it can employ what happens to it as a basis of inferring what is likely to happen later. In the degree in which it can read future results in present on-goings, its responsive choice, its partiality to this condition or that, become intelligent. Its bias grows reasonable. It can deliberately, intentionally, participate in the direction of the course of affairs. Its foresight of different futures which result according as this or that present factor predominates in the shaping of affairs permits it to partake intelligently instead of blindly and fatally in the consequences its reactions give rise to. Participate it must, and to its own weal or woe. Inference, the use of what happens, to anticipate what will—or at least may—happen, makes the difference between directed and undirected participation. And this capacity for inferring is precisely the same as that use of natural occurrences for the discovery and determination of consequences—the formation of new dynamic connections—which constitutes knowledge.

The fact that thought is an intrinsic feature of experience is fatal to the traditional empiricism which makes it an artificial by-product. But for that same reason it is fatal to the historic rationalisms whose justification was the secondary and retrospective position assigned to thought by empirical philosophy. According to the particularism of the latter, thought was inevitably only a bunching together of hard-and-fast separate items; thinking was but the gathering together and tying of items already completely given, or else an equally artificial untying—a mechanical adding and subtracting of the given. It was but a cumulative registration, a consolidated merger; generality was a matter of bulk, not of quality. Thinking was therefore treated as lacking constructive power; even its organizing capacity was but simulated, being in truth but arbitrary pigeon-holing. Genuine projection of the novel, deliberate variation and invention, are idle fictions in such a version of experience. If there ever was creation, it all took place at a remote period. Since then the world has only recited lessons.

The value of inventive construction is too precious to be disposed of in this cavalier way. Its unceremonious denial afforded an opportunity to assert that in addition to experience the subject has a ready-made faculty of thought or reason which transcends experience. Rationalism thus accepted the account of experience given by traditional empiricism, and introduced reason as extra-empirical. There are still thinkers who regard any empiricism as necessarily committed to a belief in a cut-and-dried reliance upon disconnected precedents, and who hold that all systematic organization of past experiences for new and constructive purposes is alien to strict empiricism.

Rationalism never explained, however, how a reason extraneous to experience could enter into helpful relation with concrete experiences. By definition, reason and experience were antithetical, so that the concern of reason was not the fruitful expansion and guidance of the course of experience, but a realm of considerations too sublime to touch, or be     .

touched by, experience. Discreet rationalists confined themselves to theology and allied branches of abstruse science, and to mathematics. Rationalism would have been a doctrine reserved for academic specialists and abstract formalists had it not assumed the task of providing an apologetics for traditional morals and theology, thereby getting into touch with actual human beliefs and concerns. It is notorious that historic empiricism was strong in criticism and in demolition of outworn beliefs, but weak for purposes of constructive social direction. But we frequently overlook the fact that whenever rationalism cut free from conservative apologetics, it was also simply an instrumentality for pointing out inconsistencies and absurdities in existing beliefs—a sphere in which it was immensely useful, as the Enlightenment shows. Leibniz and Voltaire were contemporary rationalists in more senses than one.[3]

The recognition that reflection is a genuine factor within experience and an indispensable factor in that control of the world which secures a prosperous and significant expansion of experience undermines historic rationalism as assuredly as it abolishes the foundations of historic empiricism. The bearing of a correct idea of the place and office of reflection upon modern idealisms is less obvious, but no less certain.

One of the curiosities of orthodox empricism is that its outstanding speculative problem is the existence of an "external world." For in accordance with the notion that experience is attached to a private subject as its exclusive possession, a world like the one in which we appear to live must be "external" to experience instead of being its subject matter. I call it a curiosity, for if anything seems adequately grounded empirically it is the existence of a world which resists the characteristic functions of the subject of experience; which goes its way, in some respects, independently of these functions, and which frustrates our hopes and intentions. Ignorance which is fatal; disappointment; the need of adjusting means and ends to the course of nature, would seem to be facts sufficiently characterizing empirical situations as to render the existence of an external world indubitable.

That the description of experience was arrived at by forcing actual empirical facts into conformity with dialectic developments from a concept of a knower outside of the real world of nature is testified to by the

[3] Mathematical science in its formal aspects, or as a branch of formal logic, has been the empirical stronghold of rationalism. But an empirical empiricism, in contrast with orthodox deductive empiricism, has no difficulty in establishing its jurisdiction as to deductive functions.

historic alliance of empiricism and idealism.[4] According to the most logically consistent editions of orthodox empiricism, all that can be experienced is the fleeting, the momentary, mental state. That alone is absolutely and indubitably present; therefore, it alone is cognitively certain. It alone is *knowledge*. The existence of the past (and of the future), of a decently stable world and of other selves—indeed, of one's own self—falls outside this datum of experience. These can be arrived at only by inference which is "ejective"—a name given to an alleged type of inference that jumps from experience, as from a springboard, to something beyond experience.

I should not anticipate difficulty in showing that this doctrine is, dialectically, a mass of inconsistencies. Avowedly it is a doctrine of desperation, and as such it is cited here to show the desperate straits to which ignoring empirical facts has reduced a doctrine of experience. More positively instructive are the objective idealisms which have been the offspring of the marriage between the "reason" of historic rationalism and the alleged immediate psychical stuff of historic empiricism. These idealisms have recognized the genuineness of connections and the impotency of "feeling." They have then identified connections with logical or rational connections, and thus treated "the real World" as a synthesis of sentient consciousness by means of a rational self-consciousness introducing objectivity: stability and universality of reference.

Here again, for present purposes, criticism is unnecessary. It suffices to point out that the value of this theory is bound up with the genuineness of the problem of which it purports to be a solution. If the basic concept is a fiction, there is no call for the solution. The more important point is to perceive how far the "thought" which figures in objective idealism comes from meeting the empirical demands made upon actual thought. Idealism is much less formal than historic rationalism. It treats thought, or reason, as constitutive of experience by means of uniting and constructive functions, not as just concerned with a realm of eternal truths apart from experience. On such a view thought certainly loses its abstractness and remoteness. But, unfortunately, in thus gaining the whole world it loses its own self. A world already, in its intrinsic structure, dominated by thought is not a world in which, save by contradiction of premises, thinking has anything to do.

[4] It is a shame to devote the word idealism, with its latent moral, practical connotations, to a doctrine whose tenets are the denial of the existence of a physical world, and the psychical character of all objects—at least as far as they are knowable. But I am following usage, not attempting to make it.

That the doctrine logically results in making change unreal and error unaccountable are consequences of importance in the technique of professional philosophy; in the denial of empirical fact which they imply they seem to many a *reductio ad absurdum* of the premises from which they proceed. But, after all, such consequences are of only professional import. What is serious, even sinister, is the implied sophistication regarding the place and office of reflection in the scheme of things. A doctrine which exalts thought in name while ignoring its efficacy in fact (that is, its use in bettering life) is a doctrine which cannot be entertained and taught without serious peril. Those who are not concerned with professional philosophy but who are solicitous for intelligence as a factor in the amelioration of actual conditions can but look askance at any doctrine which holds that the entire scheme of things is already, if we but acquire the knack of looking at it aright, fixedly and completely rational. It is a striking manifestation of the extent in which philosophies have been compensatory in quality.[5] But the matter cannot be passed over as if it were simply a question of not grudging a certain amount of consolation to one amid the irretrievable evils of life. For as to these evils no one knows how many are retrievable; and a philosophy which proclaims the ability of a dialectic theory of knowledge to reveal the world as already and eternally a self-luminous rational whole, contaminates the scope and use of thought at its very spring. To substitute the otiose insight gained by manipulation of a formula for the slow co-operative work of a humanity guided by reflective intelligence is more than a technical blunder of speculative philosophers.

A practical crisis may throw the relationship of ideas to life into an exaggerated Brocken-like spectral relief, where exaggeration renders perceptible features not ordinarily noted. The use of force to secure narrow because exclusive aims is no novelty in human affairs. The deploying of all the intelligence at command in order to increase the effectiveness of the force used is not so common, yet presents nothing intrinsically remarkable. The identification of force—military, economic, and administrative—with moral necessity and moral culture is, however, a phenomenon not likely to exhibit itself on a wide scale except where intelligence has already been suborned by an idealism which identifies "the actual with the rational," and thus finds the measure of reason in the brute event determined by superior force. If we are to have

---

[5] See Dr. Kallen's essay . . . . ["Value and Existence in Philosophy, Art and Religion" in *Creative Intelligence*.]

a philosophy which will intervene between attachment to rule of thumb muddling and devotion to a systematized subordination of intelligence to pre-existent ends, it can be found only in a philosophy which finds the ultimate measure of intelligence in consideration of a desirable future and in search for the means of bringing it progressively into existence. When professed idealism turns out to be a narrow pragmatism—narrow because taking for granted the finality of ends determined by historic conditions—the time has arrived for a pragmatism which shall be empirically idealistic, proclaiming the essential connection of intelligence with the unachieved future—with possibilities involving a transfiguration.

## IV

Why has the description of experience been so remote from the facts of empirical situations? To answer this question throws light upon the submergence of recent philosophizing in epistemology—that is, in discussions of the nature, possibility, and limits of knowledge in general, and in the attempt to reach conclusions regarding the ultimate nature of reality from the answers given to such questions.

The reply to the query regarding the currency of a nonempirical doctrine of experience (even among professed empiricists) is that the traditional account is derived from a conception once universally entertained regarding the subject or bearer or center of experience. The description of experience has been forced into conformity with this prior conception; it has been primarily a deduction from it, actual empirical facts being poured into the moulds of the deductions. The characteristic feature of this prior notion is the assumption that experience centers in, or gathers about, or proceeds from a center or subject which is outside the course of natural existence, and set over against it—it being of no importance, for present purposes, whether this antithetical subject is termed soul, or spirit, or mind, or ego, or consciousness, or just knower or knowing subject.

There are plausible grounds for thinking that the currency of the idea in question lies in the form which men's religious preoccupations took for many centuries. These were deliberately and systematically otherworldly. They centered about a Fall which was not an event in nature, but an aboriginal catastrophe that corrupted Nature; about a redemption made possible by supernatural means; about a life in another world—essentially, not merely spatially, Other. The supreme drama of destiny took place in a soul or spirit which, under the circumstances, could not be conceived other than as nonnatural—extranatural, if not, strictly speaking, supernatural. When Descartes and others broke away from medieval interests, they retained as commonplaces its intellectual apparatus: Such as, knowledge is exercised by a power that is extranatural and set over against the world to be known. Even if they had wished to make a complete break, they had nothing to put as knower in the place of the soul. It may be doubted whether there was any available empirical substitute until science worked out the fact that physical changes are functional correlations of energies, and that man is continuous with other forms of life, and until social life had developed an intellectually free and responsible individual as its agent.

But my main point is not dependent upon any particular theory as to the historic origin of the notion about the bearer of experience. The point is there on its own account. The essential thing is that the bearer was conceived as outside of the world; so that experience consisted in the bearer's being affected through a type of operations not found anywhere in the world, while knowledge consists in surveying the world, looking at it, getting the view of a spectator.

The theological problem of attaining knowledge of God as ultimate reality was transformed in effect into the philosophical problem of the possibility of attaining knowledge of reality. For how is one to get beyond the limits of the subject and subjective occurrences? Familiarity breeds credulity oftener than contempt. How can a problem be artificial when men have been busy discussing it almost for three hundred years? But if the assumption that experience is something set over against the world is contrary to fact, then the problem of how self or mind or subjective experience or consciousness can reach knowledge of an external world is assuredly a meaningless problem. Whatever questions there may be about knowledge, they will not be the kind of problems which have formed epistemology.

The problem of knowledge as conceived in the industry of epistemology is the problem of knowledge *in general*—of the possibility, extent, and validity of knowledge in general. What does this "in general" mean? In ordinary life there are problems a-plenty of knowledge in particular; every conclusion we try to reach, theoretical or practical, affords such a problem. But there is no problem of knowledge in general. I do not mean, of course, that general statements cannot be made about knowledge, or that the problem of attaining these general statements is not a genuine one. On the contrary, specific instances of success and failure in inquiry exist, and are of such a character that one can discover the conditions conducing to success and failure. Statement of these conditions constitutes logic, and is capable of being an important aid in proper guidance of further attempts at knowing. But this logical problem of knowledge is at the opposite pole from the epistemological. Specific problems are about right conclusions to be reached—which means, in effect, right ways of going about the business of inquiry. They imply a difference between knowledge and error consequent upon right and wrong methods of inquiry and testing; not a difference between experience and the world. The problem of knowledge *überhaupt* exists because it is assumed that there is a knower in general, who is outside of the world to be known, and who is defined in terms antithetical to the traits of the world. With analogous assumptions, we could invent and discuss a problem of digestion in general. All that would be required would be to conceive the stomach and food material as inhabiting different worlds. Such an assumption would leave on our hands the question of the possibility, extent, nature, and genuineness of any transaction between stomach and food.

But because the stomach and food inhabit a continuous stretch of existence, because digestion is but a correlation of diverse activities in one world, the problems of digestion are specific and plural: What are the particular correlations which constitute it? How does it proceed in different situations? What is favorable and what unfavorable to its best performance?—and so on. Can one deny that if we were to take our clue from the present empirical situation, including the scientific notion of evolution (biological continuity) and the existing arts of control of nature, subject and object would be treated as occupying the same natural world as unhesitatingly as we assume the natural conjunction of an animal and its food? Would it not follow that knowledge is one way in which natural energies co-operate? Would there be any problem save discovery of the peculiar structure of this co-operation, the conditions under which it occurs to best effect, and the consequences which issue from its occurrence?

It is a commonplace that the chief divisions of modern philosophy, idealism in its different kinds, realisms of various brands, so-called common-sense dualism, agnosticism, relativism, phenomenalism, have grown up around the epistemological problem of the general relation of subject and object. Problems not openly epistemological, such as whether the relation of changes in consciousness to physical changes is one of interaction, parallelism, or automatism have the same origin. What becomes of philosophy, consisting largely as it does of different answers to these questions, in case the assumptions which generate the questions have no empirical standing? Is it not time that philosophers turned from the attempt to determine the comparative merits of various replies to the questions to a consideration of the claims of the questions?

When dominating religious ideas were built up about the idea that the self is a stranger and pilgrim in this world; when morals, falling in line, found true good only in inner states of a self inaccessible to anything but its own private introspection; when political theory assumed the finality of disconnected and mutually exclusive personalities, the notion that the bearer of experience is antithetical to the world instead of being in and of it was congenial. It at least had the warrant of other beliefs and aspirations. But the doctrine of biological continuity or organic evolution has destroyed the scientific basis of the conception. Morally, men are now concerned with the amelioration of the conditions of the common lot in this world. Social sciences recognize that associated life is not a matter of physical juxtaposition, but of genuine intercourse—of community of experience in a non-metaphorical sense of community. Why should we longer try to patch up and refine and stretch the old solutions till they seem to cover the change of thought and practice? Why not recognize that the trouble is with the problem?

A belief in organic evolution which does not extend unreservedly to the way in which the subject of experience is thought of, and which does not strive to bring the entire theory of experience and knowing into line with biological and social facts, is hardly more than Pickwickian. There are many, for example, who hold that dreams, hallucinations, and errors cannot be accounted for at all except on the theory that a self (or "consciousness") exercises a modifying influence upon the "real object." The logical assumption is that consciousness is outside of the real object; that it is something different in kind, and therefore has the power of changing "reality" into appearance, of introducing "relativities" into things as they are in themselves—in short, of infecting real things with subjectivity. Such writers seem unaware of the fact that this assumption makes consciousness supernatural in the literal sense of the word; and that, to say the least, the conception can be accepted by one who accepts the doctrine of biological continuity only after every other way of dealing with the facts has been exhausted.

Realists, of course (at least some of the Neorealists), deny any such miraculous intervention of consciousness. But they[6] admit the reality of

[6] The "they" means the "some" of the prior sentence—those whose realism is epistemological, instead of being a plea for taking the facts of experience as we find them without refraction through epistemological apparatus.

the problem; denying only this particular solution, they try to find some other way out, which will still preserve intact the notion of knowledge as a relationship of a general sort between subject and object.

Now dreams and hallucinations, errors, pleasures, and pains, possibly "secondary" qualities, do not occur save where there are organic centers of experience. They cluster about a subject. But to treat them as things which inhere exclusively in the subject; or as posing the problem of a distortion of *the* real object by a knower set over against the world, or as presenting facts to be explained primarily as cases of contemplative knowledge, is to testify that one has still to learn the lesson of evolution in its application to the affairs in hand.

If biological development be accepted, the subject of experience is at least an animal, continuous with other organic forms in a process of more complex organization. An animal in turn is at least continuous with chemico-physical processes which, in living things, are so organized as really to constitute the activities of life with all their defining traits. And experience is not identical with brain action; it is the entire organic agent-patient in all its interaction with the environment, natural and social. The brain is primarily an organ of a certain kind of behavior, not of knowing the world. And to repeat what has already been said, experiencing *is* just certain modes of interaction, of correlation, of natural objects among which the organism happens, so to say, to be one. It follows with equal force that experience means primarily not knowledge, but ways of doing and suffering. Knowing must be described by discovering what particular mode—qualitatively unique—of doing and suffering it is. As it is, we find experience assimilated to a nonempirical concept of knowledge, derived from an antecedent notion of a spectator outside of the world.[7]

In short, the epistemological fashion of conceiving dreams, errors, "relativities," etc., depends upon the isolation of mind from intimate participation with other changes in the same continuous nexus. Thus it is like contending that when a bottle bursts, the bottle is, in some self-

---

[7] It is interesting to note that some of the realists who have assimilated the cognitive relation to other existential relations in the world (instead of treating it as an unique or epistemological relation) have been forced in support of their conception of knowledge as a "presentative" or spectatorial affair to extend the defining features of the latter to all relations among things, and hence to make all the "real" things in the world pure "simples," wholly independent of one another. So conceived the doctrine of external relations appears to be rather the doctrine of complete externality of *things*. Aside from this point, the doctrine is interesting for its dialectical ingenuity and for the elegant development of assumed premises, rather than convincing on account of empirical evidence supporting it.

contained miraculous way, exclusively responsible. Since it is the nature of a bottle to be whole so as to retain fluids, bursting is an abnormal event—comparable to a hallucination. Hence it cannot belong to the "real" bottle; the "subjectivity" of glass is the cause. It is obvious that since the breaking of glass is a case of specific correlation of natural energies, its accidental and abnormal character has to do with *consequences,* not with causation. Accident is interference with the consequences for which the bottle is intended. The bursting considered apart from its bearing on these consequences is on a plane with any other occurrence in the wide world. But from the standpoint of a desired future, bursting is an anomaly, an interruption of the course of events.

The analogy with the occurrence of dreams, hallucinations, etc., seems to me exact. Dreams are not something outside of the regular course of events; they are in and of it. They are not cognitive distortions of real things; they are *more* real things. There is nothing abnormal in their existence, any more than there is in the bursting of a bottle.[8] But they may be abnormal, from the standpoint of their influence, of their operation as stimuli in calling out responses to modify the future. Dreams have often been taken as prognostics of what is to happen; they have modified conduct. A hallucination may lead a man to consult a doctor; such a consequence is right and proper. But the consultation indicates that the subject regarded it as an indication of consequences which he feared: as a symptom of a disturbed life. Or the hallucination may lead him to anticipate consequences which in fact flow only from the possession of great wealth. Then the hallucination is a disturbance of the normal course of events; the occurrence is wrongly *used* with reference to eventualities.

To regard reference to use and to desired and intended consequences as involving a "subjective" factor is to miss the point, for this has regard to the future. The uses to which a bottle are put are not mental; they do not consist of physical states; they are further correlations of natural existences. Consequences in use are genuine natural events; but they do not occur without the intervention of behavior involving anticipation of a future. The case is not otherwise with a hallucination. The differences it makes are in any case differences in the course of the one continuous world. The important point is whether they are good or bad differences. To use the hallucination as a sign of organic lesions that menace health means the beneficial result of seeing a physician; to respond to it as a

---

[8] In other words, there is a general "problem of error" only because there is a general problem of evil, concerning which see Dr. Kallen's essay . . . . [*Loc. cit.*]

sign of consequences such as actually follow only from being persecuted is to fall into error—to be abnormal. The persecutors are "unreal"; that is, there are no things which act as persecutors act; but the hallucination exists. Given its conditions it is as natural as any other event, and poses only the same kind of problem as is put by the occurrence of, say, a thunderstorm. The "unreality" of persecution is not, however, a subjective matter; it means that conditions do not exist for producing the *future* consequences which are now anticipated and reacted to. Ability to anticipate future consequences and to respond to them as stimuli to present behavior may well *define* what is meant by a mind or by "consciousness."[9] But this is only a way of saying just what kind of a real or natural existence the subject is; it is not to fall back on a preconception about an unnatural subject in order to characterize the occurrence of error.

Although the discussion may be already labored, let us take another example—the occurrence of disease. By definition it is pathological, abnormal. At one time in human history this abnormality was taken to be something dwelling in the intrinsic nature of the event—in its existence irrespective of future consequences. Disease was literally extranatural and to be referred to demons or to magic. No one today questions its naturalness—its place in the order of natural events. Yet it is abnormal—for it operates to effect results different from those which follow from health. The difference is a genuine empirical difference, not a mere mental distinction. From the standpoint of bearing on a subsequent course of events disease is unnatural, in spite of the naturalness of its occurrence and origin.

The habit of ignoring reference to the future is responsible for the assumption that to admit human participation in any form is to admit the "subjective" in a sense which alters the objective into the phenomenal. There have been those who, like Spinoza, regarded health and disease, good and ill, as equally real and equally unreal. However, only a few consistent materialists have included truth along with error as merely phenomenal and subjective. But if one does not regard movement toward possible consequences as genuine, wholesale denial of existential validity to all these distinctions is the only logical course. To select truth as objective and error as "subjective" is, on this basis, an unjustifiably partial procedure. Take everything as fixedly given, and

[9] Compare the paper by Professor Bode. ["Consciousness and Psychology" in *Creative Intelligence*.]

both truth and error are arbitrary insertions into fact. Admit the genuineness of changes going on, and capacity for its direction through organic action based on foresight, and both truth and falsity are alike existential. It is human to regard the course of events which is in line with our own efforts as the *regular* course of events, and interruptions as abnormal, but this partiality of human desire is itself a part of what actually takes place.

It is now proposed to take a particular case of the alleged epistemological predicament for discussion, since the entire ground cannot be covered. I think, however, the instance chosen is typical, so that the conclusion reached may be generalized.

The instance is that of so-called relativity in perception. There are almost endless instances; the stick bent in water; the whistle changing pitch with change of distance from the ear; objects doubled when the eye is pushed; the destroyed star still visible, etc., etc. For our consideration we may take the case of a spherical object that presents itself to one observer as a flat circle, to another as a somewhat distorted elliptical surface. This situation gives empirical proof, so it is argued, of the difference between a real object and mere appearance. Since there is but one object, the existence of two *subjects* is the sole differentiating factor. Hence the two appearances of the one real object [are] proof of the intervening distorting action of the subject. And many of the Neorealists who deny the difference in question, admit the case to be one of knowledge and accordingly to constitute an epistemological problem. They have in consequence developed wonderfully elaborate schemes of sundry kinds to maintain "epistemological monism" intact.

Let us try to keep close to empirical facts. In the first place the two unlike appearances of the one sphere are physically necessary because of the laws of reaction of light. If the one sphere did *not* assume these two appearances under given conditions, we should be confronted with a hopelessly irreconcilable discrepancy in the behavior of natural energy. That the result is natural is evidenced by the fact that two cameras—or other arrangements of apparatus for reflecting light—yield precisely the same results. Photographs are as genuinely physical existence as the original sphere; and they exhibit the two geometrical forms.

The statement of these facts makes no impression upon the confirmed epistemologist; he merely retorts that as long as it is admitted that the organism is the cause of a sphere being seen, from different points, as a circular and as an elliptical surface, the essence of his contention—the modification of the real object by the subject—is admitted. To the question why the same logic does not apply to photographic records he makes, as far as I know, no reply at all.

The source of the difficulty is not hard to see. The objection assumes that the alleged modifications of *the* real object are cases of *knowing* and hence attributable to the influence of a *knower*. Statements which set forth the doctrine will always be found to refer to the organic factor, to the eye, as an observer or a percipient. Even when reference is made to a lens or a mirror, language is sometimes used which suggests that the writer's naïveté is sufficiently gross to treat these physical factors as if they were engaged in perceiving the sphere. But as it is evident that the lens operates as a physical factor in correlation with other physical factors—notably light—so it ought to be evident that the intervention of the optical apparatus of the eye is a purely noncognitive matter. The relation in question is not one between a sphere and a would-be knower of it, unfortunately condemned by the nature of the knowing apparatus to alter the thing he would know; it is an affair of the dynamic interaction of two physical agents in producing a third thing, an effect—an affair of precisely the same kind as in any physical conjoint action, say the operation of hydrogen and oxygen in producing water. To regard the eye as primarily a knower, an observer, of things, is as crass as to assign that function to a camera. But unless the eye (or optical apparatus, or brain, or organism) be so regarded, there is absolutely no problem of observation or of knowledge in the case of the occurrence of elliptical and circular surfaces. Knowledge does not enter into the affair at all till *after* these forms of refracted light have been produced. About them there is nothing unreal. Light is really, physically, existentially, refracted into these forms. If the same spherical form upon refracting light to physical objects in two quite different positions produced the same geometric forms, there would, indeed, be something to marvel at—as there would be if wax produced the same results in contact simultaneously with a cold body and with a warm one. Why talk about *the real* object in relation to *a knower* when what is given is one real thing in dynamic connection with another real thing?

The way of dealing with the case will probably meet with a retort; at least, it has done so before. It has been said that the account given above and the account of traditional subjectivism differ only verbally. The essential thing in both, so it is said, is the admission that an activity of a self or subject or organism makes a difference in the real object. Whether the subject makes this difference in the very process of knowing or makes it prior to the act of knowing is a minor matter; what is important is that the known thing has, by the time it is known, been "subjectified."

The objection gives a convenient occasion for summarizing the main points of the argument. On the one hand, the retort of the objector depends upon talking about *the* real object. Employ the term "*a* real object," and the change produced by the activity characteristic of the optical apparatus is of just the same kind as that of the camera lens or that of any other physical agency. Every event in the world marks a difference made to one existence in active conjunction with some other existence. And, as for the alleged subjectivity, if subjective is used merely as an adjective to designate the specific activity of a particular existence, comparable, say, to the term feral, applied to tiger, or metallic, applied to iron, then of course reference to subjective is legitimate. But it is also tautological. It is like saying that flesh eaters are carnivorous. But the term "subjective" is so consecrated to other uses, usually implying invidious contrast with objectivity (while subjective in the sense just suggested means specific mode *of* objectivity), that it is difficult to maintain this innocent sense. Its use in any disparaging way in the situation before us—any sense implicating contrast with a real object—assumes that the organism *ought* not to make any difference when it operates in conjunction with other things. Thus we run to earth that assumption that the subject is heterogeneous from every other natural existence; it is to be the one otiose, inoperative thing in a moving world—our old assumption of the self as outside of things.[10]

What and where is knowledge in the case we have been considering? Not, as we have already seen, in the production of forms of light having a circular and elliptical surface. These forms are natural happenings. They may enter into knowledge or they may not, according to circumstances. Countless such refractive changes take place without being noted. [11] When they become subject matter for knowledge, the inquiry

---

[10] As the attempt to retain the epistemological problem and yet to reject idealistic and relativistic solutions has forced some Neorealists into the doctrine of isolated and independent simples, so it has also led to a doctrine of Eleatic pluralism. In order to maintain the doctrine [that] the subject makes no difference to anything else, it is held that *no* ultimate real makes any difference to anything else—all this rather than surrender once for all the genuineness of the problem and to follow the lead of empirical subject matter.

[11] There is almost no end to the various dialectic developments of the epistemological situation. When it is held that all the relations of the type in question are cognitive, and yet it is recognized (as it must be) that many such "transformations" go unremarked, the theory is supplemented by introducing "unconscious" psychical modifications.

they set on foot may take on an indefinite variety of forms. One may be interested in ascertaining more about the structural peculiarities of the forms themselves; one may be interested in the mechanism of their production; one may find problems in projective geometry, or in drawing and painting—all depending upon the specific matter-of-fact context. The forms may be *objectives* of knowledge—of reflective examination—or they may be means of knowing something else. It may happen—under some circumstances it does happen—that the objective of inquiry is the nature of the geometric form which, when refracting light, gives rise to these other forms. In this case the sphere is the thing known, and in this case, the forms of light are signs or evidence of the conclusion to be drawn. There is no more reason for supposing that they *are* (mis)knowledges of the sphere—that the sphere is necessarily and from the start what one is trying to know—than for supposing that the position of the mercury in the thermometer tube is a cognitive distortion of atmospheric pressure. In each case (that of the mercury and that of, say, a circular surface) the primary datum is a physical happening. In each case it may be used, upon occasion, as a sign or evidence of the nature of the causes which brought it about. Given the position in question, the circular form would be an intrinsically *unreliable* evidence of the nature and position of the spherical body only in case it, as the direct datum of perception, were *not* what it is—a circular form.

I confess that all this seems so obvious that the reader is entitled to inquire into the motive for reciting such plain facts. Were it not for the persistence of the epistemological problem it would be an affront to the reader's intelligence to dwell upon them. But as long as such facts as we have been discussing furnish the subject matter with which philosophizing is peculiarly concerned, these commonplaces must be urged and reiterated. They bear out two contentions which are important at the juncture, although they will lose special significance as soon as these are habitually recognized: Negatively, a prior and nonempirical notion of the self is the source of the prevailing belief that experience as such is primarily cognitional—a knowledge affair; positively, *knowledge is always a matter of the use that is made of experienced natural events,* a use in which given things are treated as indications of what will be experienced under different conditions.

Let us make one effort more to clear up these points. Suppose it is a question of knowledge of water. The thing to be known does not present itself primarily as a matter of knowledge-and-ignorance at all. It occurs as a stimulus to action and as the source of certain undergoings. It is something to react to—to drink, to wash with, to put out fire with, and also something that reacts unexpectedly to our reactions, that makes us undergo disease, suffocation, drowning. In this two-fold way, water or anything else enters into experience. Such presence in experience has of itself nothing to do with knowledge or consciousness; nothing that is in the sense of depending upon them, though it has everything to do with knowledge and consciousness in the sense that the latter depends upon prior experience of this noncognitive sort. Man's experience is what it is because his response to things (even successful response) and the reactions of things to his life, are so radically different from knowledge. The difficulties and tragedies of life, the stimuli to acquiring knowledge, lie in the radical disparity of presence-in-experience and presence-in-knowing. Yet the immense importance of knowledge experience, the fact that turning presence-in-experience over into presence-in-a-knowledge-experience is the sole mode of control of nature, has systematically hypnotized European philosophy since the time of Socrates into thinking that all experiencing is a mode of knowing, if not good knowledge, then a low-grade or confused or implicit knowledge.

When water is an adequate stimulus to action or when its reactions oppress and overwhelm us, it remains outside the scope of knowledge. When, however, the bare presence of the thing (say, as optical stimulus) ceases to operate directly as stimulus to response and begins to operate in connection with a forecast of the consequences it will effect when responded to, it begins to acquire meaning—to be known, to be an object. It is noted as something which is wet, fluid, satisfies thirst, allays uneasiness, etc. The conception that we begin with a known visual quality which is thereafter enlarged by adding on qualities apprehended by the other senses does not rest upon experience; it rests upon making experience conform to the notion that every experience *must* be a cognitive noting. As long as the visual stimulus operates as a stimulus on its own account, there is no apprehension, no noting, of color or light at all. To much the greater portion of sensory stimuli we react in precisely this wholly noncognitive way. In the attitude of suspended response in which consequences are anticipated, the direct stimulus becomes a sign or index of something else—and thus matter of noting or apprehension or acquaintance, or whatever term may be employed. This difference (together, of course, with the consequences which go with it) is the difference which the natural event of knowing makes to the natural event of direct organic stimulation. It is no change of a reality into an unreality, of an object into something subjective; it is no secret, illicit, or epistemological transformation; it is a genuine acquisition of new and distinctive features through entering into relations with things with which it was not formerly connected—namely, possible and future things.

But, replies some one so obsessed with the epistemological point of view that he assumes that the prior account is a rival epistemology in disguise, all this involves no change in Reality, no difference made to Reality. Water was all the time all the things it is ever found out to be. Its real nature has not been altered by knowing it; any such alteration means a misknowing.

In reply let it be said—once more and finally—there is no assertion or implication about *the* real object or *the* real world or *the* reality. Such an assumption goes with that epistemological universe of discourse which has to be abandoned in an empirical universe of discourse. The change is of *a* real object. An incident of the world operating as a physiologically direct stimulus is assuredly a reality. Responded to, it produces specific consequences in virtue of the response. Water is not drunk unless somebody drinks it; it does not quench thirst unless a thirsty person drinks it—and so on. Consequences occur whether one is aware of them or not; they are integral facts in experience. But let one of these consequences be anticipated and let it, as anticipated, become an indispensable element in the stimulus, and then there is a known object. It is not that knowing *produces* a change, but that it *is* a change of the specific kind described. A serial process, the successive portions of which are as such incapable of simultaneous occurrence, is telescoped and condensed into an object, a unified interreference of con- temporaneous properties, most of which express potentialities rather than completed data.

Because of this change, an *object* possesses truth or error (which the physical occurrence as such never has); it is classifiable as fact or fan- tasy; it is of a sort or kind, expresses an essence or nature, possesses implications, etc., etc. That is to say, it is marked by specifiable *logical* traits not found in physical occurrences as such. Because objective idealisms have seized upon these traits as constituting the very essence of Reality is no reason for proclaiming that they are ready-made features of physical happenings, and hence for maintaining that know- ing is nothing but an appearance of things on a stage for which "consciousness" supplies the footlights. For only the epistemological predicament leads to "presentations" being regarded as cognitions of things which were previously unpresented. In any empirical situation of everyday life or of science, knowledge signifies something stated or in- ferred of another thing. Visible water is not a more or less erroneous presentation of $H_2O$, but $H_2O$ is a knowledge about the thing we see, drink, wash with, sail on, and use for power.

A further point and the present phase of discussion terminates. Treating knowledge as a presentative relation between the knower and object makes it necessary to regard the mechanism of *presentation* as constituting the act of knowing. Since things may be presented in sense-perception, in recollection, in imagination and in conception, and since the mechanism in every one of these four styles of presentation is sensory-cerebral the problem of knowing becomes a mind-body problem.[12] The psychological, or physiological, mechanism of presentation involved in seeing a chair, remembering what I ate yesterday for luncheon, imagining the moon the size of a cart wheel, conceiving a mathematical continuum is identified with the operation of knowing. The evil consequences are two-fold. The problem of the relation of mind and body has become a part of the problem of the possibility of knowledge in general, to the further complication of a matter already hopelessly constrained. Meantime the actual process of knowing, namely, operations of controlled observation, inference, reasoning, and testing, the only process with *intellectual* import, is dismissed as irrelevant to the theory of knowing. The methods of knowing practiced in daily life and science are excluded from consideration in the philosophical theory of knowing. Hence the constructions of the latter become more and more elaborately artificial because there is no definite check upon them. It would be easy to quote from epistemological writers statements to the effect that these processes (which supply the only empirically verifiable facts of knowing) are *merely* inductive in character, or even that they are of purely psychological significance. It would be difficult to find a more complete inversion of the facts than in the latter statement, since presentation constitutes in fact the psychological affair. A confusion of logic with physiological [psychology] has bred hybrid epistemology, with the amazing result that the technique of effective inquiry is rendered irrelevant to the theory of knowing, and those physical events involved in the occurrence of data for knowing are treated as if they constituted the act of knowing.

---

[12] Conception-presentation has, of course, been made by many in the history of speculation an exception to this statement: "pure" memory is also made an exception by Bergson. To take cognizance of this matter would, of course, accentuate, not relieve, the difficulty remarked upon in the text.

V

What are the bearings of our discussion upon the conception of the present scope and office of philosophy? What do our conclusions indicate and demand with reference to philosophy itself? For the philosophy which reaches such conclusions regarding knowledge and mind must apply them, sincerely and wholeheartedly, to its idea of its own nature. For philosophy claims to be one form or mode of knowing. If, then, the conclusion is reached that knowing is a way of employing empirical occurrences with respect to increasing power to direct the consequences which flow from things, the application of the conclusion must be made to philosophy itself. It, too, becomes not a contemplative survey of existence nor an analysis of what is past and done with, but an outlook upon future possibilities with reference to attaining the better and averting the worse. Philosophy must take, with good grace, its own medicine.

It is easier to state the negative results of the changed idea of philosophy than the positive ones. The point that occurs to mind most readily is that philosophy will have to surrender all pretension to be peculiarly concerned with ultimate reality, or with reality as a complete (i.e., completed) whole: with *the* real object. The surrender is not easy of achievement. The philosophic tradition that comes to us from classic Greek thought and that was reinforced by Christian philosophy in the Middle Ages discriminates philosophical knowing from other modes of knowing by means of an alleged peculiarly intimate concern with supreme, ultimate, true reality. To deny this trait to philosophy seems to many to be the suicide of philosophy; to be a systematic adoption of skepticism or agnostic positivism.

The pervasiveness of the tradition is shown in the fact that so vitally a contemporary thinker as Bergson, who finds a philosophic revolution involved in abandonment of the traditional identification of the truly real with the fixed (an identification inherited from Greek thought), does not find it in his heart to abandon the counterpart identification of philosophy with search for the truly Real; and hence he finds it necessary to substitute an ultimate and absolute flux for an ultimate and absolute permanence. Thus his great empirical services in calling attention to the fundamental importance of considerations of time for problems of life and mind get compromised with a mystic, nonempirical "Intuition"; and we find him preoccupied with solving, by means of his new idea of ultimate reality, the traditional problems of realities-in-themselves and phenomena, matter and mind, free will and determinism, God and the world. Is not that another evidence of the influence of the classic idea about philosophy?

Even the new realists are not content to take their realism as a plea for approaching subject matter directly instead of through the intervention of epistemological apparatus; they find it necessary first to determine the status of *the* real object. Thus they too become entangled in the problem of the possibility of error, dreams, hallucinations, etc., in short, the problem of evil. For I take it that an uncorrupted realism would accept such things as real events, and find in them no other problems than those attending the consideration of any real occurrence—namely, problems of structure, origin, and operation.

It is often said that pragmatism, unless it is content to be a contribution to mere methodology, must develop a theory of Reality. But the chief characteristic trait of the pragmatic notion of reality is precisely that no theory of Reality in general, *überhaupt*, is possible or needed. It occupies the position of an emancipated empiricism or a thoroughgoing naïve realism. It finds that "reality" is a *denotative* term, a word used to designate indifferently everything that happens. Lies, dreams, insanities, deceptions, myths, theories are all of them just the events which they specifically are. Pragmatism is content to take its stand with science; for science finds all such events to be subject matter of description and inquiry—just like stars and fossils, mosquitoes and malaria, circulation and vision. It also takes its stand with daily life, which finds that such things really have to be reckoned with as they occur interwoven in the texture of events.

The only way in which the term reality can ever become more than a blanket denotative term is through recourse to specific events in all their diversity and thatness. Speaking summarily, I find that the retention by philosophy of the notion of a Reality feudally superior to the events of everyday occurrence is the chief source of the increasing isolation of philosophy from common sense and science. For the latter do not operate in any such region. As with them of old, philosophy in dealing with real difficulties finds itself still hampered by reference to realities more real, more ultimate, than those which directly happen.

I have said that identifying the cause of philosophy with the notion of superior reality is the cause of an *increasing* isolation from science and practical life. The phrase reminds us that there was a time when the enterprise of science and the moral interests of men both moved in a universe invidiously distinguished from that of ordinary occurrence. While all that happens is equally real—since it really happens—happenings are not of equal worth. Their respective consequences, their import, varies tremendously. Counterfeit money, although real (or rather *because* real) is really different from valid circulatory medium, just as disease is really different from health; different in specific structure and so different in consequences. In occidental thought, the Greeks were the first to draw the distinction between the genuine and the spurious in a generalized fashion and to formulate and enforce its tremendous significance for the conduct of life. But since they had at command no technique of experimental analysis and no adequate technique of mathematical analysis, they were compelled to treat the difference of the true and the false, the dependable and the deceptive, as signifying two kinds of existence, the truly real and the apparently real.

Two points can hardly be asserted with too much emphasis. The Greeks were wholly right in the feeling that questions of good and ill, as far as they fall within human control, are bound up with discrimination of the genuine from the spurious, of "being" from what only pretends to be. But because they lacked adequate instrumentalities for coping with this difference in specific situations, they were forced to treat the difference as a wholesale and rigid one. Science was concerned with vision of ultimate and true reality; opinion was concerned with getting along with apparent realities. Each had its appropriate region permanently marked off. Matters of opinion could never become matters of science; their intrinsic nature forbade. When the practice of science went on under such conditions, science and philosophy were one and the same thing. Both had to do with ultimate reality in its rigid and insuperable difference from ordinary occurrences.

We have only to refer to the way in which medieval life wrought the philosophy of an ultimate and supreme reality into the context of practical life to realize that for centuries political and moral interests were bound up with the distinction between the absolutely real and the relatively real. The difference was no matter of a remote technical philosophy, but one which controlled life from the cradle to the grave, from the grave to the endless life after death. By means of a vast institution, which in effect was state as well as church, the claims of ultimate reality were enforced; means of access to it were provided. Acknowledgment of The Reality brought security in this world and salvation in the next. It is not necessary to report the story of the change which has since taken place. It is enough for our purposes to note that none of the modern philosophies of a superior reality, or *the* real object, idealistic or realistic, holds that its insight makes a difference like that between sin and holiness, eternal condemnation and eternal bliss. While in its own context the philosophy of ultimate reality entered into the vital concerns of men, it now tends to be an ingenious dialectic exercised in professorial corners by a few who have retained ancient premises while rejecting their application to the conduct of life.

The increased isolation from science of any philosophy identified with the problem of *the* real is equally marked. For the growth of science has consisted precisely in the invention of an equipment, a technique of appliances and procedures, which, accepting all occurrences as homogeneously real, proceeds to distinguish the authenticated from the spurious, the true from the false, by specific modes of treatment in specific situations. The procedures of the trained engineer, of the competent physician, of the laboratory expert, have turned out to be the only ways of discriminating the counterfeit from the valid. And they have revealed that the difference is not one of antecedent fixity of existence, but one of mode of treatment and of the consequences thereon attendant. After mankind has learned to put its trust in specific procedures in order to make its discriminations between the false and the true, philosophy arrogates to itself the enforcement of the distinction at its own cost.

More than once, this essay has intimated that the counterpart of the idea of invidiously real reality is the spectator notion of knowledge. If the knower, however defined, is set over against the world to be known, knowing consists in possessing a transcript, more or less accurate but otiose, of real things. Whether this transcript is presentative in character (as realists say) or whether it is by means of states of consciousness which represent things (as subjectivists say), is a matter of great importance in its own context. But, in another regard, this difference is negligible in comparison with the point in which both agree. Knowing is viewing from outside. But if it be true that the self or subject of experience is part and parcel of the course of events, it follows that the self *becomes* a knower. It becomes a mind in virtue of a distinctive way of partaking in the course of events. The significant distinction is no longer between the knower *and* the world; it is between different ways of being in and of the movement of things; between a brute physical way and a purposive, intelligent way.

There is no call to repeat in detail the statements which have been advanced. Their net purport is that the directive presence of future possibilities in dealing with existent conditions is what is meant by knowing; that the self becomes a knower or mind when anticipation of future consequences operates as its stimulus. What we are now concerned with is the effect of this conception upon the nature of philosophic knowing.

As far as I can judge, popular response to pragmatic philosophy was moved by two quite different considerations. By some it was thought to provide a new species of sanctions, a new mode of apologetics, for certain religious ideas whose standing had been threatened. By others, it was welcomed because it was taken as a sign that philosophy was about to surrender its otiose and speculative remoteness; that philosophers were beginning to recognize that philosophy is of account only if, like everyday knowing and like science, it affords guidance to action and thereby makes a difference in the event. It was welcomed as a sign that philosophers were willing to have the worth of their philosophizing measured by responsible tests.

I have not seen this point of view emphasized, or hardly recognized, by professional critics. The difference of attitude can probably be easily explained. The epistemological universe of discourse is so highly technical that only those who have been trained in the history of thought think in terms of it. It did not occur, accordingly, to non-technical readers to interpret the doctrine that the meaning and validity of thought are fixed by differences made in consequences and in satisfactoriness, to mean consequences in personal feelings. Those who were professionally trained, however, took the statement to mean that consciousness or mind in the mere act of looking at things modifies them. It understood the doctrine of test of validity by consequences to mean that apprehensions and conceptions are true if the modifications affected by them were of an emotionally desirable tone.

Prior discussion should have made it reasonably clear that the source of this misunderstanding lies in the neglect of temporal considerations. The change made in things by the self in knowing is not immediate and, so to say, cross-sectional. It is longitudinal—in the redirection given to changes already going on. Its analogue is found in the changes which take place in the development of, say, iron ore into a watch spring, not in those of the miracle of transubstantiation. For the static, cross-sectional, nontemporal relation of subject and object, the pragmatic hypothesis substitutes apprehension of a thing in terms of the results in other things which it is tending to effect. For the unique epistemological relation, it substitutes a practical relation of a familiar type—responsive behavior which changes in time the subject matter to which it applies. The unique thing about the responsible behavior which constitutes knowing is the specific difference which marks it off from other modes of response, namely, the part played in it by anticipation and prediction. Knowing is the act, stimulated by this foresight, of securing and averting consequences. The success of the achievement measures the standing of the foresight by which response is directed. The popular impression that pragmatic philosophy means that philosophy shall develop ideas relevant to the actual crises of life, ideas influential in dealing with them and tested by the assistance they afford, is correct.

Reference to practical response suggests, however, another misapprehension. Many critics have jumped at the obvious association of the word pragmatic with practical. They have assumed that the intent is to limit all knowledge, philosophic included, to promoting "action," understanding by action either just any bodily movement, or those bodily movements which conduce to the preservation and grosser well-being of the body. James's statement that general conceptions must "cash in" has been taken (especially by European critics) to mean that the end and measure of intelligence lies in the narrow and coarse utilities which it produces. Even an acute American thinker, after first criticizing pragmatism as a kind of idealistic epistemology, goes on to treat it as a doctrine which regards intelligence as a lubricating oil facilitating the workings of the body.

One source of the misunderstanding is suggested by the fact that "cashing in" to James meant that a general idea must always be capable of verification in specific existential cases. The notion of "cashing in" says nothing about the breadth or depth of the specific consequences. As an empirical doctrine, it could not say anything about them in general; the specific cases must speak for themselves. If one conception is verified in terms of eating beefsteak, and another in terms of a favorable credit balance in the bank, that is not because of anything in the theory, but because of the specific nature of the conceptions in question, and because there exist particular events like hunger and trade. If there are also existences in which the most liberal esthetic ideas and the most generous moral conceptions can be verified by specific embodiment, assuredly so much the better. The fact that a strictly empirical philosophy was taken by so many critics to imply an *a priori* dogma about the kind of consequences capable of existence is evidence, I think, of the inability of many philosophers to think in concretely empirical terms. Since the critics were themselves accustomed to get results by manipulating the concepts of "consequences" and of "practice," they assumed that even a would-be empiricist must be doing the same sort of thing. It will, I suppose, remain for a long time incredible to some that a philosopher should really intend to go to specific experiences to determine of what scope and depth practice admits, and what sort of consequences the world permits to come into being. Concepts are so clear; it takes so little time to develop their implications; experiences are so confused, and it requires so much time and energy to lay hold of them. And yet these same critics charge pragmatism with adopting subjective and emotional standards!

As a matter of fact, the pragmatic theory of intelligence means that the function of mind is to project new and more complex ends—to free experience from routine and from caprice. Not the use of thought to accomplish purposes already given either in the mechanism of the body or in that of the existent state of society, but the use of intelligence to liberate and liberalize action, is the pragmatic lesson. Action restricted to given and fixed ends may attain great technical efficiency; but efficiency is the only quality to which it can lay claim. Such action is mechanical (or becomes so), no matter what the scope of the preformed end, be it the Will of God or *Kultur*. But the doctrine that intelligence develops within the sphere of action for the sake of possibilities not yet given is the opposite of a doctrine of mechanical efficiency. Intelligence *as* intelligence is inherently forward-looking; only by ignoring its primary function does it become a mere means for an end already given. The latter *is* servile, even when the end is labeled moral, religious, or esthetic. But action directed to ends to which the agent has not previously been attached inevitably carries with it a quickened and enlarged spirit. A pragmatic intelligence is a creative intelligence, not a routine mechanic.

All this may read like a defense of pragmatism by one concerned to make out for it the best case possible. Such is not, however, the intention. The purpose is to indicate the extent to which intelligence frees action from a mechanically instrumental character. Intelligence is, indeed, instrumental *through* action to the determination of the qualities of future experience. But the very fact that the concern of intelligence is with the future, with the as-yet-unrealized (and with the given and the established only as conditions of the realization of possibilities), makes the action in which it takes effect generous and liberal; free of spirit. Just that action which extends and approves intelligence has an intrinsic value of its own in being instrumental—the intrinsic value of being informed with intelligence in behalf of the enrichment of life. By the same stroke, intelligence becomes truly liberal: knowing is a human undertaking, not an esthetic appreciation carried on by a refined class or a capitalistic possession of a few learned specialists, whether men of science or of philosophy.

More emphasis has been put upon what philosophy is not than upon what it may become. But it is not necessary, it is not even desirable, to set forth philosophy as a scheduled program. There are human difficulties of an urgent, deep-seated kind which may be clarified by trained reflection, and whose solution may be forwarded by the careful development of hypotheses. When it is understood that philosophic thinking is caught up in the actual course of events, having the office of guiding them toward a prosperous issue, problems will abundantly present themselves. Philosophy will not solve these problems; philosophy is vision, imagination, reflection—and these functions, apart from action, modify nothing and hence resolve nothing. But in a complicated and perverse world, action which is not informed with vision, imagination, and reflection, is more likely to increase confusion and conflict than to straighten things out. It is not easy for generous and sustained reflection to become a guiding and illuminating method in action. Until it frees itself from identification with problems which are supposed to depend upon Reality as such, or its distinction from a world of Appearance, or its relation to a Knower as such, the hands of philosophy are tied. Having no chance to link its fortunes with a responsible career by suggesting things to be tried, it cannot identify itself with questions which actually arise in the vicissitudes of life. Philosophy recovers itself when it ceases to be a device for dealing with the problems of philosophers and becomes a method, cultivated by philosophers, for dealing with the problems of men.

Emphasis must vary with the stress and special impact of the troubles which perplex men. Each age knows its own ills, and seeks its own remedies. One does not have to forecast a particular program to note that the central need of any program at the present day is an adequate conception of the nature of intelligence and its place in action. Philosophy cannot disavow responsibility for many misconceptions of the nature of intelligence which now hamper its efficacious operation. It has at least a negative task imposed upon it. It must take away the burdens which it has laid upon the intelligence of the common man in struggling with his difficulties. It must deny and eject that intelligence which is naught but a distant eye, registering in a remote and alien medium the spectacle of nature and life. To enforce the fact that the emergence of imagination and thought is relative to the connection of the sufferings of men with their doings is of itself to illuminate those sufferings and to instruct those doings. To catch mind in its connection with the entrance of the novel into the course of the world is to be on the road to see that intelligence is itself the most promising of all novelties, the revelation of the meaning of that transformation of past into future which is the reality of every present. To reveal intelligence as the organ for the guidance of this transformation, the sole director of its quality, is to make a declaration of present untold significance for action. To elaborate these convictions of the connection of intelligence with what men undergo because of their doings and with the emergence and direction of the creative, the novel, in the world is of itself a program which will keep philosophers busy until something more worth while is forced upon them. For the elaboration has to be made through application to all the disciplines which have an intimate connection with human conduct: to logic, ethics, esthetics, economics, and the procedure of the sciences formal and natural.

I also believe that there is a genuine sense in which the enforcement of the pivotal position of intelligence in the world and thereby in control of human fortunes (so far as they are manageable) is the peculiar problem in the problems of life which come home most closely to ourselves—to ourselves living not merely in the early twentieth century but in the United States. It is easy to be foolish about the connection of thought with national life. But I do not see how any one can question the distinctively national color of English, or French, or German philosophies. And if of late the history of thought has come under the domination of the German dogma of an inner evolution of ideas, it requires but a little inquiry to convince oneself that that dogma itself testifies to a particularly nationalistic need and origin. I believe that philosophy in America will be lost between chewing a historic cud long since reduced to woody fiber, or an apologetics for lost causes (lost to natural science), or a scholastic, schematic formalism, unless it can somehow bring to consciousness America's own needs and its own implicit principle of successful action.

This need and principle, I am convinced, is the necessity of a deliberate control of policies by the method of intelligence, an intelligence which is not the faculty of intellect honored in textbooks and neglected elsewhere, but which is the sum-total of impulses, habits, emotions, records, and discoveries which forecast what is desirable and undesirable in future possibilities, and which contrive ingeniously in behalf of imagined good. Our life has no background of sanctified categories upon which we may fall back; we rely upon precedent as authority only to our own undoing—for with us there is such a continuously novel situation that final reliance upon precedent entails some class interest guiding us by the nose whither it will. British empiricism, with its appeal to what has been in the past, is, after all, only a kind of *a priorism*. For it lays down a fixed rule for future intelligence to follow; and only the immersion of philosophy in technical learning prevents our seeing that this is the essence of *a priorism*.

We pride ourselves upon being realistic, desiring a hard-headed cognizance of facts, and devoted to mastering the means of life. We pride ourselves upon a practical idealism, a lively and easily moved faith in possibilities as yet unrealized, in willingness to make sacrifice for their realization. Idealism easily becomes a sanction of waste and carelessness, and realism a sanction of legal formalism in behalf of things as they are—the rights of the possessor. We thus tend to combine a loose and ineffective optimism with assent to the doctrine of take who take can: a deification of power. All peoples at all times have been narrowly realistic in practice and have then employed idealization to cover up in sentiment and theory their brutalities. But never, perhaps, has the tendency been so dangerous and so tempting as with ourselves. Faith in the power of intelligence to imagine a future which is the projection of the desirable in the present, and to invent the instrumentalities of its realization, is our salvation. And it is a faith which must be nurtured and made articulate: surely a sufficiently large task for our philosophy.

# II

## Earlier Psychological Writings

The material in this section illustrates Dewey's philosophical development from the perspective of his concern with psychology. In his attempt to bring the concerns and methods of psychology to bear upon philosophical issues, Dewey himself undergoes significant changes in outlook, methodology, and above all, terminology. These essays provide us not only with an insight into the evolution of Dewey's thought but also into the impact of the new psychology, particularly that of William James, on philosophical language at the turn of the century.

## 7. The Psychological Standpoint*

In this early essay (1886) Dewey's position is that British philosophy has deserted the psychological standpoint. He laments this, for he contends that "the nature of all objects of philosophical inquiry is to be fixed by finding out what experience says about them. And psychology is the scientific and systematic account of this experience." Of course, at that time Dewey's understanding of psychology, even when dealing with British philosophy, was still characterized by the problems germane to philosophical idealism, such as the unity of consciousness and the "thing in itself." And despite his attempt to abandon the "old ontological man," he can still say that "the individual consciousness is but the process of realization of the universal consciousness through itself." At this point in his career Dewey's approach was empirical, but he lacked the behavioral data to make a real break with the language of idealism.

* From *Mind*, XI (January, 1886), pp. 1-19.

1

It is a good omen for the future of philosophy that there is now a disposition to avoid discussion of particular cases in dispute, and to examine instead the fundamental presuppositions and method. This is the sole condition of discussion which shall be fruitful, and not word-bandying. It is the sole way of discovering whatever of fundamental agreement there is between different tendencies of thought, as well as of showing on what grounds the radical differences are based. It is therefore a most auspicious sign that, instead of eagerly clamoring forth our views on various subjects, we are now trying to show *why* we hold them and *why* we reject others. It is hardly too much to say that it is only within the past ten years that what is vaguely called Transcendentalism has shown to the English reading world just why it holds what it does, and just what are its objections to the method most characteristically associated with English thinking. Assertion of its results, accompanied with attacks upon the results of Empiricism, and *vice versa*, we had before; but it is only recently that the grounds, the reasons, the method, have been stated. And no one can deny that the work has been done well, clearly, conscientiously, and thoroughly. English philosophy cannot now be what it would have been, if (to name only one of the writers) the late Professor Green´ had not written. And now that the differences and the grounds for them have been so definitely and clearly stated, we are in a condition, I think, to see a fundamental agreement, and that just where the difference has been most insisted upon, *viz.,* in the standpoint. It is the *psychological* standpoint which is the root of all the difference, as Professor Green has shown with such admirable lucidity and force. Yet I hope to be able to suggest, if not to show, that after all the psychological standpoint is what both sides have in common. In this present paper, I wish to point out that the defects and contradictions so powerfully urged against the characteristic tendency of British Philosophy are due—not to its psychological standpoint but—to its *desertion* of it. In short, the psychological basis of English philosophy has been its strength: its weakness has been that it has left this basis—that it has not been psychological enough.

In stating what is the psychological standpoint, care has to be taken that it be not so stated as to prejudge at the outset the whole matter. This can be avoided only by stating it in a very general manner. Let Locke do it. "I thought that the first step towards satisfying several inquiries the mind of man was very apt to run into was to take a view of our own understandings, examine our own powers, and see to what things they were adapted." This, with the further statement that "What-soever is the object of the understanding when a man thinks" is an Idea, fixed the method of philosophy. We are not to determine the nature of reality or of any object of philosophical inquiry by examining it as it is in itself, but only as it is an element in our knowledge, in our experience, only as it is related to our mind, or is an "idea." As Professor Fraser well puts it, Locke's way of stating the question "involves the fundamental assumption of philosophy, that real things as well as imaginary things, whatever their absolute existence may involve, exist for us only through becoming involved in what we mentally experience in the course of our self-conscious lives." Or, in the ordinary way of putting it, the nature of all objects of philosophical inquiry is to be fixed by finding out what experience says about them. And psychology is the scientific and systematic account of this experience. This and this only do I understand to be essential to the psychological standpoint, and, to avoid misunderstanding from the start, I shall ask the reader not to think any more into it, and especially to avoid reading into it any assumption regarding its "individual" and "introspective" character. The further development of the standpoint can come only in the course of the article.

Now that Locke, having stated his method, immediately deserted it will, I suppose, be admitted by all. Instead of determining the nature of objects of experience by an account of our knowledge, he proceeded to explain our knowledge by reference to certain unknowable substances, called by the name of matter, making impressions on an unknowable substance, called mind. While, by his method, he should explain the nature of "matter" and of "mind"—two "inquiries the mind of man is very apt to run into"—from our own understandings, from "ideas," he actually explains the nature of our ideas, of our consciousness, whether sensitive or reflective, from that whose characteristic, whether mind or matter, is to be *not* ideas nor consciousness nor in any possible relation thereto, because utterly unknowable. Berkeley, in effect, though not necessarily, as it seems to me, in intention, deserted the method in his reference of ideas to a purely transcendent spirit. Whether or not he conceived it as purely transcendent, yet at all events, he did not show its necessary immanence *in* our conscious experience. But Hume? Hume, it must be confessed, is generally thought to stand on purely psychological ground. This is asserted as his merit by those who regard the theory of the association of ideas as the basis of all philosophy; it is asserted as his defect by those who look at his skeptical mocking of knowledge as following necessarily from his method. But according to both, he, at least, was consistently psychological. Now the psychological standpoint is this: nothing shall be admitted into philosophy which does not show itself in experience, and its nature, that is, its place in experience, shall be fixed by an account of the process of knowledge—by Psychology. Hume reversed this. He started with a theory as to the nature of reality and determined experience from that. The only reals for him were certain irrelated sensations and out of these knowledge arises or becomes. But if knowledge or experience becomes from them, then *they* are never known and never can be. If experience *originates from* them, they never were and never can be elements *in* experience. Sensations as known or experienced are always related, classified sensations. That which is known as existing only in experience, which has its existence only as an element of knowledge, cannot be the same when transported out of knowledge, and made its origin. A known sensation has its sole existence *as* known; and to suppose that it can be regarded as *not* known, as prior to knowledge, and still be what it is *as* known, is a logical feat which it is hoped few are capable of. Hume, just as much as Locke, assumes that something exists out of relation to knowledge or consciousness, and that this something is ultimately the only real, and that from it knowledge, consciousness, experience, come to be. If this is not giving up the psychological standpoint, it would be difficult to tell what is. Hume's "distinct perceptions which are distinct existences," and which give rise to knowledge only as they are related to each other, are so many things-in-themselves. They existed prior to knowledge, and therefore are not for or within it.

But it will be objected that all this is a total misapprehension. Hume did not assume them *because* they were prior to and beyond knowledge. He examined experience and found, as any one does who analyzes it, that it is made up of sensations; that, however complex or immediate it appears to be, on analysis it is always found to be but an aggregate of grouped sensations. Having found this by analysis, it was his business, as it is that of every psychologist, to show *how* by composition these sensations produce knowledge and experience. To call them things-in-themselves is absurd—they are the simplest and best-known things in all our experience. Now this answer, natural as it is, and conclusive as it seems, only brings out the radical defect of the procedure. The dependence of our knowledge upon sensations—or rather that knowledge is nothing but sensations as related to each other—is not denied. What is denied is the correctness of the procedure which, discovering a certain element *in* knowledge to be necessary for knowledge, therefore concludes that this element has an existence prior to or apart from knowledge. The alternative is not complex. Either these sensations are the sensations which are known—sensations which are elements in knowledge—and then they cannot be employed to account for its origin; or they can be employed to account for its origin, and then are not sensations as they are known. In this case, they must be something of which nothing can be said except that they are *not* known, *are* not in consciousness—that they are things-in-themselves. If, in short, these sensations are not to be made "ontological," they must be sensations known, sensations which are elements in experience; and if they exist only for knowledge, then knowledge is wherever they are, and they cannot account for its origin. The supposed objection rests upon a distinction between sensations as they are known, and sensations as they exist. And this means simply that existence—the only real existence—is not for consciousness, but that consciousness comes about from it; it makes no difference that one calls it sensations, and another the "real existence" of mind or matter. If one is anxious for a thing-in-itself in one's philosophy, this will be no objection. But we who are psychological, who believe in the relativity of knowledge, should we not make a halt before we declare a fundamental disparity between a thing as it is and a thing as it is known—whether that thing be sensation or what not?

As this point is fundamental, let me dwell upon it a little. All our knowledge originates from sensations. Very good. But what are these sensations? Are they the sensations which we know: the classified related sensations; *this* smell, or *this* color? No, these are the results of knowledge. They too presuppose sensations as their origin. What about these original sensations? They existed before knowledge, and knowledge originated and was developed by their grouping themselves together. Now, waiving the point that knowledge *is* precisely this grouping together and that therefore to tell us that it originated from grouping sensations is a good deal like telling us that knowledge originated knowledge, that experience is the result of experience—I must inquire again what these sensations are. And I can see but this simple alternative: either they are known, are, from the first, elements in knowledge, and hence cannot be used to account for the origin of knowledge; or they are not, and, what is more to the point, they never can be. As soon as they are known, they cease to be the pure sensation we are after and become an element *in* experience, *of* knowledge. The conclusion of the matter is, that sensations which can be used to account for the *origin* of knowledge or experience, are sensations which cannot be known, are things-in-themselves which are not relative to consciousness. I do not here say that there are not such: I only say that, if there are, we have given up our psychological standpoint and have become "ontologists" of the most pronounced character.

But the confusion is deeply rooted, and I cannot hope that I have yet shown that any attempt to show the *origin* of knowledge or of conscious experience presupposes a division between things as they are for knowledge or experience and as they are in themselves, and is therefore non-psychological in character. I shall be told that I am making the whole difficulty for myself; that I persist in taking the standpoint of an adult whose experience is already formed; that I must become as an infant to enter the true psychological kingdom. If I will only go back to that stage, I shall find a point where knowledge has not yet begun, but where sensations must be supposed to exist. Owing to our different standing, since these sensations have to us been covered with the residues of thousands of others and have become symbolic of them, we cannot tell what these sensations are; though in all probability they are to be conceived in some analogy to nervous shocks. But the truth of our psychological analysis does not depend upon this. The fact that sensations exist before knowledge and that knowledge comes about by their organic registration and integration is undisputed. And I can imagine that I am told that if I would but confine myself to the analysis of given facts, I should find this whole matter perfectly simple—that the sensations have not the remotest connection with any sort of "metaphysics" or analogy with things-in-themselves, and that we are all the time on positive scientific ground. I hope so. We are certainly approaching some degree of definiteness in our conception of what constitutes a sensation. But I am afraid that in thus defining the nature of a sensation, in taking it out of the region of vagueness, my objector has taken from it all those qualities which would enable it to serve as the origin of knowledge or of conscious experience. It is no longer a thing-in-itself, but neither is it, I fear, capable of accounting for experience. For, alas, we have to use experience to account for it. An infant, whether I think myself back to my early days or select some other baby, is, I suppose, a known object existing in the world of experience; and his nervous organism and the objects which affect it, these too, I suppose, are known objects which exist for consciousness. Surely it is not a baby thing-in-itself which is affected, nor a world thing-in-itself which calls forth the sensation. It is the known baby and a known world in definite action and reaction upon each other, and this definite relation is precisely a sensation. Yes, we are on positive scientific ground, and for that very reason we are on ground where the origin of knowledge and experience cannot be accounted for. Such a sensation I can easily form some conception of. I can even imagine how such sensations may by their organic registration and integration bring about that knowledge which I may myself possess. But such a sensation is not prior to consciousness or knowledge. It is but an element in the world of conscious experience. Far from being that from which all relations spring, it is itself but one relation—the relation between an organic body, and one acting upon it. Such a sensation, a sensation which exists only within and for experience, is not one which can be used to account for experience. It is but one element in an organic whole, and can no more account for the whole, than a given digestive act can account for the existence of a living body, although this digestive act and others similar to it may no doubt be shown to be all-important in the formation of a given living body. In short, we have finally arrived at the root of the difficulty. Our objector has been supposing that he could account for the origin of consciousness or knowledge because he could account for the process by which the given knowledge of a given individual came about. But if he accounts for this by something which is not known, which does not exist for consciousness, he is leaving the psychological standpoint to take the ontological; if he accounts for it by a known something, as a sensation produced by the reaction of a nervous organism upon a stimulus, he is accounting for its origin from something which exists only for and within consciousness. Consequently he is not accounting for the origin of consciousness or knowledge as such at all. He is simply accounting for the origin of an individual consciousness, or a specific group of known facts, by reference to the larger group of known facts or universal consciousness. Hence also the historic impotency of all forms of materialism. For either this matter is unknown, is a thing-in-itself, and hence may be called anything else as well as matter; or it is known, and then becomes but one set of the relations which in their completeness constitute mind—when to account for mind from it is to assume as ultimate reality that which has existence only as substantiated by mind. To the relations of the individual to the universal consciousness, I shall return later. At present, I am concerned only to point out that, if a man comes to the conclusion that *all* knowledge is relative, that existence means existence for consciousness, he is bound to apply this conclusion to his starting point and to his process. If he does this, he sees that the starting point (in this case, sensations) and the process (in this case, integration of sensations) exist for consciousness also—in short, that the *becoming* of consciousness exists for consciousness only, and hence that consciousness can never have become at all. That for which all origin and change exists, can never have originated or changed.

I hope that my objector and myself have now got within sight of each other so that we can see our common ground, and the cause of our difference. We both admit that the becoming of certain definite forms of knowledge, say Space, Time, Body, External World, etc., etc., may (in ideal, at least, if not yet as matter of actual fact) be accounted for as the product of a series of events. Now he supposes that, because the origin of some or all of our knowledge or conscious experience, knowledge of all particular things and of all general relations, can be thus accounted for, he has thereby accounted for the origin of consciousness or knowledge itself. All I desire to point out is that he is always accounting for their origin *within* knowledge or conscious experience, and that he cannot take his first step or develop this into the next, cannot have either beginning or process, without presupposing known elements—the whole sphere of consciousness, in fact. In short, what he has been doing is not to show the origin of consciousness or knowledge, but simply how consciousness or knowledge has differentiated itself into various forms. It is indeed the business of the psychologist to show how (not the *ideas of* space and time, etc., but) space, time, etc., arise, but since this origin is only within or for consciousness, it is but the showing of how knowledge develops *itself;* it is but the showing of how consciousness specifies itself into various given forms. He has not been telling us how knowledge became, but how it came to be in a certain way, that is, in a certain set of relations. In making out the origin of any or all particular knowledges (if I may be allowed the word), he is but showing the elements of knowledge. And in doing this, he is performing a twofold task. He is showing on the one hand what place they hold within experience, *i.e.,* he is showing their special adequacy or validity, and on the other he is explicating the nature of consciousness or experience. He is showing that it is not a bare form, but that, since these different elements arise necessarily within it, it is an infinite richness of relations. Let not the psychologist imagine then that he is showing the *origin* of consciousness, or of experience. There is nothing but themselves from which they can originate. He is but showing *what they are,* and, since they *are,* what they always have been.

I hope that it has now been made plain that the polemic against the attempt of the psychologist to account for the origin of conscious experience does not originate in any desire to limit his sphere but simply to call him away from a meaningless and self-contradictory conception of the psychological standpoint to an infinitely fruitful one. The psychological standpoint as it has developed itself is this: all that is, is for consciousness or knowledge. The business of the psychologist is to give a genetic account of the various elements within this consciousness, and thereby fix their place, determine their validity, and at the same time show definitely what the real and eternal nature of this consciousness is. If we actually believe in experience, let us be in earnest with it, and believe also that if we only ask, instead of assuming at the outset, we shall find what the infinite content of experience is. How experience became we shall never find out, for the reason that experience always is. We shall never account for it by referring it to something else, for "something else" always is only for and in experience. *Why* it is, we shall never discover, for it is a whole. But how the elements within the whole become we may find out, and thereby account for them by referring them to each other and to the whole, and thereby also discover why they are.

We have now reached positive ground, and, in the remainder of the paper, I wish to consider the relations, within this whole, of various specific elements which have always been "inquiries into which the mind of man was very apt to run," *viz.*: the relations of Subject and Object, and the relations of Universal and Individual, or Absolute and Finite.

## II

From the psychological standpoint the relation of Subject and Object is one which exists within consciousness. And its nature or meaning must be determined by an examination of consciousness itself. The duty of the psychologist is to show how it arises for consciousness. Put from the positive side, he must point out how consciousness differentiates itself so as to give rise to the existence within, that is for, itself of subject and object. This operation fixes the nature of the two (for they have no nature aside from their relation in consciousness), and at the same time explicates or develops the nature of consciousness itself. In this case, it reveals that consciousness is precisely the unity of subject and object.

Now psychology has never been so false to itself as to utterly forget that this is its task. From Locke downwards we find it dealing with the problems of the origin of space, time, the "ideas" of the external world, of matter, of body, of the *Ego*, etc., etc. But it has interpreted its results so as to deprive them of all their meaning. It has most successfully avoided seeing the necessary implications of its own procedure. There are in particular two interpretations by which it has evaded the necessary meaning of its own work.

The first of these I may now deal with shortly, as it is nothing but our old friend *x*, the thing-in-itself in a new guise. It is Reasoned or Transfigured Realism. It sees clearly enough that everything which we know is relative to our consciousness, and it sees also clearly enough that *our* consciousness is also relative. All that we can know exists for our consciousness; but when we come to account for our consciousness we find that this too is dependent. It is dependent on a nervous organism; it is dependent upon objects which affect this organism. It is dependent upon a whole series of past events formulated by the doctrine of evolution. But this body, these objects, this series of events, they too exist but for our consciousness. Now there is no *"metaphysics"* about all this. It is positive science. Still there is a contradiction. Consciousness at once depends upon objects and events, and these depend upon, or are relative to consciousness. Hence the fact of the case must be this: The nervous organism, the objects, the series of events *as known,* are relative to our consciousness, but since this itself is dependent, is a product, there is a reality behind the processes, behind our consciousness, which has produced them both. Subject and object as known *are* relative to consciousness, but there is a larger circle, a real object from which both of them emerge, but which can never be known, since to know is to relate to our consciousness. This is the problem: on one hand, the relativity of all knowledge to our consciousness; on the other, the dependence of our consciousness on something not itself. And this is the solution: a real not related to consciousness, but which has produced both consciousness itself, and the objects which as known are relative to consciousness. Now all that has been said in the first part of this article has gone for naught if it is not seen that such an argument is not a solution of the contradiction, but a statement of it. The problem is to reconcile the undoubted relativity of all existence as known, to consciousness, and the undoubted dependence of our own consciousness. And it ought to be evident that the only way to reconcile the apparent contradiction, to give each its rights without denying the truth of the other, is to think them together. If this is done, it will be seen that the solution is that the consciousness to which all existence is relative is not our consciousness, and that our consciousness is itself relative to consciousness in general. But Reasoned Realism attempts to solve the problem not by bringing the elements together, but by holding them apart. It does not seek the higher unity which enables each to be seen as indeed true, but it attempts to divide. It attributes one element of the contradiction to our consciousness, and another to a thing-in-itself—the unknown reality. But this is only an express statement of the contradiction. If all *be* relative to consciousness, there is no thing-in-itself, just consciousness itself. If there be a thing-in-itself then all is not relative to consciousness. Let a man hold the latter if he will, but let him expressly recognize that thereby he has put himself on "ontological" ground and adopted an "ontological" method. Psychology he has forever abandoned.

The other evasion is much more subtle and "reasoned." It is a genuine attempt to untie the Gordian knot, as the other was a slashing attempt to cut it with the sword of a thing-in-itself. It is Subjective Idealism. And I wish now to show that Subjective Idealism is *not* the meaning of the psychological standpoint applied to the relation of subject and object. It is rather a misinterpretation of it based upon the same refusal to think two undoubted facts in their unity, the same attempt to divide the contradiction instead of solving it, which we have seen in the case of attempts to determine the origin of knowledge, and of Transfigured Realism. The position is this: The necessary relation of the world of existences to consciousness is recognized. [Thus Bain:] "There is no possible knowledge of a world except in reference to our minds—knowledge is a state of mind. The notion of material things is a mental fact. We are incapable even of discussing the existence of an independent material world; the very fact is a contradiction. We can speak only of a world presented to our own minds." But this being stated, consciousness is now separated into two parts—one of which is the subject, which is identified with mind, *Ego*, the Internal; while the other is the object, which is identified with the External, the *Non-Ego*, Matter. "Mind is definable, in the first instance, by the *method of contrast*, or as a remainder arising from *subtracting the object world from the totality of conscious experience.*" "The totality of our mental life is made up of *two kinds* of consciousness—the object consciousness and the subject consciousness. The first is the external world, or *Non-Ego;* the second is our *Ego*, or mind proper." Consciousness "includes our object states as well as our subject states. The object and subject are *both parts* of our being, as I conceive, and hence we have a subject consciousness, which is in a special sense Mind (*the scope of mental science*), and an object consciousness in which all other sentient beings participate, and which gives us the extended and material universe." It is, of course, still kept in view (which constitutes the logical superiority of Subjective Idealism over Realism) that "the object consciousness, which we call Externality, is still a mode of self in the most comprehensive sense." "Object experience is still conscious experience, that is Mind." I have quoted at this length because the above passages seem to me an admirable statement of a representative type of Subjective Idealism.

The logic of the process seems to be as follows. It is recognized that all existence with which philosophy or anything else has to do must be known existence—that is, that all existence is for consciousness. If we examine this consciousness, we shall find it testifying to "two kinds of consciousness"—one, a series of sensations, emotions, and ideas, etc., the other, objects determined by spatial relations. We have to recognize then two parts in consciousness, a subject part, mind more strictly speaking, and an object part, commonly called the external world or matter. But it must not be forgotten that this after all is a part of my own being, my consciousness. The subject swallows up the object. But this subject, again, "segregates" itself into "two antithetical halves," into "two parts," the subject and the object. Then again the object vanishes into the subject, and again the subject divides itself. And forever the process is kept up. Now the point I wish to make is that consciousness is here used in two entirely different senses, and that the apparent plausibility of the argument rests upon their confusion. There is consciousness in the broad sense, consciousness which includes subject and object; and there is consciousness in the narrow sense, in which it is equivalent to "mind," "Ego," that is, to the series of conscious states. The whole validity of the argument rests, of course, upon the supposition that ultimately these two are just the same—that it is the individual consciousness, the "Ego" which differentiates itself into the "two kinds of consciousness," subject and object. If not, "mind," as well as "matter"—the series of psychical states or events which constitute the Ego and are "the scope of mental science," as well as that in which all "sentient beings participate"—is but an element in consciousness. If this be so, Subjective Idealism is abandoned and Absolute Idealism (to which I hardly need say this article has been constantly pointing) is assumed. The essence of Subjective Idealism is that the subject consciousness or mind, which remains after the "object world has been subtracted," is that for which after all this object world exists. Were this not so—were it admitted that this subject, mind, and the object, matter, are both but elements within, and both exist only for, consciousness—we should be in the sphere of an eternal absolute consciousness, whose partial realization both the individual "subject" and the "external world" are. And I wish to show that this is the only meaning of the facts of the case; that Subjective Idealism is but the bald statement of a contradiction.

This brief digression is for the purpose of showing that, to Subjective

Idealism, the consciousness for which all exists is the consciousness which is called mind, *Ego,* "my being." The point which I wished to make was that this identification is self-contradictory, although it is absolutely necessary to this form of Idealism. I shall be brief here in order not to make a simple matter appear complicated. How can consciousness which gives rise to the "two kinds" of consciousness which in its primary aspect exists in time as a series of psychical events or states be the consciousness for which a permanent world of spatially related objects, in which "all sentient beings participate," exists? How can the "mind" which is defined by way of "contrast," which exists after the object world has been "subtracted," be the mind which is the whole, of which subject and object are alike elements? To state that the mind, in the first instance, is but the remainder from the totality of conscious experience "minus the object world," and to state also "that this object world is itself a part of mind"—what is that but to state in terms a self-contradiction? Unless it be to state that this way of looking at mind, "in the first instance," is but a partial and unreal way of looking at it, and that mind in truth is the unity of subject and object, one of which cannot be subtracted from the other, because it has absolutely no existence without the other. Is it not a self-contradiction to declare that the "scope of mental science" is subject consciousness or mind, and at the same time to declare that "both subject and object are parts of our being," are but "two kinds" of consciousness? Surely Psychology ought to be the science of our whole being, and of the whole consciousness. But no words can make the contradiction clearer than the mere statement of it. The only possible hypothesis upon which to reconcile the two statements that mind is consciousness with the object world subtracted, and that it is the whole of our conscious experience, including both subject and object world, is that the term "Mind" is used in two entirely different senses in the two cases. In the first it must be individual mind, or consciousness, and in the second it must be absolute mind or consciousness, for and in which alone the individual or subject consciousness and the external world or object consciousness exist and get their reality.

The root of the whole difficulty is this. It is the business of Psychology to take the whole of conscious experience for its scope. It is its business to determine within this whole what the nature of subject and object are. Now Subjective Idealism identifies at the outset, as may be seen in the passages quoted, subject with "Mind," "*Ego,*" and object with "Matter," "*Non-Ego,*" "External World," and then goes on to hold that the "scope" of Psychology is the former only. In short, the psychological standpoint, according to which the nature of subject and object was to be determined from the nature of conscious experience, was abandoned at the outset. It is presumed that we already know what the "subject" is, and Psychology is confined to treatment of that. It is assumed that we know already what the "object" is, and Psychology is defined by its elimination. This method, as psychology, has two vices. It is "ontological," for it sets up some external test to fix upon the nature of subject and object; and it is arbitrary, for it dogmatically presupposes the limitation of Psychology to a series of subjective states. It assumes that Psychology instead of being the criterion of all, has some outside criterion from which its own place and subject matter is determined, and more specifically, *it assumes that the standpoint of Psychology is necessarily individual or subjective*. Why should we be told that the scope of Psychology is subject consciousness, and subject consciousness be defined as the totality of conscious experience *minus* the object world, unless there is presupposed a knowledge of what subject and object are? How different is the method of the true psychological standpoint! It shows how subject and object arise within conscious experience, and thereby develops the nature of consciousness. It shows it to be the unity of subject and object. It shows therefore that there cannot be "two kinds" of consciousness, one subject, the other object, but that all consciousness whether of "Mind," or of "Matter," is, *since* consciousness, the unity of subject and object. Consciousness may, and undoubtedly does, have two aspects—one aspect in which it appears as an individual, and another in which it appears as an external world over against the individual. But there are not two kinds of consciousness, one of which may be subtracted from the whole and leave the other. They are but consciousness in one phase, and how it is that consciousness assumes this phase, how it is that this division into the individual and the external world arises for consciousness (in short, how consciousness in one stage appears as perception)—that is precisely the business of Psychology to determine. But it does not determine it by assuming at the outset that the subject is "me," and the object is the world. And if this be not assumed at the outset it certainly will not be reached at the conclusion. The conclusion will show that the distinction of consciousness into the individual and the world is but one form in which the *relation* of subject and object, which everywhere constitutes consciousness, appears. This brings us definitely to the relation of the individual and the universal consciousness.

## III

We have seen that the attempt to account for the origin of knowledge, at bottom, rests on the undoubted fact that the individual consciousness does become, but also that the only way to account for this becoming, without self-contradiction, is by the postulate of a universal consciousness. We have seen again that the truth at the bottom of subjective idealism is the undoubted fact that all existence is relative to our consciousness, but also that the only consistent meaning of this fact is that our consciousness as individual is itself relative to a universal consciousness. And now I am sure that my objector, for some time silent, will meet me with renewed vigor. He will turn one of these arguments against the other and say: "After all, this consciousness for which all exists is your individual consciousness. The universal consciousness itself exists only for it. You may say indeed that this individual consciousness, which has now absorbed the universal again, shows the universal as necessary to its own existence, but this is only to fall into the contradiction which you have already urged against a similar view on the part of Subjective Idealism. Your objection in that case was that consciousness divided into subject consciousness and object consciousness, of which the former immediately absorbed the latter, and again subdivided itself into the subject and object consciousness. You objected that this was the express statement of a contradiction—the statement that the subject consciousness was and was not the whole of conscious experience. It was only as it was asserted to be the whole that any ground was found for subjective idealism; but only as it was regarded as a remainder left over from subtraction of the object world does it correspond to actual experience. Now you have yourself fallen into precisely this contradiction. You do but state that the individual consciousness is and is not the universal consciousness. Only so far as it is not, do you escape subjective idealism; only so far as it is, do you escape the thing-in-itself. If this universal consciousness is not for our individual consciousness, if it is not a part of our conscious experience, it is unknowable, a thing-in-itself. But if it be a part of our individual consciousness, then after all the individual consciousness is the ultimate. By your own argument you have no choice except between the acceptance of an unknowable unrelated reality or of subjective idealism."

This objection amounts to the following disjunction: Either the universal consciousness is the individual and we have subjective idealism; or, it is something beyond the individual consciousness, and we have a thing-in-itself. Now this dilemma looks somewhat formidable, yet its statement shows that the objector has not yet put himself upon the psychological ground: there is something of the old "ontological" man left in him yet, for it assumes that he has, prior to its determination by Psychology, an adequate idea of what "individual" is and means. If he will take the psychological standpoint, he will see that nature of the individual as well as of the universal must be determined within and through conscious experience. And if this is so, all ground for the disjunction falls away at once. This disjunction rests upon the supposition that the individual and the universal consciousness are something opposed to each other. If one were to assert that the meaning of the individual consciousness is that it is universal, the whole objection loses not only its ground but its meaning; it becomes nonsense. But I am not concerned just at present to state this; I am concerned only to point out that, if one starts with a presupposition regarding the nature of the individual consciousness, one is leaving the psychological standpoint. In forming the parallel between the position attributed to the writer and that of subjective idealism, the supposed objector was building wiser than perhaps he knew. The trouble with the latter view is that it supposes that consciousness may be divided into "two kinds," one subjective, the other objective; that it presupposes, at the start, the nature of subject and object. The fact of the case is that, since consciousness is the unity of subject and object, there is no purely subjective or purely objective. So here. It is presupposed that there are "two kinds" of consciousness, one individual, the other universal. And the fact will be found to be, I imagine, that consciousness is the unity of the individual and the universal; that there is no purely individual or purely universal. So the disjunction made is meaningless. But however that may be, at all events it leaves the psychological basis, for it assumes that the nature of the individual is already known.

This has been said that it may be borne in mind from the outset that Psychology must determine within consciousness the nature of the individual and the universal consciousness, thereby determining at once their place within experience, and explicating the nature of consciousness itself. And this, stated in plain terms, means simply that, since consciousness does show the origin of individual and universal consciousness *within itself*, consciousness is therefore both universal and individual. *How* this is, the present article, of course, does not undertake to say. Its more modest function is simply to point out that it is the business of psychology to show the nature of the individual and the universal and of the relation existing between them. These must not be presupposed, and then imported bodily to determine the nature of psychologic experience. There has now been rendered explicit what was implied concerning the psychological standpoint from the first, *viz.*, that it is a universal standpoint. If the nature of all objects of philosophical inquiry is to be determined from fixing their place within conscious experience, then there is no criterion outside of or beyond or behind just consciousness itself. To adopt the psychological standpoint is to assume that consciousness itself is the only possible absolute. And this is tacitly assumed all the while by subjective idealism. The most obvious objection to subjective idealism is, of course, that it presupposes that, if "mind were to become extinct, the annihilation of matter, space, time would result." And the equally obvious reply of subjective idealism is: "My conception of the universe even though death may have overtaken all its inhabitants, would not be an independent reality, I should merely take on the object-consciousness of a supposed mind then present" (Bain). In short, the reality of the external world, though I should imagine all finite minds destroyed, would be that I cannot imagine consciousness destroyed. As soon as I imagine an external world, I imagine a consciousness in relation to which it exists. One may put the objection from a side which gets added force with every advance of physical science. The simplest physiology teaches that all our sensations originate from bodily states—that they are conditioned upon a nervous organism. The science of biology teaches that this nervous organism is not ultimate but had its origin; that its origin lies back in indefinite time, and that as it now exists it is a result of an almost infinite series of processes; all these events, through no one knows how much time, having been precedent to your and my mind, and being the condition of their existence. Now is all this an illusion, as it must be, if its only existence is for a consciousness which is "but a transition from one state to another"? The usual answer to this argument is that it is an *ignoratio elenchi:* that it has presupposed a consciousness for which these events existed; and that they have no meaning except when stated in terms of consciousness. This answer I have no call to rebut. But it must be pointed out that this is to suppose the individual consciousness capable of transcending itself and assuming a universal standpoint—a standpoint whence it can see its own becoming, as individual. It is this *implication* of the universal nature of the individual consciousness which has constituted the strength of English philosophy; it is its lack of *explication* which has constituted its weakness. Subjective idealism has "admitted of no answer and produced no conviction" because of just this confusion. That which has admitted of no answer is the existence of all *for* consciousness; that which has produced no conviction is the existence of all for our consciousness as merely individual. English philosophy can assume its rightful position only when it has become fully aware of its own presuppositions; only when it has become conscious of that which constitutes its essential characteristic. It must see that the psychological standpoint is necessarily a universal standpoint and consciousness necessarily the only absolute, before it can go on to develop the nature of consciousness and of experience. It must see that the individual consciousness, the consciousness which is but "transition," but a process of becoming, which, in its primary aspect, has to be defined by way of "contrast," which is but a "part" of conscious experience, nevertheless is when viewed in its finality, in a perfectly concrete way, the universal consciousness, the consciousness which has never become and which *is* the totality; and that it is only because the individual consciousness is, in its ultimate reality, the universal consciousness that it affords any basis whatever for philosophy.

The case stands thus: We are to determine the nature of everything, subject and object, individual and universal, as it is found within conscious experience. Conscious experience testifies, in the primary aspect, my individual self is a "transition," is a process of becoming. But it testifies also that this individual self is conscious of the transition, that it knows the process by which it has become. In short, the individual self can take the universal self as its standpoint, and thence know its own origin. In so doing, it knows that it has its origin in processes which exist for the universal self, and that therefore the universal self never has become. Consciousness testifies that consciousness is a result, but that it is the result of consciousness. Consciousness is the self-related. Stated from the positive side, consciousness has shown that it involves *within* itself a process of becoming, and that this process becomes conscious of itself. This process is the individual consciousness; but since it is conscious of itself, it is consciousness of the universal consciousness. All consciousness, in short, is self-consciousness, and the self is the universal consciousness, for which all process is and which, therefore, always is. The individual consciousness is but the process of realization of the universal consciousness through itself. Looked at as process, as realizing, it is individual consciousness; looked at as produced or realized, as conscious of the process, that is, of itself, it is universal consciousness.

It must not be forgotten that the object of this paper is simply to develop the presuppositions which have always been latent or implicit in the psychological standpoint. What has been said in the way of positive result has been said, therefore, only as it seemed necessary to develop the meaning of the standpoint. It must also be remembered that it is the work of Psychology itself to determine the exact and concrete relations of subject and object, individual and universal, within consciousness. What has been said here, if said only for the development of the standpoint, is therefore exceedingly formal. To some of the more concrete problems I hope to be able to return at another time.

# 8. Psychology as Philosophic Method*

In some ways a clarification of the previous article, "The Psychological Standpoint," Dewey, in the following selection, takes on a more positive tone in defending psychology as a viable philosophic method. Dewey reads the state of the problem in 1886 as follows: "There is an absolute self-consciousness. The science of this is philosophy. This absolute self-consciousness manifests itself in the knowing and acting of individual men. The science of this manifestation, a phenomenology, is psychology." But Dewey considers this distinction to be merely functional and not substantive, and so the burden of the present paper is to show that "what else can philosophy in its fullness be but psychology, and psychology but philosophy."

In "The Psychological Standpoint," I endeavored to point out that the characteristic English development in philosophy—the psychological movement since Locke—had been neither a "threshing of old straw," nor a movement of purely negative meaning, whose significance for us was exhausted when we had learned how it necessarily led to the movement in Germany—the so-called "transcendental" movement. Its positive significance was found to consist in the fact that it declared consciousness to be the sole content, account and criterion of all reality; and psychology, as the science of this consciousness, to be the explicit and accurate determination of the nature of reality in its wholeness, as well as the determination of the value and validity of the various elements or factors of this whole. It is the ultimate science of reality, because it declares what experience in its totality is; it fixes the worth and meaning of its various elements by showing their development and place within this whole. It is, in short,

* From *Mind*, XI (April, 1886), pp. 153-73.

*philosophic method*. But that paper was necessarily largely negative, for it was necessary to point out that as matter of fact the movement had not been successful in presenting psychology as the method of philosophy, for it had not been true to its own basis and ideal. Instead of determining all, both in its totality and its factors, through consciousness, it had endeavored to determine consciousness from something out of and beyond necessary relation to consciousness. It had determined its psychology from a dogmatically presupposed ontology, instead of getting at its ontology from a critical examination of the nature and contents of consciousness, as its standpoint required. It had a thing-in-itself, something whose very existence was to be opposed to consciousness, as in the unknowable "substances" of Locke, the transcendent Deity of Berkeley, the sensations or impressions of Hume and Mill, the "transfigured real" of Spencer; and it used this thing-in-itself as the cause and criterion of conscious experience. Thus it contradicted itself; for, if psychology as method of philosophy means anything, it means that nothing shall be assumed except just conscious experience itself, and that the nature of all shall be ascertained from and within this.

It is to the positive significance of psychology as philosophic method—its significance when it is allowed to develop itself free from self-contradictory assumptions—that this present paper is directed. It was suggested in the previous paper that this method, taken in its purity, would show substantial identity with the presuppositions and results of the "transcendental" movement. And as the principal attacks upon the pretensions of psychology to be method for philosophy, or anything more than one of the special sciences, have come from representatives of this movement, this paper must be occupied with treating psychology in reference to what we may call German philosophy, as the other treated it in reference to English philosophy. In so far as the criticisms from this side have been occupied with pointing out the failure of the actual English psychology to be philosophy, there is of course no difference of opinion. That arises only in so far as these criticisms have seemed (*seemed*, I repeat) to imply that the same objections must hold against every *possible* psychology; while it seems to the writer that psychology is the only *possible* method.

It is held, or seems to be held, by representatives of the post-Kantian movement, that man may be regarded in two aspects, in one of which he is an object of experience like other objects: he is a finite thing among other finite things; with these things he is in relations of action and reaction, but possesses the additional characteristic that he is a knowing, feeling, willing *phenomenon*. As such, he forms the object of a special science, psychology, which, like every other special science, deals with its material as pure object, abstracting from that creative synthesis *of subject and object,* self-consciousness, through which all things are and are known. It is therefore, like all the special sciences, partial and utterly inadequate to determining the nature and meaning of that whole with which philosophy has to deal. Nay more, it is itself ultimately dependent upon philosophy for the determination of the meaning, validity, and limits of the principles, categories, and method which it unconsciously assumes. To regard psychology therefore as philosophic method is to be guilty of the same error as it would be to regard the highest generalizations of, say, physics as adequate to determining the problems of philosophy. It is an attempt to determine the unconditioned whole, self-consciousness, by that which has no existence except as a conditioned part of this very whole.

> Metaphysics [says Professor Caird] has to deal with conditions of the knowable, and hence with self-consciousness or that unity which is implied in all that is and is known. Psychology has to inquire how this self-consciousness is realized or developed in man, in whom the consciousness of self grows with the consciousness of a world in time and space, of which he individually is only a part, and to parts of which only he stands in immediate relation. In considering the former question we are considering the sphere within which all knowledge and all objects of knowledge are contained. In considering the latter, we are selecting one particular object or class of objects within this sphere. . . . It is possible to have a *purely objective* anthropology or psychology—which abstracts from the relation of man to the mind that knows him—just as it is possible to have a purely objective science of nature.[1]

The other aspect of man is that in which he, as self-conscious, has manifested in him the unity of all being and knowing, and is not finite, *i.e.*, an object or event, but is, in virtue of his self-conscious nature, infinite, the bond, the living union of all objects and events. With this infinite, universal self-consciousness, philosophy deals; with man as the object of experience, psychology deals.

In stating the position of the post-Kantian movement, I used the

[1] Art. "Metaphysic," *Ency. Britt.*, xvi, 89. Cp. Professor Adamson, *Philosophy of Kant*, pp. 22 ff., *Fichte*, pp. 109 ff.; *Essays in Philosophical Criticism*, pp. 44 ff.; Professor A. Seth, *Ency. Britt.*, art. "Philosophy."

word *seemed,* and used it advisedly, as I do not conceive that at bottom there is any difference of opinion. But it seems to me that there are invariably involved in the reasonings of this school certain presuppositions regarding the real science of psychology which, probably for the reason that the writers have seen such misuse made of a false psychology, are not distinctly stated, and which, accordingly, not only lessen the convincing force with which their reasonings are received by those unacquainted with the necessity and rationality of these presuppositions, but which also, as not distinctly thought out, tend at times to involve these reasonings in unnecessary obscurity and even contradictions. It is these presuppositions regarding the nature of a real psychology, lying at the basis of all the work of the post-Kantian school, conditioning it and giving it its worth, which it is the object of this paper to examine.

The start is made accordingly from the supposed distinction of aspects in man's nature, according to one of which he is an object of experience and the subject of psychology, and according to the other of which, he, as self-consciousness, is the universal condition and unity of all experience, and hence not an object of experience. As I have already referred to Professor Adamson's treatment of this distinction, let me refer to a later writing of his which seems to retract all that gave validity to this distinction. After pointing out that the subject matter of psychology *cannot* be *pure* objects but must always be the reference of an individual subject to a content which is universal, he goes on with the following most admirable statement:

> It is in and through the conscious life of the individual that all the thinking and acting which form the material for other treatment is realised. When we isolate the content and treat it as having a *quasi*-experience *per se*, we are in the attitude of objective or natural science. When we endeavour to interpret the significance of the whole, to determine the meaning of the connective links that bind it together, we are in the attitude of philosophy. But when we regard the modes through which knowledge and acting are realised in the life of an individual subject, we are in the position of the psychological inquirer.

Now, when psychology is defined as the science of the realization of the universe in and through the individual, all pretense of regarding psychology as merely one of the special sciences, whose subject matter by necessity is simply some one department of the universe, considered out of relation to the individual, is, of course, abandoned. With this falls, as a matter of course, the supposed twofold character of man's nature. If the essence of his nature is to be the realization of the universe, there is no aspect in which, *as man,* it appears as a mere object or event in the universe. The distinction is now transferred to the two ways of looking at the same material, and no longer concerns two distinct materials. Is this distinction, however, any more valid? Is there any reason for distinguishing between the modes through which the universe is realized in an individual, and the significance of this universe as a whole? At first sight there may appear to be, but let us consider the following questions. Does the whole have any significance beyond itself? If we consider experience in its absolute totality so far as realized in the individual, can the "significance of the whole" be determined beyond what itself testifies to as a whole; and do the "connective links which bind together" have any "meaning" except just as they do bind together? And since this whole and these connective links are given to us by the science of psychology, what is this except completed philosophic method, and what more has philosophy to do except to abstract from this totality, and regard it, on its material side, as philosophy of nature, and on its formal as real logic? Psychology, as science of the realization through the individual of the universe, answers the question as to the significance of the whole, by giving that whole, and at the same time gives the meaning of the parts and of their connection by showing just their place within this whole.

It would be fatal to the existence of philosophy as well as of psychology to make any distinction here. Were not the universe realized in the individual, it would be impossible for the individual to rise to a universal point of view, and hence to philosophize. That the universe has not been completely realized in man is no more an objection to the employment of psychology as the determination of the nature of this universe, than it is to any treatment of philosophy whatever. In no way can the individual philosophize about a universe which has not been realized in his conscious experience. The universe, except as realized in an individual, has no existence. In man it is partially realized, and man has a partial science; in the absolute it is completely realized, and God has a complete science. Self-consciousness means simply an individualized universe; and if this universe has *not* been realized in man, if man be not self-conscious, then no philosophy whatever is possible. If it *has* been realized, it is in and through psychological experience that this realization has occurred. Psychology is the scientific account of this realization, of this individualized universe, of this self-consciousness.

What other account can be given? It is the object of this paper to show that no other account can be given. Not only is any final distinction or dualism, even of aspects, in man's nature utterly untenable, but no distinction even of aspects can be made in the *treatment* of man's nature. Psychology has to do with just the consciousness which constitutes man's experience, and all further determinations of experience fall within this psychological determination of it, and are hence abstract. More definitely, Psychology, and not Logic, is the method of Philosophy. Let us deal *seriatim* with these two questions.

I

No such distinction in the nature of man, as that in one aspect he is "part of the partial world," and hence the subject of a purely natural science, psychology, and in another the conscious subject for which all exists, the subject of philosophy, can be maintained. This is our first assertion. Let us turn again to that most lucid and comprehensive statement of philosophic doctrine by Professor Caird, from which extract has already been made. The distinction to be upheld is that between the "sphere in which all knowledge and all objects of knowledge are contained" and "one particular object within this sphere." The question which at once arises is, How does this distinction come about? Granted that it is valid, how is man known as requiring in his nature this distinction for his proper comprehension? There is but one possible answer: it is a distinction which has arisen within and from conscious experience itself. In the course of man's realization of the universe there is necessitated this distinction. This distinction therefore falls within the sphere of psychology, and cannot be used to fix the position of psychology. Much less can psychology be identified with some one aspect of experience which has its origin only within that experience which in its wholeness constitutes the material of psychology. The distinction, as we shall immediately see, cannot be an absolute one: by no possibility or contingency can man be regarded as *merely* one of objects of experience; but so far as the distinction has relative validity it is a purely psychological one, originating because man in his experience, at different *stages* of it, finds it necessary to regard himself in two lights—in one of which he is a particular space- and time-conditioned being (we cannot say object or event) or activity, and in the other the unconditioned eternal synthesis of all. At most the distinction is only one of various stages in one and the same experience, both of which, as stages of experience—one, indeed, of experience in its partiality and the other of experience in its totality—fall within the science of experience, *viz.*, psychology.

We will see how the question stands if we state it otherwise. Does or does not the self-consciousness of man fall within the science of psychology? What reason can be given for excluding it? Certainly few would be found so thoroughgoing as to deny that perception is a matter which that science must treat; those however who admit perception would find themselves hard put to it to give a reason for excluding memory, imagination, conception, judgment, reasoning. Why having reached the stage of reasoning, where the original implicit individual with which we began has been broken up into the greatest possible number of explicit relations, shall we rule out self-consciousness where these relations are again seen united into an individual unity? There is no possible break: either we must deny the possibility of treating perception in psychology, and then our "purely objective science of psychology" can be nothing more than a physiology; or, admitting it, we must admit what follows directly from and upon it—self-consciousness. Self-consciousness is indeed a *fact* (I do not fear the word) of experience, and must therefore find its treatment in psychology.

But this is not all. Not only does self-consciousness appear as one of the stages of psychological experience, but the explanation of the simplest psychological fact—say one of perception, or feeling, or impulse—involves necessary reference to self-consciousness. Self-consciousness is involved in every simpler process, and no one of them can be scientifically described or comprehended except as this involution is brought out. In fact, their comprehension or explanation is simply bringing to light this implication of self-consciousness within them. This would be the last thing that the upholders of self-consciousness as the final unity and synthesis, the absolute meaning of experience, could deny. The organic nature of self-consciousness being their thesis, it must indeed reveal itself in, or rather constitute, each of its members and phases. The very *existence* of any idea or feeling being ultimately its relation to self-consciousness, what other account of it can be given except its organic placing in the system? If there be such an act as perception, a candid, careful examination of it, *not of its logical conditions*, but of itself as *matter of experienced fact*, will reveal what it is; and this revelation will be the declaration of its relation to that organic system which in its wholeness is self-consciousness. We may then abstract from this relation, which constitutes its very being, and consider it as an *object of perception*, and, generalizing the case, produce a philosophy of nature; or, considering it as conditioned by thought, we may thus produce a logic. But both of these proceedings go on in abstraction from its real being, and cannot give the real method of philosophy. In short, the real *esse* of things is neither their *percipi*, nor their *intelligi* alone; it is their *experiri*. Logic may give us the science of the *intelligi*, the philosophy of nature of the *percipi*, but only psychology can give us the systematic connected account of the *experiri*, which is also in its wholeness just the *experior*—self-consciousness itself.

We may see how the matter stands by inquiring what would be the effect upon philosophy if self-consciousness were not an *experienced fact, i.e.*, if it were not one actual stage in that realization of the universe by an individual which is defined as constituting the sphere of psychology. The result would be again, precisely, that no such thing as philosophy, under any theory of its nature whatever, is possible. Philosophy, it cannot be too often repeated, consists simply in viewing things *sub specie aeternitatis* or *in ordine ad universum*. If man, as matter of fact, does not realize the nature of the eternal and the universal *within* himself, as the essence of his own being; if he does not at one stage of his experience consciously, and in all stages implicitly, lay hold of this universal and eternal, then it is a mere matter of words to say that he can give no account of things as they universally and eternally are. To deny, therefore, that self-consciousness is a matter of psychological experience is to deny the possibility of any philosophy.

What the denial comes to we have had historically demonstrated in Kant. He admits perception and conception as matters of experience, but he draws the line at self-consciousness. It is worth noticing that his reason for denying it is not psychological at all, but logical. It is not because self-consciousness *is* not a fact, but because it *cannot* be a fact according to his logical presuppositions. The results following the denial are worthy of notice as corresponding exactly to what we might be led to expect: first, with the denial of the fact of self-consciousness comes the impossibility of solving the problem of philosophy, expressed in the setting up of an unknown thing-in-itself as the ultimate ground and condition of experience; and, secondly, comes the failure to bring perception and conception into any organic connection with experience, that is, the failure to really comprehend and explain them, manifested in the limitation of both perception, through the forms of space and time, and thinking, through the categories, to phenomena which are in no demonstrable connection with reality. The failure to recognize self-consciousness as a stage of psychological experience leads not only to a failure to reach the alternate synthesis of experience, but renders it impossible to explain the simpler forms of psychological experience. This failure of Kant teaches us another lesson also, in that, as already stated, it was due to abandoning his real method, which was *psychological*, consisting in the self-knowledge of reason as an organic system by reason itself, and setting up a *logical* standard (in this latter case the principles of non-contradiction and identity), by which to determine the totality of experience. The work of Hegel consisted essentially in showing that Kant's *logical* standard was erroneous, and that, as matter of logic, the only true criterion or standard was the organic notion, or *Begriff*, which is a systematic totality, and accordingly able to explain both itself and also the simpler processes and principles. That Hegel accomplished this work successfully and thoroughly there can be to the writer no doubt; but it seems equally clear that the work of Kant is in need of another complement, following more closely his own conception of method and of philosophy, which shall consist in showing self-consciousness as a fact of experience, as well as perception through organic forms and thinking through organic principles. And it seems further that, only when this has been done, will, for the first time, the presuppositions latent in the work of Hegel, which give it its convincing force and validity, be brought out.

Again, it seems worthy of note that the late Professor Green (of whom the writer would not speak without expressing his deep, almost reverential gratitude), when following out Kant's work from its logical side, hardly escaped Kant's negative results. (By Kant's logical method we mean the inquiry into the *necessary conditions* of experience; by his psychological method the inquiry into the *actual nature* of experience.) After his complete demonstration of consciousness as the final condition, synthesis and unity of all that is or is knowable, he finds himself obliged to state: "As to what that consciousness in itself or in its completeness is, we can only make negative statements. *That* there is such a consciousness is implied in the existence of the world; but *what* it is we can only know through its so far acting in us as to enable us, however partially and interruptedly, to have knowledge of a world or an intelligent experience." Had he begun from the latter statement, and shown as matter of fact that this universal consciousness *had* realized itself, though only partially and interruptedly, in us, he certainly would have been able to make very positive statements regarding it, and would also have furnished a basis in fact for his logical method, which now seems to hang upon nothing but a unity of which all that can be said is that it *is* a unity, and that it *is not* anything in particular. When one reflects that it is not only upon the existence of this unity, but upon its working in and through us, that all philosophy and philosophizing depend, one cannot conceal the apprehension that too great a load of philosophy has been hung upon too feeble a peg.

So, too, after his victorious demonstration that upon the existence of this spiritual unity depends the possibility of all moral experience, he finds himself obliged to state, with that candor so characteristic of all his thinking: "Of a life of completed development, of activity with the end attained, we can only speak or think in negatives, and thus only can we speak or think of that state of being in which, according to our theory, the ultimate moral good must consist." Once more, had he started from the fact that as matter of actual realization this absolute good has been reproduced in our lives and the end attained (for surely the good is a matter of quality and not of quantity, and the end a power, not a sum), he would not have found himself in this difficulty. But with a purely logical method, one can end only with the *must be* or the *ought:* the *is* vanishes, because it has been abstracted from. The psychological method starts from the *is*, and thereby also gives the basis *and* the ideal for the *ought* and *must be*.

But it is time that we returned to our thesis, which, in brief, was that no distinction which maintains that psychology is the science of man as "part of this partial world" can be maintained. The following reasons for this denial have been given: it was pointed out that the relative validity which this distinction in man's nature undoubtedly possesses is itself the product and manifestation of psychological experience; that man as man, or as the conscious experience whose science is psychology, is self-conscious, and that therefore self-consciousness as the unity of subject and object, not as "purely objective," as the totality, not as a "part," must be included in the science of psychology; and that furthermore this treatment of self-consciousness is necessary for the explanation and comprehension of any partial fact of conscious experience. And finally, it was pointed out that the denial of self-consciousness as constituting matter of experience, and hence of psychology, was the denial of the possibility of philosophy itself; and this was illustrated by historic examples. Before passing on to the second topic, I wish briefly to return to Professor Caird's exposition, and shelter myself somewhat beneath the wings of his authority. In the article already referred to, he goes on to state that the natural objective science of man after all "omits the distinctive characteristic of man's being"; that while we may treat inorganic nature and even organic with purely natural objective methods and principles, because "they are not unities for *themselves,* but only *for us,*" such treatment cannot be applied to man, for man *is for himself, i.e.,* is not a pure object, but is self-consciousness. Thus, he continues:

> In man, in so far as he is self-conscious—*and it is self-consciousness that makes him man*—the unity through which all things are and are known is manifested. . . . Therefore to treat him as a simply natural being is *even more inaccurate and misleading* than to forget or deny his relation to nature altogether. A true psychology must avoid both errors: it must conceive man as at once spiritual and natural; it must find a reconciliation of freedom and necessity. It must face *all the difficulties involved in the conception of the absolute principle of self-consciousness*—through which all things are and are known—*as manifesting itself in the life of a being like man,* who "comes to himself" only by a long process of development out of the unconsciousness of a merely animal existence.

When it is stated, later on, that the natural science of man "is necessarily abstract and imperfect, as it omits from its view the central fact in the life of the object of which it treats," it is hardly worth while discussing whether there be any such science or not. But there is suggested for us in the quotation just made our second problem—the final relation of psychology, which confessedly must deal with self-consciousness, to philosophy. For there the problem of psychology was stated to be the question of the "absolute principle of self-consciousness, manifesting itself in the life of a being like man." That is, it is here suggested that psychology does not deal with the absolute principle in itself, but only with the modes by which this is manifested or realized in the life of man. Psychology no longer appears as an objective science; it now comes before us as a phenomenology, presupposing a science of the absolute reality itself. It is to this question that I now turn. Is psychology the science *merely* of the manifestation of the Absolute, or is it the science of the Absolute itself?

II

The relation of Psychology to Philosophy now stands, I suppose, something like this: There is an absolute self-consciousness. The science of this is philosophy. This absolute self-consciousness manifests itself in the knowing and acting of individual men. The science of this manifestation, a phenomenology, is psychology. The distinction is no longer concerned with man's being itself; it is a distinction of treatment, of ways of looking at the same material. Before going to its positive consideration the following questions may suggest the result we desire to reach. How does there come about this distinction between the "spiritual" and the "natural," between "freedom" and "necessity"? How does there come into our knowledge the notion of a distinction between the "absolute principle of self-consciousness" and "man coming to himself only by a long process of development out of the unconsciousness of a merely animal existence"? Is this a distinction which falls outside the subject matter of psychology, and which may therefore be used to determine it; or is it one which has originated *within* psychological experience, and whose nature therefore, instead of being capable of fixing the character of psychology, must itself be determined *by* psychology? Furthermore, what *is* this distinction between the absolute self-consciousness and its manifestation in a being like man? Is the absolute self-consciousness complete in itself, or does it involve this realization and manifestation in a being like man? If it is complete in itself, how can any philosophy which is limited to "this absolute principle of self-consciousness" face and solve the difficulties involved in its going beyond itself to manifest itself in self-consciousness? This cannot be what is meant. The absolute self-consciousness must involve within itself, as organic member of its very being and activity, this manifestation and revelation. Its being must be this realization and manifestation. Granted that this realization and manifestation is an act not occurring in time, but eternally completed in the nature of the Absolute, and that it occurs only "partially" and "interruptedly" *through* (not *in*) time, in a being like man—the fact none the less remains that philosophy, under any theory of its nature, can deal with this absolute self-consciousness only so far as it has partially and interruptedly realized itself in man. For man, as object of his philosophy, this Absolute has existence only so far as it has manifested itself in his conscious experience. To return to our questions: If the material of philosophy be the absolute self-consciousness, and this absolute self-consciousness *is* the realization and manifestation of itself, and as material for philosophy exists only in so far as it has realized and manifested itself in man's conscious experience, and if psychology be the science of this realization in man, what else can philosophy in its fullness be but psychology, and psychology but philosophy?

These questions are stated only to suggest the end which we shall endeavor to reach. I shall not attempt to answer them directly, but to consider first the relations of Psychology to Science, and hence to Philosophy; and secondly to Logic.

(1) *The Relation of Psychology to Science.* Psychology is the completed method of philosophy, because in it science and philosophy, fact and reason, are one. Philosophy seems to stand in a double relation to Science. In its first aspect it is *a* science—the highest of all sciences. We take one sphere of reality and ask certain questions regarding it, and the answers give us some one science; we find in the process that this sphere of reality can only artificially be thus isolated, and we broaden and deepen our question, until finally, led by the organic connection of science with science, we ask after the nature of all reality, as one connected system. The answer to this question constitutes philosophy as one science amid the circle of sciences. But to continue to regard it in this way is to fail to grasp the meaning of the process which has forced us into philosophy. At the same time that philosophy is seen as the completion of the sciences, it is seen as their basis. It is no longer *a* science; it is Science. That is to say, the same movement of thought and reality which forces upon us the conception of a science which shall deal with the totality of reality forces us to recognize that no one of our previous sciences was in strict truth science. Each abstracted from certain larger aspects of reality, and was hence hypothetical. Its truth was conditioned upon the truth of its relations to that whole which that science, as special science, could not investigate without giving up its own independent existence. Only in this whole is categorical truth to be found, and only as categorical truth is found in this whole is the basis found for the special sciences. Philosophy as the science of this whole appears no longer therefore as *a* science, but as all science taken in its organic systematic wholeness—not merely to which every so-called special science is something subordinate, but of which it constitutes an organic member. Philosophy has no existence except as the organic living unity and bond of these sciences; they have no existence except through their position in this living synthesis.

Now the question is, where does psychology stand within this organism? On the one hand, psychology is certainly a positive science. It finds its materials in certain facts and events. As to systematic observation, experiment, conclusion and verification, it can differ in no essential way from any one of them. It is based upon and deals with fact, and aims at the ordered comprehension and explanation of fact as any special science does. Yet the whole drift of this paper has been to show that in some way psychology does differ very essentially from any one of them. Where shall we find this difference? In one word, its relation to them is precisely that which we have discovered philosophy to bear: it is not only *a* science, but it turns out to be science as an organic system, in which every special science has its life, and from which it must abstract when it sets up for an independent existence of its own. We begin with any special science. That turns out to be not only some one department or sphere of reality, but also some one department of conscious experience. From one science to another we go, asking for some explanation of conscious experience, until we come to psychology, which gives us an account of it, in its own behalf, as neither mathematics, nor physics, nor biology does. So far we have only *a* special science, though the highest and most concrete of all. But the very process that has made necessary this new science reveals also that each of the former sciences existed only in abstraction from it. Each dealt with some one phase of conscious experience, and for that very reason could not deal with the totality which gave it its being, consciousness. But in psychology we have the manifestation and explication of this consciousness. It gives in its wholeness what each of them would give in part, *viz.,* the nature of experience, and hence is related to them as the whole is to the part. It appears no longer, therefore, as the highest *of* sciences: it appears as Science itself, that is, as systematic account and comprehension of the nature of conscious experience. Mathematics, physics, biology, exist, because conscious experience reveals itself to be of such a nature, that one may make virtual abstraction from the whole, and consider a part by itself, without damage, so long as the treatment is purely scientific, that is, so long as the implicit connection with the whole is left undisturbed, and the attempt is not made to present this partial science as metaphysic, or as an explanation of the whole, as is the usual fashion of our uncritical so-called "scientific philosophies." Nay more, this abstraction of some one sphere is itself a living function of the psychologic experience. It is not merely something which it allows: it is something which it *does*. It is the analytic aspect of its own activity, whereby it deepens and renders explicit, realizes its own nature; just as their connection with each other is the synthetic aspect of the same self-realizing movement, whereby it returns to itself: while psychology in its completeness is the whole self-developing activity itself, which shows itself as the organic unity of both synthetic and analytic movements, and thus the condition of their possibility and ground of their validity. The analytic movement constitutes the special sciences; the synthetic constitutes the philosophy of nature; the self-developing activity itself, as psychology, constitutes philosophy.

What other position can be given psychology, so soon as we recognize the absurdity and impossibility of considering it a purely objective science? It is the science of the modes by which, in and through the individual, the universe is realized, it is said. But that the universe has no existence except as absolutely realized in an individual, *i.e.*, except as self-consciousness, is precisely the result of philosophy, and can therefore be no objection to such a consideration of the universe: in fact, such a statement only amounts to saying that psychology considers the universe as it really is. If the assertion is varied again, to read that philosophy treats of this individualized universe as it eternally *is*, while psychology can treat of it only as it partially and interruptedly *becomes*, this loses sight of two very important facts. First, philosophy can treat of absolute self-consciousness only in so far as it *has become* in a being like man, for otherwise it is not material for philosophy at all; and, secondly, it falls into the error of regarding this realization in man as a time-conditioned product, which it is not. Time is not something outside of the process of conscious experience; it is a form within it, one of the functions by which it organically constitutes its own being. In fact, psychology as philosophic method has an immense advantage at just this point over any other method of treating this problem. To any philosophy attempting to consider the absolute self-consciousness by itself, it must remain forever an insoluble problem why the *is* should ever appear as *becoming*, why the eternal should ever appear through the temporal. Psychology solves the problem by avoiding the assumption which makes it a problem. For, dealing with an individualized universe, one of whose functions of realization *is* time, it knows nothing about any consciousness which is out of relation to time. The case is just here: if philosophy will deal with the absolute consciousness conceived as purely eternal, out of relation to time, then the existence of that which constitutes the actual content of man's experience is utterly inexplicable; it is not only a mystery, but a mystery which contradicts the very nature of that which is, *ex hypothesi*, the absolute. If philosophy does deal with the eternal absolute consciousness as forever realized, yet as forever having time as one of its organic functions, it is not open to anyone to bring charges against psychology as philosophy, for this and no more psychology does.

The question just comes to this: If we start from reason alone we shall never reach fact. If we start with fact, we shall find it revealing itself as reason. The objection to an account of fact or experience as philosophy is but a prejudice, though historically considered a well-grounded one. On the one hand, it has arisen because some partial account of experience, or rather account of partial experience, has been put forth as the totality, and just because thus put forth as absolute, has lost even the relative validity which it possessed as partial. Such is the procedure of Empiricism. On the other hand, we have had put forth as matter of fact certain truths declared to be immediate and necessary and intuitive, coming no one knows whence and meaning no one knows what. The aversion to immediacy, to "undeduced" fact, as given us by the Intuitionalists, is certainly a well-grounded one. But neither of these objections lies against psychology as account of the facts of experience. Men are mortal, and every actual account of experience will suffer from the defects of mortals, and be but partial, no doubt; unfortunately we are none of us omniscient yet. But the very essence of psychology as method is that it treats of experience in its absolute totality, not setting up some one aspect of it to account for the whole, as, for example, our physical evolutionists do, nor yet attempting to determine its nature from something outside of and beyond itself, as, for example, our so-called empirical psychologists have done. The vice of the procedure of both is at bottom precisely the same—the abstracting of some one element from the organism which gives it meaning, and setting it up as absolute. It is no wonder that the organism always has its revenge by pronouncing this abstracted element "unknowable." The only wonder is that men should still bow in spirit before this creation of their own abstracting thought, and reverence it as the cause and ground of all reality and knowledge. There is indeed an anthropomorphism which is degrading, but it is the anthropormorphism which sets up the feeblest element of its own thinking, pure being, as Mr. Spencer does, or the poorest element of its own feeling, a sensation, and reverences that as its own and the universe's cause. That is the anthropomorphism of the enslaved thought which has not yet awakened to the consciousness of its own totality and spiritual freedom.

Now does the account of fact given by psychology have anything in common with the "ultimate, inexplicable, necessary" mental facts called intuitions. The fact of psychology reveals itself as precisely reason, which thereby accounts for itself, and in accounting for itself accounts for all its members. The fact of psychology is not isolated "truths," but the organic system of self-consciousness. This fact is indeed "immediate," but it is immediate only in and through a process, hence of mediation. It is indeed self-evidencing, but what it evidences is simply, of the parts, relation to and dependence upon the whole, and of the whole, that it is self-conditioned and self-related. Of the whole fact it may be said indeed that it is inexplicable. "It is true that we cannot explain the spiritual principle which is implied in all experience by reference to anything else than itself.''[2] "Because all we can experience is included in this one world, and all our inferences and explanations relate only to its details, neither it as a whole, nor the one consciousness which constitutes it, can be accounted for in the ordinary sense of the word. They cannot be accounted for by what they include; and being all-inclusive, there remains nothing else by which they can be accounted for.''[3] In short, any system of philosophy must ultimately fall back on the fact for which no reason can be given except precisely just that it is what it is. This implication of fact[4] is latent in all philosophy whatever, and all that psychology as philosophic method does is to render this necessary implication explicit. It alone starts from the completed fact, and it alone is therefore completed philosophy.

If it may have seemed at times in the course of the discussion that the nominal subject—the relation of psychology to science—had been left, it will now appear, I think, that we have all the time been dealing with just that subject. Science is the systematic account, or *reason* of *fact;* Psychology is the completed systematic account of the ultimate fact, which, as fact, reveals itself as reason, and hence accounts for itself, and gives the "reasons" of all sciences. The other point, the relation of psychology to logic, has already been dealt with by implication, and need not detain us long again.

(2) *The Relation of Psychology to Logic.* The whole course of philosophic thought, so far as the writer can comprehend it, has consisted in showing that any distinction between the form and the matter of philosophic truth, between the content and the method, is fatal to the reaching of truth. Self-consciousness is the final truth, and in self-consciousness the form as organic system and the content as organized system are exactly equal to each other. It is a process which, as form, has produced itself as matter. Psychology as the account of this self-consciousness must necessarily fulfill all the conditions of true method. Logic, since it necessarily abstracts from the ultimate fact, cannot reach in matter what it points to in form. While its content, if it be true philosophy, must be the whole content of self-consciousness or spirit, its form is only one process within this content, that of thought-conditions, the *Idee.* While the content is the eternal nature of the universe, its form

---

[2] Professor E. Caird, *Mind*, viii, 560.

[3] Green, *Prolegomena to Ethics*, p. 52.

[4] The insistence upon this seems to have been Lotze's great work as a philosopher.

is adequate only to "thinking what God thought and was before the creation of the world," that is, the universe in its unreality, in its abstraction. It is this contradiction between content and form in logic which makes it not philosophic method, but only one moment within that method. No contradiction results as soon as logic is given its proper place *within* the system. The contradiction occurs when, at the same moment that it is said that logic is "abstract," the logical method is still said to be the method of philosophy.

Such contradictions certainly appear to exist, for example, in the philosophy of Hegel. They have been often pointed out, and I shall only summarize them, following for the most part a recent writer.[5] There is no way of getting from logic to the philosophy of nature *logically*. The only way is to fall back upon the fact; "we know from experience" that we have nature as well as the *Idee*. In truth we do not go from logic to nature at all. The movement is a reverse movement. "In reality, the necessity for any such transition is purely factitious, because *the notions never existed otherwise than in nature and spirit*. . . . They were got by abstraction from the concrete. . . . We owe, therefore, no apology for a return to the reality from which we took them." In short, it is necessity of fact, a necessity of conscious experience, which takes us from the realm of the *Idee* to the realm of nature, from the sphere of thought-conditions to the sphere of existent relations. "The same is true when we pass to the philosophy of spirit. The general *form* of personality is deducible, but not a living human spirit with its individual thoughts, feelings and actions." This remains "the incomprehensible and inexplicable point in philosophy." And so it does undoubtedly while we regard logic as method of philosophy. But this "inexplicability" is but the express condemnation of the method, not a fact to be contented with. If we go deeper and inquire not how is the transition from logic to the philosophy of nature or to the philosophy of spirit made, but how is any transition whatever possible, we find the same difficulty. It exists only by reason of the presupposed fact. "We cannot in strictness say that the result has been independently proved, because it has been reached in this fashion by the method. It was presupposed *in* the method all along." In a definite case, how is the transition, say from the category of quality to that of quantity, made? It occurs not by virtue of the category of quality in itself, but by virtue of the fact that the whole *Idee* is implicitly contained in the principle of quality, and must manifest itself, which it does by forcing quality, as an inadequate expression of its own

[5] Professor A. Seth, "Hegel: an Exposition and Criticism," *Mind*, 24.

nature, into quantity, which expresses its being more fully. And thus the process continues until the *Idee* has manifested itself as the whole organic system, which has expressed explicitly all that which in *Idee* it is. But this movement itself depends on spirit, and on the manifestation of spirit in nature, as already seen. Every purely logical transition therefore occurs at bottom because of fact, *i.e.*, seen in its wholeness it is not a logical transition but a factual. Psychology, as philosophic method, merely starts from this everywhere presupposed fact, and by so doing, for the first time, gives logic its basis and validity.

There can be no escape from this result by saying that after all in the philosophy of spirit, spirit is shown to be the *prius* and condition of the whole, as it undoubtedly is· by Hegel himself. This merely brings the contradiction itself into clearer light. For logic, being thus confessedly determined as abstract, is still retained to determine the nature of the concrete. Logic, while it is thus declared to be only one moment of spirit, is still used to determine the nature of the whole. Thus is revealed the contradiction between form and content involved in the use of logic as the method of philosophy. Spirit is reached by a *logical* process, and the *logical* result is that as fact it is not reached at all. As concrete, it is beyond the reach of any abstract process. Either one must call in the aid of the presupposed but suppressed Fact, and recognize that after all the process has been going on within a further and higher determination; or, failing to see this, must recognize Spirit as only one factor or moment of the logical movement, that is, give up the notion of self-consciousness as subject, and fall back into Spinozistic pantheism. The logical movement, considered by itself, is always balancing in unstable equilibrium between dualism and pantheism. Set up as absolute method, it either recognizes the fact, but being unable to comprehend it, has to regard this fact, as foreign element over against it, as the matter of Plato and Aristotle, the thing-in-itself of Kant, and *Anstoss* of Fichte,[6] or endeavors to absorb the Fact as a mere element in its own logical being, and falls into Pantheism.

This is the reason why Hegel, although the very center of his system is self-conditioned spirit, lends himself so easily to pantheistic treatment. Logic cannot reach, however much it may point to, an actual individual. The gathering up of the universe into the one self-conscious individuality it may assert as *necessary*, it cannot give it as *reality*. It is only as logic contradicts itself and faces back on the constant presup-

---

[6] The inability to go from the "because" of reason to the "cause" of fact, from logic to reality, when logic is not taken simply as one movement *within* reality, is clearly set forth in the closing chapters of Mr. Bradley's *Principles of Logic*.

position of this reality that it can demonstrate what it asserts. Taken purely by itself it must issue in a pantheism where the only real is the *Idee*, and where all its factors and moments, including spirit and nature, are real only at different stages or phases of the *Idee*, but vanish as imperfect ways of looking at things, or as illusions, when we reach the *Idee*. And thus the *Idee* itself vanishes, as an organic system, as a unity which lives through its distinctions, and becomes a dead identity, in no way distinguishable from the substance of Spinoza. Logic set up as absolute method reveals its self-contradiction by destroying itself. In a purely logical method the distinctions, the process, must disappear in the final unity, the product. Only a living actual Fact can preserve within its unity that organic system of differences in virtue of which it lives and moves and has its being. It is with this fact, conscious experience in its entirety, that psychology as method begins. It thus brings to clear light of day the presupposition implicit in every philosophy, and thereby affords logic, as well as the philosophy of nature, its basis, ideal and surety. If we have determined the nature of reality, by a process whose content equals its form, we can show the meaning, worth and limits of any one moment of this reality.

The conclusion of the whole matter is that a "being like man," since self-conscious, is an individualized universe, and hence that his nature is the proper material of philosophy, and in its wholeness the only material. Psychology is the science of this nature, and no dualism in it, or in ways of regarding it, is tenable. Whatever the dualism may be, it is only relative, and one which occurs within, not without, psychological experience. Psychology, as the complete systematic account of man, at the same time shows the value and meaning, and affords the condition, of the special sciences, the philosophy of nature and of logic. Or, in a word, if the reality of spirit be the presupposition, the *prius* and the goal, the condition and the end of all reality, the science of spirit must occupy a corresponding position with relation to all science. Surely then, as the Editor of *Mind* formerly urged, "the method of psychological approach is not philosophically valueless," and we have "ground for the belief that it has only to be more systematically followed out for the attaining of as great results as have been claimed for another way, while in this way the results are more likely to secure general acceptance"[7] because, we may add, it simply expresses in a scientific way that which lies at the basis of all that has been otherwise secured.

[7] "Psychology and Philosophy," *Mind*, Vol. viii, 20.

# 9. The Reflex Arc Concept in Psychology*

This article, with some changes, was reprinted by Dewey in *Philosophy and Civilization* (1930), under the new title of "The Unit of Behavior." We reprint the earlier version as an indication of Dewey's thought in the 1890's, although the use of the word "behavior" in the second edition is instructive, for it is precisely Dewey's awareness of the behavioral dimensions in psychology that characterizes "The Reflex Arc Conception in Psychology" and differentiates it sharply from his earlier psychological writings.

Without doubt, the decisive factor in enabling Dewey to break with the language of Kant in his consideration of psychology was the publication in 1890 of William James' *Principles of Psychology*. In "The Development of American Pragmatism," Dewey wrote that the *Principles* enabled him to criticize Locke and Hume, as well as Kant and the neo-Kantians.

As for the essay itself, regarded by Gordon W. Allport as "the most important psychological paper of the nineties" (Schilpp, p. 269), it is Dewey's effort to criticize the reflex arc concept as being inadequate as a principle of behavioral unity with regard to sensory stimulus and motor responses.

That the greater demand for a unifying principle and controlling working hypothesis in psychology should come at just the time when all generalizations and classifications are most questioned and questionable is natural enough. It is the very cumulation of discrete facts creating the demand for unification that also breaks down previous lines of classification. The material is too great in mass and too varied in style to fit into existing pigeonholes, and the cabinets of science break of their own dead weight. The idea of the reflex arc has upon the whole come nearer to meeting this demand for a general working hypothesis than any other single concept. It being admitted that the sensorimotor apparatus represents both the unit of nerve structure and the type of nerve function, the image of this relationship passed over into psychology, and became an organizing principle to hold together the multiplicity of fact.

In criticizing this conception it is not intended to make a plea for the

* From *Psychological Review*, III (July, 1896), pp. 357-70.

principles of explanation and classification which the reflex arc idea has replaced; but, on the contrary, to urge that they are not sufficiently displaced, and that in the idea of the sensorimotor circuit, conceptions of the nature of sensation and of action derived from the nominally displaced psychology are still in control.

The older dualism between sensation and idea is repeated in the current dualism of peripheral and central structures and functions; the older dualism of body and soul finds a distinct echo in the current dualism of stimulus and response. Instead of interpreting the character of sensation, idea and action from their place and function in the sensorimotor circuit, we still incline to interpret the latter from our preconceived and preformulated ideas of rigid distinctions between sensations, thoughts and acts. The sensory stimulus is one thing, the central activity, standing for the idea, is another thing, and the motor discharge, standing for the act proper, is a third. As a result, the reflex arc is not a comprehensive, or organic, unity, but a patchwork of disjointed parts, a mechanical conjunction of unallied processes. What is needed is that the principle underlying the idea of the reflex arc as the fundamental psychical unity shall react into and determine the values of its constitutive factors. More specifically, what is wanted is that sensory stimulus, central connections and motor responses shall be viewed, not as separate and complete entities in themselves, but as divisions of labor, functioning factors, within the single concrete whole, now designated the reflex arc.

What is the reality so designated? What shall we term that which is not sensation-followed-by-idea-followed-by-movement, but which is primary; which is, as it were, the psychical organism of which sensation, idea and movement are the chief organs? Stated on the physiological side, this reality may most conveniently be termed co-ordination. This is the essence of the facts held together by and subsumed under the reflex arc concept. Let us take, for our example, the familiar child-candle instance. The ordinary interpretation would say the sensation of light is a stimulus to the grasping as a response, the burn resulting is a stimulus to withdrawing the hand as response and so on. There is, of course, no doubt that is a rough practical way of representing the process. But when we ask for its psychological adequacy, the case is quite different. Upon analysis, we find that we begin not with a sensory stimulus, but with a sensorimotor co-ordination, the optical-ocular, and that in a certain sense it is the movement which is primary, and the sensation which is secondary, the movement of body, head and eye muscles determining the quality of what is experienced. In other words, the real beginning is with the act of seeing; it is looking, and not a sensation of light. The sensory quale gives the value of the act, just as the movement furnishes its mechanism and control, but both sensation and movement lie inside, not outside, the act.

Now if this act, the seeing, stimulates another act, the reaching, it is because both of these acts fall within a larger co-ordination; because seeing and grasping have been so often bound together to reinforce each other, to help each other out, that each may be considered practically a subordinate member of a bigger co-ordination. More specifically, the ability of the hand to do its work will depend, either directly or indirectly, upon its control, as well as its stimulation, by the act of vision. If the sight did not inhibit as well as excite the reaching, the latter would be purely indeterminate, it would be for anything or nothing, not for the particular object seen. The reaching, in turn, must both stimulate and control the seeing. The eye must be kept upon the candle if the arm is to do its work; let it wander and the arm takes up another task. In other words, we now have an enlarged and transformed co-ordination; the act is seeing no less than before, but it is now seeing-for-reaching purposes. There is still a sensorimotor circuit, one with more content or value, not a substitution of a motor response for a sensory stimulus.

Now take the affairs at its next state, that in which the child gets burned. It is hardly necessary to point out again that this is also a sensorimotor co-ordination and not a mere sensation. It is worth while, however, to note especially the fact that it is simply the completion, or fulfilment, of the previous eye-arm-hand co-ordination and not an entirely new occurrence. Only because the heat-pain quale enters into the same circuit of experience with the optical-ocular and muscular quales, does the child learn from the experience and get the ability to avoid the experience in the future.

More technically stated, the so-called response is not merely *to* the stimulus; it is *into* it. The burn is the original seeing, the original optical-ocular experience enlarged and transformed in its value. It is no longer mere seeing; it is seeing-of-a-light-that-means-pain-when-contact-occurs. The ordinary reflex arc theory proceeds upon the more or less tacit assumption that the outcome of the response is a totally new experience; that it is, say, the substitution of a burn sensation for a light sensation through the intervention of motion. The fact is that the sole meaning of the intervening movement is to maintain, reinforce or transform (as the case may be) the original quale; that we do not have the replacing of one sort of experience by another, but the development or (as it seems convenient to term it) the mediation of an experience.

The seeing, in a word, remains to control the reaching, and is, in turn, interpreted by the burning.[1]

The discussion up to this point may be summarized by saying that the reflex arc idea, as commonly employed, is defective in that it assumes sensory stimulus and motor response as distinct psychical existences, while in reality they are always inside a co-ordination and have their significance purely from the part played in maintaining or reconstituting the co-ordination; and (secondly) in assuming that the quale of experience which precedes the "motor" phase and that which succeeds it are two different states, instead of the last being always the first reconstituted, the motor phase coming in only for the sake of such mediation. The result is that the reflex arc idea leaves us with a disjointed psychology, whether viewed from the standpoint of development in the individual or in the race, or from that of the analysis of the mature consciousness. As to the former, in its failure to see that the arc of which it talks is virtually a circuit, a continual reconstitution, it breaks continuity and leaves us nothing but a series of jerks, the origin of each jerk to be sought outside the process of experience itself, in either an external pressure of "environment," or else in an unaccountable spontaneous variation from within the "soul" or the "organism."[2] As to the latter, failing to see the unity of activity, no matter how much it may prate of unity, it still leaves us with sensation or peripheral stimulus; idea, or central process (the equivalent of attention); and motor response, or act, as three disconnected existences, having to be somehow adjusted to each other, whether through the intervention of an extra-experimental soul, or by mechanical push and pull.

Before proceeding to a consideration of the general meaning for psychology of the summary, it may be well to give another descriptive analysis, as the value of the statement depends entirely upon the universality of its range of application. For such an instance we may conveniently take Baldwin's analysis of the reactive consciousness. In this there are, he says, "three elements corresponding to the three elements of the nervous arc. First, the receiving consciousness, the stimulus—say

[1] See, for a further statement of mediation, my *Syllabus of Ethics*, p. 15.

[2] It is not too much to say that the whole controversy in biology regarding the source of variation, represented by Weismann and Spencer respectively, arises from beginning with stimulus or response instead of with the co-ordination with reference to which stimulus or response are functional divisions of labor. The same may be said, on the psychological side, of the controversy between the Wundtian "apperceptionists" and their opponents. Each has a *disjectum membrum* of the same organic whole, whichever is selected being an arbitrary matter of personal taste.

a loud, unexpected sound; second, the attention involuntarily drawn, the registering element; and, third, the muscular reaction following upon the sound—say flight from fancied danger.'' Now, in the first place, such an analysis is incomplete; it ignores the status prior to hearing the sound. Of course, if this status is irrelevant to what happens afterwards, such ignoring is quite legitimate. But is it irrelevant either to the quantity or the quality of the stimulus?

If one is reading a book, if one is hunting, if one is watching in a dark place on a lonely night, if one is performing a chemical experiment; in each case, the noise has a very different psychical value; it is a different experience. In any case, what proceeds the "stimulus" is a whole act, a sensorimotor co-ordination. What is more to the point, the "stimulus" emerges out of this co-ordination; it is born from it as its matrix; it represents as it were an escape from it. I might here fall back upon authority, and refer to the widely accepted sensation continuum theory, according to which the sound cannot be absolutely *ex abrupto* from the outside, but is simply a shifting of focus of emphasis, a redistribution of tensions within the former act; and declare that unless the sound activity had been present to some extent in the prior co-ordination, it would be impossible for it now to come to prominence in consciousness. And such a reference would be only an amplification of what has already been said concerning the way in which the prior activity influences the value of the sound sensation. Or, we might point to cases of hypnotism, mono-ideism and absent-mindedness, like that of Archimedes, as evidences that if the previous co-ordination is such as rigidly to lock the door, the auditory disturbance will knock in vain for admission to consciousness. Or, to speak more truly in the metaphor, the auditory activity must already have one foot over the threshold, if it is ever to gain admittance.

But it will be more satisfactory, probably, to refer to the biological side of the case, and point out that as the ear activity has been evolved on account of the advantage gained by the whole organism, it must stand in the strictest histological and physiological connection with the eye, or hand, or leg, or whatever other organ has been the overt center of action. It is absolutely impossible to think of the eye center as monopolizing consciousness and the ear apparatus as wholly quiescent. What happens is a certain relative prominence and subsidence as between the various organs which maintain the organic equilibrium.

Furthermore, the sound is not a mere stimulus, or mere sensation; it again is an act, that of hearing. The muscular response is involved in this as well as sensory stimulus; that is, there is a certain definite set of

the motor apparatus involved in hearing just as much as there is in subsequent running away. The movement and posture of the head, the tension of the ear muscles, are required for the "reception" of the sound. It
is just as true to say that the sensation of sound arises from a motor
response as that the running away is a response to the sound. This may
be brought out by reference to the fact that Professor Baldwin, in the
passage quoted, has inverted the real order as between his first and second elements. We do not have first a sound and then activity of attention, unless sound is taken as mere nervous shock or physical event, not
as conscious value. The conscious sensation of sound depends upon the
motor response having already taken place; or, in terms of the previous
statement (if stimulus is used as a conscious fact, and not as a mere
physical event) it is the motor response or attention which constitutes
that which finally becomes the stimulus to another act. Once more, the
final "element," the running away, is not merely motor, but is sensorimotor, having its sensory value and its muscular mechanism. It is also a co-ordination. And, finally, this sensorimotor co-ordination is not a
new act, supervening upon what preceded. Just as the "response" is
necessary to constitute the stimulus, to determine it as sound and as this
kind of sound, of wild beast or robber, so the sound experience must
persist as a value in the running, to keep it up, to control it. The motor
reaction involved in the running is, once more, into, not merely to, the
sound. It occurs to change the sound, to get rid of it. The resulting
quale, whatever it may be, has its meaning wholly determined by
reference to the hearing of the sound. It is that experience mediated.[3]
What we have is a circuit; not an arc or broken segment of a circle. This
circuit is more truly termed organic than reflex, because the motor
response determines the stimulus, just as truly as sensory stimulus
determines movement. Indeed, the movement is only for the sake of
determining the stimulus, of fixing what kind of a stimulus it is, of interpreting it.

I hope it will not appear that I am introducing needless refinements
and distinctions into what, it may be urged, is after all an undoubted

---

[3] In other words, every reaction is of the same type as that which Professor
Baldwin ascribes to imitation alone, *viz.*, circular. Imitation is simply that particular form of the circuit in which the "response" lends itself to comparatively
unchanged maintenance of the prior experience. I say comparatively unchanged,
for as far as this maintenance means additional control over the experience, it is
being psychically changed, becoming more distinct. It is safe to suppose,
moreover, that the "repetition" is kept up only so long as this growth or mediation
goes on. There is the new-in-the-old, if it is only the new sense of power.

fact, that movement as response follows sensation as stimulus. It is not a question of making the account of the process more complicated, though it is always wise to beware of that false simplicity which is reached by leaving out of account a large part of the problem. It is a question of finding out what stimulus or sensation, what movement and response mean; a question of seeing that they mean distinctions of flexible function only, not of fixed existence; that one and the same occurrence plays either or both parts, according to the shift of interest; and that because of this functional distinction and relationship, the supposed problem of the adjustment of one to the other, whether by superior force in the stimulus or an agency *ad hoc* in the center or the soul, is a purely self-created problem.

We may see the disjointed character of the present theory, by calling to mind that it is impossible to apply the phrase "sensorimotor" to the occurrence as a simple phrase of description; it has validity only as a term of interpretation, only, that is, as defining various functions exercised. In terms of description, the whole process may be sensory or it may be motor, but it cannot be sensorimotor. The "stimulus," the excitation of the nerve ending and of the sensory nerve, the central change, are just as much, or just as little, motion as the events taking place in the motor nerve and the muscles. It is one uninterrupted, continuous redistribution of mass in motion. And there is nothing in the process, from the standpoint of description, which entitles us to call this reflex. It is redistribution pure and simple; as much so as the burning of a log, or the falling of a house or the movement of the wind. In the physical process, as physical, there is nothing which can be set off as stimulus, nothing which reacts, nothing which is response. There is just a change in the system of tensions.

The same sort of thing is true when we describe the process purely from the psychical side. It is now all sensation, all sensory quale; the motion, as psychically described, is just as much sensation as is sound or light or burn. Take the withdrawing of the hand from the candle flame as example. What we have is a certain visual-heat-pain-muscular-quale, transformed into another visual-touch-muscular-quale—the flame now being visible only at a distance, or not at all, the touch sensation being altered, etc. If we symbolize the original visual quale by v, the temperature by h, the accompanying muscular sensation by m, the whole experience may be stated as vhm-vh$m$-$vhm'$; $m$ being the quale of withdrawing, $m'$ the sense of the status after the withdrawal. The motion is not a certain kind of existence; it is a sort of sensory experience interpreted, just as is candle flame, or burn from candle flame. All are on a par.

But, in spite of all this, it will be urged, there is a distinction between stimulus and response, between sensation and motion. Precisely; but we ought now to be in a condition to ask of what nature is the distinction, instead of taking it for granted as a distinction somehow lying in the existence of the facts themselves. We ought to be able to see that the ordinary conception of the reflex arc theory, instead of being a case of plain science, is a survival of the metaphysical dualism, first formulated by Plato, according to which the sensation is an ambiguous dweller on the borderland of soul and body, the idea (or central process) is purely psychical, and the act (or movement) purely physical. Thus the reflex arc formulation is neither physical (or physiological) nor psychological; it is a mixed materialistic-spiritualistic assumption.

If the previous descriptive analysis has made obvious the need of a reconsideration of the reflex arc idea, of the nest of difficulties and assumptions in the apparently simple statement, it is now time to undertake an explanatory analysis. The fact is that stimulus and response are not distinctions of existence, but teleological distinctions, that is, distinctions of function, or part played, with reference to reaching or maintaining an end. With respect to this teleological process, two stages should be discriminated, as their confusion is one cause of the confusion attending the whole matter. In one case, the relation represents an organization of means with reference to a comprehensive end. It represents an accomplished adaptation. Such is the case in all well developed instincts, as when we say that the contact of eggs is a stimulus to the hen to set; or the sight of corn a stimulus to pick; such also is the case with all thoroughly formed habits, as when the contact with the floor stimulates walking. In these instances there is no question of consciousness of stimulus as stimulus, of response as response. There is simply a continuously ordered sequence of acts, all adapted in themselves and in the order of their sequence, to reach a certain objective end, the reproduction of the species, the preservation of life, locomotion to a certain place. The end has got thoroughly organized into the means. In calling one stimulus, another response, we mean nothing more than that such an orderly sequence of acts is taking place. The same sort of statement might be made equally well with reference to the succession of changes in a plant, so far as these are considered with reference to their adaptation to, say, producing seed. It is equally applicable to the series of events in the circulation of the blood, or the sequence of acts occurring in a self-binding reaper.[4]

Regarding such cases of organization viewed as already attained, we may say, positively, that it is only the assumed common reference to an inclusive end which marks each member off as stimulus and response, that apart from such reference we have only antecedent and consequent;[5] in other words, the distinction is one of interpretation. Negatively, it must be pointed out that it is not legitimate to carry over, without change, exactly the same order of considerations to cases where it is a question of *conscious* stimulation and response. We may, in the above case, regard, if we please, stimulus and response each as an entire act, having an individuality of its own, subject even here to the qualification that individuality means not an entirely independent whole, but a division of labor as regards maintaining or reaching an end. But in any case, it is an act, a sensorimotor co-ordination, which stimulates the response, itself in turn sensorimotor, not a sensation which stimulates a movement. Hence the illegitimacy of identifying, as is so often done, such cases of organized instincts or habits with the so-called reflex arc, or of transferring, without modification, considerations valid of this serial co-ordination of acts to the sensation-movement case.

The fallacy that arises when this is done is virtually the psychological or historical fallacy. A set of considerations which hold good only because of a completed process, is read into the content of the process which conditions this completed result. A state of things characterizing an outcome is regarded as a true description of the events which led up to this outcome; when, as a matter of fact, if this outcome had already been in existence, there would have been no necessity for the process. Or, to make the application to the case in hand, considerations valid of an attained organization or co-ordination, the orderly sequence of minor acts in a comprehensive co-ordination, are used to describe a process, *viz.*, the distinction of mere sensation as stimulus and of mere

---

[4] To avoid misapprehension, I would say that I am not raising the question as to how far this teleology is real in any one of these cases; real or unreal, my point holds equally well. It is only when we regard the sequence of acts *as if* they were adapted to reach some end that it occurs to us to speak of one as stimulus and the other as response. Otherwise, we look at them as a *mere* series.

[5] Whether, even in such a determination, there is still not a reference of a more latent kind to an end is, of course, left open.

movement as response, which takes place only because such an attained organization is no longer at hand, but is in process of constitution. Neither mere sensation, nor mere movement, can ever be either stimulus or response; only an act can be that; the *sensation* as stimulus means the lack of and search for such an objective stimulus, or orderly placing of an act; just as mere movement as response means the lack of and search for the right act to complete a given co-ordination.

A recurrence to our example will make these formulae clearer. As long as the seeing is an unbroken act, which is as experienced no more mere sensation than it is mere motion (though the onlooker or psychological observer can interpret it into sensation and movement), it is in no sense the sensation which stimulates the reaching; we have, as already sufficiently indicated, only the serial steps in a co-ordination of *acts*. But now take a child who, upon reaching for bright light (that is, exercising the seeing-reaching co-ordination), has sometimes had a delightful exercise, sometimes found something good to eat and sometimes burned himself. *Now the response is not only uncertain, but the stimulus is equally uncertain; one is uncertain only in so far as the other is.* The real problem may be equally well stated as either to discover the right stimulus, to constitute the stimulus, or to discover, to constitute, the response. The question of whether to reach or to abstain from reaching is the question what sort of a bright light have we here? Is it the one which means playing with one's hands, eating milk, or burning one's fingers? The stimulus must be constituted for the response to occur. Now it is at precisely this juncture and because of it that the distinction of sensation as stimulus and motion as response arises.

The sensation or conscious stimulus is not a thing or existence by itself; it is that phase of a co-ordination requiring attention because, by reason of the conflict within the co-ordination, it is uncertain how to complete it. It is doubt as to the next act, whether to reach or no, which gives the motive to examining the act. The end to follow is, in this sense, the stimulus. It furnishes the motivation to attend to what has just taken place; to define it more carefully. From this point of view the discovery of the stimulus is the "response" to possible movement as "stimulus." We must have an anticipatory sensation, an image, of the movements that may occur, together with their respective values, before attention will go to the seeing to break it up as a sensation of light, and of light of this particular kind. It is the initiated activities of reaching, which, inhibited by the conflict in the co-ordination, turn round, as it were, upon the seeing, and hold it from passing over into further act until its quality is determined. Just here the act as objective stimulus becomes transformed into sensation as possible, as conscious, stimulus. Just here also, motion as conscious response emerges.

In other words, sensation as stimulus does not mean any particular psychical *existence*. It means simply a function, and will have its value shift according to the special work requiring to be done. At one moment the various activities of reaching and withdrawing will be the sensation, because they are that phase of activity which sets the problem, or creates the demand for, the next act. At the next moment the previous act of seeing will furnish the sensation, being, in turn, that phase of activity which sets the pace upon which depends further action. Generalized, sensation as stimulus is always that phase of activity requiring to be defined in order that a co-ordination may be completed. What the sensation will be in particular at a given time, therefore, will depend entirely upon the way in which an activity is being used. It has no fixed quality of its own. The search for the stimulus is the search for exact conditions of action; that is, for the state of things which decides how a beginning co-ordination should be completed.

Similarly, motion, as response, has only a functional value. It is whatever will serve to complete the disintegrating co-ordination. Just as the discovery of the sensation marks the establishing of the problem, so the constitution of the response marks the solution of this problem. At one time, fixing attention, holding the eye fixed, upon the seeing and thus bringing out a certain quale of light is the response, because that is the particular act called for just then; at another time, the movement of the arm away from the light is the response. There is nothing in itself which may be labeled response. That one certain set of sensory quales should be marked off by themselves as "motion" and put in antithesis to such sensory quales as those of color, sound and contact, as legitimate claimants to the title of sensation, is wholly inexplicable unless we keep the difference of function in view. It is the eye and ear sensations which fix for us the problem; which report to us the conditions which have to be met if the co-ordination is to be successfully completed; and just the moment we need to know about our movements to get an adequate report, just that moment, motion miraculously (from the ordinary standpoint) ceases to be motion and become "muscular sensation." On the other hand, take the change in values of experience, the transformation of sensory quales. Whether this change will or will not be interpreted as movement, whether or not any consciousness of movement will arise, will depend upon whether this change is satisfactory, whether or not it is regarded as a harmonious development of a co-ordination, or whether the change is regarded as simply a means in solving a problem, an instrument in reaching a more satisfactory co-ordination. So long as our experience runs smoothly we are no more conscious of motion as motion than we are of this or that color or sound by itself.

To sum up: the distinction of sensation and movement as stimulus and response respectively is not a distinction which can be regarded as descriptive of anything which holds of psychical events or existences as such. The only events to which the terms stimulus and response can be descriptively applied are to minor acts serving by their respective positions to the maintenance of some organized co-ordination. The conscious stimulus or sensation, and the conscious response of motion, have a special genesis or motivation, and a special end or function. The reflex arc theory, by neglecting, by abstracting from, this genesis and this function gives us one disjointed part of a process as if it were the whole. It gives us literally an arc, instead of the circuit; and not giving us the circuit of which it is an arc, does not enable us to place, to center, the arc. This arc, again, falls apart into two separate existences having to be either mechanically or externally adjusted to each other.

The circle is a co-ordination, some of whose members have come into conflict with each other. It is the temporary disintegration and need of reconstitution which occasions, which affords the genesis of, the conscious distinction into sensory stimulus on one side and motor response on the other. The stimulus is that phase of the forming co-ordination which represents the conditions which have to be met in bringing it to a successful issue; the response is that phase of one and the same forming co-ordination which gives the key to meeting these conditions, which serves as instrument in effecting the successful co-ordination. They are therefore strictly correlative and contemporaneous. The stimulus is something to be discovered; to be made out; if the activity affords its own adequate stimulation, there is no stimulus save in the objective sense already referred to. As soon as it is adequately determined, then and then only is the response also complete. To attain either, means that the co-ordination has completed itself. Moreover, it is the motor response which assists in discovering and constituting the stimulus. It is the holding of the movement at a certain stage which creates the sensation, which throws it into relief.

It is the co-ordination which unifies that which the reflex arc concept gives us only in disjointed fragments. It is the circuit within which fall distinctions of stimulus and response as functional phases of its own mediation or completion. The point of this story is in its application; but the application of it to the question of the nature of psychical evolution, to the distinction between sensational and rational consciousness, and the nature of judgment must be deferred to a more favorable opportunity.

## 10. The Psychology of Effort*

This essay should be read as more than an isolated piece of technical analysis of an aspect of human activity, for Dewey here prefigures a lifelong concern. He was extremely fascinated with the problematic character of human life and with the process of bringing something off—that is, of harmonizing means and ends. He writes in this essay of the effort involved in "the mastery of novel acts," while in his later works on education he focuses on the stresses involved while inquiring into new areas, and in his writing on art he points to the tension between anticipation and consummation. In this essay, the language is of a descriptive psychology but the setting is one that he returns to over and over—namely, the description of man as struggling to achieve a functional resolution of a problem, whether it be of immediate or more extensive significance.

There are three distinguishable views regarding the psychical quales experienced in cases of effort. One is the conception that effort, as such, is strictly "spiritual" or "intellectual," unmediated by any sensational element whatever; it being admitted, of course, that the expression or putting forth of effort, in so far as it occurs through the muscular system, has sensational correlates. This view shades into the next in so far as its upholders separate "physical" from "moral" effort, and admit that in the former the consciousness of effort is more or less sensational in character, while in the latter remaining wholly non-sensuous in quality. The third view declines to accept the distinction made between moral and physical effort as a distinction of genesis, and holds that all sense of effort is sensationally (peripherally) determined. For example, the first theory, in its extreme or typical form, would say that when we put forth effort, whether to lift a stone, to solve a refractory problem, or to resist temptation, the sense of effort is the consciousness of pure psychical activity, to be carefully distinguished from any sense of the

* From *Philosophical Review* VI (January, 1897), pp. 43-56.

muscular and organic changes occurring from the actual putting forth of effort, the latter being a return wave of resulting sensations. The second view would discriminate between the cases alluded to, drawing a line between effort in lifting the stone, which is considered as itself due to sense of strain and tension arising from the actual putting forth of energy (and hence sensuously conditioned), and the two other cases. Various writers would, however, apparently draw the line at different places, some conceding the sense of effort in intellectual attention to be sensational, mediated through feeling the contraction of muscles of forehead, fixation of eyes, changes in breathing, etc. Others would make the attention, as such, purely spiritual (*i.e.*, in this use, non-sensational), independently of whether the outcome is intellectual or moral in value. But the third view declares unambiguously that the sense of effort is, in any case, due to the organic reverberations of the act itself, the "muscular," visceral, and breathing sensations.[1]

In the following paper I propose, for the most part, to approach this question indirectly rather than directly, my underlying conviction being that the difference between the "sensational" and "spiritual" schools is due to the fact that one is thinking of a distinctly psychological fact, the way in which the sense or *consciousness* of effort is mediated, while the other is, in reality, discussing a logical or moral problem—the interpretation of the category of effort, the value which it has as a part of experience. To the point that the distinction between "physical" and "spiritual" effort is one of interpretation, of function, rather than of kind of existence, I shall return to the sequel. Meantime, I wish to present a certain amount of introspective evidence for the position that the sense of effort (as distinguished from the fact or the category) is sensationally mediated; and then to point out that if this is admitted, the real problem of the psychology of effort is only stated, not solved; this problem being to find the sensational *differentia* between the cases in which there is, and those in which there is not, a sense of effort.

The following material was gathered, it may be said, not with reference to the conscious examination of the case in hand, but in the course of a study of the facts of choice; this indirect origin makes it, I believe, all the more valuable. The cases not quoted are identical in kind

---

[1] Professor James, to whom, along with Ferrier, we owe, for the most part the express recognition of the sensational quales concerned in effort, appears to accept the second of these three types of views. I do not know that the question has been raised as to how this distinction is reconcilable with his general theory of emotion; nor yet how his ground for making it—the superiority of the spiritual over the physical—is to be adjusted to his assertion (*Psychology*, II, p. 453) that the sensational theory of emotions does not detract from their spiritual significance.

with those quoted, there being no reports of a contrary sense. "In decid-ing a question that had to be settled in five minutes, I found myself turned in the chair, till I was sitting on its edge, with the left arm on the back of the chair, hand clenched so tightly that the marks on the nails were left in the palm, breathing so rapid that it was oppressive, winking rapid, jaws clenched, leaning far forward and supporting my head by the right hand. The question was whether I should go to the city that day. When I decided to go I felt more like resting than starting."

The next instance relates to an attempt to recall lines of poetry for-merly memorized. "There is a feeling of strain. This I found to be imme-diately dependent upon a hard knitting of the brows and forehead—especially upon a fixing and converging of the eyes. At the same time there is a general contraction of the system as a whole. The breathing is quiet, slow, and regular, save where emotional accompani-ments break it up. The meter is usually kept by a slight movement of the toes in the shoes or by a finger of the hand. As the recollection pro-ceeds, there is a sensation of peering, of viewing the whole scene. The fixation exhausts the eyes much more than hard reading."

The succeeding instance relates to the effort involved in understand-ing an author. "First, I am conscious of drawing myself together, my forehead contracts, my eyes and ears seem to draw themselves in and shut themselves off. There is tension of the muscles of limbs. Secondly, a feeling of movement or plunge forward occurs. My particular sensa-tions differ in different cases, but all have this in common: First, a feeling of tension, and then movement forward. Sometimes the forward movement is accompanied by a muscular feeling in the arms as if throw-ing things to right and left, in clearing a road to a desired object. Sometimes it is a feeling of climbing, and planting my foot firmly as on a height attained."[2]

Now of course I am far from thinking that these cases, or any number of such cases, prove the sensational character of the consciousness of effort. Logically, the statements are all open to the interpretation that we are concerned here with products or incidental *sequelae* of effort, rather than with its essence. But I have yet to find a student who, with growing power of introspection, did not report that to him such sensa-tions seemed to constitute the "feel" of effort. Moreover, the cumulative force of such statements is very great, if not logically con-clusive. Many state that if they relax their muscles entirely it is impossi-

---

[2] A number of cases, on further questioning, reported a similar rhythm of con-traction and movement accompanying mental effort. This topic would stand spe-cial inquiry.

ble to keep up the effort. Sensations frequently mentioned are those connected with breathing—stopping the respiration, breathing more rapidly, contracted chest and throat; others are contraction of brow, holding head fixed, or twisting it, compression of lips, clenching of fist, contraction of jaws, sensations in pit of stomach, goneness in legs, shoulders higher, head lower than usual, fogginess or mistiness in visual field, trying to see something which eludes vision, etc.

But upon the whole I intend rather to assume that the sense of effort is, in all its forms, sensationally conditioned. We have in this fact (if it be a fact) no adequate psychology of effort, but only the preliminary of such theory. The conception up to this point has, for theoretical purposes, negative value only; it is useful in overthrowing other theories of effort, but throws no positive light upon its nature. The problem of interest, as soon as the rival theories are dismissed, comes to be this: Granted the sensational character of the consciousness of effort, what is its specific *differentia?* What we wish now to know is what set of sensory values marks off experiences of effort from those closely resembling, but not felt as cases of effort. So far as I know this question has not been raised.

How then does, say, a case of perception with effort differ from a case of "easy" or effortless perception? The difference, I repeat, shall be wholly in sensory quale; but in *what* sensory quale?

At this point a reversion to a different point of view, and the introduction of a different order of ideas is likely to occur. We may be told, as an explanation of the difference, that in one case we have a feeling of activity, a feeling of the putting forth of energy. I found that persons who in special cases have become thoroughly convinced of the sensational quality of all consciousness of effort, will make this answer. The explanation is, I think, that the point of view unconsciously shifts from effort as a psychical fact, as fact of direct consciousness, to effort as an objective or teleological fact. We stop thinking of the sense of effort, and think of the reference or import of the experience. Effort, as putting forth of energy, is involved equally in all psychical occurrences. It exists with a sense of ease just as much as with a sense of strain. There may be more of it in cases of extreme absorption and interest, where no effort is felt, than in cases of extreme sense of effort. Compare, for example, the psychophysical energy put forth in listening to a symphony, or in viewing a picture gallery, with that exercised in trying to fix a small moving speck on the wall; compare the energy, that is, as objectively measured. In the former case, the whole being may be intensely active, and yet there may be, at the time, absolutely no consciousness of effort or strain. The latter may be, objectively, a very trivial activity, and yet the consciousness of strain may be the chief thing in the conscious experience. In some cases it seems almost as if the relation between effort as an objective fact, and effort as a psychical fact, were an inverse one. If a monotonous physical movement be indefinitely repeated, it will generally be found that as long as "activity" is put forth, and accomplishes something objectively (as measured in some dynometric register), there is little sense of effort. Let the energy be temporarily exhausted and action practically cease, then the sense of effort will be at its maximum. Let a wave of energy recur, and there is at once a sense of lightness, of ease. And in all cases, the sense of effort and ease follows, never precedes, the change in activity as objectively measured.

We are not concerned, accordingly, with any question of the existence or non-existence of spiritual activity, or even of psychophysical activity. The reference to this, as furnishing the *differentia* of cases of consciousness of effort from those of ease, is not so much false as irrelevant.

Where, then, shall we locate the discriminative factor? Take the simplest possible case: I try to make out the exact form, or the nature, of a faint marking on a piece of paper a few feet off, at about the limit of distinct vision. What is the special sensation carrier of the sense of effort here? Introspectively I believe the answer is very simple. In the case of felt effort, certain sensory quales, usually fused, fall apart in consciousness, and there is an alternation, an oscillation, between them, accompanied by a disagreeable tone when they are apart, and an agreeable tone when they become fused again. Moreover, the separation in consciousness during the period when the quales are apart is not complete, but the image of the fused quale is at least dimly present. Specifically, in ordinary or normal vision, there is no distinction within consciousness of the ocular-motor sensation which corresponds to fixation, from the optical sensations of light and color. The two are so intimately fused that there is but one quale in consciousness. In these cases, there is feeling of ease, or at least absence of sense of effort. In other cases, the sensations corresponding to frowning, to holding the head steady, the breathing fixed—the whole adjustment of motor apparatus—come into consciousness of themselves on their own account. Now we are not accustomed to find satisfaction in the experience of motor adjustment; the relevant sensations have value and interest, not in themselves, but in the specific quales of sound, color, touch, or whatever they customarily introduce. In at least ninety-nine onehundreths of our experience, the "muscular" sensations are felt simply as passing over into some other experience which is either aimed at, or which, when experienced, affords satisfaction. A habit of expectation, of looking forward to some other experience, thus comes to be the normal associate of motor experience. It is felt as fringe, as "tendency," not as psychical resting place. Whenever it persists as motor, whenever the expectation of other sensory quales of positive value is not met, there is at least a transitory feeling of futility, of thwartedness, or of irritation at a failure. Hence the disagreeable tone referred to. But in the type of cases taken as our illustration, more is true than a failure of an expected consequent through mere inertia of habit. The image of the end aimed at persists, and, through its contrast with the partial motor quale, emphasizes and reinforces the sense of incompleteness. That is to say, one is continually imaging the speck as having some particular form—an oval or an angular form; as having a certain nature—an inkspot, a flyspeck. Then this image is as continually interfered with by the sensations of motor adjustment coming to consciousness by themselves. Each experience breaks into, and breaks up, the other before it has attained fullness. Let the image of a five-sided inkspot be acquiesced in apart from the motor adjustment (in other words, let one pass into the state of reverie), or let the "muscular" sensations be given complete sway by themselves (as when one begins to study them in his capacity as psychologist), and all sense of effort disappears. It is the rivalry, with the accompanying disagreeable tone due to failure of habit, that constitutes the sense of effort.

It will be useful to apply the terms of this analysis to some attendant phenomena of effort. First, it enables us to account for the growing sense of effort with fatigue, without having to resort to a set of conceptions lying outside the previously used ideas. The sense of fatigue increases effort, just because it marks the emergence into consciousness of a distinct new set of sensations which resist absorption into, or fusion with, the dominant images of the current habit or purpose. Upon the basis of other theories of effort, fatigue increases sense of effort because of sheer exhaustion; upon this theory, because of the elements introduced which distract attention. Other theories, in other words, have to fall back upon an extrapsychical factor, and something which is heterogeneous with the other factors concerned. Moreover, they fail to account for the fact that if the feeling of fatigue is surrendered to, it ceases to be disagreeable, and may become a delicious languor.

In a similar way certain facts connected with sense of effort, as related to the mastery of novel acts, may be explained. Take the alternation of ridiculous excess of effort, with total collapse of effort in learning to ride a bicycle. Before one mounts one has perhaps a pretty definite visual image of himself in balance and in motion. This image persists as a desirability. On the other hand, there comes into play at once the consciousness of the familiar motor adjustments—for the most part, related to walking. The two sets of sensations refuse to coincide, and the result is an amount of stress and strain relevant to the most serious problems of the universe. Or, again, the conflict becomes so unregulated that the image of the balance disappears, and one finds himself with only a lot of "muscular" sensations at hand; the effort entirely vanishes. I have taken an extreme case, but surely everyone is familiar, in dealing with unfamiliar occupations, of precisely this alternation of effort, out of all proportion to the objective significance of the end, with the complete mind-wandering and failure of endeavor. If the sense of effort is the sense of incompatibility between two sets of sensory images, one of which stands for an end to be reached, or a fulfillment of a habit, while the other represents the experiences which intervene in reaching the end, these phenomena are only what are to be expected. But if we start from a "spiritual" theory of effort, I know of no explanation which is anything more than an hypostatized repetition of the facts to be explained.

It probably has already occurred to the reader, that when the theory of the sensational character of the consciousness of effort is analyzed, instead of being merely thrown out at large, the feeling that it deals common sense a blow in the face disappears. If we state the foregoing analysis in objective, instead of in psychical, terms, it just says that effort is the feeling of opposition existing between end and means. The kinesthetic image of qualitative nature (*i.e.*, of color, sound, contact) stands for the end, whether consciously desired, or as furnishing the culmination of habit. The "muscular" sensations[3] represent the means, the experiences to which value is not attached on their own account, but as intermediaries to an intrinsically valuable consciousness.

Practically stated, this means that effort is nothing more, and also nothing less, than tension between means and ends in action, and that the sense of effort is the awareness of this conflict. The sensational character of this experience, which has been such a stumbling block to some, means that this tension of adjustment is not merely ideal, but is actual (*i.e.*, practical); it is one which goes on in a struggle for existence. Be-

[3] Perhaps it would be well to state that sensations of tendons, joints, internal contacts, etc., are what is meant by this term—the whole report of the motor adjustment.

ing a struggle for realization in the world of concrete quales and values, it makes itself felt in the only media possible—specific sensations, on the one hand, and muscular sensations, on the other. Instead of denying, or slurring over, effort, such an account brings it into prominence. Surely what common sense values in effort is not some transcendental act, occurring before any change in the actual world of qualities, but precisely this readjustment within the concrete region. And if one is somewhat scandalized at being told that the awareness of effort is a sense of changes of breathing, of muscular tensions, etc., it is not, I conceive, because of what is said, but rather because of what is left unsaid—that these sensations report the state of things as regards effective realization.

It is difficult to see, upon a more analytic consideration than common sense is called upon to make, what is gained for the "spiritual" nature of effort by relegating it to a purely extrasensational region. That "spiritual" is to be so interpreted as to mean existence in a sphere transcending space and time determinations is, at best, a piece of metaphysics, and not a piece of psychology; and as a piece of metaphysics, it cannot escape competition with the theory which finds the meaning of the spiritual in the whole process of realizing the concrete values of life. I do not find that any of the upholders of the non-sensational quality of effort has ever made a very specific analysis of the experience. Professor Baldwin's account, however, being perhaps the most thoroughgoing statement of effort as preceding sensation, in "physical" as well as "spiritual" effort, is, perhaps, as explicit as any. In one passage, effort is "distinct consciousness of opposition between what we call self and muscular resistance." Now a consciousness of muscular resistance, whatever else it may or may not be, would seem to involve sensations, and the consciousness of effort to be, so far forth, sensationally mediated—which is contrary to the hypothesis. Moreover, it is extremely difficult to see how there can be any consciousness of opposition between the self in general, and the muscles in general. Until the "self" actually starts to do something (and then, of course, there are sensations), how can the muscles offer any opposition to it? And even when it does begin to do something, how can the muscles, as muscles, offer opposition? If because the act is unfamiliar, then certainly what we get is simply a case of difficulty in the having of a unified consciousness—the kinesthetic image of the habitual movement will not unify with the proposed sensory image, and there is rivalry. But this is not a case of muscles resisting the self; it is a case of divided activity of the self. It means that the activity already going on (and, therefore, reporting itself sensationally) resists displacement, or transformation, by or into another activity which is beginning, and thus making its sensational report.

But Professor Baldwin gives another statement which is apparently different. "In all voluntary movement, therefore, there is an earlier fiat than the will to move, *i.e.*, the fiat of attention to the particular idea of movement." And it is repeatedly intimated that the real difficulty in effort is, not in the muscular execution, but in holding a given idea in consciousness. (In fact, it is distinctly stated that, even in muscular effort, the real effort is found in "attending" to the idea.) Now, this statement is certainly preferable to the other, in that it avoids the appearance of making the muscles offer resistance to the self. But now, what has become of the resistance, and, hence, of the effort? Is there anything left to offer opposition *to* the self? Can an idea, *qua* pure idea, offer resistance and demand effort? And is it the self, as barely self, to which resistance is made? Such questions may, perhaps, serve to indicate the abstractness of the account, and suggest the fact that effort is never felt, save when a *change of existing activity is proposed*. In this case, the effort may be centered in the introduction of the new idea as against the persistence of the present doing, or it may be to maintain the existing habit against the suggested change. In the former, the new activity will probably be categorized as duty; in the latter case, as temptation or distraction. But in either alternative, effort is felt with reference to the adjustment of factors in an action. Neither of these is exclusively self, neither the old nor the new factor; and the one which happens to be especially selected as self varies with the state of action. At one period, the end or aim is regarded as self, and the existing habit, or mode of action, as the obstruction to the realization of the desired self; at the next stage, the end having been pretty well defined, the habit, or existing line of action, since the only means or instrument for attaining this end, is conceived as self, and the ideal as "beyond," and at once as resisting and as soliciting the self.

I do not suppose anyone will question this account, so far as relates to the fact that the sense of effort arises only with reference to a proposed change in the existing activity, and that at least the existing activity has its sensational counterpart. Doubt is more likely to arise as regards the proposed end, or the intruding distraction. This, it may be said, is pure idea, not activity, and, hence, has no sensational report. But whoever takes this position must be able to explain the *differentia* between instances of logical manipulation of an idea, aesthetic contemplation, and cases of sense of effort. I may take the idea of something I ought to do, but which is repulsive to me; may say that I ought to do it, and may then hold the idea as an idea or object in consciousness, may revolve it in all lights, may turn it over and over, may chew it as a sweet or a bitter cud, and yet have absolutely no sense of effort. It is only, so far as I can trust my own observation, when this idea passes into at least nascent or partial action, and thus comes head up against some other line of action, that the sense of effort arises.

In other words, the sense of effort arises, not because there is an activity struggling against resistance, or a self which is endeavoring to overcome obstacles outside of it; but it arises within activity, marking the attempt to co-ordinate separate factors within a single whole. Activity is here taken not as formal, but as actual and specific. It means an act, definitely doing something definite. An act, as something which occupies time, necessarily means conflict of acts. The demand for time is simply the result of a lack of unity. The intervening process of execution, the use of means, is the process of disintegrating acts hitherto separate and independent, and putting together the result, or fragments, into a single piece of conduct. Were it not for the division of acts and results in conflict, the deed, or co-ordination, would be accomplished at once.

One of the conflicting acts stands for the end or aim. This, at first, is the sensory image which gives the cue and motive to the reaction or response. In the case previously cited, it is the image of the colored speck, as determining the movements of the head and eye muscles.[4] That we are inclined to view only the motor response as act, and regard the image, either as alone psychical, or as pure idea, is because the image is already in existence, and, therefore, its active side may be safely neglected. Being already in possession of the field, it does not require any conscious activity to keep it in existence. The movement of the muscles, being the means by which the desired end may be reached, becomes the all-important thing, or *the* act; in accordance with the general principle that attention always goes to the weakest part of a co-ordination in process of formation, meaning by weakest, that part least under the immediate control of habit. This being conceived alone as act, everything lying outside of it is conceived as resistance; thus recognition is avoided of the fact, that the real state of things is, that there are two acts mutually opposing each other, during their transformation over into a third new and inclusive act.

We have here, I think, an adequate explanation of all that can be said

---

[4] It must not be forgotten that both sensory stimulus and motor response are both in reality sensorimotor, and, therefore, each is itself an act or psychical whole. On this point, see my "The Reflex Arc Concept."

about the tremendous importance of effort, of all that Professor James has so conclusively said. This importance is not due to the fact that effort is the one sole evidence of a free spiritual activity struggling against outward and material resistance. It is due to the fact that effort is the critical point of progress in action, arising whenever old habits are in process of reconstruction, or of adaptation to new conditions; unless they are so readapted, life is given over to the rule of conservatism, routine, and over-inertia. To make a new co-ordination the old co-ordination must, to some extent, be broken up, and the only way of breaking it up is for it to come into conflict with some other co-ordination; that is, a conflict of two acts, each representing a habit, or end, is the necessary condition of reaching a new act which shall have a more comprehensive end. That sensations of the bodily state report to us this conflict and readjustment, merely indicates that the reconstruction going on is one of acts, and not mere ideas. The whole prejudice which supposes that the spiritual sense of effort is lost when it is given sensational quality, is simply a survival of the notion that an idea is somehow more spiritual than an act.

Up to this time I have purposely avoided any reference to the attempt to explain effort by attention. My experience has been that this mode of explanation does not explain, but simply shifts the difficulty, at the same time making it more obscure by claiming to solve it. There is some danger that attention may become a psychological pool of Bethesda. If we have escaped the clutch of associationalism, only to fall into attentionalism, we have hardly bettered our condition in psychology. But the preceding account would apply to any concrete analyses of effort in terms of attention. The psychological fallacy besets us here. We confuse attention as an objective fact, attention for the observer, with attention as consciously experienced. During complete absorption an onlooker may remark how attentive such a person is, or after such an absorption one may look back and say how attentive one was; but taking the absorption when it occurs, it means that only the subject matter is present in consciousness, not attention itself. We are conscious of being attentive only when our attention is divided, only when there are two centers of attention competing with each other, only when there is an oscillation from one group of ideas to another, together with a tendency to a third group of ideas, in which the two previous groups are included. The sense of strain in attention, instead of being coincident with the activity of attention, is proof that attention itself is not yet complete.

To establish the identity of attention with the formation of a new act, through the mutual adaptation of two existing habits, would take us too far away from our present purpose; but there need be no hesitation, I believe, in admitting that the sense of attention arises only under the conditions of conflict already stated.

# III

## The Experience
## of Knowing

The five essays in this section present the origins and development of Dewey's pragmatic epistemology. The early essays show Dewey's struggle to divest himself of the absolutistic claims of objective idealism and to move in the direction of a logic of inquiry in which the experience of knowing becomes as much the focus of concern as that which is known. This position is presented clearly in the last essay of this section, "The Pattern of Inquiry."

## 11. "Consciousness" and Experience*

At the turn of the century, Dewey was still very much concerned with the relative responsibilities of psychology and philosophy. In this essay, he attempts to bring their functions close together while being especially critical of that type of philosophy which continues to make judgments about human behavior, although innocent of important behavioral data. In a note at the conclusion of this essay, Dewey points to the developments in the first decade of the twentieth century, which bear out his earlier judgments and which provide the basis for a "pragmatic empiricism." Dewey, of course, participated in those developments, and several of the essays in which he articulated his positions are reprinted below—namely, "The Experimental Theory of Knowledge," "Experience and Objective Idealism," and "The Postulate of Immediate Empiricism."

* From John Dewey, *The Influence of Darwin on Philosophy: And Other Essays on Contemporary Thought*, pp. 242-270. Copyright 1910 by Holt, Rinehart and Winston, Inc. Copyright 1938 by John Dewey. Reprinted by permission of Holt, Rinehart and Winston, Inc. (Published originally as "Psychology and Philosophic Method," May, 1899.)

Every science in its final standpoint and working aims is controlled by conditions lying outside itself—conditions that subsist in the practical life of the time. With no science is this as obviously true as with psychology. Taken without nicety of analysis, no one would deny that psychology is specially occupied with the individual; that it wishes to find out those things that proceed peculiarly from the individual, and the mode of their connection with him. Now, the way in which the individual is conceived, the value that is attributed to him, the things in his make-up that arouse interest, are not due at the outset to psychology. The scientific view regards these matters in a reflected, a borrowed, medium. They are revealed in the light of social life. An autocratic, an aristocratic, a democratic society propound such different estimates of the worth and place of individuality; they procure for the individual as an individual such different sorts of experience; they aim at arousing such different impulses and at organizing them according to such different purposes, that the psychology arising in each must show a different temper.

In this sense, psychology is a political science. While the professed psychologist, in his conscious procedure, may easily cut his subject-matter loose from these practical ties and references, yet the starting point and goal of his course are none the less socially set. In this conviction I venture to introduce to an audience that could hardly be expected to be interested in the technique of psychology, a technical subject, hoping that the human meaning may yet appear.

There is at present a strong, apparently a growing tendency to conceive of psychology as an account of the consciousness of the individual, considered as something in and by itself; consciousness, the assumption virtually runs, being of such an order that it may be analyzed, described, and explained in terms of just itself. The statement, as commonly made, is that psychology is an account of consciousness, *qua* consciousness; and the phrase is supposed to limit psychology to a certain definite sphere of fact that may receive adequate discussion for scientific purposes, without troubling itself with what lies outside. Now if this conception be true, there is no intimate, no important connection of psychology and philosophy at large. That philosophy, whose range is comprehensive, whose problems are catholic, should be held down by a discipline whose voice is as partial as its material is limited, is out of the range of intelligent discussion.

But there is another possibility. If the individual of whom psychology treats be, after all, a social individual, any absolute setting off and apart of a sphere of consciousness as, even for scientific purposes, self-sufficient, is condemned in advance. All such limitation, and all inquiries, descriptions, explanations that go with it, are only preliminary. "Consciousness" is but a symbol, an anatomy whose life is in natural and social operations. To know the symbol, the psychical letter, is important; but its necessity lies not within itself, but in the need of a language for reading the things signified. If this view be correct, we cannot be so sure that psychology is without large philosophic significance. Whatever meaning the individual has for the social life that he both incorporates and animates, that meaning has psychology for philosophy.

This problem is too important and too large to suffer attack in an evening's address. Yet I venture to consider a portion of it, hoping that such things as appear will be useful clues in entering wider territory. We may ask what is the effect upon psychology of considering its material as something so distinct as to be capable of treatment without involving larger issues. In this inquiry we take as representative some such account of the science as this: Psychology deals with consciousness "as such" in its various modes and processes. It aims at an isolation of each such as will permit accurate description: at statement of its place in the serial order such as will enable us to state the laws by which one calls another into being, or as will give the natural history of its origin, maturing, and dissolution. It is both analytic and synthetic—analytic in that it resolves each state into its constituent elements; synthetic in that it discovers the processes by which these elements combine into complex wholes and series. It leaves alone—it shuts out—questions concerning the validity, the objective import of these modifications: of their value in conveying truth, in effecting goodness, in constituting beauty. For it is just with such questions of worth, of validity, that philosophy has to do.

Some such view as this is held by the great majority of working psychologists to-day. A variety of reasons have conspired to bring about general acceptance. Such a view seems to enroll one in the ranks of the scientific men rather than of the metaphysicians—and there are those who distrust the metaphysicians. Others desire to take problems piecemeal and in detail, avoiding that excursion into ultimates, into that never-ending panorama of new questions and new possibilities that seems to be the fate of the philosopher. While no temperate mind can do other than sympathize with this view, it is hardly more than an expedient. For, as Mr. James remarks, after disposing of the question of free-will by relegating it to the domain of the metaphysician:—"Metaphysics means only an unusually obstinate attempt to think clearly and consistently"—and clearness and consistency are not things to be put off beyond a certain point. When the metaphysician chimes in with this new-found modesty of the psychologist, so different from the disposition of Locke and Hume and the Mills, salving his metaphysical conscience with the remark—it hardly possesses the dignity of a conviction—that the partial sciences, just because they are partial, are not expected to be coherent with themselves nor with one another; when the metaphysician, I say, praises the psychologist for sticking to his last, we are reminded that another motive is also at work. There is a half-conscious irony in this abnegation of psychology. It is not the first time that science has assumed the work of Cinderella; and, since Mr. Huxley has happily reminded her, she is not altogether oblivious, in her modesty, of a possible future check to the pride of her haughty sister, and of a certain coronation that shall mark her coming to her own.

But, be the reasons as they may, there is little doubt of the fact. Almost all our working psychologists admit, nay, herald this limitation of their work. I am not presumptuous enough to set myself against this array. I too proclaim myself of those who believe that psychology has to do (at a certain point, that is) with "consciousness as such." But I do not believe that the limitation is final. Quite the contrary: if "consciousness" or "state of consciousness" be given intelligible meaning, I believe that this conception is the open gateway into the fair fields of philosophy. For, note you, the phrase is an ambiguous one. It may mean one thing to the metaphysician who proclaims: Here finally we have psychology recognizing her due metes and bounds, giving bonds to trespass no more. It may mean quite another thing to the psychologist in his work—whatever he may happen to say about it. It may be that the psychologist deals with states of consciousness as the significant, the analyzable and describable form, to which he reduces the things he is studying. Not that they *are* that existence, but that they are its indications, its clues, in shape for handling by scientific methods. So, for example, does the paleontologist work. Those curiously shaped and marked forms to which he is devoted are not life, nor are they the literal termini of his endeavor; but through them as signs and records he construes a life. And again, the painter-artist might well say that he is concerned only with colored paints as such. Yet none the less through them as registers and indices, he reveals to us the mysteries of sunny meadow, shady forest, and twilight wave. These are the things-in-themselves of which the oils on his palette are phenomena.

So the preoccupation of the psychologist with states of consciousness may signify that they are the media, the concrete conditions to which he purposely reduces his material, in order, *through them*, as methodological helps, to get at and understand that which is anything but a state of consciousness. To him, however, who insists upon the fixed and final limitation of psychology, the state of consciousness is not the shape some fact takes from the exigency of investigation; it is literally the full fact itself. It is not an intervening term; it bounds the horizon. Here, then, the issue defines itself. I conceive that states of consciousness (and I hope you will take the phrase broadly enough to cover all the specific data of psychology) have no existence before the psychologist begins to work. He brings them into existence. What we are really after is the process of experience, the way in which it arises and behaves. We want to know its course, its history, its laws. We want to know its various typical forms; how each originates; how it is related to others; the part it plays in maintaining an inclusive, expanding, connected course of experience. Our problem as psychologists is to learn its *modus operandi*, its method.

The paleontologist is again summoned to our aid. In a given district he finds a great number and variety of footprints. From these he goes to work to construct the structure and the life habits of the animals that made them. The tracks exist undoubtedly; they are there; but yet he deals with them not as final existences but as signs, phenomena in the literal sense. Imagine the hearing that the critic would receive who should inform the paleontologist that he is transcending his field of scientific activity; that his concern is with footprints as such, aiming to describe each, to analyze it into its simplest forms, to compare the different kinds with one another so as to detect common elements, and finally, thereby, to discover the laws of their arrangement in space!

Yet the immediate data are footprints, and footprints only. The paleontologist does in a way do all these things that our imaginary critic is urging upon him. The difference is not that he arbitrarily lugs in other data; that he invents entities and faculties that are not there. The difference is in his standpoint. His interest is in the animals, and the data are treated in whatever way seems likely to serve this interest. So with the psychologist. He is continually and perforce occupied with minute and empirical investigation of special facts—states of consciousness, if you please. But these neither define nor exhaust his scientific problem. They are his footprints, his clues through which he places before himself the life-process he is studying—with the further difference that his footprints are not after all given to him, but are developed by his investigation.[1]

The supposition that these states are somehow existent by themselves and in this existence provide the psychologist with ready-made material is just the supreme case of the "psychological fallacy": the confusion of experience as it is to the one experiencing with what the psychologist makes out of it with his reflective analysis.

The psychologist begins with certain operations, acts, functions as his data. If these fall out of sight in the course of discussion, it is only because having been taken for granted, they remain to control the whole development of the inquiry, and to afford the sterling medium of redemption. Acts such as perceiving, remembering, intending, loving give the points of departure; they alone are concrete experiences. To understand these experiences, under what conditions they arise, and what effects they produce, analysis into states of consciousness occurs. And the modes of consciousness that are figured remain unarranged and unimportant, save as they may be translated back into acts.

To remember is to do something, as much as to shoe a horse, or to cherish a keepsake. To propose, to observe, to be kindly affectioned, are terms of value, of practice, of operation; just as digestion, respiration, locomotion express functions, not observable "objects." But there is an object that may be described: lungs, stomach, leg-muscles, or whatever. Through the structure we present to ourselves the function; it appears laid out before us, spread forth in detail—objectified in a word. The anatomist who devotes himself to this detail may, if he please (and he probably does please to concentrate his devotion) ignore the function: to discover what is there, to analyze, to measure, to describe, gives him outlet enough. But nevertheless it is the function that fixed the point of departure, that prescribed the problem and that set the limits, physical as well as intellectual, of subsequent investigation. Reference to function makes the details discovered other than a jumble of in-

---

[1] This is a fact not without its bearings upon the question of the nature and value of introspection. The objection that introspection "alters" the reality and hence is untrustworthy, most writers dispose of by saying that, after all, it need not alter the reality so very much—not beyond repair— and that, moreover, memory assists in restoring the ruins. It would be simpler to admit the fact: that the purpose of introspection is precisely to effect the right sort of alteration. If introspection should give us the original experience again, we should just be living through the experience over again in direct fashion; as psychologists we should not be forwarded one bit. Reflection upon this obvious proposition may bring to light various other matters worthy of note.

coherent trivialities. One might as well devote himself to the minute description of a square yard of desert soil were it not for this translation. States of consciousness are the morphology of certain functions.[2] What is true of analysis, of description, is true equally of classification. Knowing, willing, feeling, name states of consciousness not in terms of themselves, but in terms of acts, attitudes, found in experience.[3]

Explanation, even of an "empirical sort" is as impossible as determination of a "state" and its classification, when we rigidly confine ourselves to modifications of consciousness as a self-existent. Sensations are always defined, classified, and explained by reference to conditions which, according to the theory, are extraneous—sense-organs and stimuli. The whole physiological side assumes a ludicrously anomalous aspect on this basis.[4] While experimentation is retained, and even made much of, it is at the cost of logical coherence. To experiment with reference to a bare state of consciousness is a performance of which one cannot imagine the nature, to say nothing of doing it; while to experiment with reference to acts and the conditions of their occurrence is a natural and straightforward undertaking. Such simple processes as association are concretely inexplicable when we assume states of consciousness as existences by themselves. As recent psychology testifies,

[2] Thus to divorce "structure psychology" from "function psychology" is to leave us without possibility of scientific comprehension of function, while it deprives us of all standard of reference in selecting, observing, and explaining the structure.

[3] The following answer may fairly be anticipated: "This is true of the operations cited, but only because complex processes have been selected. Such a term as 'knowing' does of course express a function involving a system of intricate references. But, for that very reason, we go back to the sensation which is the genuine type of the 'state of consciousness' as such, pure and unadulterate and unsophisticated." The point is large for a footnote, but the following considerations are instructive: (1) The same psychologist will go on to inform us that sensations, as we experience them, are networks of reference—they are perceptual, and more or less conceptual even. From which it would appear that whatever else they are or are not, the sensations, for which self-inclosed existence is claimed, are *not* states of consciousness. And (2) we are told that these are reached by scientific abstraction in order to account for complex forms. From which it would appear that they are hypothecated as products of interpretation and for purposes of further interpretation. Only the delusion that the more complex forms are just aggregates (instead of being acts, like seeing, hoping, etc.) prevents recognition of the point in question—that the "state of consciousness" is an instrument of inquiry or methodological appliance.

[4] On the other hand, if what we are trying to get at is just the course and procedure of experiencing, of course any consideration that helps distinguish and make comprehensible that process is thoroughly pertinent.

we again have to resort to conditions that have no place nor calling on the basis of the theory—the principle of habit, of neural action, or else some connection in the object.[5]

We have only to note that there are two opposing schools in psychology to see in what an unscientific status is the subject. We have only to consider that these two schools are the result of assuming states of consciousness as existences *per se* to locate the source of the scientific scandal. No matter what the topic, whether memory or association or attention or effort, the same dualisms present themselves, the same necessity of choosing between two schools. One, lost in the distinctions that it has developed, denies the function because it can find objectively presented only states of consciousness. So it abrogates the function, regarding it as a mere aggregate of such states, or as a purely external and factitious relation between them. The other school, recognizing that this procedure explains away rather than explains, the values of experience, attempts to even up by declaring that certain functions are themselves immediately given data of consciousness, existing side by side with the "states," but indefinitely transcending them in worth, and apprehended by some higher organ. So against the elementary contents and external associations of the analytic school in psychology, we have the complicated machinery of the intellectualist school, with its pure self-consciousness as a source of ultimate truths, its hierarchy of intuitions, its ready-made faculties. To be sure, these "spiritual faculties" are now largely reduced to some one comprehensive form—Apperception, or Will, or Attention, or whatever the fashionable term may be. But the principle remains the same; the assumption of a function as a given existent, distinguishable in itself and acting upon other existences—as if the functions digestion and vision were regarded as separate from organic structures, somehow acting upon them from the outside so as to bring co-operation and harmony into them![6] This division into psychological schools is as reasonable as would be one of botanists into rootists and flowerists; of those proclaiming the root to be the rudimentary and essential structure, and those asserting that since

[5] It may avoid misunderstanding if I anticipate here a subsequent remark: that my point is not in the least that "states of consciousness" require some "synthetic unity" or faculty of substantial mind to effect their association. Quite the contrary; for this theory also admits the "states of consciousness" as existences in themselves also. My contention is that the "state of consciousness" as such is always a methodological product, developed in the course and for the purposes of psychological analysis.

* The "functions" are in truth ordinary everyday acts and attitudes: seeing, smelling, talking, listening, remembering, hoping, loving, fearing.

the function of seed-bearing is the main thing, the flower is really the controlling "synthetic" principle. Both sensationalist and intellectualist suppose that psychology has some special sphere of "reality" or of experience marked off for it within which the data are just lying around, self-existent and ready-made, to be picked up and assorted as pebbles await the visitor on the beach. Both alike fail to recognize that the psychologist first has experience to deal with; the same experience that the zoologist, geologist, chemist, mathematician, and historian deal with, and that what characterizes his specialty is not some data or existences which he may call uniquely his own; but the problem raised—the problem of the *course* of the acts that constitute experiencing.

Here psychology gets its revenge upon those who would rule it out of possession of important philosophical bearing. As a matter of fact, the larger part of the questions that are being discussed in current epistemology and what is termed metaphysic of logic and ethic arise out of (and are hopelessly compromised by) this original assumption of "consciousness as such"—in other words, are provoked by the exact reason that is given for denying to psychology any essential meaning for epistemology and metaphysic. Such is the irony of the situation. The epistemologist's problem is, indeed, usually put as the question of how the subject can so far "transcend" itself as to get valid assurance of the objective world. The very phraseology in which the problem is put reveals the thoroughness of the psychologist's revenge. Just and only because experience has been reduced to "states of consciousness" as independent existences, does the question of self-transcendence have any meaning. The entire epistemological industry is one—shall I say it—of a Sisyphean nature. *Mutatis mutandis*, the same holds of the metaphysic of logic, ethic, and esthetic. In each case, the basic problem has come to be how a mere state of consciousness can be the vehicle of a system of truth, of an objectively valid good, of beauty which is other than agreeable feeling. We may, indeed, excuse the psychologist for not carrying on the special inquiries that are the business of logical, ethical, and esthetical philosophy; but can we excuse ourselves for forcing his results into such a shape as to make philosophic problems so arbitrary that they are soluble only by arbitrarily wrenching scientific facts?

Undoubtedly we are between two fires. In placing upon psychology the responsibility of discovering the method of experience, as a sequence of acts and passions, do we not destroy just that limitation to concrete detail which now constitutes it a science? Will not the psychologist be the first to repudiate this attempt to mix him up in matters philosophical? We need only to keep in mind the specific facts involved in the term Course or Process of Experience to avoid this danger. The immediate preoccupation of the psychologist is with very definite and empirical facts—questions like the limits of audition, of the origin of pitch, of the structure and conditions of the musical scale, etc. Just so the immediate affair of the geologist is with particular rock-structures, of the botanist with particular plants, and so on. But through the collection, description, location, classification of rocks the geologist is led to the splendid story of world-forming. The limited, fixed, and separate piece of work is dissolved away in the fluent and dynamic drama of the earth. So, the plant leads with inevitableness to the whole process of life and its evolution.

In form, the botanist still studies the genus, the species, the plant—hardly, indeed, that; rather the special parts, the structural elements, of the plant. In reality, he studies life itself; the structures are the indications, the signature through which he renders transparent the mystery of life growing in the changing world. It was doubtless necessary for the botanist to go through the Linnean period—the period of engagement with rigid detail and fixed classifications; of tearing apart and piecing together; of throwing all emphasis upon peculiarities of number, size, and appearance of matured structure; of regarding change, growth, and function as external, more or less interesting, attachments to form. Examination of this period is instructive; there is much in contemporary investigation and discussion that is almost unpleasantly reminiscent in its suggestiveness. The psychologist should profit by the intervening history of science. The conception of evolution is not so much an additional law as it is a face-about. The fixed structure, the separate form, the isolated element, is henceforth at best a mere stepping-stone to knowledge of process, and when not at its best, marks the end of comprehension, and betokens failure to grasp the problem.

With the change in standpoint from self-included existence to including process, from structural unit of composition to controlling unity of function, from changeless form to movement in growth, the whole scheme of values is transformed. Faculties are definite directions of development; elements are products that are starting-points for new processes; bare facts are indices of change; static conditions are modes of accomplished adjustment. Not that the concrete, empirical phenomenon loses in worth, much less that unverifiable "metaphysical" entities are impertinently introduced; but that our aim is the discovery of a process of actions in its adaptations to circumstance. If we apply this evolutionary logic in psychology, where shall we stop? Questions of limits of stimuli in a given sense, say hearing, are in reality questions of temporary arrests, adjustments marking the favorable equilibrium of the whole organism; they connect with the question of the use of sensation in general and auditory sensations in particular for life-habits; of the origin and use of localized and distinguished perception; and this, in turn, involves within itself the whole question of space and time recognition; the significance of the thing-and-quality experience, and so on. And when we are told that the question of the origin of space experience has nothing at all to do with the question of the nature and significance of the space experienced, the statement is simply evidence that the one who makes it is still at the static standpoint; he believes that things, that relations, have existence and significance apart from the particular conditions under which they come into experience, and apart from the special service rendered in those particular conditions.

Of course, I am far from saying that every psychologist must make the whole journey. Each individual may contract, as he pleases, for any section or subsection he prefers; and undoubtedly the well-being of the science is advanced by such division of labor. But psychology goes over the whole ground from detecting every distinct act of experiencing, to seeing what need calls out the special organ fitted to cope with the situation, and discovering the machinery through which it operates to keep a-going the course of action.

But, I shall be told, the wall that divides psychology from philosophy cannot be so easily treated as non-existent. Psychology is a matter of natural history, even though it may be admitted that it is the natural history of the course of experience. But philosophy is a matter of values; of the criticism and justification of certain validities. One deals, it is said, with genesis, with conditions of temporal origin and transition; the other with analysis, with eternal constitution. I shall have to repeat that just this rigid separation of genesis and analysis seems to me a survival from a pre-evolutionary, a pre-historic age. It indicates not so much an assured barrier between philosophy and psychology as the distance dividing philosophy from all science. For the lesson that mathematicians first learned, that physics and chemistry pondered over, in which the biological disciplines were finally tutored, is that sure and delicate analysis is possible only through the patient study of conditions of origin and development. The method of analysis in mathematics is the method of construction. The experimental method is the method of making, of following the history of production; the term "cause" that has (when taken as an existent entity) so hung on the heels of science as to impede its progress, has universal meaning when read as condition of appearance in a process. And, as already intimated, the conception of evolution is no more and no less the discovery of a general law of life than it is the generalization of all scientific method. Everywhere analysis that cannot proceed by examining the successive stages of its subject, from its beginning up to its culmination, that cannot control this examination by discovering the conditions under which successive stages appear, is only preliminary. It may further the invention of proper tools of inquiry, it may help define problems, it may serve to suggest valuable hypotheses. But as science it breathes an air already tainted. There is no way to sort out the results flowing from the subject-matter itself from those introduced by the assumptions and presumptions of our own reflection. Not so with natural history when it is worthy of its name. Here the analysis is the unfolding of the existence itself. Its distinctions are not pigeon-holes of our convenience; they are stakes that mark the parting of the ways in the process itself. Its classifications are not a grasp at factors resisting further analysis; they are the patient tracings of the paths pursued. Nothing is more out of date than to suppose that interest in genesis is interest in reducing higher forms to cruder ones: it is interest in locating the exact and objective conditions under which a given fact appears, and in relation to which accordingly it has its meaning. Nothing is more naïve than to suppose that in pursuing "natural history" (term of scorn in which yet resides the dignity of the world-drama) we simply learn something of the temporal conditions under which a given value appears, while its own eternal essential quality remains as opaque as before. Nature knows no such divorce of quality and circumstance. Things come when they are wanted and as they are wanted; their quality is precisely the response they give to the conditions that call for them, while the furtherance they afford to the movement of their whole is their meaning. The severance of analysis and genesis, instead of serving as a ready-made test by which to try out the empirical, temporal events of psychology from the rational abiding constitution of philosophy, is a brand of philosophic dualism: the supposition that values are externally obtruded and statically set is irrelevant rubbish.

There are those who will admit that "states of consciousness" are but the cross-sections of flow of behavior, arrested for inspection, made in order that we may reconstruct experience in its life-history. Yet in the knowledge of the course and method of our experience, they will hold that we are far from the domain proper of philosophy. Experience, they say, is just the historic achievement of finite individuals; it tells the tale of approach to the treasures of truth, of partial victory, but larger defeat, in laying hold of the treasure. But, they say, reality is not the path to reality, and record of devious wanderings in the path is hardly a a safe account of the goal. Psychology, in other words, may tell us something of how we mortals lay hold of the world of things and truths; of how we appropriate and assimilate its contents; and how we react. It may trace the issues of such approaches and apprehensions upon the course of our own individual destinies. But it cannot wisely ignore nor sanely deny the distinction between these individual strivings and achievements, and the "Reality" that subsists and supports its own structure outside these finite futilities. The processes by which we turn over The Reality into terms of our fragmentary unconcluded, inconclusive experiences are so extrinsic to the Reality itself as to have no revealing power with reference to it. There is the *ordo ad universum*, the subject of philosophy; there is the *ordo ad individuum*, the subject of psychology.

Some such assumption as this lies latent, I am convinced, in all forswearings of the kinship of psychology and philosophy. Two conceptions hang together. The opinion that psychology is an account only and finally of states of consciousness, and therefore can throw no light upon the objects with which philosophy deals, is twin to the doctrine that the whole conscious life of the individual is not organic to the world. The philosophic basis and scope of this doctrine lie beyond examination here. But even in passing one cannot avoid remarking that the doctrine is almost never consistently held; the doctrine logically carried out leads so directly to intellectual and moral scepticism that the theory usually prefers to work in the dark background as a disposition and temper of thought rather than to make a frank statement of itself. Even in the half-hearted expositions of the process of human experience as something merely annexed to the reality of the universe, we are brought face to face to the consideration with which we set out: the dependence of theories of the individual upon the position at a given time of the individual practical and social. The doctrine of the accidental, futile, transitory significance of the individual's experience as compared with eternal realities; the notion that at best the individual is simply realizing for and in himself what already has fixed completeness in itself is congruous only with a certain intellectual and political scheme and must modify itself as that shifts. When such rearrangement comes, our estimate of the nature and importance of psychology will mirror the change.

When man's command of the methods that control action was pre-carious and disturbed; when the tools that subject the world of things and forces to use and operation were rare and clumsy, it was una-voidable that the individual should submit his perception and purpose blankly to the blank reality beyond. Under such circumstances, external authority must reign; the belief that human experience in itself is ap-proximate, not intrinsic, is inevitable. Under such circumstances, reference to the individual, to the subject, is a resort only for explaining error, illusion, and uncertainty. The necessity of external control and external redemption of experience reports itself in a low valuation of the self, and of all the factors and phases of experience that spring from the self. That the psychology of medievalism should appear only as a por-tion of its theology of sin and salvation is as obvious as that the psy-chology of the Greeks should be a chapter of cosmology.

As against all this, the assertion is ventured that psychology, sup-plying us with knowledge of the behavior of experience, is a conception of democracy. Its postulate is that since experience fulfils itself in in-dividuals, since it administers itself through their instrumentality, the account of the course and method of this achievement is a significant and indispensable affair.

Democracy is possible only because of a change in intellectual condi-tions. It implies tools for getting at truth in detail, and day by day, as we go along. Only such possession justifies the surrender of fixed, all-embracing principles to which, as universals, all particulars and individ-uals are subject for valuation and regulation. Without such possession, it is only the courage of the fool that would undertake the venture to which democracy has committed itself—the ordering of life in response to the needs of the moment in accordance with the ascertained truth of the moment. Modern life involves the deification of the here and the now; of the specific, the particular, the unique, that which happens once and has no measure of value save such as it brings with itself. Such deification is monstrous fetishism, unless the deity be there; unless the universal lives, moves, and has its being in experience as individ-ualized.[7] This conviction of the value of the individualized finds its

[6] This is perhaps a suitable moment to allude to the absence, in this discussion, of reference to what is sometimes termed rational psychology—the assumption of a separate, substantialized ego, soul, or whatever, existing side by side with par-ticular experiences and "states of consciousness," acting upon them and acted upon by them. In ignoring this and confining myself to the "states of consciousness"

further expression in psychology, which undertakes to show how this individualization proceeds, and in what aspect it presents itself.

Of course, such a conception means something for philosophy as well as for psychology; possibly it involves for philosophy the larger measure of transformation. It involves surrender of any claim on the part of philosophy to be the sole source of some truths and the exclusive guardian of some values. It means that philosophy be a method; not an assurance company, nor a knight errant. It means an alignment with science. Philosophy may not be sacrificed to the partial and superficial clamor of that which sometimes officiously and pretentiously exhibits itself as Science. But there is a sense in which philosophy must go to school to the sciences; must have no data save such as it receives at their hands; and be hospitable to no method of inquiry or reflection not akin to those in daily use among the sciences. As long as it claims for itself special territory of fact, or peculiar modes of access to truth, so long must it occupy a dubious position. Yet this claim it has to make until psychology comes to its own. There is something in experience, something in things, which the physical and the biological sciences do not touch; something, moreover, which is not just more experiences or more existences; but without which their materials are inexperienced, unrealized. Such sciences deal only with what *might* be experienced; with the content of experience, provided and assumed there be experience. It is psychology which tells us how this possible experience loses its barely hypothetical character, and is stamped with categorical unquestioned experiencedness; how, in a word, it becomes here and

---

theory and the "natural history" theory, I may appear not only to have unduly narrowed the concerns at issue, but to have weakened my own point, as this doctrine seems to offer a special vantage ground whence to defend the close relationship of psychology and philosophy. The "narrowing," if such it be, will have to pass—from limits of time and other matters. But the other point I cannot concede. The independently existing soul restricts and degrades individuality, making of it a separate thing outside of the full flow of things, alien to things experienced and consequently in either mechanical or miraculous relations to them. It is vitiated by just the quality already objected to—that psychology has a separate piece of reality apportioned to it, instead of occupying itself with the manifestation and operation of any and all existences in reference to concrete action. From this point of view, the "states of consciousness" attitude is a much more hopeful and fruitful one. It ignores certain considerations, to be sure; and when it turns its ignoring into denial, it leaves us with curious hieroglyphics. But after all, there is a key; these symbols can be read; they may be translated into terms of the course of experience. When thus translated, selfhood, individuality, is neither wiped out nor set up as a miraculous and foreign entity; it is seen as the unity of reference and function involved in all things when fully experienced—the pivot about which they turn.

now in some uniquely individualized life. Here is the necessary transition of science into philosophy; a passage that carries the verified and
solid body of the one into the large and free form of the other.*

## 12. The Experimental Theory of Knowledge*

An earlier version of this essay appeared in *Mind* in 1906.
Along with approximately a dozen other essays published between 1905 and 1907, Dewey attempts in this selection to
frame out a metaphysics of experience, with particular emphasis on the meaning of relations in the knowing process.
These efforts of Dewey correspond thematically with those of
William James between 1904 and 1906 to also develop a
metaphysics of relations, called by James a "radical empiricism."

In this essay, "The Experimental Theory of Knowledge,"
Dewey cites his opposition to those for whom the knowing
process is "a strictly 'mental' thing" and to those for whom
"our 'mental states' are bare transitory hints" of absolute
reality. To the contrary, Dewey stresses the "intending"
character of knowing and the relational character of truth.

* [Note: I have let this paper stand much as written, though now conscious that
much more is crowded into it than could properly be presented in one paper. The
drift of the ten years from '99 to '09 has made, I venture to believe, for increased
clearness in the main positions of the paper: The revival of a naturalistic realism,
the denial of the existence of "consciousness," the development of functional and
dynamic psychology (accompanied by aversion to interpretation of functions as
faculties of a soul-substance)—all of these tendencies are sympathetic with the
aim of the paper. There is another reason for letting it stand: the new functional
and pragmatic empiricism proffered in this volume has been constantly objected to
on the ground that its conceptions of knowledge and verification lead only to subjectivism and solipsism. The paper may indicate that the identification of experience with bare states of consciousness represents the standpoint of the critic,
not of the empiricism criticised, and that it is for him, not for me, to fear the subjective implications of such a position. The paper also clearly raises the question as
to how far the isolation of "consciousness" from nature and social life, which
characterizes the procedure of many psychologists of to-day, is responsible for
keeping alive quite unreal problems in philosophy.]

* From John Dewey, *The Influence of Darwin on Philosophy: And Other Essays in Contemporary Thought*, pp. 77-111. Copyright 1910 by Holt,
Rinehart and Winston, Inc. Copyright 1938 by John Dewey. Reprinted by permission of Holt, Rinehart and Winston, Inc. (Published originally in July, 1906.)

Dewey writes that "fulfillment, completion are always relative terms. Hence the criterion of the truth or falsity of the meaning, of the adequacy, of the cognitional thing lies within the relationships of the situation and not without." He prefers the adverb "truly" to the abstract noun "truth," but perhaps it can be said that what he points to are our attempts at "trueing."

It should be possible to discern and describe a knowing as one identifies any object, concern, or event. It must have its own marks; it must offer characteristic features—as much so as a thunder-storm, the constitution of a State, or a leopard. In the search for this affair, we are first of all desirous for something which is for itself, contemporaneously with its occurrence, a cognition, not something called knowledge by another and from without—whether this other be logician, psychologist, or epistemologist. The "knowledge" may turn out false, and hence no knowledge; but this is an after-affair; it may prove to be rich in fruitage of wisdom, but if this outcome be only wisdom after the event, it does not concern us. What we want is just something which takes itself as knowledge, rightly or wrongly.

I

This means a specific case, a sample. Yet instances are proberbially dangerous—so naïvely and graciously may they beg the questions at issue. Our recourse is to an example so simple, so much on its face as to be as innocent as may be of assumptions. This case we shall gradually complicate, mindful at each step to state just what new elements are introduced. Let us suppose a smell, just a floating odor. This odor may be anchored by supposing that it moves to action; it starts changes that end in picking and enjoying a rose. This description is intended to apply to the course of events witnessed and recounted from without. What sort of a course must it be to constitute a knowledge, or to have somewhere within its career that which deserves this title? The smell, *imprimis*, is there; the movements that it excites are there; the final plucking and gratification are experienced. But, let us say, the smell is not the smell *of* the rose; the resulting change of the organism is not a sense of walking and reaching; the delicious finale is not the fulfilment of the movement, and, through that, of the original smell; "is not," in each case meaning is "not experienced as" such. We may take, in short, these experiences in a brutely serial fashion. The smell, $S$, is replaced (and displaced) by a felt movement, $K$, this is replaced by the gratification, $G$. Viewed from without, as we are now regarding it, there is $S$-$K$-$G$. But from within, for itself, it is now $S$, now $K$, now $G$, and so on to the end of the chapter. Nowhere is there looking before and after; memory and anticipation are not born. Such an experience neither is, in whole or in part, a knowledge, nor does it exercise a cognitive function.

Here, however, we may be halted. If there is anything present in "consciousness" at all, we may be told (at least we constantly are so told) there must be knowledge of it as present—present, at all events, in "consciousness." There is, so it is argued, knowledge at least of a simple apprehensive type, knowledge of the acquaintance order, knowledge *that*, even though not knowledge *what*. The smell, it is admitted, does not know *about* anything else, nor is anything known *about* the smell (the same thing, perhaps); but the smell is known, either by itself, or by the mind, or by some subject, some unwinking, unremitting eye. No, we must reply; there is no apprehension without some (however slight) context; no acquaintance which is not either recognition or expectation. Acquaintance is presence honored with an escort; presence is introduced as familiar, or an associate springs up to greet it. Acquaintance always implies a little friendliness; a trace of re-knowing, of anticipatory welcome or dread of the trait to follow.

This claim cannot be dismissed as trivial. If valid, it carries with it the distance between being and knowing: and the recognition of an element of mediation, that is, of art, in all knowledge. This disparity, this transcendence, is not something which holds of *our* knowledge, of finite knowledge, just marking the gap between our type of consciousness and some other with which we may contrast it after the manner of the agnostic or the transcendentalist (who hold so much property in joint ownership!), but exists because knowing is knowing, that way of bringing things to bear upon things which we call reflection—a manipulation of things experienced in the light one of another.

"Feeling," I read in a recent article, "feeling is immediately acquainted with its own quality, with its own subjective being."[1] How

---

[1] I must remind the reader again of a point already suggested. It is the identification of presence in consciousness with knowledge as such that leads to setting up *a* mind (*ego*, subject) which has the peculiar property of knowing (only so often it knows wrong!), or else that leads to supplying "sensations" with the peculiar property of surveying their own entrails. Given the correct feeling that knowledge involves relationship, there being, by supposition, no other *thing* to which the thing in consciousness is related, it is forthwith related to a soul substance, or to its ghostly offspring, a "subject," or to "consciousness" itself.

and whence this duplication in the inwards of feeling into feeling the knower and feeling the known? into feeling as being and feeling as acquaintance? Let us frankly deny such monsters. Feeling *is* its own quality; is its own *specific* (whence and why, once more, *subjective?*) being. If this statement be dogmatism, it is at least worth insistent declaration, were it only by way of counter-irritant to that other dogmatism which asserts that being in "consciousness" is always presence for or in knowledge. So let us repeat once more, that to *be* a smell (or anything else) is one thing, to be *known* as smell, another; to be a "feeling" one thing, to be *known* as a "feeling" another.[2] The first is thinghood; existence indubitable, direct; in this way all things *are* that are in "consciousness" at all.[3] The second is *reflected* being, things indicating and calling for other things—something offering the possibility of truth and hence of falsity. The first is genuine immediacy; the second is (in the instance discussed) a pseudo-immediacy, which in the same breath that it proclaims its immediacy smuggles in another term (and one which is unexperienced both in itself and in its relation) the subject or "consciousness," to which the immediate is related.[4]

But we need not remain with dogmatic assertions. To be acquainted with a thing or with a person has a definite empirical meaning; we have only to call to mind what it is to be genuinely and empirically acquainted, to have done forever with this uncanny presence which, though bare and simple presence, is yet known, and thus is clothed upon and complicated. To be acquainted with a thing is to be assured (from the standpoint of the experience itself) that it is of such and such a character; that it will behave, if given an opportunity, in such and such a

---

[2] Let us further recall that this theory requires either that things present shall already be psychical things (feelings, sensations, etc.), in order to be assimilated to the knowing mind, subject to consciousness; or else translates genuinely naïve realism into the miracle of a mind that gets outside itself to lay its ghostly hands upon the things of an external world.

[3] This means that things may be present *as* known, just as they be present as hard or soft, agreeable or disgusting, hoped for or dreaded. The mediacy, or the art of intervention, which characterizes knowledge, indicates precisely the way in which known things as known are immediately present.

[4] If Hume had had a tithe of the interest in the *flux* of perceptions and in *habit*—principles of continuity and of organization—which he had in distinct and isolated existences, he might have saved us both from German *Erkenntnisstheorie*, and from that modern miracle play, the psychology of elements of consciousness, that under the aegis of science, does not hesitate to have psychical elements compound and breed, and in their agile intangibility put to shame the performances of their less acrobatic cousins, physical atoms.

way; that the obviously and flagrantly present trait is associated with fellow traits that will show themselves, if the leadings of the present trait are followed out. To be acquainted is to anticipate to some extent, on the basis of prior experience. I am, say, barely acquainted with Mr. Smith: then I have no extended body of associated qualities along with those palpably present, but at least some one suggested trait occurs; his nose, his tone of voice, the place where I saw him, his calling in life, an interesting anecdote about him, etc. To be acquainted is to know what a thing is *like* in some particular. If one is acquainted with the smell of a flower it means that the smell is not just smell, but reminds one of some other experienced thing which stands in continuity with the smell. There is thus supplied a condition of control over or purchase upon what is present, the possibility of translating it into terms of some other trait not now sensibly present.

Let us return to our example. Let us suppose that $S$ is not just displaced by $K$ and then by $G$. Let us suppose it persists; and persists not as an unchanged $S$ alongside $K$ and $G$, nor yet as fused with them into a new further quale $J$. For in such events, we have only the type already considered and rejected. For an observer the new quale might be more complex, or fuller of meaning, than the original $S$, $K$, or $G$, but might not be experienced *as* complex. We might thus suppose a composite photograph which should suggest nothing of the complexity of its origin and structure. In this case we should have simply another picture.

But we may also suppose that the blur of the photograph suggests the superimposition of pictures and something of their character. Then we get another, and for our problem, much more fruitful kind of persistence. We will imagine that the final $G$ assumes this form: Gratification-terminating-movement-induced-by-smell. The smell is still present; it has persisted. It is not present in its original form, but is represented with a quality, an office, that of having excited activity and thereby terminating its career in a certain quale of gratification. It is not $S$, but   ; that is $S$ with an increment of meaning due to maintenance and fulfilment through a process. $S$ is no longer just smell, but smell which has excited and thereby secured.

Here we have a cognitive, but not a cognitional thing. In saying that the smell is finally experienced as *meaning* gratification (through intervening handling, seeing, etc.) and meaning it not in a hapless way, but in a fashion which operates to effect what is meant, we retrospectively attribute intellectual force and function to the smell—and this is what is signified by "cognitive." Yet the smell is not cognitional, because it did not knowingly intend to mean this; but is found, after the event, to have meant it. Nor again is the final experience, the    or transformed $S$, a knowledge.

Here again the statement may be challenged. Those who agree with the denial that bare presence of a quale in "consciousness" constitutes acquaintance and simple apprehension, may now turn against us, saying that experience of fulfilment of meaning is just what we mean by knowledge, and this is just what the    of our illustration is. The point is fundamental. As the smell at first was presence or being, less than knowing, so the fulfilment is an experience that is more than knowing. Seeing and handling the flower, enjoying the full meaning of the smell as the odor of just this beautiful thing, is not knowledge because it is more than knowledge.

As this may seem dogmatic, let us suppose that the fulfilment, the realization, experience, is a knowledge. Then how shall it be distinguished from and yet classed with other things called knowledge, viz., reflective, discursive cognitions? Such knowledges are what they are precisely because they are not fulfilments, but intentions, aims, schemes, symbols of overt fulfilment. Knowledge, perceptual and conceptual, of a hunting dog is prerequisite in order that I may really hunt with the hounds. The hunting in turn may increase my knowledge of dogs and their ways. But the knowledge of the dog, *qua* knowledge, remains characteristically marked off from the use of that knowledge in the fulfilment experience, the hunt. The hunt is a *realization* of knowledge; it alone, if you please, verifies, validates, knowledge, or supplies tests of truth. The prior knowledge of the dog, was, if you wish, hypothetical, lacking in assurance or categorical certainty. The hunting, the fulfilling, realizing experience alone *gives* knowledge, because it alone completely assures; makes faith good in works.

Now there is and can be no objection to this definition of knowledge, *provided it is consistently adhered to*. One has as much right to identify knowledge with complete assurance, as I have to identify it with anything else. Considerable justification in the common use of language, in common sense, may be found for defining knowledge as complete assurance. But even upon this definition, the fulfilling experience is not, as such, complete assurance, and hence not a knowledge. Assurance, cognitive validation, and guaranteeship, follow from it, but are not coincident with its occurrence. It *gives*, but *is* not, assurance. The concrete construction of a story, the manipulation of a machine, the hunting with the dogs, is not, so far as it *is* fulfilment, a confirmation of meanings previously entertained as cognitional; that is, is not contemporaneously experienced as such. To think of prior schemes, symbols, meanings, as fulfilled in a subsequent experience, is reflectively to present in their relations to one another both the meanings and the experiences in which they are, as a matter of fact, embodied. This reflective attitude cannot be identical with the fulfilment experience itself; it occurs only in retrospect when the worth of the meanings, or cognitive ideas, is critically inspected in the light of their fulfilment; or it occurs as an interruption of the fulfilling experience. The hunter stops his hunting as a fulfilment to reflect that he made a mistake in his idea of his dog, or again, that his dog is everything he thought he was—that his notion of him is confirmed. Or, the man stops the actual construction of his machine and turns back upon his plan in correction or in admiring estimate of its value. *The fulfilling experience is not of itself knowledge*, then, even if we identify knowledge with fulness of assurance or guarantee. Moreover it gives, affords, assurance only in reference to a situation which we have not yet considered.[5]

Before the category of confirmation or refutation can be introduced, there must be something which *means* to mean something and which therefore can be guaranteed or nullified by the issue—and this is precisely what we have not as yet found. We must return to our instance and introduce a further complication. Let us suppose that the smell quale recurs at a later date, and that it recurs neither as the original $S$ nor yet as the final , but as an $S'$ which is fated or charged with the sense of the possibility of a fulfilment like unto . The $S'$ that recurs is aware of something else which it means, which it intends to effect through an operation incited by it and without which its own presence is abortive, and, so to say, unjustified, senseless. Now we have an experience which is *cognitional*, not merely cognitive; which is contemporaneously aware of meaning something beyond itself, instead of having this meaning ascribed by another at a later period. *The odor knows the rose; the rose is known by the odor; and the import of each term is constituted by the relationship in which it stands to the other.* That is, the import of the smell is the indicating and demanding relation which it sustains to the enjoyment of the rose as its fulfilling experience; while this enjoyment is just the content or definition of what the smell consciously meant, *i.e.*, meant to mean. Both the thing meaning and the thing meant are elements in the same situation. Both are present, but both are not present in the same way. In fact, one is present as-*not-*

---

[5] In other words, the situation as described is not to be confused with the case of hunting on purpose to test an idea regarding the dog.

present-in-the-same-way-in-which-the-other-is. It is present as some-thing to be rendered present in the same way through the intervention of an operation. We must not balk at a purely verbal difficulty. It suggests a verbal inconsistency to speak of a thing present-as-absent. But all ideal contents, all aims (that is, things aimed at) are present in just such fashion. Things can be presented as absent, just as they can be presented as hard or soft, black or white, six inches or fifty rods away from the body. The assumption that an ideal content must be either totally absent, or else present *in just the same fashion* as it will be when it is realized, is not only dogmatic, but self-contradictory. The only way in which an ideal content can be experienced at all is to be presented as *not-present-in-the-same-way* in which something else is present, the lat-ter kind of presence affording the standard or type of *satisfactory* presence. When present in the same way it ceases to be an ideal content. Not a contrast of bare existence over against non-existence, or of pres-ent consciousness over against reality out of present consciousness, but of a satisfactory with an unsatisfactory mode of presence makes the dif-ference between the "really" and the "ideally" present.

In terms of our illustration, handling and enjoying the rose are pres-ent, but they are not present in the same way that the smell is present. They are present as *going* to be there in the same way, through an operation which the smell stands sponsor for. The situation is inherently an uneasy one—one in which everything hangs upon the performance of the operation indicated; upon the adequacy of movement as a con-necting link, or real adjustment of the thing meaning and the thing meant. Generalizing from the instance, we get the following definition: An experience is a knowledge, if in its quale there is an experienced distinction and connection of two elements of the following sort: *one means or intends the presence of the other in the same fashion in which itself is already present, while the other is that which, while not present in the same fashion, must become so present if the meaning or intention of its companion or yoke-fellow is to be fulfilled through the operation it sets up.*

II

We now return briefly to the question of knowledge as acquaintance, and at greater length to that of knowledge as assurance, or as fulfilment which confirms and validates. With the recurrence of the odor as mean-ing something beyond itself, there is apprehension, knowledge *that*. One may now say I know what a *rose* smells like; or I know what *this* smell is like; I am acquainted with the rose's agreeable odor. In short, on the basis of a present quality, the odor anticipates and forestalls some further trait.

We have also the conditions of knowledge of the confirmation and refutation type. In the working out of the situation just described, in the transformation, self-indicated and self-demanded, of the tensional into a harmonious or satisfactory situation, fulfilment *or* disappointment results. The odor either does or does not fulfil itself in the rose. The smell as intention is borne out by the facts, or is nullified. As has already been pointed out, the subsequent experience of the fulfilment type is not primarily a confirmation or refutation. Its import is too vital, too urgent to be reduced *in itself* just to the value of testing an intention or meaning.[6] But it gets *in reflection* just such verificatory significance. If the smell's intention is unfulfilled, the discrepancy may throw one back, in reflection, upon the original situation. Interesting developments then occur. The smell meant a rose; and yet it did not (so it turns out) mean a rose; it meant another flower, or something, one can't just tell what. Clearly there is *something else* which enters in; something else beyond the odor as it was first experienced determined the validity of its meaning. Here then, perhaps, we have a transcendental, as distinct from an experimental reference? *Only if this something else makes no difference, or no detectable difference, in the smell itself.* If the utmost observation and reflection can find no difference in the smell quales that fail and those that succeed in executing their intentions, then there is an outside controlling and disturbing factor, which, since it is outside of the situation, can never be utilized in knowledge, and hence can never be employed in any concrete testing or verifying. In this case, knowing depends upon an extra-experimental or transcendental factor. But this very transcendental quality makes both confirmation and refutation, correction, criticism, of the pretensions or meanings of things, impossible. For the conceptions of truth and error, we must, upon the transcendental basis, substitute those of accidental success or

---

[6] Dr. Moore, in an essay in "Contributions to Logical Theory" has brought out clearly, on the basis of a criticism of the theory of meaning and fulfilment advanced in Royce's "World and Individual," the full consequences of this distinction. I quote one sentence (p. 350): "Surely there is a pretty discernible difference between experience as a purposive idea, and the experience which fulfils this purpose. To call them both 'ideas' is at least confusing." The text above simply adds that there is also a discernible and important difference between experiences which, *de facto*, are purposing and fulfilling (that is, are seen to be such *ab extra*), and those which meant to be such, and are found to be what they meant.

failure. Sometimes the intention chances upon one, sometimes upon another. Why or how, the gods only know—and they only if to them the extra-experimental factor is not extra-experimental, but makes a concrete ·difference in the concrete smell. But fortunately the situation is not one to be thus described. The factor that determines the success or failure, does institute a difference in the thing which means the object, and this difference is detectable, once attention, through failure, has been called to the need of its discovery. At the very least, it makes this difference: the smell is infected with an element of uncertainty of meaning—and this as a part of the thing experienced, not for an observer. This additional *awareness* at least brings about an additional *wariness*. Meaning is more critical, and operation more cautious.

But we need not stop here. Attention may be fully directed to the subject of smells. Smells may become the object of knowledge. They may take, *pro tempore*,[7] the place which the rose formerly occupied. One may, that is, observe the cases in which odors mean other things than just roses, may voluntarily produce new cases for the sake of further inspection, and thus account for the cases where meanings had been falsified in the issue; discriminate more carefully the peculiarities of those meanings which the event verified, and thus safeguard and bulwark to some extent the employing of similar meanings in the future. Superficially, it may then seem as if odors were treated after the fashion of Locke's simple ideas, or Hume's "distinct ideas which are separate existences." Smells apparently assume an independent, isolated status during this period of investigation. "Sensations," as the laboratory psychologist and the analytic psychologist generally study them, are examples of just such detached things. But egregious error results if we forget that this seeming isolation and detachment is the outcome of a deliberate scientific device—that it is simply a part of the scientific technique of an inquiry directed upon securing *tested* conclusions. Just and only because odors (or any group of qualities) are parts of a connected world are they signs of things beyond themselves; and only because they are signs is it profitable and necessary to study them *as if* they were complete, self-enclosed entities.

In the reflective determination of things with reference to their specifically meaning other things, experiences of fulfilment, disap-

[7] The association of science and philosophy with leisure, with a certain economic surplus, is not accidental. It is practically worth while to postpone practice; to substitute theorizing, to develop a new and fascinating mode of practice. But it is the excess achievement of practice which makes this postponement and substitution possible.

pointment, and going astray inevitably play an important and recurrent *rôle*. They also are realistic facts, related in realistic ways to the things that intend to mean other things and to the things intended. When these fulfilments and refusals *are reflected upon* in the determinate relations in which they stand to their relevant meanings, they obtain a quality which is quite lacking to them in their immediate occurrence as just fulfilments or disappointments; viz., the property of affording assurance and correction—of confirming and refuting. Truth and falsity are not properties of any experience or thing, in and of itself or in its first intention; *but of things where the problem of assurance consciously enters in. Truth and falsity present themselves as significant facts only in situations in which specific meanings and their already experienced fulfilments and non-fulfilments are intentionally compared and contrasted with reference to the question of the worth, as to reliability of meaning, of the given meaning or class of meanings.* Like knowledge itself, truth is an experienced relation of things, and it has no meaning outside of such relation,[8] any more than such adjectives as comfortable applied to a lodging, correct applied to speech, persuasive applied to an orator, etc., have worth apart from the *specific* things to which they are applied. It would be a great gain for logic and epistemology, if we were always to translate the noun "truth" back into the adjective "true," and this back into the adverb "truly"; at least, if we were to do so until we have familiarized ourselves thoroughly with the fact that "truth" is an abstract noun, summarizing a quality presented by specific affairs in their own specific contents.


### III


I have attempted, in the foregoing pages, a description of the function of knowledge in its own terms and on its merits—a description which in intention is realistic, if by realistic we are content to mean naturalistic, a description undertaken on the basis of what Mr. Santayana has well called "following the lead of the subject-matter." Unfortunately at the present time all such undertakings contend with a serious extraneous obstacle. Accomplishing the undertaking has difficulties enough of its

---

[8] It is the failure to grasp the coupling of truth of meaning with a *specific* promise, undertaking, or intention expressed by a thing which underlies, so far as I can see, the criticisms passed upon the experimental or pragmatic view of the truth. It is the same failure which is responsible for the wholly *at large* view of truth which characterizes the absolutists.

own to reckon with; and first attempts are sure to be imperfect, if not radically wrong. But at present the attempts are not, for the most part, even listened to on their own account, they are not examined and criticised as naturalistic attempts. *They are compared with undertakings of a wholly different nature, with an epistemological theory of knowledge, and the assumptions of this extraneous theory are taken as a ready-made standard by which to test their validity.* Literally of course, "epistemology" means only theory of knowledge; the term *might* therefore have been employed simply as a synonym for a descriptive logic; for a theory that takes knowledge as it finds it and attempts to give the same kind of an account of it that would be given of any other natural function or occurrence. But the mere mention of what *might* have been only accentuates what is. The things that pass for epistemology all assume that knowledge is not a natural function or event, but a mystery.

Epistemology starts from the assumption that certain conditions lie back of knowledge. The mystery would be great enough if knowledge were constituted by non-natural conditions back of knowledge, but the mystery is increased by the fact that the conditions are defined so as to be incompatible with knowledge. Hence the primary problem of epistemology is: How is knowledge *überhaupt*, knowledge at large, *possible?* Because of the incompatibility between the concrete occurrence and function of knowledge and the conditions back of it to which it must conform, a second problem arises: How is knowledge in general, knowledge *überhaupt, valid?* Hence the complete divorce in contemporary thought between epistemology as theory of knowledge and logic as an account of the specific ways in which particular beliefs that are better than other alternative beliefs regarding the same matters are formed; and also the complete divorce between a naturalistic, a biological and social psychology, setting forth how the function of knowledge is evolved out of other natural activities, and epistemology as an account of how knowledge is possible anyhow.

It is out of the question to set forth in this place in detail the contrast between transcendental epistemology and an experimental theory of knowledge. It may assist the understanding of the latter, however, if I point out, baldly and briefly, how, *out of the distinctively empirical situation*, there arise those assumptions which make knowledge a mystery, and hence a topic for a peculiar branch of philosophizing.

As just pointed out, epistemology makes the possibility of knowledge a problem, because it assumes back of knowledge conditions incompatible with the obvious traits of knowledge as it empirically exists. These assumptions are that the organ or instrument of knowledge is not a natural object, but some ready-made state of mind or consciousness, something purely "subjective," a peculiar kind of existence which lives, moves, and has its being in a realm different from things to be known; and that the ultimate goal and content of knowledge is a fixed, ready-made thing which has no organic connections with the origin, purpose, and growth of the attempt to know it, some kind of *Ding-an-sich* or absolute, extra-empirical "Reality."

(1) It is not difficult to see at what point in the development of natural knowledge, or the signifying of one thing by another, there arises the notion of the knowing medium as something radically different in the order of existence from the thing to be known. It arises subsequent to the repeated experience of non-fulfilment, of frustration and disappointment. The odor did not after all mean the rose; it meant something quite different; and yet its indicative function was exercised so forcibly that we could not help—or at least *did* not help—believing in the existence of the rose. This is a familiar and typical kind of experience, one which very early leads to the recognition that "things are not what they seem." There are two contrasted methods of dealing with this recognition: one is the method indicated above. We go more thoroughly, patiently, and carefully into the facts of the case. We employ all sorts of methods, invented for the purpose, of examining the things that are signs and the things that are signified, and we experimentally produce various situations, in order that we may tell *what* smells mean roses *when* roses are meant, what it is about the smell and the rose that led us into error; and that we may be able to discriminate those cases in which a suspended conclusion is all that circumstances admit. We simply do the best we can to regulate our system of signs so that they become as instructive as possible, utilizing for this purpose (as indicated above) all possible experiences of success and of failure, and deliberately instituting cases which will throw light on the specific empirical causes of success and failure.

Now it so happens that when the facts of error were consciously generalized and formulated, namely in Greek thought, such a technique of specific inquiry and rectification did not exist—in fact, it hardly could come into existence until *after* error had been seized upon as constituting a fundamental anomaly. Hence the method just outlined of dealing with the situation was impossible. We can imagine disconsolate ghosts willing to postpone any professed solution of the difficulty till subsequent generations have thrown more light on the question itself; we can hardly imagine passionate human beings exercising such reserve.

At all events, Greek thought provided what seemed a satisfactory way out: there are two orders of existence, one permanent and complete, the noumenal region, to which alone the characteristic of Being is properly applicable, the other transitory, phenomenal, sensible, a region of non-Being, or at least of mere Coming-to-be, a region in which Being is hopelessly mixed with non-Being, with the unreal. The former alone is the domain of knowledge, of truth; the latter is the territory of opinion, confusion, and error. In short, the contrast *within* experience of the cases in which things successfully and unsuccessfully maintained and executed the meanings of other things was erected into a wholesale difference of status in the intrinsic characters of the things involved in the two types of cases.

With the beginnings of modern thought, the region of the "unreal," the source of opinion and error, was located exclusively in the individual. The object was *all* real and *all* satisfactory, but the "subect" could approach the object only through his own subjective states, his "sensations" and "ideas." The Greek conception of two orders of existence was retained, but instead of the two orders characterizing the "universe" itself, one *was* the universe, the other was the individual mind trying to know that universe. This scheme would obviously easily account for error and hallucination; but how could *knowledge*, truth, ever come about on such a basis? The Greek problem of the possibility of error became the modern problem of the possibility of knowledge.

Putting the matter in terms that are independent of history, experiences of failure, disappointment, non-fulfilment of the function of meaning and contention may lead the individual to the path of science—to more careful and extensive investigation of the things themselves, with a view to detecting specific sources of error, and guarding against them, and regulating, so far as possible, the conditions under which objects are bearers of meanings beyond themselves. But impatient of such slow and tentative methods (which insure not infallibility but increased probability of valid conclusions), by reason of disappointment a person may turn epistemologist. He may then take the discrepancy, the failure of the smell to execute its own intended meaning, as a wholesale, rather than as a specific fact: as evidence of a contrast in general between things meaning and things meant, instead of as evidence of the need of a more cautious and thorough inspection of odors and execution of operations indicated by them. One may then say: Woe is me; smells are only *my* smells, subjective states existing in an order of being made out of consciousness, while roses exist in another order made out of a radically different sort of stuff; or, odors are made out of "finite" consciousness as their stuff, while the real things, the objects which fulfil them, are made out of an "infinite" consciousness as their material. Hence some purely metaphysical tie has to be called in to bring them into connection with each other. And yet this tie does not concern knowledge; it does not make the meaning of one odor any more correct than that of another, nor enable us to discriminate relative degrees of correctness. As a principle of control, this transcendental connection is related to all alike, and hence condemns and justifies all alike.[9]

It is interesting to note that the transcendentalist almost invariably first falls into the psychological fallacy; and then having himself taken the psychologist's attitude (the attitude which is interested in meanings as themselves self-inclosed "ideas") accuses the empiricist whom he criticises of having confused mere psychological existence with logical validity. That is, he begins by supposing that the smell of our illustration (and all the cognitional objects for which this is used as a symbol) is a purely mental or psychical state, so that the question of logical reference or intention is the problem of how the merely mental can "know" the extra-mental. But from a strictly empirical point of view, the smell which knows is no more merely mental than is the rose known. We may, if we please, say that the smell when involving conscious meaning or intention is "mental," but this term "mental" does not denote some separate type of existence—existence as a state of consciousness. It denotes only the fact that the smell, a real and non-psychical object, now exercises an intellectual *function*. This new property involves, as James has pointed out, an *additive* relation—a new

[10] The belief in the *metaphysical* transcendence of the object of knowledge seems to have its real origin in an *empirical* transcendence of a very specific and describable sort. The thing meaning is one thing; the thing meant is another thing, and is (as already pointed out) a thing presented as not given in the same way as is the thing which means. It is something *to be* so given. No amount of careful and thorough inspection of the indicating and signifying things can remove or annihilate this gap. The *probability* of correct meaning may be increased in varying degrees—and this is what we mean by control. But final certitude can never be reached except experimentally—except by performing the operations indicated and discovering whether or no the intended meaning is fulfilled *in propria persona*. In this experimental sense, truth or the object of any given meaning is always beyond or outside of the cognitional thing that means it. Error as well as truth is a necessary function of knowing. But the non-empirical account of this transcendent (or beyond) relationship puts *all* the error in one place (*our* knowledge), and *all* the truth in another (absolute consciousness or else a thing-in-itself).

property possessed by a non-mental object, when that object, occurring in a new context, assumes a further office and use.[10] To be "in the mind" means to be in a situation in which the function of intending is directly concerned.[11] Will not some one who believes that the knowing experience is *ab origine* a strictly "mental" thing, explain how, as matter of fact, it does get a specific, extra-mental reference, capable of being tested, confirmed, or refuted? Or, if he believes that viewing it as merely mental expresses only the form it takes for psychological analysis, will he not explain why he so persistently attributes the inherently "mental" characterization of it to the empiricist whom he criticises? An object *becomes* meaning when used empirically in a certain way; and, under certain circumstances, the exact character and worth of this meaning *becomes* an object of solicitude. But the transcendental epistemologist with his purely psychical "meanings" and his purely extra-empirical "truths" assumes a *Deus ex Machina* whose mechanism is preserved a secret. And as if to add to the arbitrary character of his assumption, he has to admit that the transcendental *a priori* faculty by which mental states get objective reference does not in the least help us to discriminate, *in the concrete*, between an objective reference that is false and one that is valid.

(2) The counterpart assumption to that of pure aboriginal "mental states" is, of course, that of an Absolute Reality, fixed and complete in itself, of which our "mental states" are bare transitory hints, their true meaning and their transcendent goal being the Truth *in rerum natura*. If the organ and medium of knowing is a self-inclosed order of existence different in kind from the Object to be known, then that Object must stand out there in complete aloofness from the concrete purpose and procedure of knowing it. But if we go back to the knowing as a natural occurrence, capable of description, we find that just as a smell does not mean Rose in general (or anything else at large), but means a *specific* group of qualities whose experience is intended and anticipated, so the function of knowing is always expressed in connections between a given experience and a specific possible wanted experience. The "rose" that is meant in a particular situation *is* the rose of that situation. When this experience is consummated, it is achieved as the fulfilment of the conditions in which just *that* intention was entertained—not as the

[10] Compare his essay, "Does Consciousness Exist?" in the *Journal of Philosophy, Psychology, and Scientific Methods*, Vol. I., p. 480.

[11] Compare the essay on the "Problem of Consciousness," by Professor Woodbridge, in the Garman Memorial Volume, entitled "Studies in Philosophy and Psychology."

fulfilment of a faculty of knowledge or a meaning in general. Subsequent meanings and subsequent fulfilments may increase, may enrich the consummating experience; the object or content of the rose as known may be other and fuller next time and so on. But we have no right to set up "a rose" at large or in general as the object of the knowing odor; the object of a knowledge is always strictly correlative to that particular thing which means it. It is not something which can be put in a wholesale way over against that which cognitively refers to it, as when the epistemologist puts the "real" rose (object) over against a merely phenomenal or empirical rose which *this* smell happens to mean. As the meaning gets more complex, fuller, more finely discriminated, the object which realizes or fulfils the meaning grows similarly in quality. But we cannot set up a rose, an object of fullest, complete, and exhaustive content as that which is really meant by any and every odor of a rose, whether it consciously meant to mean it or not. The test of the cognitional rectitude of the odor lies in the *specific* object which it sets out to secure. This is the meaning of the statement that the import of *each* term is found in its relationship to the other. It applies to object meant as well as to the meaning. Fulfilment, completion are always relative terms. *Hence the criterion of the truth or falsity of the meaning, of the adequacy, of the cognitional thing lies within the relationships of the situation and not without.* The thing that means another by means of an intervening operation either succeeds or fails in accomplishing the operation indicated, while this operation either gives or fails to give the object meant. Hence the truth or falsity of the original cognitional object.

## IV

From this excursion, I return in conclusion to a brief general characterization of those situations in which we are aware that things mean other things and are so critically aware of it that, in order to increase the probability of fulfilment and to decrease the chance of frustration, all possible pains are taken to regulate the meanings that attach to things. These situations define that type of knowing which we call *scientific*. There are things that claim to mean other experiences; in which the trait of meaning other objects is not discovered *ab extra*, and after the event, but is part of the thing itself. This trait of the thing is as realistic, as specific, as any other of its traits. It is, therefore, as open to inspection and determination as to its nature, as is any other trait. Moreover, since it is upon this trait that assurance (as distinct from accident) of fulfilment depends, an especial interest, an absorbing interest, attaches to its determination. Hence the scientific type of knowledge and its growing domination over other sorts.

We *employ* meanings in all intentional constructions of experience—in all anticipations, whether artistic, utilitarian or technological, social or moral. The success of the anticipation is found to depend upon the character of the meaning. Hence the stress upon a right determination of these meanings. Since they are the instruments upon which fulfilment depends *so far as that is controlled* or other than accidental, they become themselves objects of surpassing interest. For all persons at some times, and for one class of persons (scientists) at almost all times, the determination of the meanings employed in the control of fulfilments (of acting upon meanings) is central. The experimental or pragmatic theory of knowledge explains the dominating importance of science; it does not depreciate it or explain it away.

Possibly pragmatic writers are to blame for the tendency of their critics to assume that the practice they have in mind is utilitarian in some narrow sense, referring to some preconceived and inferior use—though I cannot recall any evidence for this admission. But what the pragmatic theory has in mind is precisely the fact that all the affairs of life which need regulation—*all values of all types*—depend upon utilizations of meanings. Action is not to be limited to anything less than the carrying out of ideas, than the execution, whether strenuous or easeful, of meanings. Hence the surpassing importance which comes to attach to the careful, impartial construction of the meanings, and to their constant survey and resurvey with reference to their value as evidenced by experiences of fulfilment and deviation.

That truth denotes *truths*, that is, specific verifications, combinations of meanings and outcomes reflectively viewed, is, one may say, the central point of the experimental theory. Truth, in general or in the abstract, is a just name for an experienced relation among the things of experience: that sort of relation in which intents are retrospectively viewed from the standpoint of the fulfilment which they secure through their own natural operation or incitement. Thus the experimental theory explains directly and simply the absolutistic tendency to translate concrete true things into the general relationship, Truth, and then to hypostatize this abstraction into identity with real being, Truth *per se* and *in se*, of which all transitory things and events—that is, all experienced realities—are only shadowy futile approximations. This type of relationship is central for man's will, for man's conscious endeavor. To select, to conserve, to extend, to propagate those meanings which the course of events has generated, to note their peculiarities, to be in advance on the alert for them, to search for them anxiously, to substitute them for meanings that eat up our energy in vain, defines the aim of rational effort and the goal of legitimate ambition. The absolutistic theory is the transfer of this moral or voluntary law of selective action into a quasi-physical (that is, metaphysical) law of indiscriminate being. Identify metaphysical being with *significant excellent* being—that is, with those relationships of things which, in our moments of deepest insight and largest survey, we would continue and reproduce—and the experimentalist, rather than the absolutist, is he who has a right to proclaim the supremacy of Truth, and the superiority of the life devoted to Truth for its own sake over that of "mere" activity. But to read back into an order of things which exists without the participation of our reflection and aim, the quality which defines the purpose of our thought and endeavor is at one and the same stroke to mythologize reality and to deprive the life of thoughtful endeavor of its ground for being.

## 13. Experience and Objective Idealism*

This essay is extremely telescoped in style, as witness the fact that some twenty years later Dewey devoted several hundred pages of *Experience and Nature* to an explication of the same themes. His fundamental concern is with the misleading presentation of the meaning of "experience" in the history of philosophy. Dewey believes that objective idealism owes its influence in great measure to its description of experiencing as a purely subjective human activity. Dewey denies this allegation and cites Locke, Peirce, and James to support his position. He points to a mediation between idealism seen as a process of "idealization" and an empiricism that acknowledges "the transitive character of experience" and "the possible control of the character of the transition by means of intelligent effort." Students who have found irreducible

* From John Dewey, *The Influence of Darwin on Philosophy: And Other Essays in Contemporary Thought*, pp. 198-225. Copyright 1910 by Holt, Rinehart and Winston, Inc. Copyright 1938 by John Dewey. Reprinted by permission of Holt, Rinehart and Winston, Inc. (Originally published in 1906.)

strains of idealism in the development of pragmatism will find this essay a primary source for such a claim.

I

Idealism as a philosophic system stands in such a delicate relation to experience as to invite attention. In its subjective form, or sensationalism, it claims to be the last word of empiricism. In its objective, or rational form, it claims to make good the deficiencies of the subjective type, by emphasizing the work of thought that supplies the factors of objectivity and universality lacking in sensationalism. With reference to experience *as it now is*, such idealism is half opposed to empiricism and half committed to it,—antagonistic, so far as existing experience is regarded as tainted with a sensational character; favorable, so far as this experience is even now prophetic of some final, all-comprehensive, or absolute experience, which in truth is one with reality.

That this combination of opposition to present experience with devotion to the cause of experience in the abstract leaves objective idealism in a position of unstable equilibrium from which it can find release only by euthanasia in a thorough-going empiricism seems evident. Some of the reasons for this belief may be readily approached by a summary sketch of three historic episodes in which have emerged important conceptions of experience and its relation to reason. The first takes us to classic Greek thought. Here experience means the preservation, through memory, of the net result of a multiplicity of particular doings and sufferings; a preservation that affords positive skill in maintaining further practice, and promise of success in new emergencies. The craft of the carpenter, the art of the physician are standing examples of its nature. It differs from instinct and blind routine or servile practice because there is some knowledge of materials, methods, and aims, in their adjustment to one another. Yet the marks of its passive, habitual origin are indelibly stamped upon it. On the knowledge side it can never aspire beyond opinion, and if true opinion be achieved, it is only by happy chance. On the active side it is limited to the accomplishment of a special work or a particular product, following some unjustified, because assumed, method. Thus it contrasts with the true knowledge of reason, which is direct apprehension, self-revealing and self-validating, of an eternal and harmonious content. The regions in which experience and reason respectively hold sway are thus explained. Experience has to do with production, which, in turn, is relative to decay. It deals with generation, becoming, not with finality, being. Hence it is infected with the trait of relative non-being, of mere imitativeness; hence its multiplicity, its logical inadequacy, its relativity to a standard and end beyond itself. Reason, *per contra*, has to do with meaning, with significance (ideas, forms), that is eternal and ultimate. Since the meaning of anything is the worth, the good, the end of that thing, experience presents us with partial and tentative efforts to achieve the embodiment of purpose, under conditions that doom the attempt to inconclusiveness. It has, however, its meed of reality in the degree in which its results *participate* in meaning, the good, reason.

From this classic period, then, comes the antithesis of experience as the historically achieved *embodiments* of meaning, partial, multiple, insecure, to reason as the source, author, and container of *meaning*, permanent, assured, unified. Idealism means ideality, experience means brute and broken facts. That things exist because of and for the sake of meaning, and that experience gives us meaning in a servile, interrupted, and inherently deficient way—such is the standpoint. Experience gives us meaning in process of becoming; special and isolated instances in which it *happens*, temporally, to appear, rather than meaning pure, undefiled, independent. Experience presents purpose, the good, struggling against obstacles, "involved in matter."

Just how much the vogue of modern Neo-Kantian idealism, professedly built upon a strictly epistemological instead of upon a cosmological basis, is due, in days of a declining theology, to a vague sense that affirming the function of reason in the constitution of a knowable world (which in its own constitution as logically knowable may be, morally and spiritually, anything you please), carries with it an assurance of the superior reality of the good and the beautiful as well as of the "true," it would be hard to say. Certainly unction seems to have descended upon epistemology, in apostolic succession, from classic idealism; so that neo-Kantianism is rarely without a tone of edification, as if feeling itself the patron of man's spiritual interests in contrast to the supposed crudeness and insensitiveness of naturalism and empiricism. At all events, we find here one element in our problem: Experience considered as the summary of past episodic adventures and happenings in relation to fulfilled and adequately expressed meaning.

The second historic event centers about the controversy of innate ideas, or pure concepts. The issue is between empiricism and rationalism as theories of the origin and validation of scientific knowledge. The empiricist is he who feels that the chief obstacle which prevents scientific method from making way is the belief in pure thoughts, not derived from particular observations and hence not responsible to the course of experience. His objection to the "high *a priori* road" is that it introduces in irresponsible fashion a mode of presumed knowledge which may be used at any turn to stand sponsor for mere tradition and prejudice, and thus to nullify the results of science resting upon and verified by observable facts. Experience thus comes to mean, to use the words of Peirce, "that which is forced upon a man's recognition will-he, nill-he, and shapes his thoughts to something quite different from what they naturally would have taken."[1] The same definition is found in James, in his chapter on Necessary Truths: "Experience means experience of something foreign supposed to impress us whether spontaneously or in consequence of our own exertions and acts."[2] As Peirce points out, this notion of experience as the foreign element that forces the hand of thought and controls its efficacy, goes back to Locke. Experience is "observation employed either about external sensible objects, or about the internal operations of our minds"[3] as furnishing in short all the valid data and tests of thinking and knowledge. This meaning, thinks Peirce, should be accepted "as a landmark which it would be a crime to disturb or displace."

The contention of idealism, here bound up with rationalism, is that perception and observation cannot guarantee knowledge in its honorific sense (science); that the peculiar differentia of scientific knowledge is a constancy, a universality, and necessity that contrast at every point with perceptual data, and that indispensably require the function of conception.[4] In short, *qualitative transformation of facts* (data of perception), not their mechanical subtraction and recombination, is the difference between scientific and perceptual knowledge. Here the problem which emerges is, of course, the significance of perception and of conception in respect to experience.[5]

The third episode reverses in a curious manner (which confuses pres-

---

[1] C. S. Peirce, *Monist*, Vol. XVI., p. 150.

[2] *Psychology*, Vol. II., p. 618.

[3] "Essay concerning Human Understanding," Book II, Chapter II, §2. Locke doubtless derived this notion from Bacon.

[4] It is hardly necessary to refer to the stress placed upon mathematics, as well as upon fundamental propositions in logic, ethics, and cosmology.

[5] Of course there are internal historic connections between experience as effective "memory," and experience as "observation." But the motivation and stress, the problem, has quite shifted. It may be remarked that Hobbes still writes under the influence of the Aristotelian conception. "Experience is nothing but Memory" ("Elements of Philosophy," Part I, Chapter I, §2), and hence is opposed to science.

ent discussion) the notion of experience as a foreign, alien, coercive material. It regards experience as a fortuitous association, by merely psychic connections, of individualistic states of consciousness. This is due to the Humian development of Locke. The "objects" and "operations," which to Locke were just given and secured in observation, become shifting complexes of subjective sensations and ideas, whose apparent permanency is due to discoverable illusions. This, of course, is the empiricism which made Kant so uneasily toss in his dogmatic slumbers (a tossing that he took for an awakening); and which, by reaction, called out the conception of thought as a function operating both to elevate perceptual data to scientific status, and also to confer objective status, or knowable character, upon even sensational data and their associative combinations.[6] Here emerges the third element in our problem: The function of thought as furnishing objectivity to any experience that claims cognitive reference or capacity.

Summing up the matter, idealism stands forth with its assertion of thought or reason as (1) the sponsor for all significance, ideality, purpose, in experience,—the author of the good and the beautiful as well as the true; (2) the power, located in pure conceptions, required to elevate perceptive or observational material to the plane of science; and (3) the constitution that gives objectivity, even the semblance of order, system, connection, mutual reference, to sensory data that without its assistance are mere subjective flux.

---

[6] There are, of course, anticipations of Hume in Locke. But to regard Lockeian experience as equivalent to Humian is to pervert history. Locke, as he was to himself and to the century succeeding him, was not a subjectivist, but in the main a common sense objectivist. It was this that gave him his historic influence. But so completely has the Hume-Kant controversy dominated recent thinking that it is constantly projected backward. Within a few weeks I have seen three articles, all insisting that the meaning of the term experience must be subjective, and stating or implying that those who take the term objectively are subverters of established usage! But a casual study of the dictionary will reveal that experience has always meant "*what* is experienced," observation as a source of knowledge, as well as the act, fact, or mode of experiencing. In the Oxford Dictionary, the (obsolete) sense of "experimental testing," of actual "observation of facts and events," and "the fact of being consciously affected by an act" have almost contemporaneous datings, viz., 1384, 1377, and 1382 respectively. A usage almost more objective than the second, the Baconian use, is "what has been experienced; the events that have taken place within the knowledge of an individual, a community, mankind at large, either during a particular period or generally." This dates back to 1607. Let us have no more captious criticisms and plaints based on ignorance of linguistic usage. [This pious wish has not been met. J. D., 1909.]

II

I begin the discussion with the last-named function. Thought is here conceived as *a priori*, not in the sense of particular innate ideas, but of a function that constitutes the very possibility of any objective experience, any experience involving reference beyond its own mere subjective happening. I shall try to show that idealism is condemned to move back and forth between two inconsistent interpretations of this *a priori* thought. It is taken to mean both the organized, the regulated, the informed, established character of experience, an order immanent and constitutional; and an agency which organizes, regulates, forms, synthesizes, a power operative and constructive. And the oscillation between and confusion of these two diverse senses is necessary to Neo-Kantian idealism.

When Kant compared his work in philosophy to that of the men who introduced construction into geometry, and experimentation into physics and chemistry, the point of his remarks depends upon taking the *a priori* worth of thought in a regulative, directive, controlling sense, thought as consciously, intentionally, making an experience *different* in a *determinate* sense and manner. But the point of his answer to Hume consists in taking the *a priori* in the other sense, as something which is *already* immanent in *any* experience, and which accordingly makes no determinate difference to any one experience as compared with any other, or with any past or future form of itself. The concept is treated first as that which makes an experience actually different, controlling its evolution towards consistency, coherency, and objective reliability; then, it is treated as that which has already effected the organization of any and every experience that comes to recognition at all. The fallacy from which he never emerges consists in vibrating between the definition of a concept as a rule of constructive synthesis in a *differential* sense, and the definition of it as a static endowment lurking in "mind," and giving automatically a hard and fixed law for the determination of every experienced object. The *a priori* conceptions of Kant as immanent fall, like the rain, upon the just and the unjust; upon error, opinion, and hallucination. But Kant slides into these *a priori* functions the preferential values exercised by empirical reflective thought. The concept of triangle, taken geometrically, means doubtless a determinate method of construing space elements; but to Kant it also means something that exists in the mind *prior* to all such geometrical constructions and that unconsciously lays down the law not only for their conscious elaboration, but also for any space perception, even for that which takes a rectangle to be a triangle. The first of the meanings is intelligible, and marks a definite contribution to the logic of science. But it is not "objective idealism"; it is a contribution to a revised empiricism. The second is a dark saying.

That organization of some sort exists in every experience I make no doubt. That isolation, discrepancy, the fragmentary, the incompatible, are brought to recognition and to logical function only with reference to some prior existential mode of organization seems clear. And it seems equally clear that reflection goes on with profit only because the materials with which it deals have already some degree of organization, or exemplify various relationships. As against Hume, or even Locke, we may be duly grateful to Kant for enforcing acknowledgment of these facts. But the acknowledgment means simply an improved and revised empiricism.

For, be it noted, this organization, first, is not the work of reason or thought, unless "reason" be stretched beyond all identification; and, secondly, it has no sacrosanct or finally valid and worthful character. (1) Experience always carries with it and within it certain systematized arrangements, certain classifications (using the term without intellectualistic prejudice), coexistent and serial. If we attribute these to "thought" then the structure of the brain of a Mozart which hears and combines sounds in certain groupings, the psycho-physical visual habit of the Greek, the locomotor apparatus of the human body in the laying-out and plotting of space is "thought." Social institutions, established political customs, effect and perpetuate modes of reaction and of perception that compel a certain grouping of objects, elements, and values. A national constitution brings about a definite arrangement of the factors of human action which holds even physical things together in certain determinate orders. Every successful economic process, with its elaborate divisions and adjustments of labor, of materials and instruments, is just such an objective organization. Now it is one thing to say that thought has played a part in the origin and development of such organizations, and continues to have a rôle in their judicious employment and application; it is another to say that these organizations *are* thought, or are its exclusive product. Thought that functions in these ways is distinctively *reflective* thought, thought as practical, volitional, deliberately exercised for specific aims—thought as an act, an art of skilled mediation. As *reflective* thought, its end is to terminate its own first and experimental forms, and to secure an organization which, while it may evoke new reflective thinking, puts an end to the thinking that secured the organization. *As organizations*, as established, effectively controlling arrangements of objects in experience, their mark is that they are not thoughts, but habits, customs of action.[7]

Moreover, such reflective thought as does intervene in the formation and maintenance of these practical organizations harks back to prior practical organizations, biological and social in nature. It serves to *valuate* organizations already existent as biological functions and instincts, while, as itself a biological activity, it redirects them to new conditions and results. Recognize, for example, that a geometric concept is a practical locomotor function of arranging stimuli in reference to maintenance of life activities *brought into consciousness*, and then serving as a center of reorganization of such activities to freer, more varied flexible and valuable forms; recognize this, and we have the truth of the Kantian idea, without its excrescences and miracles. The concept is the practical activity doing consciously and artfully what it had aforetime done blindly and aimlessly, and thereby not only doing it better but opening up a freer world of significant activities. Thought as such a reorganization of natural functions does naturally what Kantian forms and schematizations do only supernaturally. In a word, the constructive or organizing activity of "thought" does not inhere in thought as a transcendental function, a form or mode of some supra-empirical ego, mind, or consciousness, but in thought as itself vital activity. And in any case we have passed to the idea of thought as reflectively reconstructive and directive, and away from the notion of thought as immanently constitutional and organizational. To make this passage and yet to ignore its existence and import is essential to objective idealism.

(2) No final or ultimate validity attaches to these original arrangements and institutionalizations in any case. Their value is teleological and experimental, not fixedly ontological. "Law and order" are good things, but not when they become rigidity, and create mechanical uniformity or routine. Prejudice is the acme of the *a priori*. Of the *a priori* in this sense we may say what is always to be said of habits and institutions: They are good servants, but harsh and futile masters. Organization as already effected is always in danger of becoming a *mortmain*; it may be a way of sacrificing novelty, flexibility, freedom, creation to static standards. The curious inefficiency of idealism at this point is evident in the fact that genuine thought, empirical reflective

---

[7] The relationship of organization and thought is precisely that which we find psychologically typified by the rhythmic functions of habit and attention, attention being always, *ab quo*, a sign of the failure of habit, and, *ad quem*, a reconstructive modification of habit.

thought, is required precisely for the purpose of re-forming established and set formations.

In short, (a) a priori character is no exclusive function of thought. Every biological function, every motor attitude, every vital impulse as the carrying vehicle of experience is thus apriorily regulative in prospective reference; what we call apperception, expectation, anticipation, desire, demand, choice, are pregnant with this constitutive and organizing power. (b) In so far as "thought" does exercise such reorganizing power, it is because thought is itself still a vital function. (c) Objective idealism depends not only upon ignoring the existence and capacity of vital functions, but upon a profound confusion of the constitutional a priori, the unconsciously dominant, with empirically reflective thought. In the sense in which the a priori is worth while as an attribute of thought, thought cannot be what the objective idealist defines it as being. Plain, ordinary, everyday empirical reflections, operating as centers of inquiry, of suggestion, of experimentation, exercise the valuable function of regulation, in an auspicious direction, of subsequent experiences.

The categories of accomplished systematization cover alike the just and the unjust, the false and the true, while (unlike God's rain) they exercise no specific or differential activity of stimulation and control. Error and inefficiency, as well as value and energy, are embodied in our objective institutional classifications. As a special favor, will not the objective idealist show how, in some one single instance, his immanent "reason" makes any difference as respects the detection and elimination of error, or gives even the slightest assistance in discovering and validating the truly worthful? This practical work, the life blood of intelligence in everyday life and in critical science, is done by the despised and rejected matter of concrete empirical contexts and functions. Generalizing the issue: If the immanent organization be ascribed to thought, why should its work be such as to demand continuous correction and revision? If specific reflective thought, as empirical, be subject to all the limitations supposed to inhere in experience as such, how can it assume the burden of making good, of supplementing, reconstructing, and developing meanings? The logic of the case seems to be that Neo-Kantian idealism gets its status against empiricism by first accepting the Humian idea of experience, while the express import of its positive contribution is to show the non-existence (not merely the cognitive invalidity) of anything describable as mere states of subjective consciousness. Thus in the end it tends to destroy itself and to make way for a more adequate empiricism.

## III

In the above discussion, I have unavoidably anticipated the second problem: the relation of conceptual thought to perceptual data. A distinct aspect still remains, however. Perception, as well as apriority, is a term harboring a fundamental ambiguity. It may mean (1) a distinct type of activity, predominantly practical in character, though carrying at its heart important cognitive and esthetic qualities; or (2) a distinctively cognitional experience, the function of observation as explicitly logical—a factor in science *qua* science.

In the first sense, as recent functional empiricism (working in harmony with psychology, but not itself peculiarly psychological) has abundantly shown, perception is primarily an act of adjustment of organism and environment, differing from a mere reflex or instinctive adaptation in that, in order to compensate for the failure of the instinctive adjustment, it requires an objective or discriminative presentation of conditions of action: the negative conditions or obstacles, and the positive conditions or means and resources.[8] This, of course, is its cognitive phase. In so far as the material thus presented not only serves as a direct cue to further successful activity (successful in the overcoming of obstacles to the maintenance of the function entered upon) but presents auxiliary collateral objects and qualities that give additional range and depth of meaning to the activity of adjustment, perceiving is esthetic as well as intellectual.[9]

Now such perception cannot be made antithetical to thought, for it may itself be surcharged with any amount of imaginatively supplied and reflectively sustained ideal factors—such as are needed to determine and select relevant stimuli and to suggest and develop an appropriate plan and course of behavior. The amount of such saturating intellectual material depends upon the complexity and maturity of the behaving agent. Such perception, moreover, is strictly teleological, since it arises from an experienced need and functions to fulfil the purpose indicated by this need. The cognitional content is, indeed, carried by affectional and intentional contexts.

[8] Compare, for example, Dr. Stuart's paper in the "Studies in Logical Theory," pp. 253-256. I may here remark that I remain totally unable to see how the *interpretation* of objectivity to mean controlling conditions of action (negative and positive as above) derogates at all from its naïve objectivity, or how it connotes cognitive subjectivity, or is in any way incompatible with a common-sense realistic theory of perception.

[9] For this suggested interpretation of the esthetic as surprising, or unintended, gratuitous collateral reinforcement, see Gordon, "Psychology of Meaning."

Then we have perception as scientific observation. This involves the deliberate, artful exclusion of affectional and purposive factors as exercising mayhap a vitiating influence upon the cognitive or objective content; or, more strictly speaking, a transformation of the more ordinary or "natural" emotional and purposive concomitants, into what Bain calls "neutral" emotion, and a purpose of finding out what the present conditions of the problem are. (The practical feature is not thus denied or eliminated, but the overweening influence of a present dominating end is avoided, so that *change of the character of the end* may be effected, if found desirable.) Here observation may be opposed to thought, in the sense that exact and minute description may be set over against interpretation, explanation, theorizing, and inference. In the wider sense of thought as equaling reflective process, the work of observation and description forms a constituent division of labor *within* thought. The impersonal demarcation and accurate registration of what is objectively there or present occurs for the sake (*a*) of eliminating meaning which is habitually but uncritically referred, and (*b*) of getting a basis for a meaning (at first purely inferential or hypothetical) that may be consistently referred; and that (*c*), resting upon examination and not upon mere *a priori* custom, may weather the strain of subsequent experiences. But in so far as thought is identified with the conceptual phase as such of the entire logical function, observation is, of course, set over against thought: deliberately, purposely, and artfully so.

It is not uncommon to hear it said that the Lockeian movement was all well enough for psychology, but went astray because it invaded the field of logic. If we mean by psychology a natural history of what at any time *passes* for knowledge, and by logic conscious control in the direction of grounded assurance, this remark appears to reverse the truth. As a natural history of knowledge in the sense of opinion and belief, Locke's account of discrete, simple ideas or meanings, which are compounded and then distributed, does palpable violence to the facts. But every line of Locke shows that he was interested in knowledge in its honorific sense—controlled certainty, or, where this is not feasible, measured probability. And to logic as an account of the way in which we by art build up a *tested* assurance, a rationalized conviction, Locke makes an important positive contribution. The pity is that he inclined to take it for the whole of the logic of science,[10] not seeing that it was but a correlative division of labor to the work of hypotheses or inference; and that he

[10] This, however, is not strictly true, since Locke goes far to supply the means of his own correction in his account of the "workmanship of the understanding."

tended to identify it with a natural history or psychology. The latter tendency exposed Locke to the Humian interpretation, and permanently sidetracked the positive contribution of his theory to logic, while it led to that confusion of an untrue psychology with a logic valid within limits, of which Mill is the standard example.

In analytic observation, it is a positive object to strip off all inferential meaning so far as may be—to reduce the facts as nearly as may be to derationalized data, in order to make possible a new and better rationalization. In and because of this process, the perceptual data approach the limit of a disconnected manifold, of the brutely given, of the merely sensibly present; while meaning stands out as a searched for principle of unification and explanation, that is, as a thought, a concept, an hypothesis. The extent to which this is carried depends wholly upon the character of the specific situation and problem; but, speaking generally, or of limiting tendencies, one may say it is carried to mere observation, pure brute description, on the one side, and to mere thought, that is hypothetical inference, on the other.

So far as Locke ignored this instrumental character of observation, he naturally evoked and strengthened rationalistic idealism; he called forth its assertion of the need of reason, of concepts, of universals, to constitute knowledge in its eulogistic sense. But two contrary errors do not make a truth, although they suggest and determine the nature of some relevant truth. This truth is the empirical origin, in a determinate type of situation, of the contrast of observation and conception, the empirical relevancy and the empirical worth of this contrast in controlling the character of subsequent experiences. To suppose that perception as it concretely exists, either in the early experiences of the animal, the race, or the individual, or in its later refined and expanded experiences, is identical with the sharply analyzed, objectively discriminated and internally disintegrated elements of scientific observation, is a perversion of experience; a perversion for which, indeed, professed empiricists set the example, but which idealism must perpetuate if it is not to find its end in an improved, functional empiricism.[11]

---

[11] Plato, especially in his "Theaetetus," seems to have begun the procedure of blasting the good name of perceptive experience by identifying a late and instrumental distinction, having to do with logical control, with all experience whatsoever.

## IV

We come now to the consideration of the third element in our problem; identity, important and normative value, in relation to experience; the antithesis of experience as a tentative, fragmentary, and ineffectual embodiment of meaning over against the perfect, eternal system of meanings which experience suggests even in nullifying and mutilating.

That from the *memory* standpoint experience presents itself as a multiplicity of episodic events with just enough continuity among them to suggest principles true "on the whole" or usually, but without furnishing instruction as to their exact range and bearing, seems obvious enough. Why should it not? The motive which leads to reflection on *past* experience could be satisfied in no other way. Continuities, connecting links, dynamic transitions drop out because, for the purpose of the recollection, they would be hindrances if now repeated; or because they are now available only when themselves objectified in definite terms and thus given a *quasi* atomistic standing of their own. This is the only alternative to what the psychologists term "total reminiscence," which, so far as total, leave us with an elephant on our hands. Unless we are going to have a wholesale revivification of the past, giving us just another embarrassing present experience, illusory because irrelevant, memory must work by retail—by summoning *distinct* cases, events, sequences, precedents. Dis-membering is a positively necessary part of remembering. But the resulting *disjecta membra* are in no sense experience as it was or is; they are simply elements held apart, and yet tentatively implicated together, in present experience for the sake of its most favorable evolution; evolution in the direction of the most excellent meaning or value conceived. If the remembering is efficacious and pertinent, it reveals the possibilities of the present; that is to say, it clarifies the transitive, transforming character that belongs inherently to the present. The dismembering of the vital present into the disconnected past is correlative to an anticipation, an idealization of the future.

Moreover, the contingent character of the principle or rule that emerges from a survey of cases, instances, as distinct from a fixed or necessary character, secures just what is wanted in the exigency of a prospective idealization, or refinement of excellence. It is just this character that secures flexibility and variety of outlook, that makes possible a consideration of alternatives and an attempt to select and to execute the more worthy among them. The fixed or necessary law would mean a future like the past—a dead, an unidealized future. It is exasperating to imagine how completely different would have been Aristotle's valuation of "experience" with respect to its contingency, if he had but once employed the function of developing and perfecting value, instead of the function of knowing an unalterable object, as the standard by which to estimate and measure intelligence.

The one constant trait of experience from its crudest to its most mature forms is that its contents undergo change of meaning, and of meaning in the sense of excellence, value. Every experience is in-course,[12] in course of becoming worse or better as to its contents, or in course of conscious endeavor to sustain some satisfactory level of value against encroachment or lapse. In this effort, both precedent, the reduction of the present idealization, the anticipation of the possible, though doubtful, future, emerge. Without idealization, that is, without conception of the favorable issue that the present, defined in terms of precedents, may portend in its transition, the recollection of precedents, and the formulation of tentative rules is nonsense. But without the identification of the present in terms of elements suggested by the past, without recognition, the ideal, the value projected as end, remains inert, helpless, sentimental, without means of realization. Resembling cases and anticipation, memory and idealization, are the corresponding terms in which a present experience has its transitive force analyzed into reciprocally pertinent means and ends.

*That* an experience will change in content and value is the one thing certain. *How* it will change is the one thing naturally uncertain. Hence the import of the art of reflection and invention. Control of the character of the change in the direction of the worthful is the common business of theory and practice. Here is the province of the episodic recollection of past history and of the idealized foresight of possibilities. The irrelevancy of an objective idealism lies in the fact that it totally ignores the position and function of ideality in sustained and serious endeavor. Were values automatically injected and kept in the world of experience by any force not reflected in human memories and projects, it would make no difference whether this force were a Spencerian environment

---

[12] Compare James, "Continuous transition is one sort of conjunctive relation; and to be a radical empiricist means to hold fast to this conjunctive relation of all others, for this is the strategic point, the position through which, if a hole be made, all the corruptions of dialectics and all the metaphysical fictions pour into our philosophy."—*Journal of Philosophy, Psychology, and Scientific Methods*, Vol. I, p. 536.

or an Absolute Reason. Did purpose ride in a cosmic automobile toward a predestined goal, it would not cease to be physical and mechanical in quality because labeled Divine Idea, or Perfect Reason. The moral would be "let us eat, drink, and be merry," for to-morrow—or if not this to-morrow, then upon some to-morrow, unaffected by our empirical memories, reflections, inventions, and idealizations—the cosmic automobile arrives. Spirituality, ideality, meaning as purpose, would be the last things to present themselves if objective idealism were true. Values cannot be both ideal and given, and their "given" character is emphasized, not transformed, when they are called eternal and absolute. But natural values become ideal the moment their maintenance is dependent upon the intentional activities of an empirical agent. To suppose that values are ideal because they are so eternally given is the contradiction in which objective idealism has intrenched itself. Objective ontological teleology spells machinery. Reflective and volitional, experimental teleology alone spells ideality.[13] Objective, rationalistic idealism breaks upon the fact that it can have no intermediary between a brutely achieved embodiment of meaning (physical in character or else of that peculiar quasi-physical character which goes generally by the name of metaphysical) and a total opposition of the given and the ideal, connoting their mutal indifference and incapacity. An empiricism that acknowledges the transitive character of experience, and that acknowledges the possible control of the character of the transition by means of intelligent effort, has abundant opportunity to celebrate in productive art, genial morals, and impartial inquiry the grace and the severity of the ideal.

# 14. The Practical Character of Reality*

In 1908, one year after the publication of *Pragmatism* by William James, John Dewey published the original version of this essay under the title "Does Reality Possess Practical Character?" In part, this essay was a defense of pragmatism, then defined tentatively by Dewey as "the doctrine that

---

[13] One of the not least of the many merits of Santayana's "Life of Reason" is the consistency and vigor with which is upheld the doctrine that significant idealism means idealization.

* From John Dewey, *Philosophy and Civilization* (New York, Capricorn Books, 1963) (1931), pp. 36-55. Reprinted by permission of G. P. Putnam's Sons. (Published originally as "Does Reality Possess Practical Character?" in 1908.)

reality possess practical character and that this character is
most efficaciously expressed in the function of intelligence.
. . ." But Dewey was concerned also with the heightening of his
attack on traditional epistemology, which he judged to be suffering from "intellectual lock-jaw." From Dewey's point of
view, the process of knowing is not simply a way to guide us
to an already existing "final term." To the contrary, it is the
changes generated by our inquiry which should occupy our attention, although these changes are neither "total" nor
"miraculous." Dewey states the mediating ground of
pragmatic epistemology as follows: "Transformation, readjustment, reconstruction, all imply prior existences; existences which have characters and behavior of their own
which must be accepted, consulted, humored, manipulated,
or made light of, in all kinds of differing ways in the different
contexts of different problems." And in a rhetorical conclusion, Dewey challenges philosophy to assume the risks and
instability involved in devoting itself to these shifts in context,
rather than to an abstract delineation of "prior existences."

I

Recently I have had an experience which, insignificant in itself,
seems to mean something as an index-figure of the present philosophic
situation. In a criticism of the neo-Kantian conception that *a priori* functions of thought are necessary to constitute knowledge, it became relevant to deny its underlying postulates: viz., the existence of anything
properly called mental states or subjective impressions precedent to all
objective recognitions, and which accordingly needed some transcendental function to order them into a world of stable and consistent
reference. It was argued that such so-called original mental data are in
truth turning points of the readjustment, or making over, through a state
of incompatibility and shock, of objective affairs. This doctrine was met
by the cry of "Subjectivism!" It had seemed to its author to be a
criticism, on ground at once naturalistic and ethical, of the ground proposition of subjectivism. Why this diversity of interpretations? So far as
the writer can judge, it is due to the fact that certain things characteristic of practical life, such things as lack and need, conflict and clash,
desire and effort, loss and satisfaction, had been frankly referred to
reality; and to the further fact that the function and structure of know-

ing had been systematically connected with these practical features. These conceptions are doubtless radical enough; the latter was perhaps more or less revolutionary. The probability, the antecedent probability, was that hostile critics would have easy work in pointing out specific errors of fact and interpretation. But no: the simpler, the more effective method, was to dismiss the whole thing as anarchic subjectivism.

This was and remains food for thought. I have been able to find but one explanation: In current philosophy, everything of a practical nature is regarded as "merely" personal, and the "merely" has the force of denying legitimate standing in the court of cosmic jurisdiction. This conception seems to me the great and the ignored assumption in contemporary philosophy; many who might shrink from the doctrine were it expressly formulated hang desperately to its implications. Yet as an underlying assumption, it is surely sheer prejudice, a culture-survival. If we suppose the traditions of philosophic discussion wiped out and philosophy starting afresh from the most active tendencies of to-day,—those striving in social life, in science, in literature, and art,—one can hardly imagine any philosophic view springing up and gaining credence, which did not give large place, in its scheme of things, to the practical and personal, and to them without employing disparaging terms, such as phenomenal, merely subjective, and so on. Why, putting it mildly, should what gives tragedy, comedy, and poignancy to life, be excluded from things? Doubtless, what we call life, what we take to be genuinely vital, is not all of things. But it is a part of things; and is that part which counts most with the philosopher—unless he has quite parted with his ancient dignity of lover of wisdom. What becomes of philosophy as far as humane and liberal interests are concerned, if, in an age when the person and the personal loom large in politics, industry, religion, art, and science, it contents itself with this parrot cry of phenomenalism, whenever the personal comes into view? When science is led by the idea of evolution to introduce into the world the principles of initiative, variation, struggle, and selection; and when social forces have driven into bankruptcy absolutistic and static dogmas as authorities for the conduct of life, it is trifling for philosophy to decline to look the situation in the face. The relegation, as matter of course, of need, of stress and strain, strife and satisfaction, to the merely personal and the merely personal to the limbo of something which is neither flesh, fowl, nor good red herring, seems the thoughtless rehearsal of ancestral prejudice.

When we get beyond the echoing of tradition, the sticking point seems to be the relation of knowledge to the practical function of things. Let reality be in itself as "practical" as you please, but let not this practical character lay profane hands on the ark of truth! Every new mode of interpreting life—every new gospel—is met with the charge of antinomianism. Imagination when bound by custom apprehends the restrictions that are relaxed and the checks that are removed, but not the inevitable responsibilities and tests that the new idea brings in. And so the conception that knowledge makes a difference in and to things looks licentious to those who fail to see that the necessity of doing this business well, of making the *right* difference, puts intelligence under bonds it never yet has known: most of all in philosophy, the most gayly irresponsible of the procedures, and the most irresponsively sullen, of the historic fruits of intelligence.

Why should the idea that knowledge makes a difference to and in things be antecedently objectionable? If one is already committed to a belief that Reality is neatly and finally tied up in a packet without loose ends, unfinished issues or new departures, one would object to knowledge making a difference just as one would object to any other impertinent obtruder. But if one believes that the world itself is in transformation, why should the notion that knowledge is the most important mode of its modification and the only organ of its guidance be *a priori* obnoxious?

There is, I think, no answer save that the theory of knowledge has been systematically built up on the notion of a static universe, so that even those perfectly free to feel the lessons of physics and biology concerning moving energy and evolution, and of history concerning the constant transformation of man's affairs (science included), retain an unquestioning belief in a theory of knowledge which is out of any possible harmony with their own theory of the matters to be known. Modern epistemology, having created the idea that the way to frame right conceptions is to analyze knowledge, has strengthened this view. For it at once leads to the view that realities must themselves have a theoretic and intellectual complexion—not a practical one. This view is naturally congenial to idealists; but that realists should so readily play into the hands of idealists by asserting what, on the basis of a formal theory of knowledge, realities must be, instead of accepting the guidance of things in divining what knowledge *is*, is an anomaly so striking as to support the view that the notion of static reality has taken its last stand in ideas about knowledge. Take, for example, the most striking, because the extreme case—knowledge of a past event. It is absurd to suppose that knowledge makes a difference to the final or appropriate content of knowledge: to the subject-matter which fulfils the requirements of knowing. In this case, it would get in its own way and trip itself up in endless regress. But it seems the very superstition of intellectualism to suppose that this fact about knowledge can decide what is the nature of that reference to the past which, when rightly made, is final. No doctrine about knowledge can hinder the belief—if there be sufficient specific evidence for it—that what we know as past may be something which has *irretrievably* undergone just the difference which knowledge makes.

Now arguments against pragmatism—by which I mean the doctrine that reality possesses practical character and that this character is most efficaciously expressed in the function of intelligence[1]—seem to fall blandly into this fallacy. They assume that to hold that knowledge makes a difference in existences is equivalent to holding that it makes a difference in the object *to be* known, thus defeating its own purpose; witless that the reality which is the appropriate object of knowledge in a given case may be precisely a reality in which knowing has succeeded in making the needed difference. This question is not one to be settled by manipulation of the concept of knowledge, nor by dialectic discussion of its essence or nature. It is a question of facts, a question of what knowing exists as in the scheme of existence. If things undergo change without thereby ceasing to be real, there can be no *formal* bar to knowing being one specific kind of change in things, nor to its test being found in the successful carrying into effect of the kind of change intended. If knowing be a change in a reality, then the more knowing reveals this change, the more transparent, the more adequate, it is. And if all existences are in transition, then the knowledge which treats them as if they were something of which knowledge is a kodak fixation is just the kind of knowledge which refracts and perverts them. And by the same token a knowing which actively participates in a change in the way to effect it in the needed fashion would be the type of knowing which is valid. If reality be itself in transition—and this doctrine originated not with the objectionable pragmatist but with the physicist and naturalist and historian—then the doctrine that knowledge *is* reality making a par-

---

[1] This definition, in the present state of discussion, is an arbitrary or personal one. The text does not mean that "pragmatism" is currently used exclusively in this sense; obviously there are other senses. It does not mean it is the sense in which it *ought* to be used. I have no wish to legislate either for language or for philosophy. But it marks the sense in which *is* is used in this paper; and the pragmatic movement is still so loose and variable that I judge one has a right to fix his own meaning, provided he serves notice and adheres to it.

ticular and specified sort of change in itself seems to have the best
chance at maintaining a theory of knowing which is in wholesome touch
with the genuine and valid.


## II


If the ground be cleared of *a priori* objections, and if it be evident
that pragmatism cannot be disposed of by any formal or dialectic
manipulations of "knowledge" or "truth," but only by showing that
some specific things are not of the sort claimed, we may consider some
common sense affiliations of pragmatism. Common sense regards intelligence as having a purpose, and knowledge as amounting to something. I once heard a physicist, quite innocent of the pragmatic controversy, remark that the knowledge of a mechanic or farmer was what
the Yankee calls gumption—acknowledgment of things in their belong-
ings and uses, and that to his mind natural science was gumption on a
larger scale: the convenient cataloguing and arranging of a whole lot of
things with reference to their most efficacious services. Popularly, good
judgment is judgment as to the relative values of things: good sense is
horse sense, ability to take hold of things right end up, to fit an instrument to an obstacle, to select resources apt for a task. To be reasonable
is to recognize things in their office as obstacles and as resources. Intelligence, in its ordinary use, is a practical term; ability to size up matters with respect to the needs and possibilities of the various situations
in which one is called to do something; capacity to envisage things in
terms of the adjustments and adaptations they make possible or hinder.
One objective test of the presence or absence of intelligence is influence
upon behavior. No capacity to make adjustments means no intelligence;
conduct evincing management of complex and novel conditions means
a high degree of reason. Such conditions at least suggest that a reality-
to-be-known, a reality which is the appropriate subject-matter of
knowledge is reality-of-use-and-in-use, direct or indirect, and that a
reality which is not in any sort of use, or bearing upon use, may go
hang, *so far as knowledge is concerned.*
No one, I suppose, would deny that knowledge *issues* in some action
which changes things to some extent—be the action only a more
deliberate maintenance of a course of conduct already instinctively entered upon. When I see a sign on the street corner I can turn or go on,
knowing what I am about. The perceptions of the scientist need have no
such overt or "utilitarian" uses, but surely after them he behaves dif-

ferently, as an inquirer if in no other way; and the cumulative effect of such changes finally modifies the overt action of the ordinary man. That knowing, *after the event,* makes a difference of this sort, few I suppose would deny: if that were all pragmatism means, it would perhaps be accepted as a harmless truism. But there is a further question of fact: just how is the "consequent" action related to the "precedent" knowledge? When *is* "after the event"? What degree of continuity exists? Is the difference between knowing and acting intelligently one of kind or simply one of dominant quality? How does a thing, if it is not already in change in the knowing, manage to issue at its term in action? Moreover, do not the changes actively effected constitute the whole *import* of the knowledge, and hence its final measure and test of validity? If it merely *happens* that knowing when it is done with passes into some action, by what miracle is the subsequent action so pat to the situation? Is it not rather true that the "knowledge" is instituted and framed in anticipation of the consequent issue, and, in the degree in which it is wise and prudent, is held open to revision during it? Certainly the moralist (one might quote, for example, Goethe, Carlyle, and Mazzini) and the common man often agree that full knowledge, adequate assurance of reality is found only in the issue which fulfills ideas; that we have to do a doctrine to *know* its truth; otherwise it is only dogma or doctrinaire program. Experimental science is a recognition that no idea is entitled to be termed knowledge till it has passed into such overt manipulation of physical conditions as constructs the object to which the idea refers. If one could get rid of one's traditional logical theories and set to work afresh to frame a theory of knowledge on the basis of the procedure of the common man, the moralist, and the experimentalist, would it be the forced or the natural procedure to say that the realities which we *know,* which we are sure of, are precisely those realities that have taken shape in and through the active procedures of knowing?

I turn to another type of consideration. Certainly one of the most genuine problems of modern life is the reconciliation of the scientific view of the universe with the claims of the moral life. Are judgments in terms of the redistribution of matter in motion (or some other closed formula) alone valid? Or are accounts of the universe in terms of possibility and desirability, of initiative and responsibility, also valid? There is no occasion to expatiate on the importance of the moral life, nor upon the supreme importance of intelligence within the moral life. But there does seem to be occasion for asking how moral judgments—judgments of the would and should—relate themselves to the world of scientific knowledge. To frame a theory of knowledge which makes it necessary to deny the validity of moral ideas, or else to refer them to some other and separate kind of universe from that of common sense and science, is both provincial and arbitrary. The pragmatist has at least tried to face, and not to dodge, the question of how it is that moral and scientific "knowledge" can both hold of one and the same world. And whatever the difficulties in his proffered solution, the conception that scientific judgments are to be assimilated to moral is closer to common sense than is the theory that validity is to be denied to moral judgments because they do not square with a preconceived theory of the nature of the world to which scientific judgments must refer. And all moral judgments are about changes to be made.

### III

I turn to one affiliation of the pragmatic theory with the results of recent science. The necessity, for the occurrence of an event in the way of knowledge, of an organism which reacts or behaves in a specific way, would seem to be as well established as any specific proposition. It is a peculiar fact, a fact fit to stir curiosity, that the rational function seems to be intercalated in a scheme of practical adjustments. The parts and members of the organism are certainly not there primarily for pure intellection or for theoretic contemplation. The brain, the last physical organ of thought, is a part of the same practical machinery for bringing about adaptation of the environment to the life requirements of the organism, to which belong legs and hand and eye. That the brain frees organic behavior from complete servitude to immediate physical conditions, that it makes possible the liberation of energy for remote and ever expanding ends is, indeed, a precious fact, but not one which removes the brain from the category of organic devices of behavior.[2] That the organ of thinking, of knowledge, was at least originally an organ of conduct, few, I imagine, will deny. And even if we try to believe that the cognitive function has supervened as a different operation, it is difficult to believe that the transfiguration has been so radical that knowing has lost all traces of its connection with vital impulse. But unless we so assume, have we any alternatives except to hold that this continual

---

[2] It is interesting to note how the metaphysical puzzles regarding "parallelism," "interaction," "automatism," the relation of "consciousness" to "body," evaporate when one ceases isolating the brain into a peculiar physical substrate of mind at large, and treats it simply as one portion of the body which is the instrumentality of adaptive behavior.

presence of vital impulse is a disturbing and refracting factor, which forever prevents knowledge from reaching its own aim; or else that a certain promoting, a certain carrying forward of the vital impulse, importing certain differences in things, *is* the aim of knowledge?

The problem cannot be evaded—save ostrich wise—by saying that such considerations are "merely genetic," or "psychological," having to do only with the origin and natural history of knowing. For the point is that the organic reaction, the behavior of the organism, affects the *content* of awareness. The subject-matter of all awareness is thing-related-to-organism—related as stimulus direct or indirect or as material of response, present or remote, ulterior or achieved.

No one—so far as I know—denies this with respect to the perceptual field of awareness. Pains, pleasures, hunger, and thirst, all "secondary" qualities, involve inextricably the "interaction" of organism and environment. The perceptual field is distributed and arranged as the possible field of selective reactions of the organism at its center. Up and down, far and near, before and behind, right and left, hard and soft (as well as white and black, bass and alto), involve reference to a center of behavior.

This material has so long been the stock in trade of both idealistic arguments and proclamations of the agnostic "relativity" of knowledge that philosophers have grown aweary of listening. But even this lethargy might be quickened by a moderate hospitality to the pragmatic interpretation. That red, or far and near, or hard and soft, or big and little, involves a relation between organism and environment, is no more an argument for idealism than is the fact that water involves a relation between hydrogen and oxygen.[3] It is, however, an argument for the ultimately practical value of these distinctions—that they are *differences* made in what things would have been without organic behavior —differences made not by "consciousness" or "mind," but by the organism as the active center of a system of activities. Moreover, the whole agnostic sting of the doctrine of "relativity" lies in the assumption that the ideal or aim of knowledge is to repeat or copy a prior existence—in which case, of course, the making of contemporaneous differences by the organism in the very fact of awareness would get in the way and forever hinder the knowledge function from the fulfillment of its proper end. Knowledge, awareness, in this case suffers from an impediment which no surgery can better. But if the aim of knowing be precisely to make *certain* differences in an environment, to carry on to

---

[3] I owe this illustration to my colleague, Dr. Montague.

*favorable issue,* by the readjustment of the organism, certain changes going on indifferently in the environment, then the fact that the changes of the organism enter pervasively into the subject-matter of awareness is no restriction or perversion of knowledge, but part of the fulfillment of its office.

The only question would then be whether *proper* reactions take place. The whole agnostic, positivistic controversy is flanked by a single move. The issue is no longer an ideally necessary but actually impossible copying, *versus* an improper but unavoidable modification of reality through organic inhibitions and stimulations: but it is the right, the economical, the effective, and, if one may venture, the useful and satisfactory reaction *versus* the wasteful, the enslaving, the misleading, and the confusing reaction. The presence of organic responses, influencing and modifying every content, every subject-matter of awareness, is the undoubted fact. But the significant thing is the *way* organic behavior enters in—the *way* it influences and modifies. We assign very different values to different types of "knowledge,"—or subject-matters involving organic attitudes and operations. Some are only guesses, opinions, suspicious characters; others are "knowledge" in the honorific and eulogistic sense—science; some turn out mistakes, blunders, errors. Whence and how this discrimination of quality in what is taken at its own time to be good knowledge? Why and how is the content of some "knowledge" genuine-knowing and of other mis-knowing? Awareness is itself a blanket term, covering, in the same bed, delusion, doubt, confusion, ambiguity, and definition, organization, logical conclusiveness assured by evidence and reason. Any naturalistic or realistic theory is committed to the idea that all of these terms bear impartially the same relation to things considered as sheer existence. What we must have in any case is the same existences—the same in kind—only differently arranged or linked up. But why then the tremendous difference in value? And if the un-naturalist, the non-realist, says the difference is one of existential kind, made by the working here malign, there benign, of "consciousness," "psychical" operations and states, upon the existences which are the direct subject-matter of knowledge, there is still the problem of discriminating the conditions and nature of the respective beneficent and malicious interventions of the peculiar "existence" labeled consciousness.[4] The realness of error, ambiguity, doubt and guess poses a problem. It is a problem which has perplexed philosophy

---

[4] Of course on the theory I am interested in expounding, the so-called action of "consciousness" means simply the organic releases in the way of behavior which are the conditions of awareness, and which also modify its content.

so long and has led to so many speculative adventures, that it would seem worth while, were it only for the sake of variety, to listen to the pragmatic solution according to which it is the business of the organic adaptation involved in all knowing to make a *certain* difference in reality, but *not* to make any old or casual difference. The right, the true and good, difference is that which carries out satisfactorily the specific purpose for the sake of which knowing occurs. All manufactures are the product of an activity, but it does not follow that all manufactures are equally good. And so all "knowledges" are differences made in things by knowing, but some differences are not calculated or wanted in the knowing, and hence are disturbers and interlopers when they come— while others fulfill the intent of the knowing, being in harmony with the consistent behavior of the organism and re-inforcing and enlarging its function. A mistake is literally a mishandling; a doubt is a temporary suspense and vacillation of reactions; an ambiguity is the tension of al-ternative but incompatible mode of responsive treatment; an inquiry is a tentative and retrievable (because intra-organic) mode of activity, en-tered upon prior to launching upon a knowledge which is public, ineluc-table—without anchors to windward—since it has taken physical effect through overt action.

It is practically all one to say that the norm of honorable knowing is to make no difference in *its* object, and that its aim is to attain and but-tress a specific kind of difference in reality. Knowing fails in its business if it makes a change in its *own* object—that is a mistake; but its own ob-ject is none the less a prior existence changed in a certain way. Nor is this a play upon the two senses—end and subject-matter—of "object." The organism has its appropriate functions. To maintain, to expand, adequate functioning is its business. This functioning does not occur *in vacuo*. It involves co-operative and readjusted changes in the cosmic medium. Hence the appropriate subject-matter of awareness is not reality at large, a metaphysical heaven to be mimeographed at many removes upon a badly constructed mental carbon paper which yields at best only fragmentary, blurred, and erroneous copies. Its proper and legitimate object is that relationship of organism and environment in which functioning is most amply and effectively attained; or by which, in case of obstruction and consequent needed experimentation, its later eventual free course is most facilitated. As for the other reality, meta-physical reality *at large*, it may, so far as awareness is concerned, go to its own place.

For ordinary purposes, that is for practical purposes, the truth and the realness of things are synonymous. We are all children who say "really and truly." A reality which is taken in organic response so as to lead to subsequent reactions that are off the track and aside from the mark, while it is, existentially speaking, perfectly real, is not *good* reality. It lacks the hallmark of value. Since it is a certain *kind* of object which we want, one which will be as favorable as possible to a consistent and liberal or growing functioning, it is this kind, the *true* kind, which for us monopolizes the title of reality. Pragmatically, teleologically, this identification of truth and "reality" is sound and reasonable: rationalistically, it leads to the notion of the duplicate versions of reality, one absolute and static because exhausted; the other phenomenal and kept continually on the jump because otherwise its own inherent nothingness would lead to its total annihilation. Since it is only genuine or sincere things, things which are good for what they lay claim to in the way of consequences, which we want or are after, *morally* they alone are "real."

## IV

So far we have been dealing with awareness as a fact—a fact there like any fact—and have been concerned to show that the subject-matter of awareness is, in any case, things in process of change; and in such change that the knowing function takes a hand in trying to guide it or steer it, so that *some* (and *not* other) consequences accrue. But what about the awareness itself? What happens when it is made the subject-matter of awareness? What sort of a thing is it? It is, I submit, mere sophistication (futile at that), to argue either that we cannot become aware of awareness without involving ourselves in an endless regress, or that whenever we are aware of anything we are thereby necessarily aware of awareness once for all, so that it has no character save a purely formal and empty one. Taken concretely, awareness is an event with certain specifiable conditions. We may indeed be aware of it formally, as a bare fact, just as we may be cognizant of an explosion without knowing anything of its nature. But we may also be aware of it in a curious and analytic spirit, undertaking to study it in detail. This inquiry, like any other inquiry, proceeds by determining conditions and consequences. Here awareness is a characteristic fact, presenting to inquiry its own characteristic ear-marks, and a valid knowledge of awareness is the same sort of thing as valid knowledge of the spectrum or of a trotting horse; it proceeds generically in the same way and must satisfy the same generic tests.

What, then, is awareness found to be? The following answer, dogmatically summary in form, involves positive difficulties, and glides over many points where our ignorance is still too great. But it represents a general trend of scientific inquiry, carried on, I hardly need say, on its own merits without respect to the pragmatic controversy. Awareness means *attention,* and attention means a crisis of some sort in an existent situation; a forking of the roads of some material, a tendency to go this way and that. It represents something the matter, something out of gear, or in some way menaced, insecure, problematical and strained. This state of tension, of ambiguous indications, projects and tendencies, is not merely in the "mind," it is nothing merely emotional. It is in the facts of the situation as transitive facts; the emotional or "subjective" disturbance is just a part of the larger disturbance. And if, employing the *language* of psychology, we say that attention is a phenomenon of conflicting habits, being the process of resolving this conflict by finding an act which functions for all the factors concerned, this language does not make the facts "merely psychological"—whatever that means.[5] The habits are as biologic as they are "personal," and as cosmic as they are biologic. They are the total order of things expressed in one way; just as a physical or chemical phenomenon is the same order expressed in another way. The statement in terms of conflict and readjustment of habits is at most one way of locating the disturbance in *things;* it furnishes no substitute for, or rival of, reality, and no "psychical" duplication.

If this be true, then awareness, even in its most perplexed and confused state, that of maximum doubt and precariousness of subject-matter, means things entering, *via* the particular thing known as organism, into a peculiar condition of differential—or additive—change. How can we refuse to raise and consider the question of how things in this condition are related to the prior state which emerges into it, and to the subsequent state of things into which it issues?[6]

Suppose the case to be awareness of a chair. Suppose that this

[5] What does it mean? Does the objectivity of fact disappear when the biologist gives it a biological statement? Why not object to his conclusions on the ground that they are "merely" biological?

[6] It is this question *of the relation to one another of different successive states of things* which the pragmatic method substitutes for the epistemological inquiry of how one sort of existence, purely mental, temporal but not spatial, immaterial, made of sublimated gaseous consciousness, can get beyond itself and have valid reference to a totally different kind of existence—spatial and extended; and how it can receive impressions from the latter, etc.,—all the questions which constitute that species of confirmed intellectual lock-jaw called epistemology.

awareness comes only when there is some problematic affair with which the chair is in some way—in whatever degree of remoteness—concerned. It may be a wonder whether it is a chair at all; or whether it is strong enough to stand on; or where I shall put it; or whether it is worth what I paid for it; or, as not infrequently happens, the situation involved in uncertainty may be some philosophic matter in which the perception of the chair is cited as evidence of illustration. (Humorously enough, awareness of it may even be cited in the course of a philosophic argument intended to show that awareness has nothing to do with situations of incompleteness and ambiguity.) Now what of the change the chair undergoes in entering this way into a situation of perplexed inquiry? Is this any part of the genuineness of that chair with which we are concerned? If not, where is the change found? In something totally different called "consciousness"? In that case how can the operations of inquiry, of observation and memory and reflection, ever have any assurance of getting referred back to the *right* object? Positively the presumption is that the *chair-of-which-we-are-speaking is* the chair *of-which-we-are-speaking;* it is the *same* thing that is out there which is also involved in the doubtful situation. Moreover, the reference to "consciousness" as the exclusive locus of the doubt only repeats the problem, for "consciousness," by the theory under consideration, means, after all, only the chair *as* concerned in the problematical situation. The *physical* chair remains unchanged, you say. Surely, if, as is altogether likely, what is *meant by* physical is precisely *that part* of the chair as object of total awareness which remains unaffected, for certain possible purposes, by entering for certain other actual purposes into the situation of awareness. But how can we segregate, *antecedently* to experimental inquiry, the "physical" chair from the chair which is now the object to be known; into what contradictions do we fall when we attempt to define the object of one awareness not in its own terms, but in terms of a selected type of object which is the appropriate subject-matter of some other cognizance!

But awareness means inquiry as well as doubt—there are the negative and positive, the retrospective and the prospective relationships of the thing. This means a genuinely *additive* quality—one of readjustment in prior things.[7] I know the dialectic argument that nothing can assume a new relation, because in order to do so it must

---

[7] We have arrived here, upon a more analytic platform, at the point made earlier concerning the fact that knowing *issues* in action which changes things.

already be completely related—when it comes from an absolutist I can understand why he holds it, even if I cannot understand the idea itself. But apart from this conceptual reasoning we must follow the lead of our subject-matter; and when we find a thing assuming new relations in the process of inquiry, must accept the fact, and frame our theory of things and of knowing to include it, not assert that it is impossible because we already have a theory of knowledge which precludes it. In inquiry, the existence which has become doubtful always undergoes experimental reconstruction. This may be largely imaginative or "speculative." We may view certain things *as if* placed under varying conditions, and consider what then happens to them. But such differences are really transformative as far as they go,—and besides, such inquiries never reach conclusions finally justifiable. In important and persistent inquiry, we insist upon something in the way of actual physical making—be it only a diagram. In other words, *science,* or knowing in its honorific sense, is experimental, involving physical construction. We insist upon something being *done about* it, that we may see how the idea when carried into effect comports with the other things through which our activities are hedged in and released. To avoid this conclusion by saying that knowing makes no difference in the "truth," but merely is the preliminary exercise which discovers it, is that old friend whose acquaintance we have repeatedly made in this discussion: the fallacy of confusing an existence anteceding knowing with the object which terminates and fulfills it. For knowing to make a difference in its own final term is gross self-stultification; it is none the less so when the aim of knowing is precisely to guide things straight up to this term. When "truth" means the accomplished introduction of certain new differences into conditions, why be foolish enough to introduce other differences, which are not wanted since they are irrelevant and misleading?

Were it not for the teachings of sad experience, it would not be necessary to add that the change in environment made by knowing is not a total or miraculous change. Transformation, readjustment, reconstruction, all imply prior existences: existences which have characters and behaviors of their own which must be accepted, consulted, humored, manipulated or made light of, in all kinds of differing ways in the different contexts of different problems. Making a difference in reality does not mean making any more difference than we find by experimentation can be made under the given conditions—even though we may still hope for different fortune another time under other circumstances. Still less does it mean making a thing into an unreality, though the pragmatist is sometimes criticized as if any change in reality must be a change into non-reality. There are difficulties, indeed, both dialectic, and real or practical, in the fact of change—in the fact that only a permanent can change and that change is alteration of a permanent. But till we enjoin botanists and chemists from referring to changes and transformations in their subject-matter on the ground that for anything to change means for it to part with its reality, we may as well permit the logician to make similar references.

V

*Sub specie aeternitatis?* or *sub specie generationis?* I am susceptible to the esthetic charm of the former ideal—who is not? There are moments of relaxation: there are moments when the demand for peace, to be let alone and relieved from the continual claim of the world in which we live that we be up and doing something about it, seems irresistible; when the responsibilities imposed by living in a moving universe seem intolerable. We contemplate with equal mind the thought of the eternal sleep. But, after all, this is a matter in which reality and not the philosopher is the court of final jurisdiction. Outside of philosophy, the question seems fairly settled; in science, in poetry, in social organization, in religion—wherever religion is not hopelessly at the mercy of a Frankenstein philosophy which it originally called into being to be its own slave. Under such circumstances there is danger that the philosophy which tries to escape the form of generation by taking refuge under the form of eternity will only come under the form of a bygone generation. To try to escape from the snares and pitfalls of time by recourse to traditional problems and interests:—rather than that let the dead bury their own dead. Better it is for philosophy to err in active participation in the living struggles and issues of its own age and times than to maintain an immune monastic impeccability, without relevancy and bearing in the generating ideas of its contemporary present. In the one case, it will be respected, as we respect all virtue that attests its sincerity by sharing in the perplexities and failures, as well as in the joys and triumphs, of endeavor. In the other case, it bids fair to share the fate of whatever preserves its gentility, but not its activity, in descent from better days; namely, to be snugly ensconced in the consciousness of its own respectability.

# 15. The Pattern of Inquiry*

At the beginning of Part II of his *Logic: The Theory of Inquiry*, John Dewey attempts to lay the groundwork for his operational approach to the problem of inquiry. He defines inquiry as "the controlled or directed transformation of an indeterminate situation into one that is so determinate in its constituent distinctions and relations as to convert the elements of the original situation into a unified whole."

Continuous with the theme of his earlier writings, several of which are reprinted above, Dewey focuses on the functional character of logical forms. He holds that "formal conceptions arise out of the ordinary transactions; they are not imposed upon them from on high or from any external and *a priori* source." And reminiscent of his views on "conclusions" and "consummations" in *Art as Experience*, Dewey contends that "objects" are not fixed things to be thought about but are both "outcomes of inquiries" and "*means* of attaining knowledge of something else." This chapter is the key to Dewey's book on *Logic* and in summary fashion contains the major themes and judgments of his mature theory of knowing.

The first chapter set forth the fundamental thesis of this volume: Logical forms accrue to subject-matter when the latter is subjected to controlled inquiry. It also set forth some of the implications of this thesis for the nature of logical theory. The second and third chapters stated the independent grounds, biological and cultural, for holding that logic is a theory of experiential naturalistic subject-matter. The first of the next two chapters developed the theme with reference to the relations of the logic of common sense and science, while the second discussed Aristotelian logic as the organized formulation of the language of Greek life, when that language is regarded as the expression of the meanings of Greek culture and of the significance attributed to various forms of natural existence. It was held throughout these chap-

* From John Dewey, *Logic: The Theory of Inquiry*, pp. 101-119. Copyright 1938 by Holt, Rinehart and Winston, Inc. Copyright © 1966 by Roberta L. Dewey. Reprinted by permission of Holt, Rinehart and Winston, Inc.

ters that inquiry, in spite of the diverse subjects to which it applies, and the consequent diversity of its special techniques has a common structure or pattern: that this common structure is applied both in common sense and science, although because of the nature of the problems with which they are concerned, the emphasis upon the factors involved varies·widely in the two modes. We now come to the consideration of the common pattern.

The fact that new formal properties accrue to subject-matter in virtue of its subjection to certain types of operation is familiar to us in certain fields, even though the idea corresponding to this fact is unfamiliar in logic. Two outstanding instances are provided by art and law. In music, the dance, painting, sculpture, literature and the other fine arts, subject-matters of everyday experience are *trans*formed by the development of forms which render certain products of doing and making objects of fine art. The materials of legal regulations are transactions occurring in the ordinary activities of human beings and groups of human beings; transactions of a sort that are engaged in apart from law. As certain aspects and phases of these transactions are legally formalized, conceptions such as misdemeanor, crime, torts, contracts and so on arise. These formal conceptions arise out of the ordinary transactions; they are not imposed upon them from on high or from any external and *a priori* source. But when they are formed they are also *formative*; they regulate the proper conduct of the activities out of which they develop.

All of these formal legal conceptions are operational in nature. They formulate and define *ways* of operation on the part of those engaged in the transactions into which a number of persons or groups enter as "parties," and the ways of operation followed by those who have jurisdiction in deciding whether established forms have been complied with, together with the existential consequences of failure of observation. The forms in question are not fixed and eternal. They change, though as a rule too slowly, with changes in the habitual transactions in which individuals and groups engage and the changes that occur in the consequences of these transactions. However hypothetical may be the conception that *logical* forms accrue to existential materials in virtue of the control exercised over inquiries in order that they may fulfil their end, the conception is descriptive of something that verifiably exists. The development of forms in consequence of operations is an established fact in some fields; it is not invented *ad hoc* in relation to logical forms.

The existence of inquiries is not a matter of doubt. They enter into every area of life and into every aspect of every area. In everyday living, men examine; they turn things over intellectually; they infer and judge as "naturally" as they reap and sow, produce and exchange commodities. As a mode of conduct, inquiry is as accessible to objective study as are these other modes of behavior. Because of the intimate and decisive way in which inquiry and its conclusions enter into the management of all affairs of life, no study of the latter is adequate save as it is noted how they are affected by the methods and instruments of inquiry that currently obtain. Quite apart, then, from the particular hypothesis about logical forms that is put forth, study of the objective facts of inquiry is a matter of tremendous import, practically and intellectually. These materials provide the theory of logical forms with a subject-matter that is not only objective but is objective in a fashion that enables logic to avoid the three mistakes most characteristic of its history.

1. In virtue of its concern with objectively observable subject-matter by reference to which reflective conclusions can be tried and tested, dependence upon subjective and "mentalistic" states and processes is eliminated.

2. The distinctive existence and nature of forms is acknowledged. Logic is not compelled, as historic "empirical" logic felt compelled to do, to reduce logical forms to mere transcripts of the empirical materials that antecede the existence of the former. Just as art-forms and legal forms are capable of independent discussion and development, so are logical forms, even though the "independence" in question is intermediate, not final and complete. As in the case of these other forms, they originate *out* of experiential material, and when constituted introduce new ways of operating with prior materials, which ways modify the material out of which they develop.

3. Logical theory is liberated from the unobservable, transcendental and "intuitional."

When methods and results of inquiry are studied as objective data, the distinction that has often been drawn between noting and reporting the ways in which men *do* think, and prescribing the ways in which they *ought* to think, takes on a very different interpretation from that usually given. The usual interpretation is in terms of the difference between the psychological and the logical, the latter consisting of "norms" provided from some source wholly outside of and independent of "experience."

The way in which men *do* "think" denotes, as it is *here* interpreted, simply the ways in which men at a given time carry on their inquiries. So far as it is used to register a difference from the ways in which they *ought* to think, it denotes a difference like that between good and bad farming or good and bad medical practice. Men think in ways they should not when they follow methods of inquiry that experience of past inquiries shows are not competent to reach the intended end of the inquiries in question.

Everybody knows that today there are in vogue methods of farming generally followed in the past which compare very unfavorably in their results with those obtained by practices that have already been introduced and tested. When an expert tells a farmer he *should* do thus and so, he is not setting up for a bad farmer an ideal drawn from the blue. He is instructing him in methods that have been tried and that have proved successful in procuring results. In a similar way we are able to contrast various kinds of inquiry that are in use or that have been used in respect to their economy and efficiency in reaching warranted conclusions. We know that some methods of inquiry are better than others in just the same way in which we know that some methods of surgery, farming, road-making, navigating or what-not are better than others. It does not follow in any of these cases that the "better" methods are ideally perfect, or that they are regulative or "normative" because of conformity to some absolute form. They are the methods which experience up to the present time shows to be the best methods available for achieving certain results, while abstraction of these methods does supply a (relative) norm or standard for further undertakings.

The search for the pattern of inquiry is, accordingly, not one instituted in the dark or at large. It is checked and controlled by knowledge of the kinds of inquiry that have and that have not worked; methods which, as was pointed out earlier, can be so compared as to yield reasoned or rational conclusions. For, through comparison-contrast, we ascertain *how and why* certain means and agencies have provided warrantably assertible conclusions, while others have not and *cannot* do so in the sense in which "cannot" expresses an intrinsic incompatibility between means used and consequences attained.

We may now ask: What is the *definition* of Inquiry? That is, what is the most highly generalized conception of inquiry which can be justifiably formulated? The definition that will be expanded, directly in the present chapter and indirectly in the following chapters, is as follows: *Inquiry is the controlled or directed transformation of an indeterminate situation into one that is so determinate in its constituent distinctions and relations as to convert the elements of the original situation into a unified whole.*[1]

---

[1] The word "situation" is to be understood in the sense already expounded.

The orginal indeterminate situation is not only "open" to inquiry, but it is open in the sense that its constituents do not hang together. The determinate situtation on the other hand, *qua* outcome of inquiry, is a closed and, as it were, finished situation or "universe of experience." "Controlled or directed" in the above formula refers to the fact that inquiry is competent in any given case in the degree in which the operations involved in it actually do terminate in the establishment of an objectively unified existential situation. In the intermediate course of transition and transformation of the indeterminate situation, *dis*course through use of symbols is employed as means. In received logical terminology, propositions, or terms and the relations between them, are instrinsically involved.

I. *The Antecedent Conditions of Inquiry: The Indeterminate Situation.* Inquiry and questioning, up to a certain point, are synonymous terms. We inquire when we question; and we inquire when we seek for whatever will provide an answer to a question asked. Thus it is of the very nature of the indeterminate situation which evokes inquiry to be *questionable;* or, in terms of actuality instead of potentiality, to be uncertain, unsettled, disturbed. The peculiar quality of what pervades the given materials, constituting them a situation, is not just uncertainty at large; it is a unique doubtfulness which makes that situation to be just and only the situation it is. It is this unique quality that not only evokes the particular inquiry engaged in but that exercises control over its special procedures. Otherwise, one procedure in inquiry would be as likely to occur and to be effective as any other. Unless a situation is uniquely qualified in its very indeterminateness, there is a condition of complete panic; response to it takes the form of blind and wild overt activities. Stating the matter from the personal side, we have "lost our heads." A variety of names serves to characterize indeterminate situations. They are disturbed, troubled, ambiguous, confused, full of conflicting tendencies, obscure, etc.

It is the *situation* that has these traits. *We* are doubtful because the situation is inherently doubtful. Personal states of doubt that are not evoked by and are not relative to some existential situation are pathological; when they are extreme they constitute the mania of doubting. Consequently, situations that are disturbed and troubled, confused or obscure, cannot be straightened out, cleared up and put in order, by manipulation of our personal states of mind. The attempt to settle them by such manipulations involves what psychiatrists call "withdrawal from reality." Such an attempt is pathological as far as it goes, and when it goes far it is the source of some form of actual insanity. The habit of disposing of the doubtful as if it belonged only to *us* rather than to the existential situation in which we are caught and implicated is an inheritance from subjectivisitic psychology. The biological antecedent conditions of an unsettled situation are involved in that state of imbalance in organic-environmental interactions which has already been described. Restoration of integration can be effected, in one case as in the other, only by operations which actually modify existing conditions, not by merely "mental" processes.

It is, accordingly, a mistake to suppose that a situation is doubtful only in a "subjective" sense. The notion that in actual existence everything is completely determinate has been rendered questionable by the progress of physical science itself. Even if it had not been, complete determination would not hold of existences as an *environment*. For Nature is an environment only as it is involved in interaction with an organism, or self, or whatever name be used.[2]

Every such interaction is a temporal process, not a momentary cross-sectional occurrence. The situation in which it occurs is indeterminate, therefore, with respect to its *issue*. If we call it *confused*, then it is meant that its outcome cannot be anticipated. It is called *obscure* when its course of movement permits of final consequences that cannot be clearly made out. It is called *conflicting* when it tends to evoke discordant responses. Even were existential conditions unqualifiedly determinate in and of themselves, they are indeterminate in *significance*: that is, in what they import and portend in their interaction with the organism. The organic responses that enter into the production of the state of affairs that is temporally later and sequential are just as existential as are environing conditions.

The immediate *locus* of the problem concerns, then, what kind of responses the organism shall make. It concerns the interaction of organic responses and environing conditions in their movement toward an existential issue. It is a commonplace that in any troubled state of affairs *things* will come out differently according to what is done. The farmer won't get grain unless he plants and tills; the general will win or lose the battle according to the way he conducts it, and so on. Neither

---

[2] Except of course a purely mentalistic name, like *consciousness*. The alleged problem of "interactionism" versus automatism, parallelism, etc., is a problem (and an insoluble one) because of the assumption involved in its statement—the assumption, namely, that the interaction in question is with something mental instead of with biological-cultural human beings.

the grain nor the tilling, neither the outcome of the battle nor the conduct of it, are "mental" events. Organic interaction becomes inquiry when existential consequences are anticipated; when environing conditions are examined with reference to their potentialities; and when responsive activities are selected and ordered with reference to actualization of some of the potentialities, rather than others, in a final existential situation. Resolution of the indeterminate situation is active and operational. If the inquiry is adequately directed, the final issue is the unified situation that has been mentioned.

II. *Institution of a Problem*. The unsettled or indeterminate situation might have been called a *problematic* situation. This name would have been, however, proleptic and anticipatory. The indeterminate situation becomes problematic in the very process of being subjected to inquiry. The indeterminate situation comes into existence from existential causes, just as does, say, the organic imbalance of hunger. There is nothing intellectual or cognitive in the existence of such situations, although they are the necessary condition of cognitive operations or inquiry. In themselves they are precognitive. The first result of evocation of inquiry is that the situation is taken, adjudged, to be problematic. To see that a situation requires inquiry is the initial step in inquiry.[3]

Qualification of a situation as problematic does not, however, carry inquiry far. It is but an initial step in institution of a problem. A problem is not a task to be performed which a person puts upon himself or that is placed upon him by others—like a so-called arithmetical "problem" in school work. A problem represents the partial transformation by inquiry of a problematic situation into a determinate situation. It is a familiar and significant saying that a problem well put is half-solved. To find out *what* the problem and problems are which a problematic situation presents to be inquired into, is to be well along in inquiry. To mistake the problem involved is to cause subsequent inquiry to be irrelevant or to go astray. Without a problem, there is blind groping in the dark. The way in which the problem is conceived decides what specific suggestions are entertained and which are dismissed; what data are selected and which rejected; it is the criterion for relevancy and irrelevancy of hypotheses and conceptual structures. On the other hand,

---

[3] If by "two-valued logic" is meant a logic that regards "true and false" as the sole logical values, then such a logic is necessarily so truncated that clearness and consistency in logical doctrine are impossible. Being the matter of a problem is a primary logical property.

to set up a problem that does not grow out of an actual situation is to start on a course of dead work, nonetheless dead because the work is "busy work." Problems that are self-set are mere excuses for seeming to do something intellectual, something that has the semblance but not the substance of scientific activity.

III. *The Determination of a Problem-Solution.* Statement of a problematic situation in terms of a problem has no meaning save as the problem instituted has, in the very terms of its statement, reference to a possible solution. Just because a problem well stated is on its way to solution, the determining of a genuine problem is a *progressive* inquiry; the cases in which a problem and its probable solution flash upon an inquirer are cases where much prior ingestion and digestion have occurred. If we assume, prematurely, that the problem involved is definite and clear, subsequent inquiry proceeds on the wrong track. Hence the question arises: How is the formation of a genuine problem so controlled that further inquiries will move toward a solution?

The first step in answering this question is to recognize that no situation which is *completely* indeterminate can possibly be converted into a problem having definite constituents. The first step then is to search out the *constituents* of a given situation which, as constituents, are settled. When an alarm of fire is sounded in a crowded assembly hall, there is much that is indeterminate as regards the activities that may produce a favorable issue. One may get out safely or one may be trampled and burned. The fire is characterized, however, by some settled traits. It is, for example, located *somewhere*. Then the aisles and exits are at fixed places. Since they are settled or determinate in *existence*, the first step in institution of a problem is to settle them in *observation*. There are other factors which, while they are not as temporally and spatially fixed, are yet observable constituents; for example, the behavior and movements of other members of the audience. All of these observed conditions taken together constitute "the facts of the case." They constitute the terms of the problem, because they are conditions that must be reckoned with or taken account of in any relevant solution that is proposed.

A *possible* relevant solution is then suggested by the determination of factual conditions which are secured by observation. The possible solution presents itself, therefore, as an *idea*, just as the terms of the problem (which are facts) are instituted by observation. Ideas are anticipated consequences (forecasts) of what will happen when certain operations are executed under and with respect to observed conditions.[4] Observation of facts and suggested meanings or ideas arise and develop in correspondence with each other. The more the facts of the case come to light in consequence of being subjected to observation, the clearer and more pertinent become the conceptions of the way the problem constituted by these facts is to be dealt with. On the other side, the clearer the idea, the more definite, as a truism, become the operations of observation and of execution that must be performed in order to resolve the situation.

An idea is first of all an anticipation of something that may happen; it marks a *possibility*. When it is said, as it sometimes is, that science is *prediction*, the anticipation that constitutes every idea an idea is grounded in a set of controlled observations and of regulated conceptual ways of interpreting them. Because inquiry is a progressive determination of a problem and its possible solution, ideas differ in grade according to the stage of inquiry reached. At first, save in highly familiar matters, they are vague. They occur at first simply as suggestions; suggestions just spring up, flash upon us, occur to us. They may then become stimuli to direct an overt activity but they have as yet no logical status. Every idea originates as a suggestion, but not every suggestion is an idea. The suggestion becomes an idea when it is examined with reference to its functional fitness; its capacity as a means of resolving the given situation.

This examination takes the form of reasoning, as a result of which we are able to appraise better than we were at the outset, the pertinency and weight of the meaning now entertained with respect to its functional capacity. But the final test of its possession of these properties is determined when it actually functions—that is, when it is put into operation so as to institute by means of observations facts not previously observed, and is then used to organize them with other facts into a coherent whole.

Because suggestions and ideas are of that which is not present in given existence, the meanings which they involve must be embodied in some symbol. Without some kind of symbol no idea; a meaning that is

---

[4] The theory of *ideas* that has been held in psychology and epistemology since the time of Locke's successors is completely irrelevant and obstructive in logical theory. For in treating them as copies of perceptions or "impressions," it ignores the prospective and anticipatory character that defines *being* an idea. Failure to define ideas functionally, in the reference they have to a solution of a problem, is one reason they have been treated as merely "mental." The notion, on the other hand, that ideas are fantasies is a derivative. Fantasies arise when the function an idea performs is ruled out when it is entertained and developed.

completely disembodied can not be entertained or used. Since an existence (which *is* an existence) is the support and vehicle of a meaning and is a symbol instead of a merely physical existence only in this respect, embodied meanings or ideas are capable of objective survey and development. To "look at an idea" is not a mere literary figure of speech.

"Suggestions" have received scant courtesy in logical theory. It is true that when they just "pop into our heads," because of the workings of the psycho-physical organism, they are not logical. But they are both the conditions and the primary stuff of logical ideas. The traditional empiristic theory reduced them, as has already been pointed out, to mental copies of physical things and assumed that they were *per se* identical with ideas. Consequently it ignored the function of ideas in directing observation and in ascertaining relevant facts. The rationalistic school, on the other hand, saw clearly that "facts" apart from ideas are trivial, that they acquire import and significance only in relation to ideas. But at the same time it failed to attend to the operative and functional nature of the latter. Hence, it treated ideas as equivalent to the ultimate structure of "Reality." The Kantian formula that apart from each other "perceptions are blind and conceptions empty" marks a profound logical insight. The insight, however, was radically distorted because perceptual and conceptual contents were supposed to originate from different sources and thus required a third activity, that of synthetic understanding, to bring them together. In logical fact, perceptual and conceptual materials are instituted in functional correlativity with each other, in such a manner that the former locates and describes the problem while the latter represents a possible method of solution. Both are determinations in and by inquiry of the original problematic situation whose pervasive quality controls their institution and their contents. Both are finally checked by their capacity to work together to introduce a resolved unified situation. As distinctions they represent logical divisions of labor.

IV. *Reasoning*. The necessity of developing the meaning-contents of ideas in their relations to one another has been incidentally noted. This process, operating with symbols (constituting propositions) is reasoning in the sense of ratiocination or rational discourse.[5] When a suggested meaning is immediately accepted, inquiry is cut short. Hence the conclusion reached is not grounded, even if it happens to be correct. The

---

[5] "Reasoning" is sometimes used to designate *inference* as well as ratiocination. When so used in logic the tendency is to identify inference and implication and thereby seriously to confuse logical theory.

check upon immediate acceptance is the examination of the meaning as a meaning. This examination consists in noting what the meaning in question implies in relation to other meanings in the system of which it is a member, the formulated relation constituting a proposition. If such and such a relation of meanings is accepted, then we are committed to such and such other relations of meanings because of their membership in the same system. Through a series of intermediate meanings, a meaning is finally reached which is more clearly *relevant* to the problem in hand than the originally suggested idea. It indicates operations which can be performed to test its applicability, whereas the original idea is usually too vague to determine crucial operations. In other words, the idea or meaning when developed in discourse directs the activities which, when executed, provide needed evidential material.

The point made can be most readily appreciated in connection with scientific reasoning. An hypothesis, once suggested and entertained, is developed in relation to other conceptual structures until it receives a form in which it can instigate and direct an experiment that will disclose precisely those conditions which have the maximum possible force in determining whether the hypothesis should be accepted or rejected. Or it may be that the experiment will indicate what modifications are required in the hypothesis so that it may be applicable, i.e., suited to interpret and organize the facts of the case. In many familiar situations, the meaning that is most relevant has been settled because of the eventuations of experiments in prior cases so that it is applicable almost immediately upon its occurrence. But, indirectly, if not directly, an idea or suggestion that is not developed in terms of the constellation of meanings to which it belongs can lead only to overt response. Since the latter terminates inquiry, there is then no adequate inquiry into the meaning that is used to settle the given situation, and the conclusion is in so far logically ungrounded.

V. *The Operational Character of Facts-Meanings*. It was stated that the observed facts of the case and the ideational contents expressed in ideas are related to each other, as, respectively, a clarification of the problem involved and the proposal of some possible solution; that they are, accordingly, functional divisions in the work of inquiry. Observed facts in their office of locating and describing the problem are existential; ideational subject-matter is non-existential. How, then, do they cooperate with each other in the resolution of an existential situation? The problem is insoluble save as it is recognized that both observed facts and entertained ideas are operational. Ideas are operational in that they instigate and direct further operations of observation; they are proposals and plans for acting upon existing conditions to bring new facts to light and to organize all the selected facts into a coherent whole.

What is meant by calling facts operational? Upon the negative side what is meant is that they are not self-sufficient and complete in themselves. They are selected and described, as we have seen, for a purpose, namely statement of the problem involved in such a way that its material both indicates a meaning relevant to resolution of the difficulty and serves to test its worth and validity. In regulated inquiry facts are selected and arranged with the express intent of fulfilling this office. They are not merely *results* of operations of observation which are executed with the aid of bodily organs and auxiliary instruments of art, but they are the particular facts and kinds of facts that will link up with one another in the definite ways that are required to produce a definite end. Those not found to connect with others in furtherance of this end are dropped and others are sought for. Being functional, they are necessarily operational. Their function is to serve as evidence and their evidential quality is judged on the basis of their capacity to form an ordered whole in response to operations prescribed by the ideas they occasion and support. If "the facts of the case" were final and complete in themselves, if they did not have a special operative force in resolution of the problematic situation, they could not serve as evidence.

The operative force of facts is apparent when we consider that no fact in isolation has evidential potency. Facts are evidential and are tests of an idea in so far as they are capable of being organized with one another. The organization can be achieved only as they *interact* with one another. When the problematic situation is such as to require extensive inquiries to effect its resolution, a series of interactions intervenes. Some observed facts point to an idea that stands for a possible solution. This idea evokes more observations. Some of the newly observed facts link up with those previously observed and are such as to rule out other observed things with respect to their evidential function. The new order of facts suggests a modified idea (or hypothesis) which occasions new observations whose result again determines a new order of facts, and so on until the existing order is both unified and complete. In the course of this serial process, the ideas that represent possible solutions are tested or "proved."

Meantime, the orders of fact, which present themselves in consequence of the experimental observations the ideas call out and direct, are *trial* facts. They are provisional. They are "facts" if they are observed by sound organs and techniques. But they are not on that account the *facts of the case*. They are tested or "proved" with respect to their evidential function just as much as ideas (hypotheses) are tested with reference to their power to exercise the function of resolution. The operative force of both ideas and facts is thus practically recognized in the degree in which they are connected with *experiment*. Naming them "operational" is but a theoretical recognition of what is involved when inquiry satisfies the conditions imposed by the necessity for experiment.

I recur, in this connection, to what has been said about the necessity for symbols in inquiry. It is obvious, on the face of matters, that a possible mode of solution must be carried in symbolic form since it is a possibility, not an assured present existence. Observed facts, on the other hand, are existentially present. It might seem therefore, that symbols are not required for referring to them. But if they are not carried and treated by means of symbols, they lose their provisional character, and in losing this character they are categorically asserted and inquiry comes to an end. The carrying on of inquiry requires that the facts be taken as *re*presentative and not just as *pre*-sented. This demand is met by formulating them in propositions—that is, by means of symbols. Unless they are so represented they relapse into the total qualitative situation.

VI. *Common Sense and Scientific Inquiry.* The discussion up to this point has proceeded in general terms which recognize no distinction between common sense and scientific inquiry. We have now reached a point where the community of pattern in these two distinctive modes of inquiry should receive explicit attention. It was said in earlier chapters that the difference between them resides in their respective subject-matters, not in their basic logical forms and relations; that the difference in subject-matters is due to the difference in the problems respectively involved; and, finally, that this difference sets up a difference in the ends or objective consequences they are concerned to achieve. Because common sense problems and inquiries have to do with the interactions into which living creatures enter in connection with environing conditions in order to establish objects of use and enjoyment, the symbols employed are those which have been determined in the habitual culture of a group. They form a system but the system is practical rather than intellectual. It is constituted by the traditions, occupations, techniques, interests, and established institutions of the group. The meanings that compose it are carried in the common everyday language of communication between members of the group. The meanings involved in this common language system determine what individuals of the group may and may not do in relation to physical objects and in relations to one another. They regulate *what* can be used and enjoyed and *how* use and enjoyment shall occur.

Because the symbol-meaning systems involved are connected directly with cultural life-activities and are related to each other in virtue of this connection, the specific meanings which are present have reference to the specific and limited environing conditions under which the group lives. Only those things of the environment that are taken, according to custom and tradition, as having connection with and bearing upon this life, enter into the meaning system. There is no such thing as disinterested intellectual concern with either physical or social matters. For, until the rise of science, there were no problems of common sense that called for such inquiry. Disinterestedness existed practically in the demand that group interests and concerns be put above private needs and interests. But there was no intellectual disinterestedness beyond the activities, interests and concerns of the group. In other words, there was no science as such, although, as was earlier pointed out, there did exist information and techniques which were available for the purposes of scientific inquiry and out of which the latter subsequently grew.

In scientific inquiry, then, meanings are related to one another on the ground of their character *as* meanings, freed from direct reference to the concerns of a limited group. Their intellectual abstractness is a product of this liberation, just as the "concrete" is practically identified by directness of connection with environmental interactions. Consequently a new language, a new system of symbols related together on a new basis, comes into existence, and in this new language semantic coherence, as such, is the controlling consideration. To repeat what has already been said, connection with problems of use and enjoyment is the source of the dominant role of qualities, sensible and moral, and of ends in common sense.

In science, since meanings are determined on the ground of their relation as meanings to one another, *relations* become the objects of inquiry and qualities are relegated to a secondary status, playing a part only as far as they assist in institution of relations. They are subordinate because they have an instrumental office, instead of being themselves, as in prescientific common sense, the matters of final importance. The enduring hold of common sense is testified to historically by the long time it took before it was seen that scientific objects are strictly relational. First tertiary qualities were eliminated; it was recognized that moral qualities are not agencies in determining the structure of nature. Then secondary qualities, the wet-dry, hot-cold, light-heavy, which were the explanatory principles of physical phenomena in Greek science, were ejected. But so-called primary qualities took their place, as with Newton and the Lockeian formulation of Newtonian existential postulates. It was not until the threshold of our time was reached that scientific inquiries perceived that their own problems and methods required an interpretation of "primary qualities" in terms of relations, such as position, motion and temporal span. In the structure of distinctively scientific objects these relations are indifferent to qualities.

The foregoing is intended to indicate that the different objectives of common sense and of scientific inquiry demand different subject-matters and that this difference in subject-matters is not incompatible with the existence of a common pattern in both types. There are, of course, secondary logical forms which reflect the distinction of properties involved in the change from qualitative and teleological subject-matter to non-qualitative and non-teleological relations. But they occur and operate within the described community of pattern. They are explicable, and explicable only, on the ground of the distinctive problems generated by scientific subject-matter. The independence of scientific objects from limited and fairly direct reference to the environment as a factor in activities of use and enjoyment, is equivalent, as has already been intimated, to their *abstract* character. It is also equivalent to their *general* character in the sense in which the generalizations of science are different from the generalizations with which common sense is familiar. The generality of *all* scientific subject-matter as such means that it is freed from restriction to conditions which present themselves at particular times and places. Their reference is to *any* set of time and place conditions—a statement which is not to be confused with the doctrine that they have no reference to actual existential occasions. Reference to time-place of existence is necessarily involved, but it is reference to whatever set of existences fulfils the general relations laid down in and by the constitution of the scientific object.[6]

*Summary*. Since a number of points have been discussed, it will be well to round up conclusions reached about them in a summary statement of the structure of the common pattern of inquiry. Inquiry is the directed or controlled transformation of an indeterminate situation into

[6] The consequences that follow are directly related to the statement in Ch. IV that the elimination of qualities and ends is intermediate; that, in fact, the construction of purely relational objects has enormously liberated and expanded common sense uses and enjoyments by conferring control over production of qualities, by enabling new ends to be realistically instituted, and by providing competent means for achieving them.

a determinately unified one. The transition is achieved by means of operations of two kinds which are in functional correspondence with each other. One kind of operations deals with ideational or conceptual subject-matter. This subject-matter stands for possible ways and ends of resolution. It anticipates a solution, and is marked off from fancy because, or, in so far as, it becomes operative in instigation and direction of new observations yielding new factual material. The other kind of operations is made up of activities involving the techniques and organs of observation. Since these operations are existential they modify the prior existential situation, bring into high relief conditions previously obscure, and relegate to the background other aspects that were at the outset conspicuous. The ground and criterion of the execution of this work of emphasis, selection and arrangement is to delimit the problem in such a way that existential material may be provided with which to test the ideas that represent possible modes of solution. Symbols, defining terms and propositions, are necessarily required in order to retain and carry forward both ideational and existential subject-matters in order that they may serve their proper functions in the control of inquiry. Otherwise the problem is taken to be closed and inquiry ceases.

One fundamentally important phase of the transformation of the situation which constitutes inquiry is central in the treatment of judgment and its functions. The transformation is existential and hence temporal. The pre-cognitive unsettled situation can be settled only by modification of its constituents. Experimental operations change existing conditions. Reasoning, as such, can provide means for effecting the change of conditions but by itself cannot effect it. Only execution of existential operations directed by an idea in which ratiocination terminates can bring about the re-ordering of environing conditions required to produce a settled and unified situation. Since this principle also applies to the meanings that are elaborated in science, the experimental production and re-arrangement of physical conditions involved in natural science is further evidence of the unity of the pattern of inquiry. The temporal quality of inquiry means, then, something quite other than that the process of inquiry takes time. It means that the objective subject-matter of inquiry undergoes temporal modification.

*Terminological.* Were it not that knowledge is related to inquiry as a product to the operations by which it is produced, no distinctions requiring special differentiating designations would exist. Material would merely be a matter of knowledge or of ignorance and error; that would be all that could be said. The content of any given proposition would have the values "true" and "false" as final and exclusive attributes. But if knowledge is related to inquiry as its warrantably assertible product, and if inquiry is progressive and temporal, then the material inquired into reveals distinctive properties which need to be designated by distinctive names. As *undergoing* inquiry, the material has a different logical import from that which it has as the *outcome* of inquiry. In its first capacity and status, it will be called by the general name *subject-matter*. When it is necessary to refer to subject-matter in the context of either observation or ideation, the name *content* will be used, and, particularly on account of its *representative* character, content of propositions.

The name *objects* will be reserved for subject-matter so far as it has been produced and ordered in settled form by means of inquiry; proleptically, objects are the *objectives* of inquiry. The apparent ambiguity of using "objects" for this purpose (since the word is regularly applied to things that are observed or thought of) is only apparent. For things exist *as* objects for us only as they have been previously determined as outcomes of inquiries. When used in carrying on new inquiries in new problematic situations, they are known as objects in virtue of prior inquiries which warrant their assertibility. In the new situation, they are *means* of attaining knowledge of something else. In the strict sense, they are part of the *contents* of inquiry as the word content was defined above. But retrospectively (that is, as products of prior determination in inquiry) they are objects.

# IV

## The Metaphysics
## of Experience

With the exception of the essay on "The Postulate of Immediate Empiricism," which acts as a transition between Dewey's early pragmatic epistemology and his mature philosophy of experience, the material in this section is from *Experience and Nature*. Delivered originally as the Carus Lectures in 1922, this book stands as Dewey's major effort to present a full-scale analysis of traditional philosophical concerns in the context of his own metaphysics of experience.

## 16. The Postulate of Immediate Empiricism*

Although written during the time when Dewey was attempting to frame out a pragmatic epistemology, this essay is characterized by an emphasis on the meaning of experience and thereby serves as a transition to his later views in *Experience and Nature*. Entitling his own version of the new movement in philosophy during the first decade of this century as "immediate empiricism," Dewey postulates that things—anything, everything, in the ordinary or nontechnical use of the term 'thing'—are what they are experienced as." This is not to be confused with the contention that things are what they are "known" as, for in Dewey's view, "knowing is one mode of experiencing" but not the sole or only genuine mode.

Now, more so than finding out what we know about, the primary philosophical question is "to find out *what* sort of experience knowing is—or, concretely how things are ex-

* From John Dewey, *The Influence of Darwin on Philosophy: And Other Essays on Contemporary Thought*, pp. 226-41. Copyright 1910 by Holt, Rinehart and Winston, Inc. Copyright 1938 by John Dewey. Reprinted by permission of Holt, Rinehart and Winston, Inc. (Published originally in 1905.)

perienced when they are experienced *as* known things."
Implicit, but left undeveloped in this essay, is Dewey's corollary view that experience is cognitive in a wider sense than
that conveyed by speaking of "known objects," as witness his
subsequent views on aesthetic and religious experience.

The criticisms made upon that vital but still unformed movement
variously termed radical empiricism, pragmatism, humanism, func-
tionalism, according as one or another aspect of it is uppermost, have
left me with a conviction that the *fundamental* difference is not so much
in matters overtly discussed as in a presupposition that remains tacit: a
presupposition as to what experience is and means. To do my little part
in clearing up the confusion, I shall try to make my own presupposition
explicit. The object of this paper is, then, to set forth what I understand
to be the postulate and the criterion of *immediate empiricism*.[1]

Immediate empiricism postulates that things—anything, everything,
in the ordinary or non-technical use of the term "thing"—are what they
are experienced as. Hence, if one wishes to describe anything truly, his
task is to tell what it is experienced as being. If it is a horse that is to be
described, or the *equus* that is to be defined, then must the horse-trader,
or the jockey, or the timid family man who wants a "safe driver," or the
zoologist or the paleontologist tell us what the horse is which is experienced. If these accounts turn out different in some respects, as well
as congruous in others, this is no reason for assuming the content of one
to be exclusively "real," and that of others to be "phenomenal"; for
each account of what is experienced will manifest that it is the account
*of* the horse-dealer, or *of* the zoologist, and hence will give the conditions requisite for understanding the differences as well as the agree-
ments of the various accounts. And the principle varies not a whit if we
bring in the psychologist's horse, the logician's horse, or the metaphysician's horse.

---

[1] All labels are, of course, obnoxious and misleading. I hope, however, the term
will be taken by the reader in the sense in which it is forthwith explained, and not
in some more usual and familiar sense. Empiricism, as herein used, is as antipodal
to sensationalistic empiricism, as it is to transcendentalism, and for the same
reason. Both of these systems fall back on something which is defined in non-
directly-experienced terms in order to justify that which is directly experienced.
Hence I have criticized such empiricism (*Philosophical Review*, Vol. XI, No. 4, p.
364) as essentially absolutistic in character; and also ("Studies in Logical Theory,"
pp. 30, 58) as an attempt to build up experience in terms of certain methodological
checks and cues of attaining *certainty*.

In each case, the nub of the question is, *what sort of experience* is denoted or indicated: a concrete and determinate experience, varying, when it varies, in specific real elements, and agreeing, when it agrees, in specific real elements, so that we have a contrast, not between *a* Reality, and various approximations to, or phenomenal representations of Reality, but between different reals of experience. And the reader is begged to bear in mind that from this standpoint, when "an experience" or "some sort of experience" is referred to, "some thing" or "some sort of thing" is always meant.

Now, this statement that things are what they are experienced to be is usually translated into the statement that things (or, ultimately, Reality, Being) *are* only and just what they are *known* to be or that things are, or Reality *is*, what it is for a conscious knower—whether the knower be conceived primarily as a perceiver or as a thinker being a further, and secondary, question. This is the root-paralogism of all idealisms, whether subjective or objective, psychological or epistemological. By our postulate, things are what they are experienced to be; and, unless knowing is the sole and only genuine mode of experiencing, it is fallacious to say that Reality is just and exclusively what it is or would be to an all-competent all-knower; or even that it *is*, relatively and piecemeal, what it is to a finite and partial knower. Or, put more positively, knowing is one mode of experiencing, and the primary philosophic demand (from the standpoint of immediatism) is to find out *what* sort of an experience knowing is—or, concretely how things are experienced when they are experienced *as* known things.[2] By concretely is meant, obviously enough (among other things), such an account of the experience of things as known that will bring out the characteristic traits and distinctions they possess as things of a knowing experience, as compared with things experienced esthetically, or morally, or economically, or technologically. To assume that, because from the *standpoint of the knowledge experience* things *are* what they are known to be, therefore, metaphysically, absolutely, without qualification, everything in its reality (as distinct from its "appearance,"

---

[2] I hope the reader will not therefore assume that from the empiricist's standpoint knowledge is of small worth or import. On the contrary, from the empiricist's standpoint it has *all* the worth which it is concretely experienced as possessing—which is simply tremendous. But the exact *nature* of this worth is a thing to be found out in describing what we mean by experiencing objects as known—the actual differences made or found in experience.

or phenomenal occurrence) is what a knower would find it to be, is, from the immediatist's standpoint, if not the root of all philosophic evil, at least one of its main roots. For this leaves out of account what the knowledge standpoint is itself *experienced as*.

I start and am flustered by a noise heard. Empirically, that noise is fearsome; it *really* is, not merely phenomenally or subjectively so. That *is what* it is experienced as being. But, when I experience the noise as a *known* thing, I find it to be innocent of harm. It is the tapping of a shade against the window, owing to movements of the wind. The experience has changed; that is, the thing experienced has changed—not that an unreality has given place to a reality, nor that some transcendental (unexperienced) Reality has changed,[3] not that truth has changed, but just and only the concrete reality experienced has changed. I now feel ashamed of my fright; and the noise as fearsome is changed to noise as a wind-curtain fact, and hence practically indifferent to my welfare. This is a change of experienced existence effected through the medium of cognition. The content of the latter experience cognitively regarded is doubtless *truer* than the content of the earlier; but it is in no sense more real. To call it truer, moreover, must, from the empirical standpoint, mean a concrete *difference* in actual things experienced.[4] Again, in many cases, only in retrospect is the prior experience cognitionally regarded at all. In such cases, it is only in regard to contrasted content *in* a subsequent experience that the determination "truer" has force.

Perhaps some reader may now object that as matter of fact the entire experience *is* cognitive, but that the earlier parts of it are only imperfectly so, resulting in a phenomenon that is not real; while the latter

---

[3] Since the non-empiricist believes in things-in-themselves (which he may term "atoms," "sensations," transcendental unities, *a priori* concepts, *an* absolute experience, or whatever), and since he finds that the empiricist makes much of change (as he must, since change is continuously experienced) he assumes that the empiricist means *his own* non-empirical Realities are in continual flux, and he naturally shudders at having his divinities so violently treated. But, once recognize that the empiricist doesn't have any such Realities at all, and the entire problem of the relation of change to reality takes a very different aspect.

[4] It would lead us aside from the point to try to tell just what is the nature of the experienced difference we call truth. Professor James's recent articles may well be consulted. The point to bear in mind here is just what sort of a thing the empiricist must mean by true, or truer (the noun of Truth is, of course, a generic name for all cases of "Trues"). The adequacy of any particular account is not a matter to be settled by general reasoning, but by finding out what sort of an experience the truth-experience actually is.

part, being a more complete cognition, results in what is relatively, at least, more real.[5] In short, a critic may say that, when I was frightened by the noise, I *knew* I was frightened; otherwise there would have been no experience at all. At this point, it is necessary to make a distinction so simple and yet so all-fundamental that I am afraid the reader will be inclined to pooh-pooh it away as a mere verbal distinction. But to see that to the empiricist this distinction is not verbal, but genuine, is the precondition of any understanding of him. The immediatist must, by his postulate, ask what is the fright experienced *as*. Is what is actually experienced, I-know-I-am-frightened, or I-*am*-frightened? I see absolutely no reason for claiming that the experience *must* be described by the former phrase. In all probability (and all the empiricist logically needs is just one case of this sort) the experience is simply and just of fright-at-the-noise. Later one may (or may not) have an experience describable *as* I-know-I-am- (or-was) and improperly or properly, frightened. But this is a different experience—that is, a different *thing*. And if the critic goes on to urge that the person "*really*" must have known that he was frightened, I can only point out that the critic is shifting the venue. He may be right, but, if so, it is only because the "really" is something not concretely experienced (whose nature accordingly is the critic's business); and this is to depart from the empiricist's point of view, to attribute to him a postulate he expressly repudiates.

The material point may come out more clearly if I say that we must make a distinction between a thing as *cognitive*, and one as *cognized*.[6] I should define a cognitive experience as one that has certain bearings or implications which induce, and fulfil themselves in, a subsequent experience in which the relevant thing is experienced *as* cognized, *as* a known object, and is thereby transformed, or reorganized. The fright-at-the-noise in the case cited is obviously *cognitive*, in this sense. By description, it induces an investigation or inquiry in which both noise and fright are objectively stated or presented—the noise as a shade-wind fact, the fright as an organic reaction to a sudden acoustic stimulus, a reaction that under the given circumstances was useless or

---

[5] I say, "relatively," because the transcendentalist still holds that finally the cognition is imperfect, giving us only some symbol or phenomenon of Reality (which *is* only in the Absolute or in some Thing-in-Itself)—otherwise the curtain-wind fact would have as much ontological reality as the existence of the Absolute itself: a conclusion at which the non-empiricist perhorresces, for no reason obvious to me—save that it would put an end to his transcendentalism.

[6] In general, I think the distinction between -*ive* and -*ed* one of the most fundamental of philosophic distinctions, and one of the most neglected. The same holds of -*tion* and -*ing*.

even detrimental, a maladaptation. Now, pretty much all of experience is of this sort (the "is" meaning, of course, is experienced *as*), and the empiricist is false to his principle if he does not duly note this fact.[7] But he is equally false to his principle if he permits himself to be confused as to the concrete differences in the two things experienced.

There are two little words through explication of which the empiricist's position may be brought out—"*as*" and "*that*." We may express his presupposition by saying that things are what they are experienced *as* being; or that to give a just account of anything is to tell what *that* thing is experienced to be. By these words I want to indicate the absolute, final, irreducible, and inexpugnable concrete *quale* which everything experienced not so much *has* as *is*. To grasp this aspect of empiricism is to see what the empiricist means by objectivity, by the element of control. Suppose we take, as a crucial case for the empiricist, an out and out illusion, say of Zöllner's lines. These are experienced as convergent; they are "truly" parallel. If things are what they are experienced as being, how can the distinction be drawn between illusion and the true state of the case? There is no answer to this question except by sticking to the fact that the experience of the lines as divergent is a concrete qualitative thing or *that*. It is *that* experience which it is, and no other. And if the reader rebels at the iteration of such obvious tautology, I can only reiterate that the realization of the *meaning* of this tautology is the key to the whole question of the objectivity of experience, as that stands to the empiricist. The lines of *that* experience *are* divergent; not merely *seem* so. The question of truth is not as to whether Being or Non-Being, Reality or mere Appearance, is experienced, but as to the *worth* of a certain concretely experienced thing. The only way of passing upon this question is by sticking in the most uncompromising fashion to *that* experience as real. *That* experience is that two lines with certain cross-hatchings are apprehended as convergent; only by taking that experience as real and as fully real, is there any basis for, or way of going to, an experienced knowledge that the lines are parallel. It is in the concrete thing *as experienced* that all the grounds and clues to its own intellectual or logical rectification are contained. It is because this thing, afterwards adjudged false, is a concrete *that*, that it develops into a corrected experience (that is, experience of a corrected thing—we reform things just as we reform ourselves or a bad

---

[7] What is criticised, now as "geneticism" (if I may coin the word) and now as "pragmatism" is, in its truth, just the fact that the empiricist does take account of the experienced "drift, occasion, and contexture" of things experienced—to use Hobbes's phrase.

boy) whose full content is not a whit more real, but which is true or truer.[8]

If *any* experience, then a *determinate* experience; and this determinateness is the only, and is the adequate, principle of control, or "objectivity." The experience may be of the vaguest sort. I may not see anything which I can identify as a familiar object—a table, a chair, etc. It may be dark; I may have only the vaguest impression that there is something which looks like a table. Or I may be completely befogged and confused, as when one rises quickly from sleep in a pitch-dark room. But this vagueness, this doubtfulness, this confusion is the thing experienced, and, *qua* real, is as "good" a reality as the self-luminous vision of an Absolute. It is not just vagueness, doubtfulness, confusion, at large or in general. It is *this* vagueness, and no other; absolutely unique, absolutely what *it* is.[9] Whatever gain in clearness, in fullness, in trueness of content is experienced must grow out of some element in the experience of *this* experienced *as* what it is. To return to the illusion: If the experience of the lines as convergent is illusory, it is because of some elements in the thing as experienced, not because of something defined in terms of externality to this particular experience. If the illusoriness can be detected, it is because the thing experienced is real, having within its experienced reality elements whose *own mutual* tension effects its reconstruction. Taken concretely, the experience of convergent lines contains within itself the elements of the transformation of its own content. It is *this* thing, and not some separate truth, that clamors for its own reform. There is, then, from the empiricist's point of view, no need to search for some aboriginal *that* to which all successive experiences are attached, and which is somehow thereby undergoing continuous change. Experience is always of *thats*; and the most comprehensive and inclusive experience of the universe that the philosopher himself can obtain is the experience of a characteristic *that*. From the empiricist's point of view, this is as true of the exhaustive and complete insight of a hypothetical all-knower as of the vague, blind experience of the awakened sleeper. As reals, they stand on the same level. As trues,

---

[8] Perhaps the point would be clearer if expressed in this way: Except as subsequent estimates of *worth* are introduced, "real" means only existent. The eulogistic connotation that makes the term Reality equivalent to *true* or *genuine* being has great pragmatic significance, but its confusion with reality as existence is the point aimed at in the above paragraph.

[9] One does not so easily escape medieval Realism as one thinks. Either every experienced thing has its own determinateness, its own unsubstitutable, unredeemable reality, or else "generals" *are* separate existences after all.

the latter has by definition the better of it; but if this insight is in any way the truth of the blind awakening, it is because the latter has, in its *own* determinate *quale*, elements of real continuity with the former; it is, *ex hypothesi*, transformable through a series of experienced reals without break of continuity, into the absolute thought-experience. There is no need of logical manipulation to effect the transformation, nor *could* any logical consideration effect it. If effected at all it is just by immediate experiences, each of which is just as real (no more, no less) as either of the two terms between which they lie. Such, at least, is the meaning of the empiricist's contention. So, when he talks of experience, he does not mean some grandiose, remote affair that is cast like a net around a succession of fleeting experiences; he does not mean an indefinite total, comprehensive experience which somehow engirdles an endless flux; he means that *things* are what they are experienced to be, and that every experience is *some* thing.

From the postulate of empiricism, then (or, what is the same thing, from a *general* consideration of the concept of experience), nothing can be deduced, not a single philosophical proposition.[10] The reader may hence conclude that all this just comes to the truism that experience is experience, or is what it is. If one attempts to draw conclusions from the bare concept of experience, the reader is quite right. But the real significance of the principle is that of a method of philosophical analysis—a method identical in kind (but differing in problem and hence in operation) with that of the scientist. If you wish to find out what subjective, objective, physical, mental, cosmic, psychic, cause, substance, purpose, activity, evil, being, quality—any philosophic term, in short—means, go to experience and see what the thing is experienced *as*.

Such a method is not spectacular; it permits of no offhand demonstrations of God, freedom, immortality, nor of the exclusive reality of matter, or ideas, or consciousness, etc. But it supplies a way of telling what all these terms mean. It may seem insignificant, or chillingly disap-

---

[10] Excepting, of course, some negative ones. One could say that certain views are certainly *not* true, because, by hypothesis, they refer to nonentities, *i.e.*, nonempiricals. But even here the empiricist must go slowly. From his own standpoint, even the most professedly transcendental statements are, after all, real as experiences, and hence negotiate some transaction with facts. For this reason, he cannot, in theory, reject them *in toto*, but has to show concretely how they arose and how they are to be corrected. In a word, his logical relationship to statements that profess to relate to things-in-themselves, unknowables, inexperienced substances, etc., is precisely that of the psychologist to the Zollner lines.

pointing, but only upon condition that it be not worked. Philosophic conceptions have, I believe, outlived their usefulness considered as stimulants to emotion, or as a species of sanctions; and a larger, more fruitful and more valuable career awaits them considered as specifically experienced meanings.*

* [Note: The reception of this essay proved that I was unreasonably sanguine in thinking that the foot-note of warning, appended to the title, would forfend radical misapprehension. I see now that it was unreasonable to expect that the word "immediate" in a philosophic writing could be generally understood to apply to anything except *knowledge*, even though the body of the essay is a protest against such limitation. But I venture to repeat that the essay is not a denial of the necessity of "mediation," or reflection, in knowledge, but is an assertion that the inferential factor must *exist*, or must occur, and that all existence is direct and vital, so that philosophy can pass upon its nature—as upon the nature of all of the rest of its subject-matter—only by first ascertaining what it exists or occurs *as*.

I venture to repeat also another statement of the text: I do not mean by "immediate experience" any aboriginal stuff out of which things are evolved, but I use the term to indicate the necessity of employing in philosophy the direct descriptive method that has now made its way in all the natural sciences, with such modifications, of course, as the subject itself entails.

There is nothing in the text to imply that things exist in experience atomically or in isolation. When it is said that a thing as cognized is *different* from an earlier non-cognitionally experienced thing, the saying no more implies lack of continuity between the things, than the obvious remark that a seed is different from a flower or a leaf denies their continuity. The amount and kind of continuity or discreteness that exists is to be discovered by recurring to what actually occurs in experience.

Finally, there is nothing in the text that denies the existence of things temporally prior to human experiencing of them. Indeed, I should think it fairly obvious that we experience most things *as* temporally prior to our experiencing of them. The import of the article is to the effect that we are not entitled to draw philosophic (as distinct from scientific) conclusions as to the meaning of prior temporal existence till we have ascertained what it is to experience a thing as past. These four disclaimers cover, I think, all the misapprehensions disclosed in the four or five controversial articles (noted below) that the original essay evoked. One of these articles (that of Professor Woodbridge), raised a point of fact, holding that cognitional experience tells us, without alteration, just what the things of other types of experience are, and in that sense transcend other experiences. This is too fundamental an issue to discuss in a note, and I content myself with remarking that with respect to it, the bearing of the article is that the issue must be settled by a careful descriptive survey of things as experienced, to see whether modifications do not occur in existences when they are experienced *as* known; *i.e.*, as true or false in character. The reader interested in following up this discussion is referred to the following articles: Vol. II of the *Journal of Philosophy, Psychology, and Scientific Methods*, two articles by Bakewell, p. 520 and p. 687; one by Bode, p. 658; one by Woodbridge, p. 573; Vol. III of the same *Journal*, by Leighton, p. 174.]

# 17. Experience and Philosophic Method*

This selection, from *Experience and Nature*, repeats in a detailed and passionate manner one of Dewey's lifelong concerns, the irreducible importance of everyday experience for philosophical method. Proceeding from his assertion of the continuity between experience and nature, Dewey affirms the relevance of the commonplace to the most profound philosophical speculation; indeed, as cut off from the use of experiences undergone, speculation becomes first incestuous and then trite.

In commenting on the riches of ordinary experience, for our understanding of nature as revealed in our interactions with the world, Dewey writes again and again of the reach of experience, its depth and its inferential power. To bypass the qualities revealed in the experience of "enjoyment and trouble, friendship and human association, art and industry" for the niceties of the language of reflection is to court disaster by playing into the hands of those who respond to the everyday with "cynicism, indifference and pessimism." In Dewey's version, philosophy has the task of "creating and promoting a respect for concrete human experience and its potentialities."

The title of this volume, *Experience and Nature*, is intended to signify that the philosophy here presented may be termed either empirical naturalism or naturalistic empiricism, or, taking "experience" in its usual signification, naturalistic humanism.

To many the associating of the two words will seem like talking of a round square, so engrained is the notion of the separation of man and experience from nature. Experience, they say, is important for those beings who have it, but is too casual and sporadic in its occurrence to carry with it any important implications regarding the nature of Nature. Nature, on the other hand, is said to be complete apart from experience. Indeed, according to some thinkers the case is even in worse plight: Experience to them is not only something extraneous which is occasionally super-imposed upon nature, but it forms a veil or screen which shuts us

---

* From John Dewey, *Experience and Nature* (New York, 1958) (1929), 2nd ed., Chap. 1.

off from nature, unless in some way it can be "transcended." So something non-natural by way of reason or intuition is introduced, something supra-empirical. According to an opposite school experience fares as badly, nature being thought to signify something wholly material and mechanistic; to frame a theory of experience in naturalistic terms is, accordingly, to degrade and deny the noble and ideal values that characterize experience.

I know of no route by which dialectical argument can answer such objections. They arise from associations with words and cannot be dealt with argumentatively. One can only hope in the course of the whole discussion to disclose the meanings which are attached to "experience" and "nature," and thus insensibly produce, if one is fortunate, a change in the significations previously attached to them. This process of change may be hastened by calling attention to another context in which nature and experience get on harmoniously together—wherein experience presents itself as the method, and the only method, for getting at nature, penetrating its secrets, and wherein nature empirically disclosed (by the use of empirical method in natural science) deepens, enriches and directs the further development of experience.

In the natural sciences there is a union of experience and nature which is not greeted as a monstrosity; on the contrary, the inquirer must use empirical method if his findings are to be treated as genuinely scientific. The investigator assumes as a matter of course that experience, controlled in specifiable ways, is the avenue that leads to the facts and laws of nature. He uses reason and calculation freely; he could not get along without them. But he sees to it that ventures of this theoretical sort start from and terminate in directly experienced subject-matter. Theory may intervene in a long course of reasoning, many portions of which are remote from what is directly experienced. But the vine of pendant theory is attached at both ends to the pillars of observed subject-matter. And this experienced material is the same for the scientific man and the man in the street. The latter cannot follow the intervening reasoning without special preparation. But stars, rocks, trees, and creeping things are the same material of experience for both.

These commonplaces take on significance when the relation of experience to the formation of a philosophic theory of nature is in question. They indicate that experience, if scientific inquiry is justified, is no infinitesimally thin layer or foreground of nature, but that it penetrates into it, reaching down into its depths, and in such a way that its grasp is capable of expansion; it tunnels in all directions and in so doing brings to the surface things at first hidden—as miners pile high on the surface of the earth treasures brought from below. Unless we are prepared to deny all validity to scientific inquiry, these facts have a value that cannot be ignored for the general theory of the relation of nature and experience.

It is sometimes contended, for example, that since experience is a late comer in the history of our solar system and planet, and since these occupy a trivial place in the wide areas of celestial space, experience is at most a slight and insignificant incident in nature. No one with an honest respect for scientific conclusions can deny that experience as an existence is something that occurs only under highly specialized conditions, such as are found in a highly organized creature which in turn requires a specialized environment. There is no evidence that experience occurs everywhere and everywhen. But candid regard for scientific inquiry also compels the recognition that when experience does occur, no matter at what limited portion of time and space, it enters into possession of some portion of nature and in such a manner as to render other of its precincts accessible.

A geologist living in 1928 tells us about events that happened not only before he was born but millions of years before any human being came into existence on this earth. He does so by starting from things that are now the material of experience. Lyell revolutionized geology by perceiving that the sort of thing that can be experienced now in the operations of fire, water, pressure, is the sort of thing by which the earth took on its present structural forms. Visiting a natural history museum, one beholds a mass of rock and, reading a label, finds that it comes from a tree that grew, so it is affirmed, five million years ago. The geologist did not leap from the thing he can see and touch to some event in by-gone ages; he collated this observed thing with many others, of different kinds, found all over the globe; the results of his comparisons he then compared with data of other experiences, say, the astronomer's. He translates, that is, observed coexistences into non-observed, inferred sequences. Finally he dates his object, placing it in an order of events. By the same sort of method he predicts that at certain places some things not yet experienced will be observed, and then he takes pains to bring them within the scope of experience. The scientific conscience is, moreover, so sensitive with respect to the necessity of experience that when it reconstructs the past it is not fully satisfied with inferences drawn from even a large and cumulative' mass of uncontradicted evidence; it sets to work to institute conditions of heat and pressure and moisture, etc., so as actually to reproduce in experiment that which he has inferred.

These commonplaces prove that experience is *of* as well as *in* nature. It is not experience which is experienced, but nature—stones, plants, animals, diseases, health, temperature, electricity, and so on. Things interacting in certain ways *are* experience; they are what is experienced. Linked in certain other ways with another natural object—the human organism—they are *how* things are experienced as well. Experience thus reaches down into nature; it has depth. It also has breadth and to an indefinitely elastic extent. It stretches. That stretch constitutes inference.

Dialectical difficulties, perplexities due to definitions given to the concepts that enter into the discussion, may be raised. It is said to be absurd that what is only a tiny part of nature should be competent to incorporate vast reaches of nature within itself. But even were it logically absurd one would be bound to cleave to it as a fact. Logic, however, is not put under a strain. The fact that something is an occurrence does not decide what kind of an occurrence it is; that can be found out only by examination. To argue from an experience "being an experience" to what it is of and about is warranted by no logic, even though modern thought has attempted it a thousand times. A bare event is no event at all; *something* happens. What that something is, is found out by actual study. This applies to seeing a flash of lightning and holds of the longer event called experience. The very existence of science is evidence that experience is such an occurrence that it penetrates into nature and expands without limit through it.

These remarks are not supposed to prove anything about experience and nature for philosophical doctrine; they are not supposed to settle anything about the worth of empirical naturalism. But they do show that in the case of natural science we habitually treat experience as starting-point, and as method for dealing with nature, and as the goal in which nature is disclosed for what it is. To realize this fact is at least to weaken those verbal associations which stand in the way of apprehending the force of empirical method in philosophy.

The same considerations apply to the other objection that was suggested: namely, that to view experience naturalistically is to reduce it to something materialistic, depriving it of all ideal significance. If experience actually presents esthetic and moral traits, then these traits may also be supposed to reach down into nature, and to testify to something that belongs to nature as truly as does the mechanical structure attributed to it in physical science. To rule out that possibility by some general reasoning is to forget that the very meaning and purport of empirical method is that things are to be studied on their own account, so as to find out what is revealed when they are experienced. The traits possessed by the subject-matters of experience are as genuine as the characteristics of sun and electron. They are *found*, experienced, and are not to be shoved out of being by some trick of logic. When found, their ideal qualities are as relevant to the philosophic theory of nature as are the traits found by physical inquiry.

To discover some of these general features of experienced things and to interpret their significance for a philosophic theory of the universe in which we live is the aim of this volume. From the point of view adopted, the theory of empirical method in philosophy does for experienced subject-matter on a liberal scale what it does for special sciences on a technical scale. It is this aspect of method with which we are especially concerned in the present chapter.

If the empirical method were universally or even generally adopted in philosophizing, there would be no need of referring to experience. The scientific inquirer talks and writes about particular observed events and qualities, about specific calculations and reasonings. He makes no allusion to experience; one would probably have to search a long time through reports of special researches in order to find the word. The reason is that everything designated by the word "experience" is so adequately incorporated into scientific procedures and subject-matter that to mention experience would be only to duplicate in a general term what is already covered in definite terms.

Yet this was not always so. Before the technique of empirical method was developed and generally adopted, it was necessary to dwell explicitly upon the importance of "experience" as a starting point and terminal point, as setting problems and as testing proposed solutions. We need not be content with the conventional allusion to Roger Bacon and Francis Bacon. The followers of Newton and the followers of the Cartesian school carried on a definite controversy as to the place occupied by experience and experiment in science as compared with intuitive concepts and with reasoning from them. The Cartesian school relegated experience to a secondary and almost accidental place, and only when the Galilean-Newtonian method had wholly triumphed did it cease to be necessary to mention the importance of experience. We may, if sufficiently hopeful, anticipate a similar outcome in philosophy. But the date does not appear to be close at hand; we are nearer in philosophic theory to the time of Roger Bacon than to that of Newton.

In short, it is the contrast of empirical method with other methods employed in philosophizing, together with the striking dissimilarity of results yielded by an empirical method and professed non-empirical methods that make the discussion of the methodological import of "experience" for philosophy pertinent and indeed indispensable.

This consideration of method may suitably begin with the contrast between gross, macroscopic, crude subject-matters in primary experience and the refined, derived objects of reflection. The distinction is one between what is experienced as the result of a minimum of incidental reflection and what is experienced in consequence of continued and regulated reflective inquiry. For derived and refined products are experienced only because of the intervention of systematic thinking. The objects of both science and philosphy obviously belong chiefly to the secondary and refined system. But at this point we come to a marked divergence between science and philosophy. For the natural sciences not only draw their material from primary experience, but they refer it back again for test. Darwin began with the pigeons, cattle and plants of breeders and gardeners. Some of the conclusions he reached were so contrary to accepted beliefs that they were condemned as absurd, contrary to common-sense, etc. But scientific men, whether they accepted his theories or not, employed his hypotheses as directive ideas for making new observations and experiments among the things of raw experience—just as the metallurgist who extracts refined metal from crude ore makes tools that are then set to work to control and use other crude materials. An Einstein working by highly elaborate methods of reflection, calculates theoretically certain results in the deflection of light by the presence of the sun. A technically equipped expedition is sent to South Africa so that by means of experiencing a thing—an eclipse—in crude, primary, experience, observations can be secured to compare with, and test the theory implied in, the calculated result.

The facts are familiar enough. They are cited in order to invite attention to the relationship between the objects of primary and of secondary or reflective experience. That the subject-matter of primary experience sets the problems and furnishes the first data of the reflection which constructs the secondary objects is evident; it is also obvious that test and verification of the latter is secured only by return to things of crude or macroscopic experience—the sun, earth, plants and animals of common, every-day life. But just what rôle do the objects attained in reflection play? Where do they come in? They *explain* the primary objects, they enable us to grasp them with *understanding*, instead of just having sense-contact with them. But how?

Well, they define or lay out a path by which return to experienced things is of such a sort that the meaning, the significant content, of what is experienced gains an enriched and expanded force because of the path or method by which it was reached. Directly, in immediate contact it may be just what it was before—hard, colored, odorous, etc. But when the secondary objects, the refined objects, are employed as a method or road for coming at them, these qualities cease to be isolated details; they get the meaning contained in a whole system of related objects; they are rendered continuous with the rest of nature and take on the import of the things they are now seen to be continuous with. The phenomena observed in the eclipse tested and, as far as they went, confirmed Einstein's theory of deflection of light by mass. But that is far from being the whole story. The phenomena themselves got a far-reaching significance they did not previously have. Perhaps they would not even have been noticed if the theory had not been employed as a guide or road to observation of them. But even if they had been noticed, they would have been dismissed as of no importance, just as we daily drop from attention hundreds of perceived details for which we have no intellectual use. But approached by means of theory these lines of slight deflection take on a significance as large as that of the revolutionary theory that lead to their being experienced.

This empirical method I shall call the *denotative* method. That philosophy is a mode of reflection, often of a subtle and penetrating sort, goes without saying. The charge that is brought against the non-empirical method of philosophizing is not that it depends upon theorizing, but that it fails to use refined, secondary products as a path pointing and leading back to something in primary experience. The resulting failure is three-fold.

First, there is no verification, no effort even to test and check. What is even worse, secondly, is that the things of ordinary experience do not get enlargement and enrichment of meaning as they do when approached through the medium of scientific principles and reasonings. This lack of function reacts, in the third place, back upon the philosophic subject-matter in itself. Not tested by being employed to see what it leads to in ordinary experience and what new meanings it contributes, this subject-matter becomes arbitrary, aloof—what is called "abstract" when that word is used in a bad sense to designate something which exclusively occupies a realm of its own without contact with the things of ordinary experience.

As the net outcome of these three evils, we find that extraordinary phenomenon which accounts for the revulsion of many cultivated persons from any form of philosophy. The objects of reflection in philosophy, being reached by methods that seem to those who employ them rationally mandatory are taken to be "real" in and of themselves—and supremely real. Then it becomes an insoluble problem why the things of gross, primary experience, should be what they are, or indeed why they should be at all. The refined objects of reflection in the natural sciences, however, never end by rendering the subject-matter from which they are derived a problem; rather, when used to describe a path by which some goal in primary experience is designated or denoted, they solve perplexities to which that crude material gives rise but which it cannot resolve of itself. They become means of control, of enlarged use and enjoyment of ordinary things. They may generate new problems, but these are problems of the same sort, to be dealt with by further use of the same methods of inquiry and experimentation. The problems to which empirical method gives rise afford, in a word, opportunities for more investigations yielding fruit in new and enriched experiences. But the problems to which non-empirical method gives rise in philosophy are blocks to inquiry, blind alleys; they are puzzles rather than problems, solved only by calling the original material of primary experience, "phenomenal," mere appearance, mere impressions, or by some other disparaging name.

Thus there is here supplied, I think, a first-rate test of the value of any philosophy which is offered us: Does it end in conclusions which, when they are referred back to ordinary life-experiences and their predicaments, render them more significant, more luminous to us, and make our dealings with them more fruitful? Or does it terminate in rendering the things of ordinary experience more opaque than they were before, and in depriving them of having in "reality" even the significance they had previously seemed to have? Does it yield the enrichment and increase of power of ordinary things which the results of physical science afford when applied in every-day affairs? Or does it become a mystery that these ordinary things should be what they are; and are philosophic concepts left to dwell in separation in some technical realm of their own? It is the fact, I repeat, that so many philosophies terminate in conclusions that make it necessary to disparage and condemn primary experience, leading those who hold them to measure the sublimity of their "realities" as philosophically defined by remoteness from the concerns of daily life, which leads cultivated common-sense to look askance at philosophy.

These general statements must be made more definite. We must illustrate the meaning of empirical method by seeing some of its results in contrast with those to which non-empirical philosophies conduct us. We begin by noting that "experience" is what James called a double-barrelled word. Like its congeners, life and history, it includes *what* men do and suffer, *what* they strive for, love, believe and endure, and also *how* men act and are acted upon, the ways in which they do and suffer, desire and enjoy, see, believe, imagine—in short, processes of *experiencing*. "Experience" denotes the planted field, the sowed seeds, the reaped harvests, the changes of night and day, spring and autumn, wet and dry, heat and cold, that are observed, feared, longed for; it also denotes the one who plants and reaps, who works and rejoices, hopes, fears, plans, invokes magic or chemistry to aid him, who is downcast or triumphant. It is "double-barrelled" in that it recognizes in its primary integrity no division between act and material, subject and object, but contains them both in an unanalyzed totality. "Thing" and "thought," as James says in the same connection, are single-barrelled; they refer to products discriminated by reflection out of primary experience.[2]

It is significant that "life" and "history" have the same fullness of undivided meaning. Life denotes a function, a comprehensive activity, in which organism and environment are included. Only upon reflective analysis does it break up into external conditions—air breathed, food taken, ground walked upon—and internal structures—lungs respiring, stomach digesting, legs walking. The scope of "history" is notorious: it is the deeds enacted, the tragedies undergone; and it is the human comment, record, and interpretation that inevitably follow. Objectively, history takes in rivers, mountains, fields and forests, laws and institutions; subjectively it includes the purposes and plans, the desires and emotions, through which these things are administered and transformed.

Now empirical method is the only method which can do justice to this inclusive integrity of "experience." It alone takes this integrated unity as the starting point for philosophic thought. Other methods begin with results of a reflection that has already torn in two the subject-matter experienced and the operations and states of experiencing. The problem is then to get together again what has been sundered—which is as if the king's men started with the fragments of the egg and tried to construct the whole egg out of them. For empirical method the problem is nothing so impossible of solution. Its problem is to note how and why the whole is distinguished into subject and object, nature and mental operations. Having done this, it is in a position to see *to what effect* the distinction

[1] *Essays in Radical Empiricism*, p. 10.

[2] It is not intended, however, to attribute to James precisely the interpretation given in the text.

is made: how the distinguished factors function in the further control and enrichment of the subject-matters of crude but total experience. Non-empirical method starts with a reflective product as if it were primary, as if it were the originally "given." To non-empirical method, therefore, object and subject, mind and matter (or whatever words and ideas are used) are separate and independent. Therefore it has upon its hands the problem of how it is possible to know at all; how an outer world can affect an inner mind; how the acts of mind can reach out and lay hold of objects defined in antithesis to them. Naturally it is at a loss for an answer, since its premises make the fact of knowledge both un-natural and unempirical. One thinker turns metaphysical materialist and denies reality to the mental; another turns psychological idealist, and holds that matter and force are merely disguised psychical events. Solutions are given up as a hopeless task, or else different schools pile one intellectual complication on another only to arrive by a long and tortuous course at that which naïve experience aleady has in its own possession.

The first and perhaps the greatest difference made in philosophy by adoption respectively of empirical or non-empirical method is, thus, the difference made in what is selected as original material. To a truly naturalistic empiricism, the moot problem of the relation of subject and object is the problem of what consequences follow in and for primary experience from the distinction of the physical and the psychological or mental from each other. The answer is not far to seek. To distinguish in reflection the physical and to hold it in temporary detachment is to be set upon the road that conducts to tools and technologies, to construc-tion of mechanisms, to the arts that ensue in the wake of the sciences. That these constructions make possible a better regulation of the affairs of primary experience is evident. Engineering and medicine, all the utili-ties that make for expansion of life, are the answer. There is better ad-ministration of old familiar things, and there is invention of new objects and satisfactions. Along with this added ability in regulation goes en-riched meaning and value in things, clarification, increased depth and continuity—a result even more precious than is the added power of con-trol.

The history of the development of the physical sciences is the story of the enlarging possession by mankind of more efficacious instrumen-talities for dealing with the conditions of life and action. But when one neglects the connection of these scientific objects with the affairs of primary experience, the result is a picture of a world of things indif-ferent to human interests because it is wholly apart from experience. It is more than merely isolated, for it is set in opposition. Hence when it is viewed as fixed and final in itself it is a source of oppression to the heart and paralysis to imagination. Since this picture of the physical universe and philosophy of the character of physical objects is contradicted by every engineering project and every intelligent measure of public hygiene, it would seem to be time to examine the foundations upon which it rests, and find out how and why such conclusions are come to.

When objects are isolated from the experience through which they are reached and in which they function, experience itself becomes reduced to the mere process of experiencing, and experiencing is therefore treated as if it were also complete in itself. We get the absurdity of an experiencing which experiences only itself, states and processes of consciousness, instead of the things of nature. Since the seventeenth century this conception of experience as the equivalent of subjective private consciousness set over against nature, which consists wholly of physical objects, has wrought havoc in philosophy. It is responsible for the feeling mentioned at the outset that "nature" and "experience" are names for things which have nothing to do with each other.

Let us inquire how the matter stands when these mental and psychical objects are looked at in their connection with experience in its primary and vital modes. As has been suggested, these objects are not original, isolated and self-sufficient. They represent the discriminated analysis of the process of experiencing from subject-matter experienced. Although breathing is in fact a function that includes both air and the operations of the lungs, we may detach the latter for study, even though we cannot separate it in fact. So while we always know, love, act for and against *things*, instead of experiencing ideas, emotions and mental intents, the attitudes themselves may be made a special object of attention, and thus come to form a distinctive subject-matter of reflective, although not of primary, experience.

We primarily observe things, not observations. But the *act* of observation may be inquired into and form a subject of study and become thereby a refined object; so may the acts of thinking, desire, purposing, the state of affection, reverie, etc. Now just as long as these attitudes are not distinguished and abstracted, they are incorporated into subject-matter. It is a notorious fact that the one who hates finds the one hated an obnoxious and despicable character; to the lover his adored one is full of intrinsically delightful and wonderful qualities. The connection between such facts and the fact of animism is direct.

The natural and original bias of man is all toward the objective; whatever is experienced is taken to be there independent of the attitude and act of the self. Its "thereness," its independence of emotion and volition, render the properties of things, whatever they are, cosmic. Only when vanity, prestige, rights of possession are involved does an individual tend to separate off from the environment and the group in which he, quite literally, lives, some things as being peculiarly himself. It is obvious that a total, unanalyzed world does not lend itself to control; that, on the contrary it is equivalent to the subjection of man to whatever occurs, as if to fate. Until some acts and their consequences are discriminatingly referred to the human organism and other energies and effects are referred to other bodies, there is no leverage, no purchase, with which to regulate the course of experience. The abstraction of certain qualities of things as due to human acts and states is the *pou sto* of ability in control. There can be no doubt that the long period of human arrest at a low level of culture was largely the result of failure to select the human being and his acts as a special kind of object, having his own characteristic activities that condition specifiable consequences.

In this sense, the recognition of "subjects" as centres of experience together with the development of "subjectivism" marks a great advance. It is equivalent to the emergence of agencies equipped with special powers of observation and experiment, and with emotions and desires that are efficacious for production of chosen modifications of nature. For otherwise the agencies are submerged in nature and produce qualities of things which must be accepted and submitted to. It is no mere play on words to say that recognition of subjective minds having a special equipment of psychological abilities is a necessary factor in subjecting the energies of nature to use as instrumentalities for ends.

Out of the indefinite number of possible illustrations of the consequences of reflective analysis yielding personal or "subjective" minds we cite one case. It concerns the influence of habitual beliefs and expectations in their social generation upon *what* is experienced. The things of primary experience are so arresting and engrossing that we tend to accept them just as they are—the flat earth, the march of the sun from east to west and its sinking under the earth. Current beliefs in morals, religion and politics similarly reflect the social conditions which present themselves. Only analysis shows that the *ways* in which we believe and expect have a tremendous affect upon *what* we believe and expect. We have discovered at last that these ways are set, almost abjectly so, by social factors, by tradition and the influence of education. Thus we discover that we believe many things not because the things are so, but because we have become habituated through the weight of authority, by imitation, prestige, instruction, the unconscious effect of language, etc.

We learn, in short, that qualities which we attribute to objects ought to be imputed to our own ways of experiencing them, and that these in turn are due to the force of intercourse and custom. This discovery marks an emancipation; it purifies and remakes the objects of our direct or primary experience. The power of custom and tradition in scientific as well as in moral beliefs never suffered a serious check until analysis revealed the effect of personal ways of believing upon things believed, and the extent to which these ways are unwittingly fixed by social custom and tradition. In spite of the acute and penetrating powers of observation among the Greeks, their "science" is a monument of the extent to which the effects of acquired social habits as well as of organic constitution were attributed directly to natural events. The de-personalizing and de-socializing of some objects, to be henceforth the objects of physical science, was a necessary precondition of ability to regulate experience by directing the attitudes and objects that enter into it.

This great emancipation was coincident with the rise of "individualism," which was in effect identical with the reflective discovery of the part played in experience by concrete selves, with their ways of acting, thinking and desiring. The results would have been all to the good if they had been interpreted by empirical method. For this would have kept the eye of thinkers constantly upon the origin of the "subjective" out of primary experience, and then directed it to the function of discriminating what is usable in the management of experienced objects. But for lack of such a method, because of isolation from empirical origin and instrumental use, the results of psychological inquiry were conceived to form a separate and isolated mental world in and of itself, self-sufficient and self-enclosed. Since the psychological movement necessarily coincided with that which set up physical objects as correspondingly complete and self-enclosed, there resulted that dualism of mind and matter, of a physical and a psychical world, which from the day of Descartes to the present dominates the formulation of philosophical problems.

With the dualism we are not here concerned, beyond pointing out that it is the inevitable result, logically, of the abandoning of acknowledgment of the primacy and ultimacy of gross experience —primary as it is given in an uncontrolled form, ultimate as it is given in a more regulated and significant form—a form made possible by the methods and results of reflective experience. But what we are directly concerned with at this stage of discussion is the result of the discovery of subjective objects upon philosophy in creation of wholesale subjectivism. The outcome was, that while in actual life the discovery of personal attitudes and their consequences was a great liberating instrument, psychology became for philosophy, as Santayana has well put it, "malicious." That is, mental attitudes, *ways* of experiencing, were treated as self-sufficient and complete in themselves, as that which is primarily *given*, the sole original and therefore indubitable data. Thus the traits of genuine primary experience, in which natural things are the determining factors in production of all change, were regarded either as not-given dubious things that could be reached only by endowing the only certain thing, the mental, with some miraculous power, or else were denied all existence save as complexes of mental states, of impressions, sensations, feelings.[3]

One illustration out of the multitude available follows. It is taken almost at random, because it is both simple and typical. To illustrate the nature of experience, what experience really is, an author writes: "When I look at a chair, I say I experience it. But what I actually experience is only a very few of the elements that go to make up a chair, namely the color that belongs to the chair under these particular conditions of light, the shape which the chair displays when viewed from this angle, etc." Two points are involved in any such statement. One is that "experience" is reduced to the traits connected with the *act of experiencing*, in this case the act of seeing. Certain patches of color, for example, assume a certain shape or form in connection with qualities connected with the muscular strains and adjustments of seeing. These qualities, which define the act of seeing when it is made an object of reflective inquiry, *over against what is seen*, thus become the chair itself for immediate or direct experience. Logically, the chair disappears and is replaced by certain qualities of sense attending the act of vision. There is no longer any other object, much less the chair which was bought, that is placed in a room and that is used to sit in, etc. If we ever get back to this total chair, it will not be the chair of direct experience, of use and enjoyment, a thing with its own independent origin, history and career; it will be only a complex of directly "given" sense qualities

---

[3] Because of this identification of the mental as the sole "given" in a primary, original way, appeal to experience by a philosopher is treated by many as necessarily committing one to subjectivism. It accounts for the alleged antithesis between nature and experience mentioned in the opening paragraph. It has become so deeply engrained that the empirical method employed in this volume has been taken by critics to be simply a re-statement of a purely subjective philosophy, although in fact it is wholly contrary to such a philosophy.

as a core, plus a surrounding cluster of other qualities revived imaginatively as "ideas."

The other point is that, even in such a brief statement as that just quoted, there is compelled recognition of an *object* of experience which is infinitely other and more than what is asserted to be alone experienced. There is the *chair* which is looked at; the *chair displaying* certain colors, the *light* in which they are displayed; the angle of vision implying reference to an organism that possesses an optical apparatus. Reference to these *things* is compulsory, because otherwise there would be no meaning assignable to the sense qualities—which are, nevertheless, affirmed to be the sole data experienced. It would be hard to find a more complete recognition, although an unavowed one, of the fact that in reality the account given concerns only a selected portion of the actual experience, namely that part which defines the act of experiencing, to the deliberate omission, *for the purpose of the inquiry in hand*, of *what* is experienced.

The instance cited is typical of all "subjectivism" as a philosophic position. Reflective analysis of one element in actual experience is undertaken; its result is then taken to be primary; as a consequence the subject-matter of actual experience from which the analytic result was derived is rendered dubious and problematic, although it is assumed at every step of the analysis. Genuine empirical method sets out from the actual subject-matter of primary experience, recognizes that reflection discriminates a new factor in it, the *act* of seeing, makes an object of that, and then uses that new object, the organic response to light, to regulate, when needed, further experiences of the subject-matter already contained in primary experience.

The topics just dealt with, segregation of physical and mental objects, will receive extended attention in the body of this volume. As respects *method*, however, it is pertinent at this point to summarize our results. Reference to the primacy and ultimacy of the material of ordinary experience protects us, in the first place, from creating artificial problems which deflect the energy and attention of philosophers from the real problems that arise out of actual subject-matter. In the second place, it provides a check or test for the conclusions of philosophic inquiry; it is a constant reminder that we must replace them, as secondary reflective products, in the experience out of which they arose, so that they may be confirmed or modified by the new order and clarity they introduce into it, and the new significantly experienced objects for which they furnish a method. In the third place, in seeing how they thus function in further experiences, the philosophical results themselves acquire empirical value; they are what they contribute to the common experience of man, instead of being curiosities to be deposited, with appropriate labels, in a metaphysical museum.

There is another important result for philosophy of the use of empirical method which, when it is developed, introduces our next topic. Philosophy, like all forms of reflective analysis, takes us away, for the time being, from the things had in primary experience as they directly act and are acted upon, used and enjoyed. Now the standing temptation of philosophy, as its course abundantly demonstrates, is to regard the results of reflection as having, in and of themselves, a reality superior to that of the material of any other mode of experience. The commonest assumption of philosophies, common even to philosophies very different from one another, is the assumption of the identity of objects of knowledge and ultimately real objects. The assumption is so deep that it is usually not expressed; it is taken for granted as something so fundamental that it does not need to be stated. A technical example of the view is found in the contention of the Cartesian school—including Spinoza—that emotion as well as sense is but confused thought which when it becomes clear and definite or reaches its goal is *cognition*. That esthetic and moral experience reveal traits of real things as truly as does intellectual experience, that poetry may have a metaphysical import as well as science, is rarely affirmed, and when it is asserted, the statement is likely to be meant in some mystical or esoteric sense rather than in a straightforward everyday sense.

Suppose however that we start with no presuppositions save that what is experienced, since it is a manifestation of nature, may, and indeed, must be used as testimony of the characteristics of natural events. Upon this basis, reverie and desire are pertinent for a philosophic theory of the true nature of things; the possibilities present in imagination that are not found in observation, are something to be taken into account. The features of objects reached by scientific or reflective experiencing are important, but so are all the phenomena of magic, myth, politics, painting, and penitentiaries. The phenomena of social life are as relevant to the problem of the relation of the individual and universal as are those of logic; the existence in political organization of boundaries and barriers, of centralization, of interaction across boundaries, of expansion and absorption, will be quite as important for metaphysical theories of the discrete and the continuous as is anything derived from chemical analysis. The existence of ignorance as well as of wisdom, of error and even insanity as well as of truth will be taken into account.

That is to say, nature is construed in such a way that all these things, since they are actual, are naturally possible; they are not explained away into mere "appearance" in contrast with reality. Illusions are illusions, but the occurrence of illusions is not an illusion, but a genuine reality. What is really "in" experience extends much further than that which at any time is *known*. From the standpoint of knowledge, objects must be distinct; their traits must be explicit; the vague and unrevealed is a limitation. Hence whenever the habit of identifying reality with the object of knowledge as such prevails, the obscure and vague are explained away. It is important for philosophic theory to be aware that the distinct and evident are prized and why they are. But it is equally important to note that the dark and twilight abound. For in any object of primary experience there are always potentialities which are not explicit; any object that is overt is charged with possible consequences that are hidden; the most overt act has factors which are not explicit. Strain thought as far as we may and not all consequences can be foreseen or made an express or known part of reflection and decision. In the face of such empirical facts, the assumption that nature in itself is all of the same kind, all distinct, explicit and evident, having no hidden possibilities, no novelties or obscurities, is possible only on the basis of a philosophy which at some point draws an arbitrary line between nature and experience.

In the assertion (implied here) that the great vice of philosophy is an arbitrary "intellectualism," there is no slight cast upon intelligence and reason. By "intellectualism" as an indictment is meant the theory that all experiencing is a mode of knowing, and that all subject-matter, all nature, is, in principle, to be reduced and transformed till it is defined in terms identical with the characteristics presented by refined objects of science as such. The assumption of "intellectualism" goes contrary to the facts of what is primarily experienced. For things are objects to be treated, used, acted upon and with, enjoyed and endured, even more than things to be known. They are things *had* before they are things cognized.

The isolation of traits characteristic of objects known, and then defined as the sole ultimate realities, accounts for the denial to nature of the characters which make things lovable and contemptible, beautiful and ugly, adorable and awful. It accounts for the belief that nature is an indifferent, dead mechanism; it explains why characteristics that are the valuable and valued traits of objects in actual experience are thought to create a fundamentally troublesome philosophical problem. Recognition of their genuine and primary reality does not signify that no thought and knowledge enter in when things are loved, desired and striven for; it signifies that the former are subordinate, so that the genuine problem is how and why, to what effect, things thus experienced are transformed into objects in which cognized traits are supreme and affectional and volitional traits incidental and subsidiary.

"Intellectualism" as a sovereign method of philosophy is so foreign to the facts of primary experience that it not only compels recourse to non-empirical method, but it ends in making knowledge, conceived as ubiquitous, itself inexplicable. If we start from primary experience, occurring as it does chiefly in modes of action and undergoing, it is easy to see what knowledge contributes—namely, the possibility of intelligent administration of the elements of doing and suffering. We are about something, and it is well to know what we are about, as the common phrase has it. To be intelligent in action and in suffering (enjoyment too) yields satisfaction even when conditions cannot be controlled. But when there is possibility of control, knowledge is the sole agency of its realization. Given this element of knowledge in primary experience, it is not difficult to understand how it may develop from a subdued and subsidiary factor into a dominant character. Doing and suffering, experimenting and putting ourselves in the way of having our sense and nervous system acted upon in ways that yield material for reflection, may reverse the original situation in which knowing and thinking were subservient to action-undergoing. And when we trace the genesis of knowing along this line, we also see that knowledge has a function and office in bettering and enriching the subject-matters of crude experience. We are prepared to understand what we are about on a grander scale, and to understand what happens even when we seem to be the hapless puppets of uncontrollable fate. But knowledge that is ubiquitous, all-inclusive and all-monopolizing, ceases to have meaning in losing all context; that it does not appear to do so when made supreme and self-sufficient is because it is literally impossible to exclude that context of non-cognitive but experienced subject-matter which gives what is *known* its import.

While this matter is dealt with at some length in further chapters of this volume, there is one point worth mentioning here. When intellectual experience and its material are taken to be primary, the cord that binds experience and nature is cut. That the physiological organism with its structures, whether in man or in the lower animals, is concerned with making adaptations and uses of material in the interest of maintenance of the life-process, cannot be denied. The brain and nervous system are primarily organs of action-undergoing; biologically, it can be asserted without contravention that primary experience is of a corresponding type. Hence, unless there is breach of historic and natural continuity, cognitive experience must originate within that of a noncognitive sort. And unless we start from knowing as a factor in action and undergoing we are inevitably committed to the intrusion of an extra-natural, if not a supernatural, agency and principle. That professed non-supernaturalists so readily endow the organism with powers that have no basis in natural events is a fact so peculiar that it would be inexplicable were it not for the inertia of the traditional schools. Otherwise it would be evident that the only way to maintain the doctrine of natural continuity is to recognize the secondary and derived character aspects of experience of the intellectual or cognitive. But so deeply grounded is the opposite position in the entire philosophic tradition, that it is probably not surprising that philosophers are loath to admit a fact which when admitted compels an extensive reconstruction in form and content.

We have spoken of the difference which acceptance of empirical method in philosophy makes in the problem of subject-object and in that of the alleged all-inclusiveness of cognitive experience.[4] There is an intimate connection between these two problems. When real objects are identified, point for point, with knowledge-objects, all affectional and volitional objects are inevitably excluded from the "real" world, and are compelled to find refuge in the privacy of an experiencing subject or mind. Thus the notion of the ubiquity of all comprehensive cognitive experience results by a necessary logic in setting up a hard and fast wall between the experiencing subject and that nature which is experienced. The self becomes not merely a pilgrim but an unnaturalized and unnaturalizable alien in the world. The only way to avoid a sharp separation between the mind which is the centre of the processes of experiencing and the natural world which is experienced is to acknowledge that

[4] To avoid misapprehension, it may be well to add a statement on the latter point. It is not denied that any experienced subject-matter whatever may *become* an object of reflection and cognitive inspection. But the emphasis is upon "become"; the cognitive never *is* all-inclusive: that is, when the material of a prior non-cognitive experience is the object of knowledge, it and the act of knowing are themselves included within a new and wider non-cognitive experience—and *this* situation can never be transcended. It is only when the temporal character of experienced things is forgotten that the idea of the total "transcendence" of knowledge is asserted.

all modes of experiencing are ways in which some genuine traits of nature come to manifest realization.

The favoring of cognitive objects and their characteristics at the expense of traits that excite desire, command action and produce passion, is a special instance of a principle of selective emphasis which introduces partiality and partisanship into philosophy. Selective emphasis, with accompanying omission and rejection, is the heart-beat of mental life. To object to the operation is to discard all thinking. But in ordinary matters and in scientific inquiries, we always retain the sense that the material chosen is selected for a purpose; there is no idea of denying what is left out, for what is omitted is merely that which is not relevant to the particular problem and purpose in hand.

But in philosophies, this limiting condition is often wholly ignored. It is not noted and remembered that the favored subject-matter is chosen for a purpose and that what is left out is just as real and important in its own characteristic context. It tends to be assumed that because qualities that figure in poetical discourse and those that are central in friendship do not figure in scientific inquiry, they have no reality, at least not the kind of unquestionable reality attributed to the mathematical, mechanical or magneto-electric properties that constitute matter. It is natural to men to take that which is of chief value to them at the time as *the* real. Reality and superior value are equated. In ordinary experience this fact does no particular harm; it is at once compensated for by turning to other things which since they also present value are equally real. But philosophy often exhibits a cataleptic rigidity in attachment to that phase of the total objects of experience which has become especially dear to a philosopher. *It* is real at all hazards and only it; other things are real only in some secondary and Pickwickian sense.

For example, certainty, assurance, is immensely valuable in a world as full of uncertainty and peril as that in which we live. As a result whatever is capable of certainty is assumed to constitute ultimate Being, and everything else is said to be merely phenomenal, or, in extreme cases, illusory. The arbitrary character of the "reality" that emerges is seen in the fact that very different objects are selected by different philosophers. These may be mathematical entities, states of consciousness, or sense data. That is, whatever strikes a philosopher from the angle of the particular problem that presses on him as being self-evident and hence completely assured, is selected by him to constitute reality. The honorable and dignified have ranked with the mundanely certain in determining philosophic definitions of the real. Scholasticism considered that the True and the Good, along with Unity, were the marks of Being as such. In the face of a problem, thought always seeks to unify things otherwise fragmentary and discrepant. Deliberately action strives to attain the good; knowledge is reached when truth is grasped. Then the goals of our efforts, the things that afford satisfaction and peace under conditions of tension and unrest, are converted into that which alone is ultimate real Being. Ulterior functions are treated as original properties.

Another aspect of the same erection of objects of selective preference into exclusive realities is seen in the addiction of philosophers to what is simple, their love for "elements." Gross experience is loaded with the tangled and complex; hence philosophy hurries away from it to search out something so simple that the mind can rest trustfully in it, knowing that it has no surprises in store, that it will not spring anything to make trouble, that it will stay put, having no potentialities in reserve. There is again the predilection for mathematical objects; there is Spinoza with his assurance that a true idea carries truth intrinsic in its bosom; Locke with his "simple idea"; Hume with his "impression"; the English neo-realist with his ultimate atomic data; the American neo-realist with his ready-made essences.

Another striking example of the fallacy of selective emphasis is found in the hypnotic influence exercised by the conception of the eternal. The permanent enables us to rest, it gives peace; the variable, the changing, is a constant challenge. Where things change something is hanging over us. It is a threat of trouble. Even when change is marked by hope of better things to come, that hope tends to project its object as something to stay once for all when it arrives. Moreover we can deal with the variable and precarious only by means of the stable and constant; "invariants"—for the time being—are as much a necessity in practice for bringing something to pass as they are in mathematical functions. The permanent answers genuine emotional, practical and intellectual requirements. But the demand and the response which meets it are empirically always found in a special context; they arise because of a particular need and in order to effect specifiable consequences. Philosophy, thinking at large, allows itself to be diverted into absurd search for an intellectual philosopher's stone of absolutely wholesale generalizations, thus isolating that which is permanent in a function and for a purpose, and converting it into the intrinsically eternal, conceived either (as Aristotle conceived it) as that which is the same at all times, or as that which is indifferent to time, out of time.

This bias toward treating objects selected because of their value in some special context as the "real," in a superior and invidious sense, testifies to an empirical fact of importance. Philosophical simplifications are due to choice, and choice marks an interest *moral* in the broad sense of concern for what is good. Our constant and unescapable concern is with prosperity and adversity, success and failure, achievement and frustration, good and bad. Since we are creatures with lives to live, and find ourselves within an uncertain environment, we are constructed to note and judge in terms of bearing upon weal and woe—upon value. Acknowledgment of this fact is a very different thing, however, from the transformation effected by philosophers of the traits they find good (simplicity, certainty, nobility, permanence, etc.) into fixed traits of real Being. The former presents something *to be accomplished*, to be brought about by the *actions* in which choice is manifested and made genuine. The latter ignores the need of action to effect the better and to prove the honesty of choice; it converts what is desired into antecedent and final features of a reality which is supposed to need only logical warrant in order to be contemplatively enjoyed as true Being.

For reflection the eventual is always better or worse than the given. But since it would also be better if the eventual good were now given, the philosopher, belonging by status to a leisure class relieved from the urgent necessity of dealing with conditions, converts the eventual into some kind of Being, something which *is*, even if it does not *exist*. Permanence, real essence, totality, order, unity, rationality, the *unum, verum et bonum* of the classic tradition, are eulogistic predicates. When we find such terms used to describe the foundations and proper conclusions of a philosophic system, there is ground for suspecting that an artificial simplification of existence has been performed. Reflection determining preference for an eventual good has dialectically wrought a miracle of transubstantiation.

Selective emphasis, choice, is inevitable whenever reflection occurs. This is not an evil. Deception comes only when the presence and operation of choice is concealed, disguised, denied. Empirical method finds and points to the operation of choice as it does to any other event. Thus it protects us from conversion of eventual functions into antecedent existence: a conversion that may be said to be *the* philosophic fallacy, whether it be performed in behalf of mathematical subsistences, esthetic essences, the purely physical order of nature, or God. The present writer does not profess any greater candor of intent than animates fellow philosophers. But the pursuance of an empirical method, is, he submits, the only way to secure execution of candid intent. Whatever enters into choice, determining its need and giving it guidance, an empirical method frankly indicates what it is for; and the fact of choice, with its workings and consequences, an empirical method points out with equal openness.

The adoption of an empirical method is no guarantee that all the things relevant to any particular conclusion will actually be found, or that when found they will be correctly shown and communicated. But empirical method points out when and where and how things of a designated description have been arrived at. It places before others a map of the road that has been travelled; they may accordingly, if they will, re-travel the road to inspect the landscape for themselves. Thus the findings of one may be rectified and extended by the findings of others, with as much assurance as is humanly possible of confirmation, extension and rectification. The adoption of empirical method thus procures for philosophic reflection something of that cooperative tendency toward consensus which marks inquiry in the natural sciences. The scientific investigator convinces others not by the plausibility of his definitions and the cogency of his dialectic, but by placing before them the specified course of searchings, doings and arrivals, in consequence of which certain things have been found. His appeal is for others to traverse a similar course, so as to see how what they find corresponds with his report.

Honest empirical method will state when and where and why the act of selection took place, and thus enable others to repeat it and test its worth. Selective choice, denoted as an empirical event, reveals the basis and bearing of intellectual simplifications; they then cease to be of such a self-enclosed nature as to be affairs only of opinion and argument, admitting no alternatives save complete acceptance or rejection. Choice that is disguised or denied is the source of those astounding differences of philosophic belief that startle the beginner and that become the plaything of the expert. Choice that is avowed is an experiment to be tried on its merits and tested by its results. Under all the captions that are called immediate knowledge, or self-sufficient certitude of belief, whether logical, esthetic or epistemological, there is something selected for a purpose, and hence not simple, not self-evident and not intrinsically eulogizable. State the purpose so that it may be re-experienced, and its value and the pertinency of selection undertaken in its behalf may be tested. The purport of thinking, scientific and philosophic, is not to eliminate choice but to render it less arbitrary and more significant. It loses its arbitrary character when its quality and consequences are such as to commend themselves to the reflection of others after they have betaken themselves to the situations indicated; it becomes significant when reason for the choice is found to be weighty and its consequences momentous. When choice is avowed, others can repeat the course of the experience; it is an experiment to be tried, not an automatic safety device.

This particular affair is referred to here not so much as matter of doctrine as to afford an illustration of the nature of empirical method. Truth or falsity depends upon what men find when they warily perform the experiment of observing reflective events. An empirical finding is refuted not by denial that one finds things to be thus and so, but by giving directions for a course of experience that results in finding its opposite to be the case. To convince of error as well as to lead to truth is to assist another to see and find something which he hitherto has failed to find and recognize. All of the wit and subtlety of reflection and logic find scope in the elaboration and conveying of directions that intelligibly point out a course to be followed. Every system of philosophy presents the consequences of some such experiment. As experiments, each has contributed something of worth to our observation of the events and qualities of experienceable objects. Some harsh criticisms of traditional philosophy have already been suggested; others will doubtless follow. But the criticism is not directed at the experiments; it is aimed at the denial to them by the philosophic tradition of selective experimental quality, a denial which has isolated them from their actual context and function, and has thereby converted potential illuminations into arbitrary assertions.

This discussion of empirical method has had a double content. On one hand, it has tried to make clear, from the analogy of empirical method in scientific inquiry, what the method signifies (and does *not* signify) for philosophy. Such a discussion would, however, have little definite import unless the *difference* that is made in philosophy by the adoption of empirical method is pointed out. For that reason, we have considered some typical ways and important places in which traditional philosophies have gone astray through failure to connect their reflective results with the affairs of everyday primary experience. Three sources of large fallacies have been mentioned, each containing within itself many more sub-varieties than have been hinted at. The three are the complete separation of subject and object (of *what* is experienced from *how* it is experienced); the exaggeration of the features of known objects at the expense of the qualities of objects of enjoyment and trouble, friendship and human association, art and industry; and the exclusive isolation of the results of various types of selective simplification which are undertaken for diverse unavowed purposes.

It does not follow that the products of these philosophies which have taken the wrong, because non-empirical, method are of no value or little worth for a philosophy that pursues a strictly empirical method. The contrary is the case, for no philosopher can get away from experience even if he wants to. The most fantastic views ever entertained by superstitious people had some basis in experienced fact; they can be explained by one who knows enough about them and about the conditions under which they were formed. And philosophers have been not more but less superstitious than their fellows; they have been, as a class, unusually reflective and inquiring. If some of their products have been fantasies, it was not because they did not, even unwittingly, start from empirical method; it was not wholly because they substituted unchecked imagination for thought. No, the trouble has been that they have failed to note the empirical needs that generate their problems, and have failed to return the refined products back to the context of actual experience, there to receive their check, inherit their full content of meaning, and give illumination and guidance in the immediate perplexities which originally occasioned reflection.

The chapters which follow make no pretence, accordingly, of starting to philosophize afresh as if there were no philosophies already in existence, or as if their conclusions were empirically worthless. Rather the subsequent discussions rely, perhaps excessively so, upon the main results of great philosophic systems, endeavoring to point out their elements of strength and of weakness when their conclusions are employed (as the refined objects of all reflection must be employed) as guides back to the subject-matter of crude, everyday experience.

Our primary experience as it comes is of little value for purposes of analysis and control, crammed as it is with things that need analysis and control. The very existence of reflection is proof of its deficiencies. Just as ancient astronomy and physics were of little scientific worth, because, owing to the lack of apparatus and techniques of experimental analysis, they had to take the things of primary observation at their face value, so "common-sense" philosophy usually repeats current conventionalities. What is averred to be implicit reliance upon what is given in common experience is likely to be merely an appeal to prejudice to gain support for some fanaticism or defence for some relic of conservative tradition which is beginning to be questioned.

The trouble, then, with the conclusions of philosophy is not in the least that they are results of reflection and theorizing. It is rather that philosophers have borrowed from various sources the conclusions of special analyses, particularly of some ruling science of the day, and imported them direct into philosophy, with no check by either the empirical objects from which they arose or those to which the conclusions in question point. Thus Plato trafficked with the Pythagoreans and imported mathematical concepts; Descartes and Spinoza took over the presuppositions of geometrical reasoning; Locke imported into the theory of mind the Newtonian physical corpuscles, converting them into given "simple ideas"; Hegel borrowed and generalized without limit the rising historical method of his day; contemporary English philosophy has imported from mathematics the notion of primitive indefinable propositions, and given them a content from Locke's simple ideas, which had in the meantime become part of the stock in trade of psychological science.

Well, why not, as long as what is borrowed has a sound scientific status? Because in scientific inquiry, refined methods justify themselves by opening up new fields of subject-matter for exploration; they create new techniques of observation and experimentation. Thus when the Michelson-Moley experiment disclosed, as a matter of gross experience, facts which did not agree with the results of accepted physical laws, physicists did not think for a moment of denying the validity of what was found in that experience, even though it rendered questionable an elaborate intellectual apparatus and system. The coincidence of the bands of the interferometer was accepted at its face value in spite of its incompatibility with Newtonian physics. Because scientific inquirers accepted it at its face value they at once set to work to reconstruct their theories; they questioned their reflective premises, not the full "reality" of what they saw. This task of re-adjustment compelled not only new reasonings and calculations in the development of a more comprehensive theory, but opened up new ways of inquiry into experienced subject-matter. Not for a moment did they think of explaining away the features of an object in gross experience because it was not in logical harmony with theory—as philosophers have so often done. Had they done so, they would have stultified science and shut themselves off from new problems and new findings in subject-matter. In short, the material of refined scientific method is continuous with that of the actual world as it is concretely experienced.

But when philosophers transfer into their theories bodily and as finalities the refined conclusions they borrow from the sciences, whether logic, mathematics or physics, these results are not employed to reveal new subject-matters and illuminate old ones of gross experience; they are employed to cast discredit on the latter and to generate new and artificial problems regarding the reality and validity of the things of gross experience. Thus the discoveries of psychologies taken out of their own empirical context are in philosophy employed to cast doubt upon the reality of things external to mind and to selves, things and properties that are perhaps the most salient characteristics of ordinary experience. Similarly, the discoveries and methods of physical science, the concepts of mass, space, motion, have been adopted wholesale in isolation by philosophers in such a way as to make dubious and even incredible the reality of the affections, purposes and enjoyments of concrete experience. The objects of mathematics, symbols of relations having no explicit reference to actual existence, efficacious in the territory to which mathematical technique applies, have been employed in philosophy to determine the priority of essences to existence, and to create the insoluble problem of why pure essence ever descends into the tangles and tortuosities of existence.

What empirical method exacts of philosophy is two things: First, that refined methods and products be traced back to their origin in primary experience, in all its heterogeneity and fullness; so that the needs and problems out of which they arise and which they have to satisfy be acknowledged. Secondly, that the secondary methods and conclusions be brought back to the things of ordinary experience, in all their coarseness and crudity, for verification. In this way, the methods of analytic reflection yield material which form the ingredients of a method of designation, denotation, in philosophy. A scientific work in physics or astronomy gives a record of calculations and deductions that were derived from past observations and experiments. But it is more than a record; it is also an indication, an assignment, of further observations and experiments to be performed. No scientific report would get a hearing if it did not describe the apparatus by means of which experiments were carried on and results obtained; not that apparatus is worshipped, but because this procedure tells other inquirers how they are to go to work to get results which will agree or disagree in their experience with those previously arrived at, and thus confirm, modify and rectify the latter. The recorded scientific result is in effect a *designation* of a method to be followed and a *prediction* of what will be found when specified observations are set on foot. That is all a philosophy can be or do. In the chapters that follow I have undertaken a revision and reconstruction of the conclusions, the reports, of a number of historic philosophic systems, in order that they may be usable methods by which one may go to his own experience, and, discerning what is found by use of the method, come to understand better what is already within the common experience of mankind.

There is a special service which the study of philosophy may render.

Empirically pursued it will not be a study of philosophy but a study, by means of philosophy, of life-experience. But this experience is already overlaid and saturated with the products of the reflection of past generations and by-gone ages. It is filled with interpretations, classifications, due to sophisticated thought, which have become incorporated into what seems to be fresh, naïve empirical material. It would take more wisdom than is possessed by the wisest historic scholar to track all of these absorbed borrowings to their original sources. If we may for the moment call these materials prejudices (even if they are true, as long as their source and authority is unknown), then philosophy is a critique of prejudices. These incorporated results of past reflection, welded into the genuine materials of first-hand experience, may become organs of enrichment if they are detected and reflected upon. If they are not detected, they often obfuscate and distort. Clarification and emancipation follow when they are detected and cast out; and one great object of philosophy is to accomplish this task.

An empirical philosophy is in any case a kind of intellectual disrobing. We cannot permanently divest ourselves of the intellectual habits we take on and wear when we assimilate the culture of our own time and place. But intelligent furthering of culture demands that we take some of them off, that we inspect them critically to see what they are made of and what wearing them does to us. We cannot achieve recovery of primitive naïveté. But there is attainable a cultivated naïveté of eye, ear and thought, one that can be acquired only through the discipline of severe thought. If the chapters which follow contribute to an artful innocence and simplicity they will have served their purpose.

I am loath to conclude without reference to the larger liberal humane value of philosophy when pursued with empirical method. The most serious indictment to be brought against non-empirical philosophies is that they have cast a cloud over the things of ordinary experience. They have not been content to rectify them. They have discredited them at large. In casting aspersion upon the things of everyday experience, the things of action and affection and social intercourse, they have done something worse than fail to give these affairs the intelligent direction they so much need. It would not matter much if philosophy had been reserved as a luxury of only a few thinkers. We endure many luxuries. The serious matter is that philosophies have denied that common experience is capable of developing from within itself methods which will secure direction for itself and will create inherent standards of judgment and value. No one knows how many of the evils and deficiencies that are pointed to as reasons for flight from experience are themselves due to the disregard of experience shown by those peculiarly reflective. To waste of time and energy, to disillusionment with life that attends every deviation from concrete experience must be added the tragic failure to realize the value that intelligent search could reveal and mature among the things of ordinary experience. I cannot calculate how much of current cynicism, indifference and pessimism is due to these causes in the deflection of intelligence they have brought about. It has even become in many circles a sign of lack of sophistication to imagine that life is or can be a fountain of cheer and happiness. Philosophies no more than religions can be acquitted of responsibility for bringing this result to pass. The transcendental philosopher has probably done more than the professed sensualist and materialist to obscure the potentialities of daily experience for joy and for self-regulation. If what is written in these pages has no other result than creating and promoting a respect for concrete human experience and its potentialities, I shall be content.

## 18. Existence as Precarious and Stable*

In this second chapter of *Experience and Nature*, Dewey fleshes out his notion of ordinary experience by virtue of his concentration on the "precarious." He states that "man finds himself living in an aleatory world; his existence involves, to put it baldly, a gamble. The world is a scene of risk; it is uncertain, unstable, uncannily unstable." Dewey then contends that with few exceptions, traditional philosophy has been unable or unwilling to deal adequately with the precarious, the ambiguous, or the contingent aspects of experience, preferring to dismiss them or buy them off by overarching classificatory systems. But however clever the dialectic or imposing the system, philosophy must never forget that "incompleteness and precariousness is a trait that must be given footing of the same rank as the finished and fixed."

It was suggested in the last chapter that experience has its equivalents in such affairs as history, life, culture. Reference to these other affairs enables us to put to one side the reminiscences which so readily give the

* From John Dewey, *Experience and Nature* (New York, 1958) (1929), 2nd ed., Chap. 10.

word experience a sectarian and provincial content. According to Tylor, culture is "that complex whole which includes knowledge, belief, art, morals, custom, and any other capabilities acquired by a man as a member of society." It is, in some sense, a whole, but it is a complex, a diversified whole. It is differentiated into religion, magic, law, fine and useful art, science, philosophy, language, domestic and political relations, etc. Consider the following words of an anthropologist and ask if they do not fairly define the problem of philosophy, although intended for another purpose. "Cultural reality is never wholly deterministic nor yet wholly objective, never wholly of yesterday nor yet wholly of today, but combines all of these in its existential reality. . . . A reconstructive synthesis re-establishes the synthetic unity necessarily lost in the process of analytic dismemberment."[1] I do not mean that philosophy is to be merged in an anthropological view of culture. But in a different context and by a different method, it has the task of analytic dismemberment and synthetic reconstruction of experience; the phenomena of culture as presented by the anthropologist provide, moreover, precious material to aid the performance of this office, material more pertinent to the task of philosophizing than that of psychology isolated from a theory of culture.

A feature of existence which is emphasized by cultural phenomena is the precarious and perilous. Sumner refers to Grimm as authority for the statement that the Germanic tribes had over a thousand distinct sayings, proverbs and apothegms, concerning luck. Time is brief, and this statement must stand instead of the discourse which the subject deserves. Man finds himself living in an aleatory world; his existence involves, to put it baldly, a gamble. The world is a scene of risk; it is uncertain, unstable, uncannily unstable. Its dangers are irregular, inconstant, not to be counted upon as to their times and seasons. Although persistent, they are sporadic, episodic. It is darkest just before dawn; pride goes before a fall; the moment of greatest prosperity is the moment most charged with ill-omen, most opportune for the evil eye. Plague, famine, failure of crops, disease, death, defeat in battle, are always just around the corner, and so are abundance, strength, victory, festival and song. Luck is proverbially both good and bad in its distributions. The sacred and the accursed are potentialities of the same situation; and there is no category of things which has not embodied the sacred and accursed: persons, words, places, times, directions in space, stones, winds, animals, stars.

[1] Goldenweiser.

Anthropologists have shown incontrovertibly the part played by the precarious aspect of the world in generating religion with its ceremonies, rites, cults, myths, magic; and it has shown the pervasive penetration of these affairs into morals, law, art, and industry. Beliefs and dispositions connected with them are the background out of which philosophy and secular morals slowly developed, as well as more slowly those late inventions, art for art's sake, and business is business. Interesting and instructive as is this fact, it is not the ramifications which here concern us. We must not be diverted to consider the consequences for philosophy, even for doctrines reigning today, of facts concerning the origin of philosophies. We confine ourselves to one outstanding fact: the evidence that the world of empirical things includes the uncertain, unpredictable, uncontrollable, and hazardous.

It is an old saying that the gods were born of fear. The saying is only too likely to strengthen a misconception bred by confirmed subjective habits. We first endow man in isolation with an instinct of fear and then we imagine him irrationally ejecting that fear into the environment, scattering broadcast as it were, the fruits of his own purely personal limitations, and thereby creating superstition. But fear, whether an instinct or an acquisition, is a function of the environment. Man fears because he exists in a fearful, an awful world. The *world* is precarious and perilous. It is as easily accessible and striking evidence of this fact that primitive experience is cited. The voice is that of early man; but the hand is that of nature, the nature in which we still live. It was not fear of gods that created the gods.

For if the life of early man is filled with expiations and propitiations, if in his feasts and festivals what is enjoyed is gratefully shared with his gods, it is not because a belief in supernatural powers created a need for expiatory, propitiatory and communal offerings. Everything that man achieves and possesses is got by actions that may involve him in other and obnoxious consequences in addition to those wanted and enjoyed. His acts are trespasses upon the domain of the unknown; and hence atonement, if offered in season, may ward off direful consequences that haunt even the moment of prosperity—or that most haunt that moment. While unknown consequences flowing from the past dog the present, the future is even more unknown and perilous; the present by that fact is ominous. If unknown forces that decide future destiny can be placated, the man who will not study the methods of securing their favor is incredibly flippant. In enjoyment of present food and companionship, nature, tradition and social organization have coöperated, thereby supplementing our own endeavors so petty and so feeble without this extraneous reinforcement. Goods are by grace not of ourselves. He is a dangerous churl who will not gratefully acknowledge by means of free-will offerings the help that sustains him.

These things are as true today as they were in the days of early culture. It is not the facts which have changed, but the methods of insurance, regulation and acknowledgment. Herbert Spencer sometimes colored his devotion to symbolic experiences with a fact of dire experience. When he says that every fact has two opposite sides, "the one its near or visible side and the other its remote or invisible side," he expresses a persistent trait of every object in experience. The visible is set in the invisible; and in the end what is unseen decides what happens in the seen; the tangible rests precariously upon the untouched and ungrasped. The contrast and the potential maladjustment of the immediate, the conspicuous and focal phase of things, with those indirect and hidden factors which determine the origin and career of what is present, are indestructible features of any and every experience. We may term the way in which our ancestors dealt with the contrast superstitious, but the contrast is no superstition. It is a primary datum in any experience.

We have substituted sophistication for superstition, at least measurably so. But the sophistication is often as irrational and as much at the mercy of words as the superstition it replaces. Our magical safeguard against the uncertain character of the world is to deny the existence of chance, to mumble universal and necessary law, the ubiquity of cause and effect, the uniformity of nature, universal progress, and the inherent rationality of the universe. These magic formulae borrow their potency from conditions that are not magical. Through science we have secured a degree of power of prediction and of control; through tools, machinery and an accompanying technique we have made the world more conformable to our needs, a more secure abode. We have heaped up riches and means of comfort between ourselves and the risks of the world. We have professionalized amusement as an agency of escape and forgetfulness. But when all is said and done, the fundamentally hazardous character of the world is not seriously modified, much less eliminated. Such an incident as the last war and preparations for a future war remind us that it is easy to overlook the extent to which, after all, our attainments are only devices for blurring the disagreeable recognition of a fact, instead of means of altering the fact itself.

What has been said sounds pessimistic. But the concern is not with morals but with metaphysics, with, that is to say, the nature of the existential world in which we live. It would have been as easy and more comfortable to emphasize good luck, grace, unexpected and unwon joys, those unsought for happenings which we so significantly call happiness. We might have appealed to good fortune as evidence of this important trait of hazard in nature. Comedy is as genuine as tragedy. But it is traditional that comedy strikes a more superficial note than tragedy. And there is an even better reason for appealing to misfortunes and mistakes as evidence of the precarious nature of the world. The problem of evil is a well recognized problem, while we rarely or never hear of a problem of good. Goods we take for granted; they are as they should be; they are natural and proper. The good is a recognition of our deserts. When we pull out a plum we treat it as evidence of the *real* order of cause and effect in the world. For this reason it is difficult for the goods of existence to furnish as convincing evidence of the uncertain character of nature as do evils. It is the latter we term accidents, not the former, even when their adventitious character is as certain.

What of it all, it may be asked? In the sense in which an assertion is true that uncontrolled distribution of good and evil is evidence of the precarious, uncertain nature of existence, it is a truism, and no problem is forwarded by its reiteration. But it is submitted that just this predicament of the inextricable mixture of stability and uncertainty gives rise to philosophy, and that it is reflected in all its recurrent problems and issues. If classic philosophy says so much about unity and so little about unreconciled diversity, so much about the eternal and permanent, and so little about change (save as something to be resolved into combinations of the permanent), so much about necessity and so little about contingency, so much about the comprehending universal and so little about the recalcitrant particular, it may well be because the ambiguousness and ambivalence of reality are actually so pervasive. Since these things form the problem, solution is more apparent (although not more actual), in the degree in which whatever of stability and assurance the world presents is fastened upon and asserted.

Upon their surface, the reports of the world which form our different philosophies are various to the point of stark contrariness. They range from spiritualism to materialism, from absolutism to relativistic phenomenalism, from transcendentalism to positivism, from rationalism to sensationalism, from idealism to realism, from subjectivism to bald objectivism, from Platonic realism to nominalism. The array of contradictions is so imposing as to suggest to sceptics that the mind of man has tackled an impossible job, or that philosophers have abandoned themselves to vagary. These radical oppositions in philosophers suggest however another consideration. They suggest that all their different philosophies have a common premise, and that their diversity is due to acceptance of a common premise. Variant philosophies may be looked at as different ways of supplying recipes for denying to the universe the character of contingency which it possesses so integrally that its denial leaves the reflecting mind without a clew, and puts subsequent philosophising at the mercy of temperament, interest and local surroundings.

Quarrels among conflicting types of philosphy are thus family quarrels. They go on within the limits of a too domestic circle, and can be settled only by venturing further afield, and out of doors. Concerned with imputing complete, finished and sure character to the world of real existence, even if things have to be broken into two disconnected pieces in order to accomplish the result, the character desiderated can plausibly be found in reason or in mechanism; in rational conceptions like those of mathematics, or brute things like sensory data; in atoms or in essences; in consciousness or in a physical externality which forces and overrides consciousness.

As against this common identification of reality with what is sure, regular and finished, experience in unsophisticated forms gives evidence of a different world and points to a different metaphysics. We live in a world which is an impressive and irresistible mixture of sufficiencies, tight completenesses, order, recurrences which make possible prediction and control, and singularities, ambiguities, uncertain possibilities, processes going on to consequences as yet indeterminate. They are mixed not mechanically but vitally like the wheat and tares of the parable. We may recognize them separately but we cannot divide them, for unlike wheat and tares they grow from the same root. Qualities have defects as necessary conditions of their excellencies; the instrumentalities of truth are the causes of error; change gives meaning to permanence and recurrence makes novelty possible. A world that was wholly risky would be a world in which adventure is impossible, and only a living world can include death. Such facts have been celebrated by thinkers like Heracleitus and Laotze; they have been greeted by theologians as furnishing occasions for exercise of divine grace; they have been elaborately formulated by various schools under a principle of relativity, so defined as to become itself final and absolute. They have rarely been frankly recognized as fundamentally significant for the formation of a naturalistic metaphysics.

Aristotle perhaps came the nearest to a start in that direction. But his thought did not go far on the road, though it may be used to suggest the road which he failed to take. Aristotle acknowledges contingency, but he never surrenders his bias in favor of the fixed, certain and finished.

His whole theory of forms and ends is a theory of the superiority in Being of rounded-out fixities. His physics is a fixation of ranks or grades of necessity and contingency so sorted that necessity measures dignity and equals degree of reality, while contingency and change measure degrees of deficiency of Being. The empirical impact and sting of the mixture of universality and singularity and chance is evaded by parcelling out the regions of space so that they have their natural abode in different portions of nature. His logic is one of definition and classification, so that its task is completed when changing and contingent things are distinguished from the necessary, universal and fixed, by attribution to inferior species of things. Chance appears in thought not as a calculus of probabilities in predicting the observable occurrence of any and every event, but as marking an inferior type of syllogism. Things that move are intrinsically different from things that exhibit eternal regularity. Change is honestly recognized as a genuine feature of *some* things, but the point of the recognition is avoided by imputing alteration to inherent deficiency of Being over against complete Being which never changes. Changing things belong to a purgatorial realm, where they wander aimlessly until redeemed by love of finality of form, the acquisition of which lifts them to a paradise of self-sufficient Being. With slight exaggeration, it may be said that the thoroughgoing way in which Aristotle defined, distinguished and classified rest and movement, the finished and the incomplete, the actual and potential, did more to fix tradition, *the* genteel tradition one is tempted to add, which identifies the fixed and regular with reality of Being and the changing and hazardous with deficiency of Being than ever was accomplished by those who took the shorter path of asserting that change is illusory.

His philosophy was closer to empirical facts than most modern philosophies, in that it was neither monistic nor dualistic but openly pluralistic. His plurals fall however, within a grammatical system, to each portion of which a corresponding cosmic status is allotted. Thus his pluralism solved the problem of how to have your cake and eat it too, for a classified and hierarchically ordered set of pluralities, of variants, has none of the sting of the miscellaneous and uncoördinated plurals of our actual world. In this classificatory scheme of separation he has been followed, though perhaps unwittingly, by many philosophers of different import. Thus Kant assigns all that is manifold and chaotic to one realm, that of sense, and all that is uniform and regular to that of reason. A single and all embracing dialectic problem of the combination of sense and thought is thereby substituted for the concrete problems that arise through the mixed and varied union in existence of the variable and the constant, the necessary and that which proceeds uncertainly.

The device is characteristic of a conversion such as has already been commented upon of a moral insight to be made good in action into an antecedent metaphysics of existence or a general theory of knowledge. The striving to make stability of meaning prevail over the instability of events is the main task of intelligent human effort. But when the function is dropped from the province of art and treated as a property of given things, whether cosmological or logical, effort is rendered useless, and a premium is put upon the accidental good-fortune of a class that happens to be furnished by the toil of another class with products that give to life its dignity and leisurely stability.

The argument is not forgetful that there are, from Heracleitus to Bergson, philosophies, metaphysics, of change. One is grateful to them for keeping alive a sense of what classic, orthodox philosophies have whisked out of sight. But the philosophies of flux also indicate the intensity of the craving for the sure and fixed. They have deified change by making it universal, regular, sure. To say this is not, I hope, verbal by-play. Consider the wholly eulogistic fashion in which Hegel and Bergson, and the professedly evolutionary philosophers of becoming, have taken change. With Hegel becoming is a rational process which defines logic although a new and strange logic, and an absolute, although new and strange, God. With Spencer, evolution is but the transitional process of attaining a fixed and universal equilibrium of harmonious adjustment. With Bergson, change is the creative operation of God, or *is* God—one is not quite sure which. The change of change is not only cosmic pyrotechnics, but is a process of divine, spiritual, energy. We are here in the presence of prescription, not description. Romanticism is an evangel in the garb of metaphysics. It sidesteps the painful, toilsome labor of understanding and of control which change sets us, by glorifying it for its own sake. Flux is made something to revere, something profoundly akin to what is best within ourselves, will and creative energy. It is not, as it is in experience, a call to effort, a challenge to investigation, a potential doom of disaster and death.

If we follow classical terminology, philosophy is love of wisdom, while metaphysics is cognizance of the generic traits of existence. In this sense of metaphysics, incompleteness and precariousness is a trait that must be given footing of the same rank as the finished and fixed. Love of wisdom is concerned with finding its implications for the conduct of life, in devotion to what is good. On the cognitive side, the issue is largely that of measure, of the ratio one bears to others in the situations of life. On the practical side, it is a question of the use to be made of each, of turning each to best account. Man is naturally philosophic, rather than metaphysical or coldly scientific, noting and describing. Concerned with prudence if not with what is honorifically called wisdom, man naturally prizes knowledge only for the sake of its bearing upon success and failure in attaining goods and avoiding evils. This is a fact of our structure and nothing is gained by recommending it as an ideal truth, and equally nothing is gained by attributing to intellect an intrinisc relationship to pure truth for its own sake or bare fact on its own account. The first method encourages dogma, and the second expresses a myth. The love of knowledge for its own sake is an ideal of morals; it is an integral condition of the wisdom that rightly conceives and effectually pursues the good. For wisdom as to ends depends upon acquaintance with conditions and means, and unless the acquaintance is adequate and fair, wisdom becomes a sublimated folly of self-deception.

Denial of an inherent relation of mind to truth or fact for its own sake, apart from insight into what the fact or truth exacts of us in behavior and imposes upon us in joy and suffering; and simultaneous affirmation that devotion to fact, to truth, is a necessary moral demand, involve no inconsistency. Denial relates to natural events as independent of choice and endeavor; affirmation relates to choice and action. But choice and the reflective effort involved in it are themselves such contingent events and so bound up with the precarious uncertainty of other events, that philosophers have too readily assumed that metaphysics, and science of fact and truth, are themselves wisdom, thinking thus to avoid the necessity of either exercising or recognizing choice. The consequence is that conversion of unavowed morals or wisdom into cosmology, and into a metaphysics of nature, which was termed in the last chapter *the* philosophic fallacy. It supplies the formula of the technique by which thinkers have relegated the uncertain and unfinished to an invidious state of unreal being, while they have systematically exalted the assured and complete to the rank of true Being.

Upon the side of wisdom, as human beings interested in good and bad things in their connection with human conduct, thinkers are concerned to mitigate the instability of life, to introduce moderation, temper and economy, and when worst comes to worst to suggest consolations and compensations. They are concerned with rendering more stable good things, and more unstable bad things; they are interested in how changes may be turned to account in the consequences to which they contribute. The facts of the ungoing, unfinished and ambiguously potential world give point and poignancy to the search for absolutes and finalities. Then when philosophers have hit in reflection upon a thing which is stably good in quality and hence worthy of persistent and continued choice, they hesitate, and withdraw from the effort and struggle that choice demands:—namely, from the effort to give it some such stability in observed existence as it possesses in quality when thought of. Thus it becomes a refuge, an asylum for contemplation, or a theme for dialectical elaboration, instead of an ideal to inspire and guide conduct.

Since thinkers claim to be concerned with knowledge of existence, rather than with imagination, they have to make good the pretention to knowledge. Hence they transmute the imaginative perception of the stably good object into a definition and description of true reality in contrast with lower and specious existence, which, being precarious and incomplete, alone involves us in the necessity of choice and active struggle. Thus they remove from actual existence the very traits which generate philosophic reflection and which give point and bearing to its conclusions. In briefest formula, "reality" becomes what we wish existence to be, after we have analyzed its defects and decided upon what would remove them; "reality" is what existence would be if our reasonably justified preferences were so completely established in nature as to exhaust and define its entire being and thereby render search and struggle unnecessary. What is left over, (and since trouble, struggle, conflict, and error still empirically exist, something *is* left over) being excluded by definition from full reality is assigned to a grade or order of being which is asserted to be metaphysically inferior; an order variously called appearance, illusion, mortal mind, or the merely empirical, against what really and truly is. Then the problem of metaphysics alters: instead of being a detection and description of the generic traits of existence, it becomes an endeavor to adjust or reconcile to each other two separate realms of being. Empirically we have just what we started with: the mixture of the precarious and problematic with the assured and complete. But a classificatory device, based on desire and elaborated in reflective imagination, has been introduced by which the two traits are torn apart, one of them being labelled reality and the other appearance. The genuinely moral problem of mitigating and regulating the troublesome factor by active employment of the stable factor then drops out of sight. The dialectic problem of logical reconciliation of two notions has taken its place.

The most widespread of these classificatory devices, the one of greatest popular appeal, is that which divides existence into the supernatural and the natural. Men may fear the gods but it is axiomatic that the gods have nothing to fear. They lead a life of untroubled serenity, the life that pleases them. There is a long story between the primitive forms of this division of objects of experience and the dialectical imputation to the divine of omnipotence, omniscience, eternity and infinity, in contrast with the attribution to man and experienced nature of finitude, weakness, limitation, struggle and change. But in the make-up of human psychology the later history is implicit in the early crude division. One realm is the home of assured appropriation and possession; the other of striving, transiency and frustration. How many persons are there today who conceive that they have disposed of ignorance, struggle and disappointment by pointing to man's "finite" nature—as if finitude signifies anything else but an abstract classificatory naming of certain concrete and discriminable traits of nature itself—traits of nature which generate ignorance, arbitrary appearance and disappearance, failure and striving. It pleases man to substitute the dialectic exercise of showing how the "finite" can exist with or within the "infinite" for the problem of dealing with the contingent, thinking to solve the problem by distinguishing and naming its factors. Failure of the exercise is certain, but the failure can be flourished as one more proof of the finitude of man's intellect, and the needlessness because impotency of endeavor of "finite" creatures to attack ignorance and oppressive fatalities. Wisdom then consists in administration of the temporal, finite and human in its relation to the eternal and infinite, by means of dogma and cult, rather than in regulation of the events of life by understanding of actual conditions.

It does not demand great ingenuity to detect the inversion here. The starting point is precisely the existing mixture of the regular and dependable and the unsettled and uncertain. There are a multitude of recipes for obtaining a vicarious possession of the stable and final without getting involved in the labor and pain of intellectual effort attending regulation of the conditions upon which these fruits depend.

This situation is worthy of remark as an exemplification of how easy it is to arrive at a description of existence via a theory of wisdom, of reflective insight into goods. It has a direct bearing upon a metaphysical doctrine which is not popular, like the division into the supernatural, and natural, but which is learned and technical. The philosopher may have little esteem for the crude forms assumed by the popular metaphysics of earth and heaven, of God, nature, and man. But the philosopher has often proceeded in a manner analogous to that which resulted in this popular metaphysics; some of the most cherished metaphysical distinctions seem to be but learned counterparts, dependent upon an elaborate intellectual technique, for these rough, crude notions of supernatural and natural, divine and human, in popular belief. I refer to such things as the Platonic division into ideal archetypes and physical events; the Aristotelian division into form which is actuality and matter which is potential, when that is understood as a distinction of ranks of reality; the noumenal things, things-in-themselves of Kant in contrast with natural objects as phenomenal; the distinction, current among contemporary absolute idealists, of reality and appearance.

The division however is not confined to philosophers with leanings toward spiritualistic philosophies. There is some evidence that Plato got the term Idea, as a name for essential form, from Democritus. Whether this be the case or no, the Idea of Democritus, though having a radically diverse structure from the Platonic Idea, had the same function of designating a finished, complete, stable, wholly unprecarious reality. Both philosophers craved solidity and both found it; corresponding to the Platonic phenomenal flux are the Democritean things as they are in custom or ordinary experience: corresponding to the ideal archetypes are substantial indivisible atoms. Corresponding, again to the Platonic theory of Ideas is the modern theory of mathematical structures which are alone independently real, while the empirical impressions and suggestions to which they give rise is the counterpart of his realm of phenomena.

Apart from the materialistic and spirtualistic schools, there is the Spinozistic division into attributes and modes; the old division of essence and existence, and its modern counterpart subsistence and existence. It is impossible to force Mr. Bertrand Russell into any one of the pigeonholes of the cabinet of conventional philosophic schools. But moral, or philosophical, motivation is obvious in his metaphysics when he says that mathematics takes us "into the region of absolute necessity, to which not only the actual world but every possible world must conform." Indeed with his usual lucidity, he says, mathematics "finds a habitation eternally standing, where our ideals are fully satisfied and our best hopes are not thwarted." When he adds that contemplation of such objects is the "chief means of overcoming the terrible sense of impotence, of weakness, of exile amid hostile power, which is too apt to result from acknowledging the all but omnipotence of alien forces," the presence of moral origin is explicit.

No modern thinker has pointed out so persuasively as Santayana that "every phase of the ideal world emanates from the natural," that "sense, art, religion, society express nature exuberantly." And yet unless one reads him wrong, he then confounds his would-be disciples and confuses his critics by holding that nature is *truly* presented only in an esthetic contemplation of essences reached by physical science, an envisagement reached through a dialectic which "is a transubstantiation of matter, a passage from existence to eternity." This passage moreover is so utter that there is no road back. The stable ideal meanings which are the fruit of nature are forbidden, in the degree in which they are its highest and truest fruits, from dropping seeds in nature to its further fructification.

The perception of genetic continuity between the dynamic flux of nature and an eternity of static ideal forms thus terminate in a sharp division, in reiteration of the old tradition. Perhaps it is a caricature to say that the ultimate of reason is held to be ability to behold nature as a complete mechanism which generates and sustains the beholding of the mechanism, but the caricature is not wilful. If the separation of contingency and necessity is abandoned, what is there to exclude a belief that science, while it is grasp of the regular and stable mechanism of nature, is also an organ of regulating and enriching, through its own expansion, the more exuberant and irregular expressions of nature in human intercourse, the arts, religion, industry, and politics?

To follow out the latter suggestion would take us to a theme reserved for later consideration. We are here concerned with the fact that it is the intricate mixture of the stable and the precarious, the fixed and the unpredictably novel, the assured and the uncertain, in existence which sets mankind upon that love of wisdom which forms philosophy. Yet too commonly, although in a great variety of technical modes, the result of the search is converted into a metaphysics which denies or conceals from acknowledgment the very characters of existence which initiated it, and which give significance to its conclusions. The form assumed by the denial is, most frequently, that striking division into a superior true realm of being and lower illusory, insignificant or phenomenal realm which characterizes metaphysical systems as unlike as those of Plato and Democritus, St. Thomas and Spinoza, Aristotle and Kant, Descartes and Comte, Haeckel and Mrs. Eddy.

The same jumble of acknowledgment and denial attends the conception of Absolute Experience: as if any experience could be more absolutely experience than that which marks the life of humanity. This conception constitutes the most recent device for first admitting and then denying the combinedly stable and unstable nature of the world. Its plaintive recognition of our experience as finite and temporal, as full of error, conflict and contradiction, is an acknowledgment of the precarious uncertainty of the objects and connections that constitute nature as it emerges in history. Human experience however has also the pathetic longing for truth, beauty and order. There is more than the longing: there are moments of achievement. Experience exhibits ability to possess harmonious objects. It evinces an ability, within limits, to safeguard the excellent objects and to deflect and reduce the obnoxious ones. The concept of an absolute experience which is only and always perfect and good, first explicates these desirable implications of things of actual experience, and then asserts that they alone are real. The experienced occurrences which give poignancy and pertinency to the longing for a better world, the experimental endeavors and plans which make possible actual betterments within the objects of actual experience, are thus swept out of real Being into a limbo of appearances.

The notion of Absolute Experience thus serves as a symbol of two facts. One is the ineradicable union in nature of the relatively stable and the relatively contingent. The division of the movement and leadings of things which are experienced into two parts, such that one set constitutes and defines absolute and eternal experience, while the other set constitutes and defines finite experience, tells us nothing about absolute experience. It tells us a good deal about experience as it exists: namely, that it is such as to involve permanent and general objects of reference as well as temporally changing events; the possibility of truth as well as error; conclusive objects and goods as well as things whose purport and nature is determinable only in an indeterminate future. Nothing is gained—except the delights of a dialectic problem—in labelling one assortment absolute experience and the other finite experience. Since the appeal of the adherents of the philosophy of absolute and phenomenal experience is to a logical criterion, namely, to the implication in every judgment, however erroneous, of a standard of consistency which excludes any possibility of contradictoriness, the inherent logical contradictions in the doctrine itself are worth noting.

In the first place, the contents as well as the form of ultimate Absolute Experience are derived from and based upon the natures of actual experience, the very experience which is then relegated to unreality by the supreme reality derived from its unreality. It is "real" just long enough to afford a spring-board into ultimate reality and to afford a hint of the essential contents of the latter and then it obligingly dissolves into mere appearance. If we start from the standpoint of the Absolute Experience thus reached, the contradiction is repeated from its side. Although absolute, eternal, all-comprehensive, and pervasively integrated into a whole so logically perfect that no separate patterns, to say nothing of seams and holes, can exist in it, it proceeds to play a tragic joke upon itself—for there is nothing else to be fooled—by appearing in a queer combination of rags and glittering gew-gaws, in the garb of the temporal, partial and conflicting things, mental as well as physical, of ordinary experience. I do not cite these dialectic contradictions as having an inherent importance. But the fact that a doctrine which avowedly takes logical consistence for its method and criterion, whose adherents are noteworthy for dialectic acumen in specific issues, should terminate in such thoroughgoing contradictions may be cited as evidence that after all the doctrine is merely engaged in an arbitrary sorting out of characters of things which in nature are always present in conjunction and interpenetration.

The union of the hazardous and the stable, of the incomplete and the recurrent, is the condition of all experienced satisfaction as truly as of our predicaments and problems. While it is the source of ignorance, error and failure of expectation, it is the source of the delight which fulfillments bring. For if there were nothing in the way, if there were no deviations and resistances, fulfillment would be at once, and in so being would fulfill nothing, but merely be. It would not be in connection with desire or satisfaction. Moreover when a fulfillment comes and is pronounced good, it is *judged* good, distinguished and asserted, simply because it is in jeopardy, because it occurs amid indifferent and divergent things. Because of this mixture of the regular and that which cuts across stability, a good object once experienced acquires ideal quality and attracts demand and effort to itself. A particular ideal may be an illusion, but having ideals is no illusion. It embodies features of existence. Although imagination is often fantastic it is also an organ of nature; for it is the appropriate phase of indeterminate events moving toward eventualities that are now but possibilities. A purely stable world permits of no illusions, but neither is it clothed with ideals. It just exists. To be good is to be better than; and there can be no better except where there is shock and discord combined with enough assured order to make attainment of harmony possible. Better objects when brought into existence are existent not ideal; they retain ideal quality only retrospectively as commemorative of issue from prior conflict and prospectively, in contrast with forces which make for their destruction. Water that slakes thirst, or a conclusion that solves a problem have ideal character as long as thirst or problem persists in a way which qualifies the result. But water that is not a satisfaction of need has no more ideal quality than water running through pipes into a reservoir; a solution ceases to be a solution and becomes a bare incident of existence when its antecedent generating conditions of doubt, ambiguity and search are lost from its context. While the precarious nature of existence is indeed the source of all trouble, it is also an indispensable condition of ideality, becoming a sufficient condition when conjoined with the regular and assured.

We long, amid a troubled world, for perfect being. We forget that what gives meaning to the notion of perfection is the events that create longing, and that, apart from them, a "perfect" world would mean just an unchanging brute existential thing. The ideal significance of esthetic objects is no exception to this principle. Their satisfying quality, their power to compose while they arouse, is not dependent upon definite prior desire and effort as is the case with the ideally satisfying quality of practical and scientific objects. It is part of their peculiar satisfying quality to be gratuitous, not purchased by endeavor. The contrast to other things of this detachment from toil and labor in a world where most realizations have to be bought, as well as the contrast to trouble and uncertainty, give esthetic objects their peculiar traits. If all things came to us in the way our esthetic objects do, none of them would be a source of esthetic delight.

Some phases of recent philosophy have made much of need, desire and satisfaction. Critics have frequently held that the outcome is only recurrence to an older subjective empiricism, though with substitution of affections and volitional states for cognitive sensory states. But need and desire are exponents of natural being. They are, if we use Aristotelian phraseology, actualizations of its contingencies and incompletenesses; as such nature itself is wistful and pathetic, turbulent and passionate. Were it not, the existence of wants would be a miracle. In a world where everything is complete, nothing requires anything else for its completion. A world in which events can be carried to a finish only through the coinciding assistance of other transitory events, is already necessitous, a world of begging as well as of beggarly elements. If human experience is to express and reflect this world, it must be marked by needs; in becoming aware of the needful and needed quality of things it must project satisfactions or completions. For irrespective of whether a satisfaction is conscious, a satisfaction or non-satisfaction is an objective thing with objective conditions. It means fulfillment of the demands of objective factors. Happiness may *mark* an awareness of such satisfaction, and it may *be* its culminating form. But satisfaction is not subjective, private or personal: it is conditioned by objective partialities and defections and made real by objective situations and completions.

By the same logic, necessity implies the precarious and contingent. A world that was all necessity would not be a world of necessity; it would just be. For in its being, nothing would be necessary for anything else. But where some things are indigent, other things are necessary if demands are to be met. The common failure to note the fact that a world of complete being would be a world in which necessity is meaningless is due to a rapid shift from one universe of discourse to another. First we postulate a whole of Being; then we shift to a part; now since a "part" is logically dependent as such in its existence and its properties, it is necessitated by other parts. But we have unwittingly introduced contingency in the very fact of marking off something as just a part. If the logical implications of the original notion are held to firmly, a part is already a part-of-a-whole. Its being what it is, is not necessitated by the whole or by other parts: its being what it is, is just a name for the whole being what it is. Whole and parts alike are but names for existence there as just what it is. But wherever we can say *if* so-and-so, then something else, there is necessity, because partialities are implied which are not just parts-of-a-whole. A world of "ifs" is alone a world of "musts"—the "ifs" express real differences; the "musts" real connections. The stable and recurrent is needed for the fulfillment of the possible; the doubtful can be settled only through its adaptation to stable objects. The necessary is always necessary for, not necessary in and of itself; it is conditioned by the contingent, although itself a condition of the full determination of the latter.

One of the most striking phases of the history of philosophic thought is the recurrent grouping together of unity, permanence (or "the eternal"), completeness and rational thought, while upon another side full multiplicity, change and the temporal, the partial, defective, sense and desire. This division is obviously but another case of violent separation of the precarious and unsettled from the regular and determinate. One aspect of it, however, is worthy of particular attention: the connection of thought and unity. Empirically, all reflection sets out from the problematic and confused. Its aim is to clarify and ascertain. When thinking is successful, its career closes in transforming the disordered into the orderly, the mixed-up into the distinguished or placed, the unclear and ambiguous into the defined and unequivocal, the disconnected into the systematized. It is empirically assured that the goal of thinking does not remain a mere ideal, but is attained often enough so as to render reasonable additional efforts to achieve it.

In these facts we have, I think, the empirical basis of the philosophic doctrines which assert that reality is really and truly a rational system, a coherent whole of relations that cannot be conceived otherwise than in terms of intellect. Reflective inquiry moves in each particular case from differences toward unity; from indeterminate and ambiguous position to clear determination, from confusion and disorder to system. When thought in a given case has reached its goal of organized totality, of definite relations of distinctly placed elements, its object is the accepted starting point, the defined subject matter, of further experiences; antecedent and outgrown conditions of darkness and of unreconciled differences are dismissed as a transitory state of ignorance and inadequate apprehensions. Retain connection of the goal with the thinking by which it is reached, and then identify it with true reality in contrast with the merely phenomenal, and the outline of the logic of rational and "objective" idealisms is before us. Thought like Being, has two forms, one real; the other phenomenal. It is compelled to take on *reflective* form, it involves doubt, inquiry and hypothesis, because it sets out from a subject-matter conditioned by sense, a fact which proves that thought, intellect, is not pure in man, but restricted by an animal organism that is but one part linked with other parts, of nature. But the conclusion of reflection affords us a pattern and guarantee of thought which is *constitutive;* one with the system of objective reality. Such in outline is the procedure of all ontological logics.

A philosophy which accepts the denotative or empirical method accepts at full value the fact that reflective thinking transforms confusion, ambiguity and discrepancy into illumination, definiteness and consistency. But it also points to the contextual situation in which thinking occurs. It notes that the starting point is the actually *problematic*, and that the problematic phase resides in some actual and specifiable situation.

It notes that the means of converting the dubious into the assured, and the incomplete into the determinate, is use of assured and established things, which are just as empirical and as indicative of the nature of experienced things as is the uncertain. It thus notes that thinking is no different in kind from the use of natural materials and energies, say fire and tools, to refine, re-order, and shape other natural materials, say ore. In both cases, there are matters which as they stand are unsatisfactory and there are also adequate agencies for dealing with them and connecting them. At no point or place is there any jump outside empirical, natural objects and their relations. Thought and reason are not specific powers. They consist of the procedures intentionally employed in the application to each other of the unsatisfactorily confused and indeterminate on one side and the regular and stable on the other. Generalizing from such observations, empirical philosophy perceives that thinking is a continuous process of temporal re-organization within one and the same world of experienced things, not a jump from the latter world into one of objects constituted once for all by thought. It discovers thereby the empirical basis of rational idealism, and the point at which it empirically goes astray. Idealism fails to take into account the specified or concrete character of the uncertain situation in which thought occurs; it fails to note the empirically concrete nature of the subject-matter, acts, and tools by which determination and consistency are reached; it fails to note that the conclusive eventual objects having the latter properties are themselves as many as the situations dealt with. The conversion of the logic of reflection into an ontology of rational being is thus due to arbitrary conversion of an eventual natural function of unification into a causal antecedent reality; this in turn is due to the tendency of the imagination working under the influence of emotion to carry unification from an actual, objective and experimental enterprise, limited to particular situations where it is needed, into an unrestricted, wholesale movement which ends in an all-absorbing dream.

The occurrence of reflection is crucial for dualistic metaphysics as well as for idealistic ontologies. Reflection occurs only in situations qualified by uncertainty, alternatives, questioning, search, hypotheses, tentative trials or experiments which test the worth of thinking. A naturalistic metaphysics is bound to consider reflection as itself a natural event occurring *within* nature because of traits of the latter. It is bound to inference from the empirical traits of thinking in precisely the same way as the sciences make inferences from the happening of suns, radio-activity, thunder-storms or any other natural event. Traits of reflection are as truly indicative or evidential of the traits of *other* things as are the traits of these events. A theory of the nature of the occurrence and career of a sun reached by denial of the obvious traits of the sun, or by denial that these traits are so connected with the traits of other natural events that they can be used as evidence concerning the nature of these other things, would hardly possess scientific standing. Yet philosophers, and strangely enough philosophers who call themselves realists, have constantly held that the traits which are characteristic of thinking, namely, uncertainty, ambiguity, alternatives, inquiring, search, selection, experimental reshaping of external conditions, do not possess the same existential character as do the objects of valid knowledge. They have denied that these traits are evidential of the character of the world within which thinking occurs. They have not, as realists, asserted that these traits are mere appearances; but they have often asserted and implied that such things are only personal or psychological in contrast with a world of objective nature. But the interests of empirical and denotative method and of naturalistic metaphysics wholly coincide. The world must actually be such as to generate ignorance and inquiry; doubt and hypothesis, trial and temporal conclusions; the latter being such that they develop out of existences which while wholly "real" are not as satisfactory, as good, or as significant, as those into which they are eventually re-organized. The ultimate evidence of genuine hazard, contingency, irregularity and indeterminateness in nature is thus found in the occurrence of thinking. The traits of natural existence which generate the fears and adorations of superstitious barbarians generate the scientific procedures of disciplined civilization. The superiority of the latter does not consist in the fact that they are based on "real" existence, while the former depend wholly upon a human nature different from nature in general. It consists in the fact that scientific inquiries reach *objects* which are better, because reached by method which controls them and which adds greater control to life itself, method which mitigates accident, turns contingency to account, and releases thought and other forms of endeavor.

The conjunction of problematic and determinate characters in nature renders every existence, as well as every idea and human act, an experiment in fact, even though not in design. To be intelligently experimental is but to be conscious of this intersection of natural conditions so as to profit by it instead of being at its mercy. The Christian idea of this world and this life as a probation is a kind of distorted recognition of the situation; distorted because it applied wholesale to one stretch of existence in contrast with another, regarded as original and final. But in truth anything which can exist at any place and at any time occurs subject to tests imposed upon it by surroundings, which are only in part compatible and reinforcing. These surroundings test its strength and measure its endurance. As we can discourse of change only in terms of velocity and acceleration which involve relations to other things, so assertion of the permanent and enduring is comparative. The stablest thing we can speak of is not free from conditions set to it by other things. That even the solid earth mountains, the emblems of constancy, appear and disappear like the clouds is an old theme of moralists and poets. The fixed and unchanged being of the Democritean atom is now reported by inquirers to possess some of the traits of his non-being, and to embody a temporary equilibrium in the economy of nature's compromises and adjustments. A thing may endure *secula seculorum* and yet not be everlasting; it will crumble before the gnawing tooth of time, as it exceeds a certain measure. Every existence is an event.

This fact is nothing at which to repine and nothing to gloat over. It is something to be noted and used. If it is discomfiting when applied to good things, to our friends, possessions and precious selves, it is consoling also to know that no evil endures forever; that the longest lane turns sometime, and that the memory of loss of nearest and dearest grows dim in time. The eventful character of all existences is no reason for consigning them to the realm of mere appearance any more than it is a reason for idealizing flux into a deity. The important thing is measure, relation, ratio, knowledge of the comparative tempos of change. In mathematics some variables are constants in some problems; so it is in nature and life. The rate of change of some things is so slow, or is so rhythmic, that these changes have all the advantages of stability in dealing with more transitory and irregular happenings—if we know enough. Indeed, if any one thing that concerns us is subject to change, it is fortunate that all other things change. A thing "absolutely" stable and unchangeable would be out of the range of the principle of action and reaction, of resistance and leverage as well as of friction. Here it would have no applicability, no potentiality of use as measure and control of other events. To designate the slower and the regular rhythmic events structure, and more rapid and irregular ones process, is sound practical sense. It expresses the function of one in respect to the other.

But spiritualistic idealism and materialism alike treat this relational and functional distinction as something fixed and absolute. One doctrine finds structure in a framework of ideal forms, the other finds it in matter. They agree in supposing that structure has some superlative reality. This supposition is another form taken by preference for the stable over the precarious and uncompleted. The fact is that all structure is structure *of* something; anything defined as structure is a character of *events*, not something intrinsic and *per se*. A set of traits is called structure, because of its limiting function in relation to other traits of events. A house has a structure; in comparison with the disintegration and collapse that would occur without its presence, this structure is fixed. Yet it is not something external to which the changes involved in building and using the house have to submit. It is rather an arrangement of changing events such that properties which change slowly, limit and direct a series of quick changes and give them an order which they do not otherwise possess. Structure is constancy of means, of things used for consequences, not of things taken by themselves or absolutely.

Structure is what makes construction possible and cannot be discovered or defined except in some realized construction, construction being, of course, an evident order of changes. The isolation of structure from the changes whose stable ordering it is, renders it mysterious—something that is metaphysical in the popular sense of the word, a kind of ghostly queerness.

The "matter" of materialists and the "spirit" of idealists is a creature similar to the constitution of the United States in the minds of unimaginative persons. Obviously the real constitution is certain basic relationships among the activities of the citizens of the country; it is a property or phase of these processes, so connected with them as to influence their rate and direction of change. But by literalists it is often conceived of as something external to them; in itself fixed, a rigid framework to which *all* changes must accommodate themselves. Similarly what we call matter is that character of natural events which is so tied up with changes that are sufficiently rapid to be perceptible as to give the latter a characteristic rhythmic order, the causal sequence. It is no cause or source of events or processes; no absolute monarch; no principle of explanation; no substance behind or underlying changes—save in that sense of substance in which a man well fortified with this world's goods, and hence able to maintain himself through vicissitudes of surroundings, is a man of substance. The name designates a character in operation, not an entity.

That structure, whether of the kind called material or of the kind summed up in the word mental, is stable or permanent relationally and in its office, may be shown in another way. There is no action without reaction; there is no exclusively one-way exercise of conditioning power, no mode of regulation that operates wholly from above to below or from within outwards or from without inwards. Whatever influences the changes of other things is itself changed. The idea of an activity proceeding only in one direction, of an unmoved mover, is a survival of Greek physics. It has been banished from science, but remains to haunt philosophy. The vague and mysterious properties assigned to mind and matter, the very conceptions of mind and matter in traditional thought, are ghosts walking underground. The notion of matter actually found in the practice of science has nothing in common with the matter of materialists—and almost everybody is still a materialist as to matter, to which he merely adds a second rigid structure which he calls mind. The matter of science is a character of natural events and changes as they change; their character of regular and stable order.

Natural events are so complex and varied that there is nothing surprising in their possession of different characterizations, characters so different that they can be easily treated as opposites.

Nothing but unfamiliarity stands in the way of thinking of both mind and matter as different characters of natural events, in which matter expresses their sequential order, and mind the order of their meanings in their logical connections and dependencies. Processes may be eventful for functions which taken in abstract separation are at opposite poles, just as physiological processes eventuate in both anabolic and katabolic functions. The idea that matter and mind are two sides or "aspects" of the same things, like the convex and the concave in a curve, is literally unthinkable.

A curve is an intelligible object and concave and convex are defined in terms of this object; they are indeed but names for properties involved in its meaning. We do not start with convexity and concavity as two independent things and then set up an unknown *tertium quid* to unite two disparate things. In spite of the literal absurdity of the comparison, it may be understood however in a way which conveys an inkling of the truth. That to which both mind and matter belong is the complex of events that constitute nature. This becomes a mysterious *tertium quid*, incapable of designation, only when mind and matter are taken to be static structures instead of functional characters. It is a plausible prediction that if there were an interdict placed for a generation upon the use of mind, matter, consciousness as nouns, and we were obliged to employ adjectives and adverbs, conscious and consciously, mental and mentally, material and physically, we should find many of our problems much simplified.

We have selected only a few of the variety of the illustrations that might be used in support of the idea that the significant problems and issues of life and philosophy concern the rate and mode of the conjunction of the precarious and the assured, the incomplete and the finished, the repetitious and the varying, the safe and sane and the hazardous. If we trust to the evidence of experienced things, these traits, and the modes and tempos of their interaction with each other, are fundamental features of natural existence. The experience of their various consequences, according as they are relatively isolated, unhappily or happily combined, is evidence that wisdom, and hence that love of wisdom which is philosophy, is concerned with choice and administration of their proportioned union. Structure and process, substance and accident, matter and energy, permanence and flux, one and many, continuity and discreteness, order and progress, law and liberty, uniformity and growth, tradition and innovation, rational will and impelling desires, proof and discovery, the actual and the possible, are names given to various phases of their conjunction, and the issue of living depends upon the art with which these things are adjusted to each other.

While metaphysics may stop short with noting and registering these traits, man is not contemplatively detached from them. They involve him in his perplexities and troubles, and are the source of his joys and achievements. The situation is not indifferent to man, because it forms man as a desiring, striving, thinking, feeling creature. It is not egotism that leads man from contemplative registration of these traits to interest in managing them, to intelligence and purposive art. Interest, thinking, planning, striving, consummation and frustration are a drama enacted by these forces and conditions. A particular choice may be arbitrary; this is only to say that it does not approve itself to reflection. But choice is not arbitrary, not in a universe like this one, a world which is not finished and which has not consistently made up its mind where it is going and what it is going to do. Or, if we call it arbitrary, the arbitrariness is not ours but that of existence itself. And to call existence arbitrary or by any moral name, whether disparaging or honorific, is to patronize nature. To assume an attitude of condescension toward existence is perhaps a natural human compensation for the straits of life. But it is an ultimate source of the covert, uncandid and cheap in philosophy. This compensatory disposition it is which forgets that reflection exists to guide choice and effort. Hence its love of wisdom is but an unlaborious transformation of existence by dialectic, instead of an opening and enlarging of the ways of nature in man. A true wisdom, devoted to the latter task, discovers in thoughtful observation and experiment the method of administering the unfinished processes of existence so that frail goods shall be substantiated, secure goods be extended, and the precarious promises of good that haunt experienced things be more liberally fulfilled.

## 19. Experience, Nature and Art*

This selection can be read from several points of view. Taken from *Experience and Nature*, it continues a major theme of that book, the attack on dualism. Specifically Dewey opposes the "division of everything into nature *and* experience, of experi-

---

* From John Dewey, *Experience and Nature* (New York, 1958) (1929), 2nd ed., Chap. 9.

ence into practice *and* theory, art *and* science, of art into useful *and* fine, menial *and* free.'' In fact, Dewey sees an analysis of art as providing a microcosm of the pattern of relations at work in the doing and reflecting which characterizes the human endeavor overall. Taken in this wide, philosophical sense, art is so revealing for Dewey that he can write, ''in short, the history of human experience is a history of the development of the arts.''

From another point of view, however, this chapter can be read as a prelude to Dewey's later effort, in *Art as Experience* (1934), to develop a full-scale aesthetics. In this regard, Dewey makes a beginning here, although undeveloped, by insisting on the distinction between art and aesthetic experience, a distinction that is central to his later aesthetics. But again, both art and aesthetic experience are revelatory of a morphology of experience. In Dewey's judgment, ''the doings and sufferings that form experience are, in the degree in which experience is intelligent or charged with meanings, a union of the precarious, novel, irregular with the settled, assured and uniform—a union which also defines the artistic and esthetic.''

Experience, with the Greeks, signified a store of practical wisdom, a fund of insights useful in conducting the affairs of life. Sensation and perception were its occasion and supplied it with pertinent materials, but did not of themselves constitute it. They generated experience when retention was added and when a common factor in the multitude of felt and perceived cases detached itself so as to become available in judgment and exertion. Thus understood, experience is exemplified in the discrimination and skill of the good carpenter, pilot, physician, captain-at-arms; experience is equivalent to art. Modern theory has quite properly extended the application of the term to cover many things that the Greeks would hardly have called ''experience,'' the bare having of aches and pains, or a play of colors before the eyes. But even those who hold this larger signification would admit, I suppose, that such ''experiences'' count only when they result in insight, or in an enjoyed perception, and that only thus do they define experience in its honorific sense.

Greek thinkers nevertheless disparaged experience in comparison with something called reason and science. The ground for depreciation was not that usually assigned in modern philosophy; it was not that experience is ''subjective.'' On the contrary, experience was considered to be a genuine expression of cosmic forces, not an exclusive attribute or posses-sion of animal or of human nature. It was taken to be a realization of inferior portions of nature, those infected with chance and change, the less *Being* part of the cosmos. Thus while experience meant art, art reflected the contingencies and partialities of nature, while science —theory—exhibited its necessities and universalities. Art was born of need, lack, deprivation, incompleteness, while science—theory —manifested fullness and totality of Being. Thus the depreciatory view of experience was identical with a conception that placed practical activ-ity below theoretical activity, finding the former dependent, impelled from outside, marked by deficiency of real being, while the latter was independent and free because complete and self-sufficing: that is perfect.

In contrast with this self-consistent position we find a curious mixture in modern thinking. The latter feels under no obligation to present a theory of natural existence that links art with nature; on the contrary, it usually holds that science or knowledge is the only *authentic* expression of nature, in which case art must be an arbitrary addition to nature. But modern thought also combines exaltation of science with eulogistic appreciation of art, especially of fine or creative art. At the same time it retains the substance of the classic disparagement of the practical in contrast with the theoretical, although formulating it in somewhat differ-ent language: to the effect that knowledge deals with objective reality as it is in itself, while in what is "practical," objective reality is altered and cognitively distorted by subjective factors of want, emotion and striv-ing. And yet in its encomium of art, it fails to note the commonplace of Greek observation—that the fine arts as well as the industrial technologies are affairs of practice.

This confused plight is partly cause and partly effect of an almost uni-versal confusion of the artistic and the esthetic. On one hand, there is action that deals with materials and energies outside the body, assemb-ling, refining, combining, manipulating them until their new state yields a satisfaction not afforded by their crude condition—a formula that applies to fine and useful art alike. On the other hand, there is the delight that attends vision and hearing, an enhancement of the receptive apprecia-tion and assimilation of objects irrespective of participation in the opera-tions of production. Provided the difference of the two things is recog-nized, it is no matter whether the words "esthetic" and "artistic" or other terms be used to designate the distinction, for the difference is not one of words but of objects. But in some form the difference must be acknowledged.

The community in which Greek art was produced was small; numerous and complicated intermediaries between production and consumption were lacking; producers had a virtually servile status. Because of the close connection between production and enjoyable fruition, the Greeks in their perceptive uses and enjoyments were never wholly unconscious of the artisan and his work, not even when they personally were exclusively concerned with delightful contemplation. But since the artist was an artisan (the term artist having none of the eulogistic connotations of present usage), and since the artisan occupied an inferior position, the enjoyment of works of any art did not stand upon the same level as enjoyment of those objects for the realization of which manual activity was not needed. Objects of rational thought, of contemplative insight were the only things that met the specification of freedom from need, labor, and matter. They alone were self-sufficient, self-existent, and self-explanatory, and hence enjoyment of *them* was on a higher plane than enjoyment of works of art.

These conceptions were consistent with one another and with the conditions of social life at the time. Nowadays we have a messy conjunction of notions that are consistent neither with one another nor with the tenor of our actual life. Knowledge is still regarded by most thinkers as direct grasp of ultimate reality, although the practice of knowing has been assimilated to the procedure of the useful arts;—involving, that is to say, doing that manipulates and arranges natural energies. Again while science is said to lay hold of reality, yet "art" instead of being assigned a lower rank is equally esteemed and honored. And when within art a distinction is drawn between production and appreciation, the chief honor usually goes to the former on the ground that it is "creative," while taste is relatively possessive and passive, dependent for its material upon the activities of the creative artist.

If Greek philosophy was correct in thinking of knowledge as contemplation rather than as a productive art, and if modern philosophy accepts this conclusion, then the only logical course is relative disparagement of all forms of production, since they are modes of practice which is by conception inferior to contemplation. The artistic is then secondary to the esthetic: "creation," to "taste," and the scientific *worker*—as we significantly say—is subordinate in rank and worth to the dilettante who enjoys the results of his labors. But if modern tendencies are justified in putting art and creation first, then the implications of this position should be avowed and carried through. It would then be seen that science is an art, that art is practice, and that the only distinction worth drawing is not between practice and theory, but between those modes of practice that are not intelligent, not inherently and immediately enjoyable, and those which are full of enjoyed meanings. When this perception dawns, it will be a commonplace that art—the mode of activity that is charged with meanings capable of immediately enjoyed possession—is the complete culmination of nature, and that "science" is properly a handmaiden that conducts natural events to this happy issue. Thus would disappear the separations that trouble present thinking: division of everything into nature *and* experience, of experience into practice *and* theory, art *and* science, of art into useful *and* fine, menial *and* free.

Thus the issue involved in experience as art in its pregnant sense and in art as processes and materials of nature continued by direction into achieved and enjoyed meanings, sums up in itself all the issues which have been previously considered. Thought, intelligence, science is the intentional direction of natural events to meanings capable of immediate possession and enjoyment; this direction—which is operative art—is itself a natural event in which nature otherwise partial and incomplete comes fully to itself; so that objects of conscious experience when reflectively chosen, form the "end" of nature. The doings and sufferings that form experience are, in the degree in which experience is intelligent or charged with meanings, a union of the precarious, novel, irregular with the settled, assured and uniform—a union which also defines the artistic and the esthetic. For wherever there is art the contingent and ongoing no longer work at cross purposes with the formal and recurrent but commingle in harmony. And the distinguishing feature of conscious experience, of what for short is often called "consciousness," is that in it the instrumental and the final, meanings that are signs and clews and meanings that are immediately possessed, suffered and enjoyed, come together in one. And all of these things are preëminently true of art.

First, then, art is solvent union of the generic, recurrent, ordered, established phase of nature with its phase that is incomplete, going on, and hence still uncertain, contingent, novel, particular; or as certain systems of esthetic theory have truly declared, though without empirical basis and import in their words, a union of necessity and freedom, a harmony of the many and one, a reconciliation of sensuous and ideal. Of any artistic act and product it may be said both that it is inevitable in its rightness, that nothing in it can be altered without altering all, and that its occurrence is spontaneous, unexpected, fresh, unpredictable. The presence in art, whether as an act or a product, of proportion, economy, order, symmetry, composition, is such a commonplace that it does not need to be dwelt upon. But equally necessary is unexpected combination, and the consequent revelation of possibilities hitherto unrealized. "Repose in stimulation" characterizes art. Order and proportion when they are the whole story are soon exhausted; economy in itself is a tiresome and restrictive taskmaster. It is artistic when it releases.

The more extensive and repeated are the basic uniformities of nature that give form to art, the "greater" is the art, provided—and it is this proviso that distinguishes art—they are indistinguishably fused with the wonder of the new and the grace of the gratuitous. "Creation" may be asserted vaguely and mystically; but it denotes something genuine and indispensable in art. The merely finished is not fine but ended, done with, and the merely "fresh" is that bumptious impertinence indicated by the slang use of the word. The "magic" of poetry—and pregnant experience has poetical quality—is precisely the revelation of meaning in the old effected by its presentation through the new. It radiates the light that never was on land and sea but that is henceforth an abiding illumination of objects. Music in its immediate occurrence is the most varied and etherial of the arts, but is in its conditions and structure the most mechanical. These things are commonplaces; but until they are commonly employed in their evidential significance for a theory of nature's nature, there is no cause to apologize for their citation.

The limiting terms that define art are routine at one extreme and capricious impulse at the other. It is hardly worth while to oppose science and art sharply to one another, when the deficiencies and troubles of life are so evidently due to separation between art and blind routine and blind impulse. Routine exemplifies the uniformities and recurrences of nature, caprice expresses its inchoate initiations and deviations. Each in isolation is unnatural as well as inartistic, for nature is an intersection of spontaneity and necessity, the regular and the novel, the finished and the beginning. It is right to object to much of current practice on the ground that it is routine, just as it is right to object to much of our current enjoyments on the ground that they are spasms of excited escape from the thraldom of enforced work. But to transform a just objection against the quality of much of our practical life into a description and definition of practice is on the same plane as to convert legitimate objection to trivial distraction, senseless amusement, and sensual absorption, into a Puritanical aversion to happiness. The idea that work, productive activity, signifies action carried on for merely extraneous ends, and the idea that happiness signifies surrender of mind to the thrills and excitations of the body are one and the same idea. The first notion marks the separation of activity from meaning, and the second marks the separation of receptivity from meaning. Both separations are inevitable as far as experience fails to be art:—when the regular, repetitious, and the novel, contingent in nature fail to sustain and inform each other in a productive activity possessed of immanent and directly enjoyed meaning.

Thus the theme has insensibly passed over into that of the relation of means and consequence, process and product, the instrumental and consummatory. Any activity that is simultaneously both, rather than in alternation and displacement, is art. Disunion of production and consumption is a common enough occurrence. But emphasis upon this separation in order to exalt the consummatory does not define or interpret either art or experience. It obscures their meaning, resulting in a division of art into useful and fine, adjectives which, when they are prefixed to "art," corrupt and destroy its intrinsic significance. For arts that are merely useful are not arts but routines; and arts that are merely final are not arts but passive amusements and distractions, different from other indulgent dissipations only in dependence upon a certain acquired refinement or "cultivation."

The existence of activities that have no immediate enjoyed intrinsic meaning is undeniable. They include much of our labors in home, factory, laboratory and study. By no stretch of language can they be termed either artistic or esthetic. Yet they exist, and are so coercive that they require some attentive recognition. So we optimistically call them "useful" and let it go at that, thinking that by calling them useful we have somehow justified and explained their occurrence. If we were to ask useful for what? we should be obliged to examine their actual consequences, and when we once honestly and fully faced these consequences we should probably find ground for calling such activities detrimental rather than useful.

We call them useful because we arbitrarily cut short our consideration of consequences. We bring into view simply their efficacy in bringing into existence certain commodities; we do not ask for their effect upon the quality of human life and experience. They are useful to make shoes, houses, motor cars, money, and other things which *may* then be put to use; here inquiry and imagination stop. What they also *make* by way of narrowed, embittered, and crippled life, of congested, hurried, confused and extravagant life, is left in oblivion. But to be useful is to fulfill need. The characteristic human need is for possession and appreciation of the meaning of things, and this need is ignored and unsatisfied in the traditional notion of the useful. We identify utility with the external relationship that some events and acts bear to other things that are their products, and thus leave out the only thing that is essential to the idea of utility, inherent place and bearing in experience. Our classificatory use of the conception of some arts as merely instrumental so as to dispose of a large part of human activity is no solving definition; it rather conveys an immense and urgent problem.

The same statement applies to the conception of merely fine or final arts and works of art. In point of fact, the things designated by the phrase fall under three captions. There are activities and receptivities to which the name of "self-expression" is often applied as a eulogistic qualification, in which one indulges himself by giving free outward exhibition to his own states without reference to the conditions upon which intelligible communication depends—an act also sometimes known as "expression of emotion," which is then set up for definition of all fine art. It is easy to dispose of this art by calling it a product of egotism due to balked activity in other occupations. But this treatment misses a more significant point. For all art is a process of making the world a different place in which to live, and involves a phase of protest and of compensatory response. Such art as there is in these manifestations lies in this factor. It is owing to frustration in communication of meanings that the protest becomes arbitrary and the compensatory response wilfully eccentric.

In addition to this type—and frequently mingled with it—there is experimentation in new modes or craftsmanship, cases where the seemingly bizarre and over-individualistic character of the products is due to discontent with existing technique, and is associated with an attempt to find new modes of language. It is aside from the point either to greet these manifestations as if they constituted art for the first time in human history, or to condemn them as not art because of their violent departures from received canons and methods. Some movement in this direction has always been a condition of growth of new forms, a condition of salvation from that mortal arrest and decay called academic art.

Then there is that which in quantity bulks most largely as fine art: the production of buildings in the name of the art of architecture; of pictures in the name of the art of painting; of novels, dramas, etc., in the name of literary art; a production which in reality is largely a form of commercialized industry in production of a class of commodities that find their sale among well-to-do persons desirous of maintaining a conventionally approved status. As the first two modes carry to disproportionate excess that factor of particularity, contingency and difference which is indispensable in all art, deliberately flaunting avoidance of the repetitions and order of nature; so this mode celebrates the regular and finished. It is reminiscent rather than commemorative of the meanings of experienced things. Its products remind their owner of things pleasant in memory though hard in direct-undergoing, and remind others that their owner has achieved an economic standard which makes possible cultivation and decoration of leisure.

Obviously no one of these classes of activity and product or all of them put together, mark off anything that can be called distinctively fine art. They share their qualities and defects with many other acts and objects. But, fortunately, there may be mixed with any one of them, and, still more fortunately, there may occur without mixture, process and product that are characteristically excellent. This occurs when activity is productive of an object that affords continuously renewed delight. This condition requires that the object be, with its successive consequences, indefinitely instrumental to *new* satisfying events. For otherwise the object is quickly exhausted and satiety sets in. Anyone, who reflects upon the commonplace that a measure of artistic products is their capacity to attract and retain observation with satisfaction under whatever conditions they are approached, while things of less quality soon lose capacity to hold attention becoming indifferent or repellent upon subsequent approach, has a sure demonstration that a genuinely esthetic object is not exclusively consummatory but is causally productive as well. A consummatory object that is not also instrumental turns in time to the dust and ashes of boredom. The "eternal" quality of great art is its renewed instrumentality for further consummatory experiences.

When this fact is noted, it is also seen that limitation of fineness of art to paintings, statues, poems, songs and symphonies is conventional, or even verbal. Any activity that is productive of objects whose perception is an immediate good, and whose operation is a continual source of enjoyable perception of other events exhibits fineness of art. There are acts of all kinds that directly refresh and enlarge the spirit and that are instrumental to the production of new objects and dispositions which are in turn productive of further refinements and replenishments. Frequently moralists make the acts *they* find excellent or virtuous wholly final, and treat art and affection as mere means. Estheticians reverse the performance, and see in good *acts* means to an ulterior external happiness, while esthetic appreciation is called a good in itself, or that strange thing an end in itself. But on both sides it is true that in being preëminently fructifying the things designated means are immediate satisfactions. They are their own excuses for being just because they are charged with an office in quickening apprehension, enlarging the horizon of vision, refining discrimination, creating standards of appreciation which are confirmed and deepened by further experiences. It would almost seem when their non-instrumental character is insisted upon as if what was meant were an indefinitely expansive and radiating instrumental efficacy.

The source of the error lies in the habit of calling by the name of means things that are not means at all; things that are only external and accidental antecedents of the happening of something else. Similarly things are called ends that are not ends save accidentally, since they are not fulfilments, consummatory, of means, but merely last terms closing a process. Thus it is often said that a laborer's toil is the means of his livelihood, although except in the most tenuous and arbitrary way it bears no relationship to his real living. Even his wage is hardly an end or consequence of his labor. He might—and frequently does—equally well or ill—perform any one of a hundred other tasks as a condition of receiving payment. The prevailing conception of instrumentality is profoundly vitiated by the habit of applying it to cases like the above, where, instead of an operation of means, there is an enforced necessity of doing one thing as a coerced antecedent of the occurrence of another thing which is wanted.

Means are always at least causal conditions; but causal conditions are means only when they possess an added qualification; that, namely, of being freely used, because of perceived connection with chosen consequences. To entertain, choose and accomplish anything as an end or consequence is to be committed to a like love and care for whatever events and acts are its means. Similarly, consequences, ends, are at least effects; but effects are not ends unless thought has perceived and freely chosen the conditions and processes that are their conditions. The notion that means are menial, instrumentalities servile, is more than a degradation of means to the rank of coercive and external necessities. It renders all things upon which the name of end is bestowed accompaniments of privilege, while the name of utility becomes an apologetic justification for things that are not portions of a good and reasonable life. Livelihood is at present not so much the consequence of a wage-earner's labor as it is the effect of other causes forming the economic régime, labor being merely an accidental appendage of these other causes.

Paints and skill in manipulative arrangement are means of a picture as end, because the picture is *their* assemblage and organization. Tones and susceptibility of the ear when properly interacting are the means of music, because they constitute, make, are, music. A disposition of virtue is a means to a certain quality of happiness because it is a constituent of that good, while such happiness is means in turn to virtue, as the sustaining of good in being. Flour, water, yeast are means of bread because they are ingredients of bread; while bread is a factor *in* life, not just *to* it. A good political constitution, honest police-system, and competent judiciary, are means of the prosperous life of the community because they are integrated portions of that life. Science is an instrumentality of and for art because it is the intelligent factor *in* art. The trite saying that a hand is not a hand except as an organ of the living body —except as a working coördinated part of a balanced system of activities—applies untritely to all things that are means. The connection of means-consequences is never one of bare succession in time, such that the element that is means is past and gone when the end is instituted. An active process is strung out temporarily, but there is a deposit at each stage and point entering cumulatively and constitutively into the outcome. A genuine instrumentality *for* is always an organ *of* an end. It confers continued efficacy upon the object in which it is embodied.

The traditional separation between some things as mere means and others as mere ends is a reflection of the insulated existence of working and leisure classes, of production that is not also consummatory, and consummation that is not productive. This division is not a *merely* social phenomenon. It embodies a perpetuation upon the human plane of a division between need and satisfaction belonging to brute life. And this separation expresses in turn the mechanically external relationship that exists in nature between situations of disturbed equilibrium, of stress, and strain, and achieved equilibrium. For in nature, outside of man, except when events eventuate in "development" or "evolution" (in which a cumulative carrying forward of consequences of past histories in new efficiencies occurs) antecedent events are external transitive conditions of the occurrence of an event having immediate and static qualities. To animals to whom acts have no meaning, the change in the environment required to satisfy needs has no significance on its own account; such change is a mere incident of ego-centric satisfactions. This physically external relationship of antecedents and consequents is perpetuated; it continues to hold true of human industry wherever labor and its materials and products are externally enforced necessities for securing a living. Because Greek industry was so largely upon this plane of servile labor, all industrial activity was regarded by Greek thought as a *mere* means, an extraneous necessity. Hence satisfactions due to it were conceived to be the ends or goods of purely animal nature in isolation. With respect to a truly human and rational life, they were not ends or goods at all, but merely "means," that is to say, external conditions that were antecedently enforced requisites of the life conducted and enjoyed by free men, especially by those devoted to the acme of freedom, pure thinking. As Aristotle asserted, drawing a just conclusion from the assumed premises, there are classes of men who are necessary materials of society but who are not integral parts of it. And he summed up the whole theory of the external and coerced relationship of means and ends when he said in this very connection that: "When there is one thing that is means and another thing that is end, there is *nothing common* between them, except in so far as the one, the means, produces, and the other, the end, receives the product."

It would thus seem almost self-evident that the distinction between the instrumental and the final adopted in philosophic tradition as a solving word presents in truth a problem, a problem so deep-seated and far-reaching that it may be said to be *the* problem of experience. For all the intelligent activities of men, no matter whether expressed in science, fine arts, or social relationships, have for their task the conversion of causal bonds, relations of succession, into a connection of means-consequence, into meanings. When the task is achieved the result is art: and in art everything is common between means and ends. Whenever so-called means remain external and servile, and so-called ends are enjoyed objects whose further causative status is unperceived, ignored or denied, the situation is proof positive of limitations of art. Such a situation consists of affairs in which the problem has *not* been solved; namely that of converting physical and brute relationships into connections of meanings characteristic of the possibilities of nature.

It goes without saying that man begins as a part of physical and animal nature. In as far as he reacts to physical things on a strictly physical level, he is pulled and pushed about, overwhelmed, broken to pieces, lifted on the crest of the wave of things, like anything else. His contacts, his sufferings and doings, are matters of direct interaction only. He is in a "state of nature." As an animal, even upon the brute level, he manages to subordinate some physical things to his needs, converting them into materials sustaining life and growth. But in so far things that serve as material of satisfaction and the acts that procure and utilize them are not objects, or things-with-meanings. That appetite as such is blind, is notorious; it may push us into a comfortable result instead of into disaster; but we are pushed just the same. When appetite is perceived in its meanings, in the consequences it induces, and these consequences are experimented with in reflective imagination, some being seen to be consistent with one another, and hence capable of co-existence and of serially ordered achievement, others being incompatible, forbidding conjunction at one time, and getting in one another's way serially—when this estate is attained, we live on the human plane, responding to things in their meanings. A relationship of cause-effect has been transformed into one of means-consequence. Then consequences belong *integrally* to the conditions which may produce them, and the latter possess character and distinction. The meaning of causal conditions is carried over also into the consequence, so that the latter is no longer a mere end, a last and closing term of arrest. It is marked out in perception, distinguished by the efficacy of the conditions which have entered into it. Its value as fulfilling and consummatory is measurable by subsequent fulfillments and frustrations to which it is contributory in virtue of the causal means which compose it.

Thus to be conscious of meanings or to have an idea, marks a fruition, an enjoyed or suffered arrest of the flux of events. But there are all kinds of ways of perceiving meanings, all kinds of ideas. Meaning may be determined in terms of consequences hastily snatched at and torn loose from their connections; then is prevented the formation of wider and more enduring ideas. Or, we may be aware of meanings, may achieve ideas, that unite wide and enduring scope with richness of distinctions. The latter sort of consciousness is more than a passing and superficial consummation or end: it takes up into itself meanings covering stretches of existence wrought into consistency. It marks the conclusion of long continued endeavor; of patient and indefatigable search and test. The idea is, in short, art and a work of art. As a work of art, it directly liberates subsequent action and makes it more fruitful in a creation of more meanings and more perceptions.

It is the part of wisdom to recognize how sparse and insecure are such accomplishments in comparison with experience in which physical and animal nature largely have their way. Our liberal and rich ideas, our adequate appreciations, due to productive art are hemmed in by an unconquered domain in which we are everywhere exposed to the incidence of unknown forces and hurried fatally to unforeseen consequences. Here indeed we live servilely, menially, mechanically; and we so live as much when forces blindly lead to us ends that are liked as when we are caught in conditions and ends against which we blindly rebel. To call satisfactions which happen in this blind way "ends" in a eulogistic sense, as did classic thought, is to proclaim in effect our servile submission to accident. We may indeed enjoy the goods the gods of fortune send us, but we should recognize them for what they are, not asserting them to be good and righteous *altogether*. For, since they have not been achieved by any art involving deliberate selection and arrangement of forces, we do not know with what they are charged. It is an old true tale that the god of fortune is capricious, and delights to destroy his darlings after having made them drunk with prosperity. The goods of art are not the less good in their goodness than the gifts of nature; while in addition they are such as to bring with themselves open-eyed confidence. They are fruits of means consciously employed; fulfillments whose further consequences are secured by conscious control of the causal conditions which enter into them. Art is the sole alternative to luck; and divorce from each other of the meaning and value of instrumentalities and ends is the essence of luck. The esoteric character of culture and the supernatural quality of religion are both expressions of the divorce.

The modern mind has formally abjured belief in natural teleology because it found Greek and medieval teleology juvenile and superstitious. Yet facts have a way of compelling recognition of themselves. There is little scientific writing which does not introduce at some point or other the idea of tendency. The idea of tendency unites in itself exclusion of prior design and inclusion of movement in a particular direction, a direction that may be either furthered or counteracted and frustrated, but which is intrinsic. Direction involves a limiting position, a point or goal of culminating stoppage, as well as an initial starting point. To assert a tendency and to be fore-conscious of a possible terminus of movement are two names of the same fact. Such a consciousness may be fatalistic; a sense of inevitable march toward impending doom. But it may also contain a perception of meanings such as flexibly directs a forward movement. The end is then an end-in-view and is in constant and cumulative reënactment at each stage of forward movement. It is no longer a terminal point, external to the conditions that have led up to it; it is the continually developing meaning of present tendencies—the very things which as directed we call "means." The process is art and its product, no matter at what stage it be taken, is a work of art.

To a person building a house, the end-in-view is not just a remote and final goal to be hit upon after a sufficiently great number of coerced motions have been duly performed. The end-in-view is a plan which is *contemporaneously* operative in selecting and arranging materials. The latter, brick, stone, wood and mortar, are means only as the end-in-view is actually incarnate in them, in forming them. Literally, they *are* the end in its present stage of realization. The end-in-view is present at each stage of the process; it is present as the *meaning* of the materials used and acts done; without its informing presence, the latter are in no sense "means;" they are merely extrinsic causal conditions. The statement is generic; it applies equally at every stage. The house itself, when building is complete, is "end" in no exclusive sense. It marks the conclusion of the organization of certain materials and events into effective means; but these material and events still exist in causal interaction with other things. New consequences are foreseen; new purposes, ends-in-view, are entertained; they are embodied in the coördination of the thing built, now reduced to material, although significant material, along with other materials, and thus transmuted into means. The case is still clearer, when instead of considering a process subject to as many rigid external conditions as is the building of a house, we take for illustration a flexibly and freely moving process, such as painting a picture or thinking out a scientific process, when these operations are carried on artistically. Every process of free art proves that the difference between means and end is analytic, formal, not material and chronologic.

What has been said enables us to re-define the distinction drawn between the artistic, as objectively productive, and the esthetic. Both involve a perception of meanings in which the instrumental and the consummatory peculiarly intersect. In esthetic perceptions an object interpenetrated with meanings is given; it may be taken for granted; it invites and awaits the act of appropriative enjoyment. In the esthetic object tendencies are sensed as brought to fruition; in it is embodied a means-consequence relationship, as the past work of his hands was surveyed by the Lord and pronounced good. This good differs from those gratifications to which the name sensual rather than sensuous is given, since the former are pleasing endings that occur in ways not informed with the meaning of materials and acts integrated into them. In appreciative possession, perception goes out to tendencies which *have* been brought to happy fruition in such a way as to release and arouse.

Artistic sense on the other hand grasps tendencies as possibilities; the invitation of these possibilities to perception is more urgent and compelling than that of the given already achieved. While the means-consequence relationship is directly sensed, felt, in both appreciation and artistic production, in the former the scale descends upon the side of the attained; in the latter there predominates the invitation of an existent consummation to bring into existence further perceptions. Art in being, the active productive process, may thus be defined as an esthetic perception together with an *operative* perception of the efficiencies of the esthetic object. In many persons with respect to most kinds of enjoyed perceptions, the sense of possibilities, the arousal or excitation attendant upon appreciation of poetry, music, painting, architecture or landscape remains diffuse and inchoate; it takes effect only in direct and undefined channels. The enjoyed perception of a visual scene is in any case a function of that scene in its total connections, but it does not link up adequately. In some happily constituted persons, this effect is adequately coördinated with other endowments and habits; it becomes an integral part of craft, taking effect in the creation of a new object of appreciation. The integration is, however, progressive and experimental, not momentarily accomplished. Thus every creative effort is temporal, subject to risk and deflection. In that sense the difference between the diffuse and postponed change of action due in an ordinary person to release of energies by an esthetic object, and the special and axial direction of subsequent action in a gifted person is, after all, a matter of degree.

Without a sense of moving tendencies which are operative in conjunction with a state of fruition, there is appetitive gratification, but nothing that may be termed appreciation. Sense of moving tendencies supplies thrill, stimulation, excitation; sense of completion, consummation, affords composure, form, measure, composition. Emphasize the latter, and appreciation is of the classic type. This type fits conditions where production is professionalized among technical craftsmen, as among the Greeks; it is adapted to a contemplative enjoyment of the achievements of past ages or remote places, where conditions forbid urge to emulation or productive activity of a similar kind. Any work of art that persistently retains its power to generate enjoyed perception or appreciation becomes in time classic.

In so-called romantic art, the sense of tendencies operative beyond the limits of consummation is in excess; a lively sense of unrealized potentialities attaches to the object; but it is employed to enhance immediate appreciation, not to promote further productive achievement. Whatever is peculiarly romantic excites a feeling that the possibilities suggested go beyond not merely actual present realization, but are beyond effective attainment in any experience. In so far intentionally romantic art is wilful, and in so far not art. Excited and uneasy perceptual enjoyment is made ultimate, and the work of art is accommodated to production of these feelings. The sense of unachieved possibilities is employed as a compensatory equivalent for endeavor in achievement. Thus when the romantic spirit invades philosophy the possibilities present in imaginative sentiment are declared to be the real, although "transcendental," substance of Being itself. In complete art, appreciation follows the object and moves with it to its completion; romanticism reverses the process and degrades the object to an occasion for arousing a predetermined type of appreciation. In classicism, objective achievement is primary, and appreciation not only conforms to the object, but the object is employed to compose sentiment and give it distinction. Its vice, as an 'ism, is that it turns the mind to what is given; the given is taken as if it were eternal and wholly separate from generation and movement. Art free from subjection to any "ism" has movement, creation, as well as order, finality.

To institute a difference of *kind* between useful and fine arts is, therefore, absurd, since art involves a peculiar interpenetration of means and ends. Many things are termed useful for reasons of social status, implying deprecation and contempt. Things are sometimes said to belong to the menial arts merely because they are cheap and used familiarly by common people. These things of daily use for ordinary ends may survive in later periods, or be transported to another culture, as from Japan and China to America, and being rare and sought by connoisseurs, rank forthwith as works of fine art. Other things may be called fine because their manner of use is decorative or socially ostentatious. It is tempting to make a distinction of degree and say that a thing belongs to the sphere of use when perception of its meaning is incidental to something else; and that a thing belongs to fine art when its other uses are subordinate to its use in perception. The distinction has a rough practical value, but cannot be pressed too far. For in production of a painting or a poem, as well as in making a vase or a temple, a perception is also employed as means for something beyond itself. Moreover, the perception of urns, pots and pans as commodities may be intrinsically enjoyable, although these things are primarily perceived with reference to some use to which they are put. The only *basic* distinction is that between bad art and good art, and this distinction, between things that meet the requirements of art and those that do not, applies equally to things of use and of beauty. Capacity to offer to perception meaning in which fruition and efficacy interpenetrate is met by different products in various degrees of fulness; it may be missed altogether by pans and poems alike. The difference between the ugliness of a mechanically conceived and executed utensil and of a meretricious and pretentious painting is one only of content or material; in form, both are articles, and bad articles.

Thinking is pre-eminently an art; knowledge and propositions which are the products of thinking, are works of art, as much so as statuary and symphonies. Every successive stage of thinking is a conclusion in which the meaning of what has produced it is condensed; and it is no sooner stated than it is a light radiating to other things—unless it be a fog which obscures them. The antecedents of a conclusion are as causal and existential as those of a building. They are not logical or dialectical, or an affair of ideas. While a conclusion follows from antecedents, it does not follow from "premises," in the strict, formal sense. Premises are the analysis of a conclusion into its logically justifying grounds; there are no premises till there is a conclusion. Conclusion and premise are reached by a procedure comparable to the use of boards and nails in making a box; or of paint and canvas in making a picture. If defective materials are employed or if they are put together carelessly and awkwardly, the result is defective. In some cases the result is called unworthy, in others, ugly; in others, inept; in others, wasteful, inefficient, and in still others untrue, false. But in each case, the condemnatory adjective refers to the resulting work judged in the light of its method of production. Scientific method or the art of constructing true perceptions is ascertained in the course of experience to occupy a privileged position in undertaking other arts. But this unique position only places it the more securely as an art; it does not set its product, knowledge, apart from other works of art.

The existential origin of valid cognitive perceptions is sometimes recognized in form and denied in substance; the name "psychological" is given to the events which generate valid beliefs. Then a sharp distinction is made between genesis as psychological and validity as logical. Of course lexicographic names are of no special moment; if any one wishes to call the efficient causes of knowledge and truth psychological, he is entitled to do so—provided the actual traits of these causative events are recognized. Such a recognition will note however that psychological does not mean psychic, or refer to events going on exclusively within the head or "subcutaneously." To become aware of an object cognitively as distinct from esthetically, involves external physical movements and external physical appliances physically manipulated. Some of these active changes result in unsound and defective perceptions; some have been ascertained to result usually in valid perceptions. The difference is precisely that which takes place when the art of architecture or sculpture is skilfully conducted or is carried on carelessly, and without adequate appliances. Sometimes the operations productive of tested beliefs are called "inductive;" with an implication in the naming, of discrediting them, as compared with deductive functions, which are assigned a superior exclusive status. Of deduction, when thus defined, the following assertions may be made. First, it has nothing to do with truth about any matter of existence. Secondly, it is not even concerned with consistency or correctness, save in a formal sense whose opposite (as has been previously pointed out) is not inconsistency but nonsense. Thirdly, the meanings which figure in it are the conclusions of prior inquiries which are "inductive," that is, are products of an experimental art of changing external things by appropriate external movements and appliances.

Deduction as it actually occurs in science is *not* deduction as deduction should be according to a common definition. Deduction deals directly with meanings in their relations to one another, rather than with meanings directly referred to existence. But these meanings are what they are in themselves and are related to one another by means of acts of taking and manipulating—an art of discourse. They possess intellectual import and enter fruitfully into scientific method only because they are selected, employed, separated and combined by acts extraneous to them, acts which are as existential and causative as those concerned in the experimental use of apparatus and other physical things. The *act* of knowing, whether solicitous about inference or about demonstration, is always inductive. There is only one mode of thinking, the inductive, when thinking denotes anything that actually happens. The notion that there is another kind called deduction is another evidence of the prevalent tendency in philosophy to treat functions as antecedent operations, and to take essential meanings *of* existence as if they were a kind of Being. As a concrete operation, deduction is generative, not sterile; but as a concrete operation, it contains an extraneous act of taking and using which is selective, experimental and checked constantly by consequences.

Knowledge or science, as a work of art, like any other work of art, confers upon things traits and potentialities which did not *previously* belong to them. Objection from the side of alleged realism to this statement springs from a confusion of tenses. Knowledge is not a distortion or perversion which confers upon *its* subject-matter traits which *do* not belong to it, but is an act which confers upon non-cognitive material traits which *did* not belong to it. It marks a change by which physical events exhibiting properties of mechanical energy, connected by relations of push and pull, hitting, rebounding, splitting and consolidating, realize characters, meanings and relations of meanings *hitherto* not possessed by them. Architecture does not add to stone and wood something which does not belong to them, but it does add to them properties and efficacies which they did not possess in their earlier state. It adds them by means of engaging them in new modes of interaction, having a new order of consequences. Neither engineering nor fine art limits itself to imitative reproduction or copying of antecedent conditions. Their products may nevertheless be more effectively natural, more "life like," than were antecedent states of natural existence. So it is with the art of knowing and its works.

The failure to recognize that knowledge is a product of art accounts for an otherwise inexplicable fact: that science lies today like an incubus upon such a wide area of beliefs and aspirations. To remove the deadweight, however, recognition that it is an art will have to be more than a theoretical avowal that science is made by man for man, although such recognition is probably an initial preliminary step. But the real source of the difficulty is that the art of knowing is limited to such a narrow area. Like everything precious and scarce, it has been artificially protected; and through this very protection it has been dehumanized and appropriated by a class. As costly jewels of jade and pearl belong only to a few, so with the jewels of science. The philosophic theories which have set science on an altar in a temple remote from the arts of life, to be approached only with peculiar rites, are a part of the technique of retaining a secluded monopoly of belief and intellectual authority. Till the art of achieving adequate and liberal perceptions of the meanings of events is incarnate in education, morals and industry, science will remain a special luxury for a few; for the mass, it will consist of a remote and abstruse body of curious propositions having little to do with life, except where it lays the heavy hand of law upon spontaneity, and invokes necessity and mechanism to witness against generous and free aspiration.

Every error is attended with a contrary and compensatory error, for otherwise it would soon be self-revealing. The conception that causes are metaphysically superior to effects is compensated for by the conception that ends are superior esthetically and morally to means. The two beliefs can be maintained together only by removing "ends" out of the region of the causal and efficacious. This is accomplished nowadays by first calling ends intrinsic values, and then by making a gulf between value and existence. The consequence is that science, dealing as it must, with existence, becomes brutal and mechanical, while criticism of values, whether moral or esthetic, becomes pedantic or effeminate, expressing either personal likes and dislikes, or building up a cumbrous array of rules and authorities. The thing that is needful, discriminating judgment by methods whose consequences improve the art, easily slips through such coarse meshes, and by far the greater part of life goes on in a darkness unillumined by thoughtful inquiry. As long as such a state of thing persists, the argument of this chapter that science is art—like many other propositions of this book—is largely prophetic, or more or less dialectical. When an art of thinking as appropriate to human and social affairs has grown up as that used in dealing with distant stars, it will not be necessary to argue that science is one among the arts and among the works of art. It will be enough to point to observable situations. The separation of science from art, and the division of arts into those concerned with mere means and those concerned with ends in themselves, is a mask for lack of conjunction between power and the goods of life. It will lose plausibility in the degree in which foresight of good informs the display of power.

Evidence of the interpenetration of the efficacious with the final in art is found in the slow emancipation of art from magical rite and cult, and the emergence of science from superstition. For magic and superstition could never have dominated human culture, nor poetry have been treated as insight into natural causes, if means and ends were empirically marked off from each other. The intimacy of their union in one and the same object is that which makes it easy to impute to whatever is consummatory a kind of efficacy which it does not possess. Whatever is final is important; to say this is to enunciate a truism. Lack of instrumentalities and of skill by which to analyze and follow the particular efficacies of the immediately enjoyed object lead to imputation to it of wholesale efficacy in the degree of its importance. To the short-cut pragmatism congenial to natural man, importance measures "reality" and reality in turn defines efficacious power. Loyalties evoked in the passionate citizen by sight of the flag or in the devout Christian by the cross are attributed directly to the intrinsic nature of these objects. Their share in a consummatory experience is translated into a mysterious inner sacred power, an indwelling efficacy. Thus a souvenir of the beloved one, arousing in the lover enjoyment similar to that awakened by the precious one to whom it belonged, possesses delightful, exciting, and consoling efficacies. No matter what things are directly implicated in a consummatory situation, they gain potencies for weal or woe similar to the good or evil which directly marks the situation. Obviously error here resides in the gross and undiscriminating way in which power is attributed; inquiry to reveal the specified elements which form the sequential order is lacking.

It is a commonplace of anthropologists that for the most part clothing originated in situations of unusual awe or prestigious display, rather than as a utility or protection. It was part of a consummatory object, rather than a means to specified consequences. Like the robes of priests, clothes were vestments, and investiture was believed to convey directly to the one ceremonially garbed dread potency or fascinating charm. Clothes were worn to confer authority; a man did not lend his significance to them. Similarly, a victorious hunter and warrior celebrated a triumphant return to camp by affixing to his person in conspicuous fashion claws and teeth of the wild beast or enemy that his prowess had subjugated. These signal proofs of power were integral portions of the object of admiration, loyalty and reverence. Thus the trophy became an emblem, and the emblem was endowed with mystic force. From a sign of glory it became a cause of glorification, and even when worn by another aroused the acclaim due to a hero. In time such trophies became the documented seal of prestigious authority. They had an intrinsic causal potency of their own. Legal history is full of like instances. Acts originally performed in connection with, say, the exchange of property, performed as part of the dramatic ceremony of taking possession of land, were not treated as mere evidences of title, but as having a mystic power to confer title.

Later, when such things lose their original power and become "mere matters of form," they may still be essential to the legal force of a transaction, as seals have had to be affixed to a contract to give it force, even though there was no longer sense or reason in their use. Things which have an efficacy imputed to them simply because they have shared in some eminent consummatory experience are symbols. They are called symbols, however, only afterwards and from without. To the devout in politics and religion they are other than symbols; they are articles possessed of occult potency. To one man, two crossed lines are an indication of an arithmetical operation to be performed; to another, they are evidence of the existence of Christianity as a historic fact, as a crescent is a reminder of the existence of Islam. But to another, a cross is more than a poignant reminder of a tragically significant death; it has intrinsic sacred power to protect and to bless. Since a flag stirs passionate loyalty to sudden and pervasive ebullition, the flag must have properties and potencies not possessed by other and differently configured pieces of cloth; it must be handled with reverence; it is the natural object of ceremonial adoration.

Phenomena like these when manifested in primitive culture are often interpreted as if they were attempts at a causal explanation of natural occurrences; magic is said to be science gone wrong. In reality, they are facts of direct emotional and practical response; beliefs, ideas, interpretations, only come later when responses not being direct and inevitably appropriate seem to demand explanation. As immediate responses they exemplify the fact that anything involved, no matter how incidentally, in a consummatory situation has the power of arousing the awe, excitement, relief, admiration belonging to the situation as a whole. Industry displaces magic, and science reduces myth, when the elements that enter into the constitution of the consummatory whole are discriminated, and each one has its own particular place in sequential order assigned it. Thus materials and efficacies characteristic of different kinds of arts are distinguished. But because the ceremonial, literary and poetic arts have quite other ways of working and other consequences, than industrial and scientific arts, it is far from following, as current theories assume, that they have no instrumental power at all, or that a sense of their instrumental agency is not involved in their appreciative perception. The pervasive operation of symbolism in human culture is all the proof that is needed to show that an intimate and direct sense of place and connection in a prolonged history enters into the enjoyed and suffered constituents of the history, and especially into the final or terminal members.

Further confirmation of this proposition is found in classic philosophy itself, in its theory that essential forms "make" things *what* they are, even though not causing them to occur. "Essence," as it figures in Greek theory, represents the mysterious potency of earlier "symbols" emancipated from their superstitious context and envisaged in a dialectic and reflective context. The essences of Greek-medieval science were in short poetic objects, treated as objects of demonstrative science, used to explain and understand the inner and ultimate constitution of things. While Greek thought was sufficiently emancipated from magic to deny "efficient" causality to formal and final essences, yet the latter were conceived of as making particular things to be *what* they are, members of natural kinds. Moreover, by a reversal of causal residence, intrinsic seeking for such forms was imputed to changing events. Thus the ground was prepared for the later frank return of patristic and scholastic thought to a frank animistic supernaturalism. The philosophic theory erred, as did magic and myth, regarding the nature of the efficacy involved in ends; and the error was due to the same causes, namely, failure of analysis into elements. It could not have occurred, were there that sharp division between means and ends, fruitions and instrumentalities, assumed by current thought.

In short, the history of human experience is a history of the development of arts. The history of science in its distinct emergence from religious, ceremonial and poetic arts is the record of a differentiation of arts, not a record of separation from art. The chief significance of the account just given, lies, for our present purpose, in its bearing upon the theory of experience and nature. It is not, however, without import for a theory of criticism. The present confusion, deemed chaos by some, in the fine arts and esthetic criticism seems to be an inevitable consequence of the underlying, even if unavowed, separation of the instrumental and the consummatory. The further men go in the concrete the more they are forced to recognize the logical consequence of their controlling assumptions. We owe it to theories of art prevalent to-day in one school of critics that certain implications, long obscured, of the traditional theory of art and nature have been brought to light. Gratitude for this debt should not be stinted because the adherents of the traditional theory regarding the newer views as capricious heresies, wild aberrations. For these critics, in proclaiming that esthetic qualities in works of fine art are unique, in asserting their separation from not only every thing that is existential in nature but also from all other forms of good, in proclaiming that such arts as music, poetry, painting have characters unshared with any natural things whatsoever:—in asserting such things the critics carry to its conclusion the isolation of fine art from the useful, of the final from efficacious. They thus prove that the separation of the consummation from the instrumental makes art wholly esoteric.

There are substantially but two alternatives. Either art is a continuation, by means of intelligent selection and arrangement, of natural tendencies of natural events; or art is a peculiar addition to nature springing from something dwelling exclusively within the breast of man, whatever name be given the latter. In the former case, delightfully enhanced perception or esthetic appreciation is of the same nature as enjoyment of any object that is consummatory. It is the outcome of a skilled and intelligent art of dealing with natural things for the sake of intensifying, purifying, prolonging and deepening the satisfactions which they spontaneously afford. That, in this process, new meanings develop, and that these afford uniquely new traits and modes of enjoyment is but what happens everywhere in emergent growths.

But if fine art has nothing to do with other activities and products, then of course it has nothing inherently to do with the objects, physical and social, experienced in other situations. It has an occult source and an esoteric character. It makes little difference what the source and the character be called. By strict logic it makes literally no difference. For if the quality of the esthetic experience is by conception unique, then the words employed to describe it have no significance derived from or comparable to the qualities of other experiences; their signification is hidden and specialized to a degree. Consider some of the terms which are in more or less current use among the critics who carry the isolation of art and the esthetic to its limit. It is sometimes said that art is the expression of the emotions; with the implication that, because of this fact, subject-matter is of no significance except as material through which emotion is expressed. Hence art becomes unique. For in works of science, utility and morals the character of the objects forming this subject-matter is all-important. But by this definition, subject-matter is stripped of all its own inherent characters in art in the degree in which it is genuine art; since a truly artistic work is manifest in the reduction of subject-matter to a mere medium of expression of emotion.

In such a statement emotion either has no significance at all, and it is mere accident that this particular combination of letters is employed; or else, if by emotion is meant the same sort of thing that is called emotion in daily life, the statement is demonstrably false. For emotion in its ordinary sense is something called out *by* objects, physical and personal; it is response *to* an objective situation. It is not something existing somewhere by itself which then employs material through which to express itself. Emotion is an indication of intimate participation, in a more or less excited way in some scene of nature or life; it is, so to speak, an attitude or disposition which is a function of objective things. It is intelligible that art should select and assemble objective things in such ways as to evoke emotional response of a refined, sensitive and enduring kind; it is intelligible that the artist himself is one capable of sustaining these emotions, under whose temper and spirit he performs his compositions of objective materials. This procedure may indeed be carried to a point such that the use of objective materials is economized to the minimum, and the evocation of the emotional response carried to its relative maximum. But it still remains true that the origin of the art-process lay in emotional responses spontaneously called out by a situation occurring without any reference to art, and without "esthetic" quality save in the sense in which all immediate enjoyment and suffering is esthetic. Economy in use of objective subject-matter may with experienced and trained minds go so far that what is ordinarily called "representation" is much reduced. But what happens is a highly funded and generalized representation of the formal sources of ordinary emotional experience.

The same sort of remark is to be made concerning "significant form" as a definition of an esthetic object. Unless the meaning of the term is so isolated as to be wholly occult, it denotes a selection, for sake of emphasis, purity, subtlety, of those forms which give consummatory significance to every-day subject-matters of experience. "Forms" are not the peculiar property or creation of the esthetic and artistic; they are characters in virtue of which anything meets the requirements of an enjoyable perception. "Art" does not create the forms; it is their selection and organization in such ways as to enhance, prolong and purify the perceptual experience. It is not by accident that some objects and situations afford marked perceptual satisfactions; they do so because of their structural properties and relations. An artist may work with a minimum of analytic recognition of these structures or "forms;" he may select them chiefly by a kind of sympathetic vibration. But they may also be discriminatively ascertained; and an artist may utilize his deliberate awareness of them to create works of art that are more formal and abstract than those to which the public is accustomed. Tendency to composition in terms of the formal characters marks much contemporary art, in poetry, painting; music, even sculpture and architecture. At their worst, these products are "scientific" rather than artistic; technical exercises, sterile and of a new kind of pedantry. At their best, they assist in ushering in new modes of art and by education of the organs of perception in new modes of consummatory objects; they enlarge and enrich the world of human vision.

Thus, by only a slight forcing of the argument, we reach a conclusion regarding the relations of instrumental and fine art which is precisely the opposite of that intended by seclusive estheticians; namely, that fine art *consciously* undertaken as such is peculiarly instrumental in quality. It is a device in experimentation carried on for the sake of education. It exists for the sake of a specialized use, use being a new training of modes of perception. The creators of such works of art are entitled, when successful, to the gratitude that we give to inventors of microscopes and microphones; in the end, they open new objects to be observed and enjoyed. This is a genuine service; but only an age of combined confusion and conceit will arrogate to works that perform this special utility the exclusive name of fine art.

Experience in the form of art, when reflected upon, we conclude by saying, solves more problems which have troubled philosophers and resolves more hard and fast dualisms than any other theme of thought. As the previous discussion has indicated, it demonstrates the intersection in nature of individual and generic; of chance and law, transforming one into opportunity and the other into liberation; of instrumental and final. More evidently still, it demonstrates the gratuitous falsity of notions that divide overt and executive activity from thought and feeling and thus separate mind and matter. In creative production, the external and physical world is more than a mere means or external condition of perceptions, ideas and emotions; it is subject-matter and sustainer of conscious activity; and thereby exhibits, so that he who runs may read, the fact that consciousness is not a separate realm of being, but is the manifest quality of existence when nature is most free and most active.

# 20. Existence, Value and Criticism*

In this selection, the concluding chapter of *Experience and Nature*, Dewey raises the problem of "value," only to cast

* From John Dewey, *Experience and Nature* (New York, 1958) (1929), 2nd ed., Chap. 2.

considerable doubt on the efficacy of a theory of value, at
least as it was posed at that time. In the use of the term
"value" Dewey detects a return of traditional dualism between existence and the honorific or precious. (Dewey
developed his own approach to "value" in 1939, when he
published a monograph entitled significantly *The Theory of
Valuation*.)

What does interest Dewey, however, is that "any *theory* of
values is perforce entrance into the field of criticism." And
this judgment leads to his statement that "philosophy is
inherently criticism, having its distinctive position among
various modes of criticism in its generality; a criticism of
criticisms, as it were." Dewey then proceeds to delineate the
salutary effects of philosophy utilized as the "critical method
of developing methods of criticism," all the while fending off
the more traditional claims made on behalf of philosophy.


Recent philosophy has witnessed the rise of a theory of value. Value
as it usually figures in this discussion marks a desperate attempt to combine the obvious empirical fact that objects are qualified with good and
bad, with philosophic deliverances which, in isolating man from nature,
qualitative individualities from the world, render this fact anomalous.
The philosopher erects a "realm of values" in which to place all the precious things which are extruded from natural existence because of isola-
tions artificially introduced. Poignancy, humor, zest, tragedy, beauty,
prosperity and bafflement, although rejected from a nature which is
identified with mechanical structure, remain just what they empirically
are, and demand recognition. Hence they are gathered up into the realm
of values, contradistinguished from the realm of existence. Then the
philosopher has a new problem with which to wrestle: What is the relationship of these two "worlds"? Is the world of value that of ultimate
and transcendent Being from which the world of existence is a derivation or a fall? Or is it but a manifestation of human subjectivity, a factor
somehow miraculously supervening upon an order complete and closed
in physical structure? Or are there scattered at random through objective being, detached subsistences as "real" as are physical events, but
having no temporal dates and spatial locations, and yet at times and
places miraculously united with existences?

Choice among such notions of value is arbitrary, because the problem
is arbitrary. When we return to the conceptions of potentiality and ac-

tuality, contingency and regularity, qualitatively diverse individuality, with which Greek thought operated, we find no room for a theory of values separate from a theory of nature. Yet if we are to recur to the Greek conceptions, the return must be a return with a difference. It must surrender the identification of natural ends with good and perfection; recognizing that a natural end, apart from endeavor expressing choice, has no intrinsic eulogistic quality, but is the boundary which writes "Finis" to a chapter of history inscribed by a moving system of energies. Failure by exhaustion as well as by triumph may constitute an end; death, ignorance, as well as life, are finalities.

Again, the return must abandon the notion of a predetermined limited number of ends inherently arranged in an order of increasing comprehensiveness and finality. It will have to recognize that natural termini are as infinitely numerous and varied as are the individual systems of action they delimit; and that since there is only relative, not absolute, impermeability and fixity of structure, new individuals with novel ends emerge in irregular procession. It must recognize that limits, closures, ends are experimentally or dynamically determined, presenting, like the boundaries of political individuals or states, a moving adjustment of various energy-systems in their cooperative and competitive interactions, not something belonging to them of their own right. Consequently, it will surrender the separation in nature from each other of contingency and regularity, the hazardous and the assured; it will avoid that relegation of them to distinct orders of Being which is characteristic of the classic tradition. It will note that they intersect everywhere; that it is uncertainty and indeterminateness that create the need for and the sense of order and security; that whatever is most complete and liberal in being and possession is for that very reason most exposed to vicissitude, and most needful of watchful safeguarding art.

The connotation of "value" in recent thought contains some hint of the changes which experience has compelled in the classic notion of natural ends. For by implication at least values are recognized to be fugitive and precarious, to be negative and positive, and indefinitely diversified in quality. Even that metaphysical theory of super-idealism which finds them to be eternal, and the eternal foundation and source of shifting temporal events, bases its argument upon the undeniable insecurity, the interminable elusiveness, the appearance and disappearance, of values in actual experience. Because of this sense of the evanescence and uncertainty of what used to be called ends but are now called values, the important consideration and concern is not a theory of values but a theory of criticism; a method of discriminating among goods on the basis of the conditions of their appearance, and of their consequences.

Values are values, things immediately having certain intrinsic qualities. Of them as values there is accordingly nothing to be said; they are what they are. All that can be said of them concerns their generative conditions and the consequences to which they give rise. The notion that things as direct values lend themselves to thought and discourse rests upon a confusion of causal categories with immediate qualities. Objects, for example, may be distinguished as contributory or as fulfilling, but this is distinction of place with respect to causal relationship; it is not a distinction of values. We may be interested in a thing, be concerned with it or like it, for a reason. The reason for appreciation, for an enjoyed appropriation, is often that the object in question serves as a means to something; or the reason is that it stands as the culmination of an antecedent process. But to take into account the reason for liking and enjoyment concerns the cause of the existence of a value, and has nothing to do with the intrinsicalness or nature of the value-quality, which either does or does not exist. Things that are means and things that are fulfillments have different qualities; but so do symphonies, operas and oratorios among themselves. The difference is not one that has anything to do with the immediacy or intrinsicalness of value-quality; it is a difference between one affair and quality and another.

It is self-contradictory to suppose that when a fulfillment possesses immediate value, its means of attainment do not. The person to whom the cessation of a tooth-ache has value, by that very fact finds value in going to a dentist, or in whatever else is means of fulfillment. For fulfillment is as relative to means as means are to realization. Means-consequences constitute a single undivided situation. Consequently when thought and discussion enter, when theorizing sets in, when there is anything beyond bare immediate enjoyment and suffering, it is the means-consequence relationship that is considered. Thought goes beyond immediate existence to its relationships, the conditions which mediate it and the things to which it is in turn mediatory. And such a procedure is criticism. The all but universal confusion in theories of value of determined position in causative or sequential relationship with value proper is indirect testimony to the fact that every intelligent appreciation is also criticism, judgment, of the thing having immediate value. Any *theory* of values is perforce entrance into the field of criticism. Value as such, even things having value, cannot in their immediate existence be reflected upon; they either are or are not; are or are not enjoyed. To pass beyond direct occurrence, even though the passage be restricted to an attempt to define value, is to begin a process of discrimination which implies a reflective criterion. In themselves, values may be just pointed at; to attempt a definition by complete pointing is however bootless. Sooner or later, with respect to positive or negative value, designation will have to include everything.

These remarks are preparatory to presenting a conception of philosophy; namely, that philosophy is inherently criticism, having its distinctive position among various modes of criticism in its generality; a criticism of criticisms, as it were. Criticism is discriminating judgment, careful appraisal, and judgment is appropriately termed criticism wherever the subject-matter of discrimination concerns goods or values. Possession and enjoyment of goods passes insensibly and inevitably into appraisal. First and immature experience is content simply to enjoy. But a brief course in experience enforces reflection; it requires but brief time to teach that some things sweet in the having are bitter in after-taste and in what they lead to. Primitive innocence does not last. Enjoyment ceases to be a datum and becomes a problem. As a problem, it implies intelligent inquiry into the conditions and consequences of a value-object; that is, criticism. If values were as plentiful as huckleberries, and the huckleberry-patch were always at hand, the passage of appreciation into criticism would be a senseless procedure. If one thing tired or bored us, we should have only to turn to another. But values are as unstable as the forms of clouds. The things that possess them are exposed to all the contingencies of existence, and they are indifferent to our likings and tastes.

Good things change and vanish not only with changes in the environing medium but with changes in ourselves. Continued perception, except when it has been cultivated through prior criticism, dulls itself; it is soon satiated, exhausted, blasé. The infinite flippancy of the natural man is a standing theme for discourse by shrewd observers of human nature. Cultivated taste alone is capable of prolonged appreciation of the same object; and it is capable of it because it has been trained to a discriminating procedure which constantly uncovers in the object new meanings to be perceived and enjoyed. Add to exhaustion of the organs of perception and enjoyment, all the other organic causes which render enjoyed objects unstable, and then add the external vicissitudes to which they are subjected, and there is no cause to wonder at the evanescence of immediate goods; nor at the so-called paradoxes of pleasure and virtue, according to which they are not secured by aiming at them but by attention to other things;—a fact however, which is not a paradox in a world where nothing is attained in any other way than by attention to its causal conditions.

When criticism and the critical attitude are legitimately distinguished from appreciation and taste, we are in the presence of one case of the constant rhythm of "perchings and flights" (to borrow James' terms), characteristic of alternate emphasis upon the immediate and mediate, the consummatory and instrumental, phases of all conscious experience. If we are misled into ignoring the omnipresence in all observations and ideas of this rhythm, it is largely because, under the influence of formal theories, we attach too elaborate and too remote a signification to "appreciation" and "criticism." Values of some sort or other are not traits of rare and festal occasions; they occur whenever any object is welcomed and lingered over; whenever it arouses aversion and protest; even though the lingering be but momentary and the aversion a passing glance toward something else.

Similarly, criticism is not a matter of formal treatises, published articles, or taking up important matters for consideration in a serious way. It occurs whenever a moment is devoted to looking to see what sort of value is present; whenever instead of accepting a value-object wholeheartedly, being rapt by it, we raise even a shadow of a question about its worth, or modify our sense of it by even a passing estimate of its probable future. It is well upon the whole that we use the terms "appreciation" and "criticism" honorifically, to designate conspicuous instances. But it is fatal to any understanding of them to fail to note that formally emphatic instances are of exactly the same nature as the rhythmic alternation between slight agreeable acceptances, annoyed rejections and passing questionings and estimates, which make up the entire course of our waking experience, whether in revery, in controlled inquiry or in deliberate management of affairs.

The rhythmic succession of the two modes of perception suggests that the difference is one of emphasis, or degree. Critical appreciation, and appreciative, warmly emotionalized criticism occur in every matured sane experience. After the first dumb, formless experience of a thing as a good, subsequent perception of the good contains at least a germ of critical reflection. For this reason, and only for this reason, elaborate and formulated criticism is subsequently possible. The latter, if just and pertinent, can but develop the reflective implications found within appreciation itself. Criticism would be the most wilful of undertakings if the possession and enjoyment of good objects had no element of memory and foresight in it; if it lacked all circumspection and judgment. Criticism is reasonable and to the point, in the degree in which it extends and deepens these factors of intelligence found in immediate taste and enjoyment.

Conscience in morals, taste in fine arts and conviction in beliefs pass insensibly into critical judgments; the latter pass also into a more and more generalized form of criticism called philosophy. How is the assertion of "canons" of taste and criticism compatible with the declaration that there is no discussing tastes? What is meant by a distinction between apparent good and real good? How can the distinction between seeming and being be capable of application to what is good? Is critical appraisal possible without a standard measure of values? Is the standard of values itself a value? Is it derived from the value-objects to which it is applied? If so, what authority does it possess over and beyond that of particular cases? What right has it to pass judgment upon its own source and authors? Does a standard exist transcendentally in independence of concrete cases judged? If so, what is its source, and what is the ground and guarantee of its applicability to alien material? Is taste, immediate appreciation, sense and moral sense, ultimate, its own final judge in every case as it arises? What, in that event, saves us from chaotic anarchy? Is there among men a common measure of value? If so, is it grounded outside of man, in an independent objective form of Being?

Such questions as these, which may be multiplied as one pleases, indicate that no great difficulty would attend an effort to derive all the stock issues of philosophy from the problems of value and their relationship to critical judgment. Whether it be a question of the good and bad in conviction and opinion, or in matters of conduct, or in appreciated scenes of nature and art, there occurs in every instance a conflict between the immediate value-object and the ulterior value-object: the given good, and that reached and justified by reflection; the now apparent and the eventual. In knowledge, for example there are beliefs *de facto* and beliefs *de jure*. In morals, there are immediate goods, the desired, and reasonable goods, the desirable. In esthetics, there are the goods of an undeveloped or perverted taste and there are the goods of cultivated taste. With respect to any of these distinctions, the true, real, final, or objective good is no *more* good as an immediate existence than is the contrasting good, called false, specious, illusory, showy, meretricious, *le faux bon*. The difference in adjectives designates a difference instituted in critical judgment; the validity of the difference between good which is approved and that which is good (immediately) but is *judged bad*, depends therefore upon the value of reflection in general, and of a particular reflective operation in especial. Even if good of the reflective object is different from that of the good of the non-reflective object, it does not follow that it is a better good, much less that it is such a difference in goodness as makes the non-reflective good *bad:*—except upon one proviso, namely, that there is something unique in the value or goodness of reflection.

Either, then, the difference between genuine, valid good and a counterfeit, specious good is unreal, or it is a difference consequent upon reflection, or criticism, and the significant point is that this difference is equivalent to that made by discovery of relationships, of conditions and consequences. With this conclusion are bound up two other propositions: Of immediate values as such, values which occur and which are possessed and enjoyed, there is no theory at all; they just occur, are enjoyed, possessed; and that is all. The moment we begin to discourse about these values, to define and generalize, to make distinctions in kinds, we are passing beyond value-objects themselves; we are entering, even if only blindly, upon an inquiry into causal antecedents and causative consequents, with a view to appraising the "real," that is the eventual, goodness of the thing in question. We are criticizing, not for its own sake, but for the sake of instituting and perpetuating more enduring and extensive values.

The other proposition is that philosophy is and can be nothing but this critical operation and function become aware of itself and its implications, pursued deliberately and systematically. It starts from actual situations of belief, conduct and appreciative perception which are characterized by immediate qualities of good and bad, and from the modes of critical judgment current at any given time in all the regions of value; these are its data, its subject-matter. These values, criticisms, and critical methods, it subjects to further criticism as comprehensive and consistent as possible. The function is to regulate the further appreciation of goods and bads; to give greater freedom and security in those acts of direct selection, appropriation, identification and of rejection, elimination, destruction which enstate and which exclude objects of belief, conduct and contemplation.

Such a conclusion wears an air of strangeness. It may appear to indicate an attempt by a dialectic trick to make the category of good-and-bad supreme in its jurisdiction over intellectual life and over all objects. This impression will, I think, be readily dissipated by consideration of the actual meaning of what is said. Objects of belief and of refusals to believe are value-objects; for each object is some thing acquiesced in, accepted, adopted, appropriated. This is the same as saying it is found good or satisfactory to believe or disbelieve; truistically, whatever is accepted is as such and in so far good. There is no occult significance in this statement; it is not preliminary to an argument which shall sweep away the properties which objects possess independent of their being objects of belief, or of their being values. It does not annihilate the difference among beliefs; it does not set up the *fact* that an object believed in is perforce found good as if it were a *reason* for belief. On the contrary: the statement is preliminary. The all-important matter is what lies back of and causes acceptance and rejection; whether or no there is method of discrimination and assessment which makes a difference in what is assented to and denied. Properties and relations that *entitle* an object to be found good in belief are extraneous to the qualities that are its immediate good; they are causal, and hence found only by search into the antecedent and the eventual. The conception that there are some objects or some properties of objects which carry their own adequate credentials upon their face is the snare and delusion of the whole historic tradition regarding knowledge, infecting alike sensational and rational schools, objective realisms and introspective idealisms.

Concerning beliefs and their objects taken in their immediacy *"non-disputandum"* holds, as truly as it does concerning tastes and their objects. If a man believes in ghosts, devils, miracles, fortune-tellers, the immutable certainty of the existing economic regime, and the supreme merits of his political party and its leaders, he does so believe; these are immediate goods to him, precisely as some color and tone combinations are lovely, or the mistress of his heart is charming. When the question is raised as to the "real" value of the object for belief, the appeal is to criticism, intelligence. And the court of appeal decides by the law of conditions and consequences. Inquiry duly pursued leads to the enstatement of an object which is directly accepted, good in belief, but an object whose character now depends upon the reflective operations whose conclusion it is. Like the object of dogmatic and uncritical belief, it marks an "end," a static arrest; but unlike it, the "end" is a *conclusion;* hence it carries credentials.

Were not objects of belief immediate goods, false beliefs would not be the dangerous things which they are. For it is because these objects are good to believe, to admit and assert, that they are cherished so intolerantly and unremittingly. Beliefs about God, Nature, society and man are precisely the things that men most cling to and most ardently fight for. It is easier to wean a miser from his hoard, than a man from his deeper opinions. And the tragedy is that in so many cases the *causes* which lead to the thing in question being a value are not *reasons* for its being a good, while the fact that it is an immediate good tends to preclude that search for causes, that dispassionate judgment, which is prerequisite to the conversion of goods *de facto* into goods *de jure*. Here, again and pre-eminently, since reflection is the instrumentality of securing freer and more enduring goods, reflection is a unique intrinsic good. Its instrumental efficacy determines it to be a candidate for a distinctive position as an immediate good, since beyond other goods it has power of replenishment and fructification. In it, apparent good and real good enormously coincide.

In traditional discussion the fact is overlooked that the subject-matter of belief is a good, since belief means assimilation and assertion. It is overlooked that its immediate goodness is both the obstacle to reflective examination and the source of its necessity. The "true" is indeed set up along with the good and the beautiful as a transcendent good, but the role of empirical good, of value, in the sweep of ordinary beliefs is passed by. The counterpart of this error, which isolates the subject-matter of intellect from the scope of values and valuations, is a corresponding isolation of the subject-matter of esthetic contemplation and immediate enjoyment from judgment. Between these two realms, one of intellectual objects without value and the other of value-objects without intellect, there is an equivocal mid-country in which moral objects are placed, with rival claimants striving to annex them either to the region of purely immediate goods (in this case termed pleasures) or to that of purely rational objects. Hence the primary function of philosophy at present is to make it clear that there is no such difference as this division assumes between science, morals, and esthetic appreciation. All alike exhibit the difference between immediate goods casually occurring and immediate goods which have been reflectively determined by means of critical inquiry. If bare liking is an adequate determinant of values in one case, it is in the others. If intelligence, criticism, is required in one, it is in the others. If the end to be attained in any case is an enhanced and purified immediate appreciative, experienced object, so it is in the others. All cases manifest the same duality and present the same problem; that of embodying intelligence in action which shall convert casual natural goods, whose causes and effects are unknown, into goods valid for thought, right for conduct and cultivated for appreciation.

Philosophic discourse partakes both of scientific and literary discourse. Like literature, it is a comment on nature and life in the interest of a more intense and just appreciation of the meanings present in experience. Its business is reportorial and transcriptive only in the sense in which the drama and poetry have that office. Its primary concern is to clarify, liberate and extend the goods which inhere in the naturally generated functions of experience. It has no call to create a world of "reality" *de novo*, nor to delve into secrets of Being hidden from common-sense and science. It has no stock of information or body of knowledge peculiarly its own; if it does not always become ridiculous when it sets up as a rival of science, it is only because a particular philosopher happens to be also, as a human being, a prophetic man of science. Its business is to accept and to utilize for a purpose the best available knowledge of its own time and place. And this purpose is criticism of beliefs, institutions, customs, policies with respect to their bearing upon good. This does not mean their bearing upon *the* good, as something itself attained and formulated in philosophy. For as philosophy has no private score of knowledge or of methods for attaining truth, so it has no private access to good. As it accepts knowledge of facts and principles from those competent in inquiry and discovery, so it accepts the goods that are diffused in human experience. It has no Mosaic nor Pauline authority of revelation entrusted to it. But it has the authority of intelligence, of criticism of these common and natural goods.

At this point, it departs from the arts of literary discourse. They have a freer office to perform—to perpetuate, enhance and vivify in imagination the natural goods; all things are forgiven to him who succeeds. But philosophic criticism has a stricter task, with a greater measure of responsibility to what lies outside its own products. It has to appraise values by taking cognizance of their causes and consequences; only by this straight and narrow path may it contribute to expansion and emancipation of values. For this reason the conclusions of science about matter-of-fact efficiencies of nature are its indispensable instruments. If its eventual concern is to render goods more coherent, more secure and more significant in appreciation, its road is the subject-matter of natural existence as science discovers and depicts it.

Only in verbal form is there anything novel in this conception of philosophy. It is a version of the old saying that philosophy is love of wisdom, of wisdom which is not knowledge and which nevertheless cannot be without knowledge. The need of an organon of criticism which uses knowledge of relations among events to appraise the casual, immediate goods that obtain among men is not a fact of philosophy, but of nature and life. We can conceive a happier nature and experience than flourishes among us wherein the office of critical reflection would be carried on so continuously and in such detail that no particular apparatus would be needed. But actual experience is such a jumble that a degree of distance and detachment are a pre-requisite of vision in perspective. Thinkers often withdraw too far. But a withdrawal is necessary, unless they are to be deafened by the immediate clamor and blinded by the immediate glare of the scene. What especially makes necessary a generalized instrument of criticism, is the tendency of objects to seek rigid non-communicating compartments. It is natural that nature, variegatedly qualified, should exhibit various trends when it achieves experience of itself, so that there is a distribution of emphasis such as are designated by the adjectives scientific, industrial, political, religious, artistic, educational, moral and so on.

But however natural from the standpoint of causation may be the institutionalizing of these trends, their separation effects an isolation which is unnatural. Narrowness, superficiality, stagnation follow from lack of the nourishment which can be supplied only by generous and wide interactions. Goods isolated as professionalism and institutionalization isolate them, petrify; and in a moving world solidification is always dangerous. Resistant force is gained by precipitation, but no one thing gets strong enough to defy everything. Over-specialization and division of interests, occupations and goods create the need for a generalized medium of intercommunication, of mutual criticism through all-around translation from one separated region of experience into another. Thus philosophy as a critical organ becomes in effect a messenger, a liaison officer, making reciprocally intelligible voices speaking provincial tongues, and thereby enlarging as well as rectifying the meanings with which they are charged.

The difficulty is that philosophy, even when professing catholicity, has often been suborned. Instead of being a free messenger of communication it has been a diplomatic agent of some special and partial interest; insincere, because in the name of peace it has fostered divisions that lead to strife, and in the name of loyalty has promoted unholy alliances and secret understandings. One might say that the profuseness of attestations to supreme devotion to truth on the part of philosophy is matter to arouse suspicion. For it has usually been a preliminary to the claim of being a peculiar organ of access to highest and ultimate truth. Such it is not; and it will not lose its esoteric and insincere air until the profession is disclaimed. Truth is a collection of truths; and these constituent truths are in the keeping of the best available methods of inquiry and testing as to matters-of-fact; methods, which are, when collected under a single name, science. As to truth, then, philosophy has no pre-eminent status; it is a recipient, not a donor. But the realm of meanings is wider than that of true-and-false meanings; it is more urgent and more fertile. When the claim of meanings to truth enters in, then truth is indeed pre-eminent. But this fact is often confused with the idea that truth has a claim to enter everywhere; that it has monopolistic jurisdiction. Poetic meanings, moral meanings, a large part of the goods of life are matters of richness and freedom of meanings, rather than of truth; a large part of our life is carried on in a realm of meanings to which truth and falsity as such are irrelevant. And the claim of philosophy to rival or displace science as a purveyor of truth seems to be mostly a compensatory gesture for failure to perform its proper task of liberating and clarifying meanings, including those scientifically authenticated. For, assuredly, a student prizes historic systems rather for the meanings and shades of meanings they have brought to light than for the store of ultimate truths they have ascertained. If accomplishment of the former office were made the avowed business of philosophy, instead of an incidental by-product, its position would be clearer, more intelligent and more respected.

It is sometimes suggested, however, that such a view of philosophy derogates from its dignity, degrading it into an instrument of social reforms, and that it is a view congenial only to those who are insensitive to the positive achievements of culture and over-sensitive to its evils. Such a conception overlooks outstanding facts. "Social reform" is conceived in a Philistine spirit, if it is taken to mean anything less than precisely the liberation and expansion of the meanings of which experience is capable. No doubt many schemes of social reform are guilty of precisely this narrowing. But for that very reason they are futile; they do not succeed in even the special reforms at which they aim, except at the expense of intensifying other defects and creating new ones. Nothing but the best, the richest and fullest experience possible, is good enough for man. The attainment of such an experience is not to be conceived as the specific problem of "reformers" but as the common purpose of men. The contribution which philosophy can make to this common aim is criticism. Criticism certainly includes a heightened consciousness of deficiencies and corruptions in the scheme and distribution of values that obtains at any period.

No just or pertinent criticism in its negative phase can possibly be made, however, except upon the basis of a heightened appreciation of the positive goods which human experience has achieved and offers. Positive concrete goods of science, art and social companionship are the basic subject-matter of philosophy as criticism; and only because such positive goods already exist is their emancipation and secured extension the defining aim of intelligence. The more aware one is of the richness of meanings which experience possesses, the more will a generous and catholic thinker be conscious of the limits which prevent sharing in them; the more aware will he be of their accidental and arbitrary distribution. If instrumental efficacies need to be emphasized, it is not for the sake of instruments but for the sake of that full and more secure distribution of values which is impossible without instrumentalities.

If philosophy be criticism, what is to be said of the relation of philosophy to metaphysics? For metaphysics, as a statement of the generic traits manifested by existences of all kinds without regard to their differentiation into physical and mental, seems to have nothing to do with criticism and choice, with an effective love of wisdom. It begins and ends with analysis and definition. When it has revealed the traits and characters that are sure to turn up in every universe of discourse, its work is done. So at least an argument may run. But the very nature of the traits discovered in every theme of discourse, since they are ineluctable traits of natural existence, forbids such a conclusion. Qualitative individuality and constant relations, contingency and need, movement and arrest are common traits of all existence. This fact is source both of values and of their precariousness; both of immediate possession which is casual and of reflection which is a precondition of secure attainment and appropriation. Any theory that detects and defines these traits is therefore but a ground-map of the province of criticism, establishing base lines to be employed in more intricate triangulations.

If the general traits of nature existed in water-tight compartments, it might be enough to sort out the objects and interests of experience among them. But they are actually so intimately intermixed that all important issues are concerned with their degrees and the ratios they sustain to one another. Barely to note and register that contingency is a trait of natural events has nothing to do with wisdom. To note, however, contingency in connection with a concrete situation of life is that fear of the Lord which is at least the beginning of wisdom. The detection and definition of nature's end is in itself barren. But the undergoing that actually goes on in the light of this discovery brings one close to supreme issues: life and death.

The more sure one is that the world which encompasses human life is of such and such a character (no matter what his definition), the more one is committed to try to direct the conduct of life, that of others as well as of himself, upon the basis of the character assigned to the world. And if he finds that he cannot succeed, that the attempt lands him in confusion, inconsistency and darkness, plunging others into discord and shutting them out from participation, rudimentary precepts instruct him to surrender his assurance as a delusion; and to revise his notions of the nature of nature till he makes them more adequate to the concrete facts in which nature is embodied. Man needs the earth in order to walk, the sea to swim or sail, the air to fly. Of necessity he acts within the world, and in order to be, he must in some measure adapt himself as one part of nature to other parts.

In mind, thought, this situation, this predicament becomes aware of itself. Instead of the coerced adaptation of part to part with coerced failure or success as consequence, there is search for the meaning of things with respect to acts to be performed, plans and policies to be formed; there is search for the meaning of proposed acts with respect to objects they induce and preclude. The one cord that is never broken is that between the energies and acts which compose nature. Knowledge modifies the tie. But the idea that knowledge breaks the tie, that it inserts something opaque between the interactions of things, is hardly less than infantile. Knowledge as science modifies the particular interactions that come within its reach, because it *is* itself a modification of interactions, due to taking into account their past and future. The generic insight into existence which alone can define metaphysics in any empirically intelligible sense is itself an added fact of interaction, and is therefore subject to the same requirement of intelligence as any other natural occurrence: namely, inquiry into the bearings, leadings and consequences of what it discovers. The universe is no infinite self-representative series, if only because the addition within it of a representation makes it a different universe.

By an indirect path we are brought to a consideration of the most far-reaching question of all criticism: the relationship between existence and value, or as the problem is often put, between the real and ideal.

Philosophies have usually insisted upon a wholesale relationship. Either the goods which we most prize and which are therefore termed ideal are identified completely and throughout with real Being; or the realms of existence and of the ideal are wholly severed from each other. In the European tradition in its orthodox form the former alternative has prevailed. *Ens* and *verum, bonum* are the same. Being, in the full sense, is perfection of power to be; the measure of degrees of perfection and of degrees of reality is extent of power. Evil and error are impotences; futile gestures against omnipotence—against Being. Spinoza restated to this effect medieval theology in terms of the new outlook of science. Modern professed idealisms have taught the same doctrine. After magnifying thought and the objects of thought, after magnifying the ideals of human aspiration, they have then sought to prove that after all these things are not ideal but are real—real not *as* meanings and ideals, but as existential being. Thus the assertion of faith in the ideal belies itself in the making; these "idealists" cannot trust their ideal till they have converted it into existence—that is, into the physical or the psychical, which, since it lacks the properties of the empirically physical and psycho-physical becomes a peculiar kind of existence, called metaphysical.

There are also philosophies, rarer in occurrence, which allege that the ideal is too sacredly ideal to have any point of contact whatever with existence; they think that contact is contagion and contagion infection. At first sight such a view seems to display a certain nobility of faith and fineness of abnegation. But an ideal realm that has no roots in existence has no efficacy nor relevancy. It is a light which is darkness, for shining in the void it illumines nothing and cannot reveal even itself. It gives no instruction, for it cannot be translated into the meaning and import of what actually happens, and hence it is barren; it cannot mitigate the bleakness of existence nor modify its brutalities. It thus abnegates itself in abjuring footing in natural events, and ceases to be ideal, to become whimsical fantasy or linguistic sophistication.

These remarks are made not so much by way of hostile animadversion as by way of indicating the sterility of wholesale conceptions of the relation of existence and value. By negative implication, they reveal the only kind of doctrine that can be effectively critical, taking effect in discriminations which emancipate, extend, and clarify. Such a theory will realize that the meanings which are termed ideal as truly as those which are termed sensuous are generated by existences; that as far as they continue in being they are sustained by events; that they are indications of the possibilities of existences, and are, therefore, to be used as well as enjoyed; used to inspire action to procure and buttress their causal conditions. Such a doctrine criticizes particular occurrences by the particular meanings to which they give rise; it criticizes also particular meanings and goods as their conditions are found to be sparse, accidental, incapable of conservation, or frequent, pliant, congruous, en-

during; and as their consequences are found to afford enlightenment
and direction in conduct, or to darken counsel, narrow the horizon of
vision, befog judgment and distort perspective. A good is a good
anyhow, but to reflection those goods approve themselves, whether
labelled beauty or truth or righteousness, which steady, vitalize and expand judgments in creation of new goods and conservation of old
goods. To common-sense this statement is a truism. If to philosophy it
is a stumbling-block, it is because tradition in philosophy has set
itself in stiff-necked fashion against discriminations within the realm
of existences, on account of the pluralistic implications of discrimination. It insists upon having all or none; it cannot choose in favor of
some existences and against others because of prior commitment to a
dogma of perfect unity. Such distinctions as it makes are therefore always hierarchical; degrees of greater and less, superior and inferior, in
one homogeneous order.

I gladly borrow the glowing words of one of our greatest American
philosophers; with their poetry they may succeed in conveying where
dry prose fails. Justice Holmes has written: "The mode in which the
inevitable comes to pass is through effort. Consciously or unconsciously
we all strive to make the kind of world that we like. And although with
Spinoza we may regard criticism of the past as futile, there is every
reason for doing all that we can to make a future such as we desire." He
then goes on to say, "there is every reason also for trying to make our
desires intelligent. The trouble is that our ideals for the most part are
inarticulate, and that even if we have made them definite we have very
little experimental knowledge of the way to bring them about." And this
effort to make our desires, our strivings and our ideals (which are as
natural to man as his aches and his clothes) articulate, to define them
(not in themselves which is impossible) in terms of inquiry into conditions and consequences is what I have called criticism; and when carried on in the grand manner, philosophy. In a further essay, Justice
Holmes touches upon the relation of philosophy (thus conceived) to our
scientific and metaphysical insight into the kind of a world in which we
live.

"When we come to our attitude toward the universe I do not see any
rational ground for demanding the superlative for being dissatisfied
unless we are assured that our truth is cosmic truth, if there is such a
thing. . . . . If a man sees no reason for believing that significance, consciousness and ideals are more than marks of the human, that does not
justify what has been familiar in French sceptics; getting upon a

pedestal and professing to look with haughty scorn upon a world in
ruins. The real conclusion is that the part cannot swallow the whole.
. . . If we believe that we came out of the universe, not it out of us, we
must admit that we do not know what we are talking about when we speak
of brute matter. We do know that a certain complex of energies can wag
its tail and another can make syllogisms. These are among the powers of
the unknown, and if, as may be, it has still greater powers that we cannot understand . . . why should we not be content? Why should we
employ the energy that is furnished to us by the cosmos to defy it and to
shake our fist at the sky? It seems to me silly."

"That the universe has in it more than we understand, that the private
soldiers have not been told the plan of campaign, or even that there is
one . . . has no bearing on our conduct. We still shall fight—all of us
because we want to live, some, at least, because we want to realize our
spontaneity and prove our powers, for the joy of it, and we may leave to
the unknown the supposed final valuation of that which in any event has
value to us. It is enough for us that the universe has produced us and
has within it, as less than it, all that we believe and love. If we think of
our existence not as that of a little god outside, but as that of a ganglion
within, we have the infinite behind us. It gives us our only but our adequate significance. If our imagination is strong enough to accept the vision of ourselves as parts inseparable from the rest, and to extend our
final interest beyond the boundary of our skins, it justifies even the
sacrifice of our lives for ends outside of ourselves. The motive to be sure
is the common wants and ideals that we find in man. Philosophy does
not furnish motives, but it shows men that they are not fools for doing
what they already want to do. It opens to the forlorn hopes on which we
throw ourselves away, the vista of the farthest stretch of human
thought, the chord of a harmony that breathes from the unknown."

Men move between extremes. They conceive of themselves as gods,
or feign a powerful and cunning god as an ally who bends the world to
do their bidding and meet their wishes. Disillusionized, they disown the
world that disappoints them; and hugging ideals to themselves as their
own possession, stand in haughty aloofness apart from the hard course
of events that pays so little heed to our hopes and aspirations. But a
mind that has opened itself to experience and that has ripened through
its discipline knows its own littleness and impotencies; it knows that its
wishes and acknowledgments are not final measures of the universe
whether in knowledge or in conduct, and hence are, in the end, tran-
sient. But it also knows that its juvenile assumption of power and

achievement is not a dream to be wholly forgotten. It implies a unity with the universe that is to be preserved. The belief, and the effort of thought and struggle which it inspires are also the doing of the universe, and they in some way, however slight, carry the universe forward. A chastened sense of our importance, apprehension that it is not a yardstick by which to measure the whole, is consistent with the belief that we and our endeavors are significant not only for themselves but in the whole.

Fidelity to the nature to which we belong, as parts however weak, demands that we cherish our desires and ideals till we have converted them into intelligence, revised them in terms of the ways and means which nature makes possible. When we have used our thought to its utmost and have thrown into the moving unbalanced balance of things our puny strength, we know that though the universe slay us still we may trust, for our lot is one with whatever is good in existence. We know that such thought and effort is one condition of the coming into existence of the better. As far as we are concerned it is the only condition, for it alone is in our power. To ask more than this is childish; but to ask less is a recreance no less egotistic, involving no less a cutting of ourselves from the universe than does the expectation that it meet and satisfy our every wish. To ask in good faith as much as this from ourselves is to stir into motion every capacity of imagination, and to exact from action every skill and bravery.

While, therefore, philosophy has its source not in any special impulse or staked-off section of experience, but in the entire human predicament, this human situation falls wholly within nature. It reflects the traits of nature; it gives indisputable evidence that in nature itself qualities and relations, individualities and uniformities, finalities and efficacies, contingencies and necessities are inextricably bound together. The harsh conflicts and the happy coincidences of this interpenetration make experience what it consciously is; their manifest apparition creates doubt, forces inquiry, exacts choice, and imposes liability for the choice which is made. Were there complete harmony in nature, life would be spontaneous efflorescence. If disharmony were not in both man and nature, if it were only between them, man would be the ruthless overlord of nature, or its querulous oppressed subject. It is precisely the peculiar intermixture of support and frustration of man by nature which constitutes experience. The standing antitheses of philosophic thought, purpose and mechanism, subject and object, necessity and freedom, mind and body, individual and general, are all of them attempts to formulate the fact that nature induces and partially sustains meanings and goods, and at critical junctures withdraws assistance and flouts its own creatures.

The striving of man for objects of imagination is a continuation of natural processes; it is something man has learned from the world in which he occurs, not something which he arbitrarily injects into that world. When he adds perception and ideas to these endeavors, it is not after all he who adds; the addition is again the doing of nature and a further complication of its own domain. To act, to enjoy and suffer in consequence of action, to reflect, to discriminate and make differences in what had been but gross and homogeneous good and evil, according to what inquiry reveals of causes and effects; to act upon what has been learned, thereby to plunge into new and unconsidered predicaments, to test and revise what has been learned, to engage in new goods and evils is human, the course which manifests the course of nature. They are the manifest destiny of contingency, fulfillment, qualitative individualization and generic uniformities in nature. To note, register and define the constituent structure of nature is not then an affair neutral to the office of criticism. It is a preliminary outline of the field of criticism, whose chief import is to afford understanding of the necessity and nature of the office of intelligence.

If I mistake not, the actual animus of subjectivity in modern philosophy is not where its antagonists have placed it. Its actual animus and its obnoxious burden are exemplified in the doctrine of its hostile critics. For they assign to knowledge alone valid reference to existence. Desires, beliefs, "practical" activity, values are attributed exclusively to the human subject; this division is what makes subjectivity a snare and peril. The case of belief is crucial. For it is admitted that belief involves a phase of acquiescence or assertion, it presents qualities which involve *personal* factors; and (whatever definition of value be employed) value. A sharp line of demarcation has therefore to be drawn between belief and knowledge, for the latter has been defined in terms of pure objectivity. The need to control belief is admitted; knowledge figures, even though according to these theories only *per accidens*, as the organon of such control. Practically then, in effect, knowledge, science, truth, is the method of criticizing beliefs. It is the method of determining right participation in beliefs on the part of personal factors. Why then keep up any other distinction between knowledge and beliefs, save that between methodical agencies, efficacious instrumentalities, and the accepted objects which being conclusions, are hence marked by characters due to the method of their production, in contrast with objects of belief blindly and accidentally generated? Why perturbation at the intimation that science is inherently an instrument of critically determining what is good and bad in the way of acceptance and rejection?

I can see but one answer. The realm of desire, belief, search, choice is thought of as "subjective" in a sense which isolates it from natural existence and which makes it an inexplicable irruption. This is the reason for sharp separation of belief and knowledge. Aversion to making science a means of determining the right operation of personal factors, just as the technical and material apparatus of a painter determines his product, is well grounded if the personal is outside of nature. Made a means to something personal conceived in this sense, science loses its objectivity, and becomes infected with the traits which characterize the merely private and arbitrary.

There is involved, however, in the conclusion an unexamined and uncriticized assumption. The reason for isolating doubt, striving, purpose, the variegated colored play of goods and bads, rejections and acceptances, is they do not belong in the block universe which forms the object of generalized knowledge, whether the block be conceived as mechanical or as rational in structure. The argument thus moves in a vicious circle; the question is begged at the outset. If individualized qualities, status arrests, limiting "ends," and contingent changes characterize nature, then they manifest themselves in the uses, enjoyments and sufferings, the searchings and strivings which form conscious experience. These are as realistic, as "objectively" natural, as are the constitutents of the object of cognitional experience. There is then no ground for denying or evading the full import of the fact that the latter are the means and the only means of regulative appraisals of values, of their revision, rectification, of their regulated generation and fortification.

The habitual avoidance in theories of knowledge of any reference to the fact that knowledge is a case of belief, operates as a device for ignoring the monstrous consequences of regarding the latter as existentially subjective, personal and private. No such device is available in dealing with esthetic and moral goods. Here the obnoxious one-sided conception operates in full force. The usual current procedure is to link values with likings as merely personal affairs, ignoring the inconvenient fact that the theory logically thereby makes all *beliefs* also matters of arbitrary, undiscussable preference. It is no cause for wonder therefore that there is next to no consensus in esthetic and moral theories. Since their subject-matter is totally segregated from that of science, since they are assigned to independent non-participating realms of existence, the only possible method of achieving agreement has been exiled in advance.

Practically this consequence is intolerable; accordingly it is rarely faced. "Standards" of value suddenly make their appearance to serve as criteria of taste and conscience. The distinction between likings and that which is worth liking, between the desired and the desirable, between the is and the ought, descends out of the blue. There are, it seems, immediate values, but there also are standard values, and the latter may be used to judge and measure immediate goods and bads. Thus the reflective distinction between the true and the false, the genuine and the spurious is brought upon the scene. In strict logic, however, it enters only to disappear. For if the standard is itself a value, then it is by definition only another name for the object of a particular liking, on the part of some particular subjective creature. If the liking for it conflicts with some other liking, the strongest wins. There is no question of false and true, of real and seeming, but only of stronger and weaker. The question of which one *should* be stronger is as meaningless as it would be in a cock-fight.

Such a conclusion puts an end to all attempt at consistency and organization and calls out in reaction an opposite theory. The "standard" is not, it is decided, for us at least, a good. It is rather a principle rationally apprehended. It is that which is "right" rather than that which is good; and since it is the right, it is the standard for judging all goods. If right is also good, the identification subsists in some transcendental realm; in some eternal, non-empirical realm of Being which is also a realm of values. The standard of good thus conceived as a principle of reason and as a form of supreme Being, is set over against the outside of actual desires, striving, satisfactions and frustrations. It ought to enter into their determination but for the most part it does not. The distinction between is and ought is one of kind, and a separation. It is not surprising that the wheel completes a full circle, and that the finale is a retort that the alleged standard is itself but another dignified disguise for some one's arbitrary liking—the *ipse dixit* of some one accidentally clothed with extraneous authority.

It is as irritating to have experience of beauty and moral goodness reduced to groundless whims as to have that of truth. Common-sense has an inexpugnable conviction that there are immediate goods of enjoyment and conduct, and that there are principles by which they may be appraised and rectified. Common-sense entertains this firm conviction because it is innocent of any rigid demarcation between knowledge on one side and belief, conduct and esthetic appreciation on the other. It is guiltless of the division between objective reality and subjective events. It takes striving, purposing, inquiring, wanting, the life of "practice," to be as much facts of nature as are the themes of scientific discourse; to it, indeed, the former has a more direct and urgent reality. Hence it has no difficulty with the idea of rational or objective criticism and rectification of immediate goods. If it were articulate, it would say that the same natural processes which generate goods and evils generate also the striving to secure the one and avoid the other, and generate judgments to regulate the strivings. Its weakness is that it fails to recognize that deliberate and systematized science is a precondition of adequate judgments and hence of adequate striving and adequate choice. Its organs of criticism are for the most part half-judgments, uncriticized products of custom, chance circumstance and vested interests. Hence common-sense when it begins to reflect upon its own convictions easily falls a victim to traditional theories; and the vicious circle begins over again. It is sound as to the need and possibility of objective criticism of values, it is weak as to the method of accomplishing.

Yet all this time there is an example of the way out in the case of beliefs. There was a time when beliefs about external events were largely matters of what it was found immediately good to accept or reject; as far as there was a distinction made between the immediately good in belief and the real or true, it lay chiefly in the fact that the latter was the object sanctioned by authorities of church and state. Yet it is now all but commonplace that every belief-value must be subjected to criticism; in scientific undertakings, it is a commonplace that criticism does not depend upon reference to a transcendent standard truth. The distinction between an immediate belief-value, which is but a challenge to inquiry, and an eventual object of belief that concludes critical inquiry, and has the value of fulfilling the causal relationships discovered, is made in the course of intelligent experiment. The result is a distinction between the apparent and the real good. Gradually a reluctant world is persuaded that meanings so determined define what is good for acceptance and assertion. Meantime beliefs determined by passion, class-interest, routine and authority remain sufficiently prevalent to enforce the perception that it makes all the difference in the world in the value of a belief how its object is formed and arrived at. Thus the lesson is enforced that critical valuations of immediate goods proceed in terms of the generation and consequences of objects qualified with good.

In outward forms, experimental science is infinitely varied. In principle it is simple. We know an object when we know how it is made, and we know how it is made in the degree in which we ourselves make it. Old tradition compels us to call thinking "mental." But "mental" thought is but partial experimentation, terminating in preliminary readjustments, confined within the organism. As long as thinking remained at this stage, it protected itself by regarding this introverted truncation as evidence of an immaterial reason superior to and independent of body. As long as thought was thus cooped up, overt action in the "outer" natural scene was inevitably shorn of its full meed of meaning; it was to that extent arbitrary and routine. When "outer" and "inner" activity came together in a single experimental operation, used as the only adequate method of discovery and proof, effective criticism, consistent and ordered valuation, emerged. Thought aligned itself with other arts that shape objects by informing things with meanings.

Psychology, which reflects the old dualistic separation of mind from nature, has made current the notion that the processes which terminate in knowledge fare forth from innocent sensory data, or from pure logical principles, or from both together, as original starting points and material. As a natural history of mind this notion is wholly mythological. All knowing and effort to know starts from some belief, some received and asserted meaning which is a deposit of prior experience, personal and communal. In every instance, from passing query to elaborate scientific undertaking, the art of knowing criticizes a belief which has passed current as genuine coin, with a view to its revision. It terminates when freer, richer and more secure objects of belief are instituted as goods of immediate acceptance. The operation is one of doing and making in the literal sense. Starting from one good, treated as apparent and questionable, and ending in another which is tested and substantiated, the final act of knowing is acceptance and intellectual appreciation of what is significantly conclusive.

Is there any reason for supposing that the situation is any different in the case of other values and valuations? Is there any intrinsic difference between the relation of scientific inquiry to belief-values, of esthetic criticism to esthetic values, and of moral judgments to moral goods? Is there any difference in logical method? If we adopt a current theory, and say that immediate values occur wherever there is liking, interest, bias, it is clear that this liking is an act, if not an overt one, at least a dispositional tendency and direction. But most likings, all likings in their first appearance, are blind and gross. They do not know what they are about nor why they attach themselves to this or that object.

Moreover, every such act takes a risk and assumes a liability, and does so ignorantly. For there are always in existence rival claimants for liking. To prefer *this* is to exclude *that*. Any liking is choice, unwittingly performed. There is no selection without rejection; interest and bias are selective, preferential. To take this for a good is to declare in act, though not at first in thought, that it is better than something else. This decision is arbitrary, capricious, unreasoned because made without thought of the other object, and without comparison. To say that an object is a good may seem to be an absolute and intrinsic declaration particularly when the assertion is made in direct act rather than in thought. But when we recognize that in effect the assertion is that one thing is better than another thing, the issues shift to something comparative, relational, causal, intellectual and objective. *Immediately* nothing is better or worse than anything else; it is just what it is. Comparison is comparison of things, things in their efficacies, their promotions and hindrances. The better is that which will do more in the way of security, liberation and fecundity for other likings and values.

To make a valuation, to judge appraisingly, is then to bring to conscious perception relations of productivity and resistance and thus to make value significant, intelligent and intelligible. In becoming discriminately aware of the causal conditions of the object liked and preferred, we become aware of its eventual operations. If in the case of esthetic and moral goods, the causal conditions which reflection reveals as determinants of the good object are found to lie within organic constitution in greater degree than is the case with objects of belief, this finding is of enormous importance for the technique of critical judgment. But it does not modify the logic which obtains in knowledge of the relationship of values and valuations to each other. It indicates the particular subject-matter which has to be controlled and used in the conscious art of re-making goods. As inquiries which aim at knowledge start from pre-existent beliefs, so esthetic and moral criticism start from antecedent natural goods of contemplative enjoyment and social intercourse. Its purpose is to make it possible to like and choose knowingly and with meaning, instead of blindly. All criticism worthy of the title is but another name for that revealing discovery of conditions and consequences which enables liking, bias, interest to express themselves in responsible and informed ways instead of ignorantly and fatalistically.

The meaning of the theory advanced concerning the relationship of goods and criticism may be illustrated by ethical theory. Few I suppose would deny that in spite of the attention devoted to this subject by many minds of a high order of intention and intellectual equipment, the outcome, judged from the standpoint of scientific consensus, is rather dismaying. The outcome is due in part to the importance of the subject, its intimate connection with man's deepest concerns, with his most cherished traditions and with the most acutely perplexing problems of his contemporary social life. Objective detachment and development of adequate intellectual instruments are necessarily difficult under such conditions. But I think that we find, amid all the diversity, one common intellectual preconception which inevitably defers the possibility of attainment of scientific method. This is the assumption, implicit or overt, that moral theory is concerned with ends, values rather than with criticism of ends and values; the latter being in fact not only independent of moral theory but not themselves having even moral quality. To discover and define once for all the *bonum* and the *summum bonum* in a way which rationally subserves all virtues and duties, is the traditional task of morals; to deny that moral theory has any such office will seem to many equivalent to denial of the possibility of moral philosophy. Yet in other things repeated failure of achievement is regarded as evidence that we are going at the affair in a wrong way. And to a mind willing to surrender the traditional preconception, failure to achieve consensus in method and even in generic conclusions in morals as a branch of philosophy may be similarly explained.

It is not meant of course that the tradition assumes that the good and the highest good are created by moral theory. The assumption is not so bad as that; it is to the effect that it is the province of moral theory to reveal moral goods; to bring them to consciousness and to enforce their character in perception. As empirical fact, however, the arts, those of converse and the literary arts which are the enhanced continuations of social converse, have been the means by which goods are brought home to human perception. The writings of moralists have been efficacious in this direction upon the whole not in their professed intent as theoretical doctrines, but in as far as they have genially participated in the arts of poetry, fiction, parable and drama. Conversion into doctrinal teachings of the imaginative relations of life with which great moral artists have dowered humanity has been the great cause of their ossification into harsh dogmas; illuminating insight into the relations and goods of life has been lost, and an arbitrary code of precepts and rules substituted. Direct appeal of experience concentrated, vivified and intensified by the insight of an artist and embodied in literary creations similar in kind to the revelation of meanings which is the work of any artist, has been treated as a discovery and definition of things true to scientific or philosophic reason.

Meantime the work which theoretical criticism might do has not been done; namely, discovery of the conditions and consequences, the existential relations, of goods which are accepted as goods not because of theory but because they are such in experience. The cause in large measure is doubtless because the prerequisite tools of physics, physiology and economics were not at hand. But now when these potential instrumentalities are more adequately prepared they will not be employed until it is recognized that the business of moral theory is not at all with consummations and goods as such, but with discovery of the conditions and consequences of their appearance, a work which is factual and analytic, not dialectic, hortatory, nor prescriptive. The argument does not forget that there have been would-be naturalistic and empirical ethics which have asserted that goods are such prior to moral conduct as well as to moral theory, and that they become moral only when employed in conduct as objects of reflective choice and endeavor. But the apparent exception proves the rule. For these forms of moral theory while releasing morals from the obligation of telling man what goods are, leaving that office to life itself, have failed to note that the office of moral philosophy is criticism; and that the performance of this office by discovery of existential conditions and consequences involves a qualitative transformation, a re-making in subsequent action which experimentally tests the conclusions of theory.

Therefore like the Aristotelian ethics, they have been dialectic, defining and classifying in hierarchical order antecedent goods and terminating in a notion of *the* good, the *summum bonum;* or, like hedonistic ethics, they have made a dialectic abstraction of a feature of concrete goods, their pleasantness; and instead of providing a method of analysis of concrete situations have laid down rules of calculation and prescribed policies to be pursued as fixed, not intellectually experimental, results of prior calculations. When they were, like Jeremy Bentham, persons of human sensitiveness to evils from which men suffer in virtue of institutions which may be altered; or, like John Stuart Mill, of genial insight into the constituents of a liberal and humane happiness, they have stirred their generation to beneficent action. But the connection between their theories and the practical outcome was adventitious; their ideas operated when all is said and done as literary rather than as scientific apparatus, as much so as in the case of reforms to which Charles Dickens not meanly contributed.

The implications of the position which has been taken import a "practical" element into philosophy as effective and verifiable criticism, obnoxious to the traditional view. Yet if man is within nature, not a little god outside, and is within as a mode of energy inseparably connected with other modes, interaction is the one unescapable trait of every human concern; thinking, even philosophic thinking, is not exempt. This interaction is subject to partiality because the human factor has bent and bias. But partiality is not obnoxious just because it is partial. A world characterized by qualitative histories with their own beginnings, directions and terminations is of necessity a world in which any interaction is intensive change—a world of partialities, particulars. What is obnoxious in partiality is due to the illusion that there are states and acts which are not also interactions. Immature and undisciplined mind believes in actions which have their seat and source in a particular and separate being, from which they issue. This is the very belief which the advance of intelligent criticism destroys. The latter transforms the notion of isolated one-sided acts into acknowledged interactions. The view which isolates knowledge, contemplation, liking, interest, value, or whatever from action is itself a survival of the notion that there are things which can exist and be known apart from active connection with other things.

When man finds he is not a little god in his active powers and accomplishments, he retains his former conceit by hugging to his bosom the notion that nevertheless in some realm, be it knowledge or esthetic contemplation, he is still outside of and detached from the ongoing sweep of inter-acting and changing events; and being there alone and irresponsible save to himself, is as a god. When he perceives clearly and adequately that he is within nature, a part of its interactions, he sees that the line to be drawn is not between blind, slavish, meaningless action and action that is free, significant, directed and responsible. Knowledge, like the growth of a plant and the movement of the earth, is a mode of interaction; but it is a mode which renders other modes luminous, important, valuable, capable of direction, causes being translated into means and effects into consequences.

All reason which is itself reasoned, is thus method, not substance; operative, not "end in itself." To imagine it the latter is to transport it outside the natural world, to convert it into a god, whether a big and original one or a little and derived one, outside of the contingencies of existence and untouched by its vicissitudes. This is the meaning of the "reason" which is alleged to envisage reality *sub specie aeternitatis*. It is indeed true that all relations, all universals and laws as such are timeless. Even an order of time as an order is timeless, for it is relational. But to give irrelevancy to time the name of eternal in an eulogistic sense, is but to proclaim that irrelevancy to any existence forms a higher kind of existence. Orders, relations, universals are significant and invaluable as objects of knowledge. They are so because they apply to intensive and extensive, individualized, existences; to things of spacious and temporal qualities. Application is not for the sake of something extraneous, for the sake of something designated an utility. It is for the sake of the laws, principles, ideals. Had they not been detached for the purpose of application, they would not have meaning; intent and potentiality of application in the course of events lends them all their significance. Without *actuality* of application, without effort to realise their intent, they are meanings, but they possess neither truth nor falsity, since without application they have no bearing and test. Thus they cease to be objects of knowledge, or even reflection; and become detached objects of contemplation. They may then have the esthetic value possessed by the objects of a dream. But after all we have not left temporal experience, human desire, liking, and passion behind or below us. We have merely painted nature with the colors of an all too local and transitory flight from the hardships of life. These eternal objects abstracted from the course of events, although labeled Reality, in opposition to Appearance, are in truth but the idlest and most evanescent of appearances, born of personal craving and shaped by private fantasy.

Because intelligence is critical method applied to goods of belief, appreciation and conduct, so as to construct freer and more secure goods, turning assent and assertion into free communication of shareable meanings, turning feeling into ordered and liberal sense, turning reaction into response, it is the reasonable object of our deepest faith and loyalty, the stay and support of all reasonable hopes. To utter such a statement is not to indulge in romantic idealization. It is not to assert that intelligence will ever dominate the course of events; it is not even to imply that it will save from ruin and destruction. The issue is one of choice, and choice is always a question of alternatives. What the method of intelligence, thoughtful valuation will accomplish, if once it be tried, is for the result of trial to determine. Since it is relative to the intersection in existence of hazard and rule, of contingency and order, faith in a wholesale and final triumph is fantastic. But some procedure has to be tried; for life is itself a sequence of trials. Carelessness and routine, Olympian aloofness, secluded contemplation are themselves choices. To claim that intelligence is a better method than its alternatives, authority, imitation, caprice and ignorance, prejudice and passion, is hardly an excessive claim. These procedures have been tried and have worked their will. The result is not such as to make it clear that the method of intelligence, the use of science in criticizing and recreating the casual goods of nature into intentional and conclusive goods of art, the union of knowledge and values in production, is not worth trying. There may be those to whom it is treason to think of philosophy as the critical method of developing methods of criticism. But this conception of philosophy also waits to be tried, and the trial which shall approve or condemn lies in the eventual issue. The import of such knowledge as we have acquired and such experience as has been quickened by thought is to evoke and justify the trial.